Hope for Creation

This latest volume from the Korean Global Mission Leaders Forum (KGMLF) deals with the pressing issues of ecological and human calamity, and in so doing, offers an unusual richness of biblical reflection and practical wisdom. Wide-ranging, diverse, and hopeful, *Hope for Creation* is the fruit of the unique space KGMLF creates by bringing together Korean and international scholars in conversation with mission practitioners.

PAUL BENDOR-SAMUEL MRCGP, MBE
Executive Director, Oxford Centre for Mission Studies
Director, Regnum Books
Sundo Kim Research Tutor in Global Mission

Far too many Christians write off environmental concerns as marginal to the gospel or simply expressions of left-wing ideology. With solid biblical, theological, scientific, and practical grounding, *Hope for Creation* compellingly challenges those assumptions and offers a hopeful and urgently needed corrective: love of God and love of neighbor require care for God's creation of which humanity is only a part.

RUTH PADILLA DEBORST, PhD
Richard C. Oudersluys Associate Professor of World Christianity,
Western Theological Seminary
Member, Asociación Casa Adobe, Costa Rica

Hope for Creation represents a milestone in mission thinking: churches in the Global South collaborating on a series of international mission discussions and cooperation, and Christian mission now takes creation care as a major agenda. This urgent topic also promises a broader interaction with various institutions and even different faiths for the common future of humanity. This book will serve churches and mission communities as a road map for local reflections and applications.

WONSUK MA, PhD
Executive Director, Center for Spirit-Empowered Research
Distinguished Professor of Global Christianity, Oral Roberts University

Hope for Creation

Missional Responses to Environmental and Human Calamities

Editors

Jonathan J. Bonk

Michel G. Distefano

J. Nelson Jennings

Jinbong Kim

Jae Hoon Lee

WILLIAM
CAREY
PUBLISHING

visit us at missionbooks.org

Published by William Carey Publishing | 10 W. Dry Creek Cir | Littleton, CO 80120 | www.missionbooks.org

William Carey Publishing is a ministry of Frontier Ventures | Pasadena, CA | www.frontierventures.org

Cover and Interior Designer: Mike Riester
Copyeditor: Michel G. Distefano
Indexer: Michel G. Distefano
Translators: Gihong Park and Youngmi Shin

ISBNs: 978-1-64508-558-4 (paperback), 978-1-64508-560-7 (epub)

Printed Worldwide   28 27 26 25 24   1 2 3 4 5   IN

Library of Congress Control Number: 2024933046

OTHER TITLES IN THE KGMLF SERIES

Accountability in Missions:
Korean and Western Case Studies

Family Accountability in Missions:
Korean and Western Case Studies

Megachurch Accountability in Missions:
Critical Assessment through Global Case Studies

People Disrupted:
Doing Mission Responsibly among Refugees and Migrants

Missionaries, Mental Health, and Accountability:
Support Systems in Churches and Agencies

The Realities of Money & Missions:
Global Challenges & Case Studies

Contents

Figures

Tables

Foreword

by J. Nelson Jennings

"Accountability" and "Christian Mission": those two themes have guided the biennial Korean Global Mission Leaders Forum (KGMLF) since it began in 2011. While each of the now seven KGMLF forums and resulting books has had a particular focus, in one way or another the intertwined threads that have run through all seven KGMLF events have been accountability and Christian mission. The November 2023 KGMLF wrestled with how churches, agencies, missionaries, and others involved in Christian mission are accountable to God, fellow human beings, and indeed all of creation with regard to the well-being of the world God has made.

The title of the book you are now reading, consisting of the papers prepared for KGMLF 2023, is *Hope for Creation: Missional Responses to Environmental and Human Calamities*. Clearly the themes of creation care, environmental disasters, hope-driven Christian mission efforts, and how those realities interrelate are massive and daunting! Even so, with pre-prepared papers, emphasis on case studies, preparation by its relatively small number of participants (in 2023 around seventy, many recognized experts in related fields), and discussion-oriented format, KGMLF is designed to tackle challenging and even intractable topics.

The previous six KGMLF publications demonstrate the difficult and often sensitive themes that have been addressed:

1. *Accountability in Missions: Korean and Western Case Studies* (Wipf & Stock, 2011)

2. *Family Accountability in Missions: Korean and Western Case Studies* (OMSC Publications, 2013)

3. *Megachurch Accountability in Missions: Critical Assessment through Global Case Studies* (William Carey Library, 2016)

4. *People Disrupted: Doing Mission Responsibly among Refugees and Migrants* (William Carey Library, 2018)

5. *Missionaries, Mental Health, & Accountability: Support Systems in Churches and Agencies* (William Carey Publishing, 2020)

6. *The Realities of Money & Missions: Global Challenges & Case Studies* (William Carey Publishing, 2022)

KGMLF forums and books have not attempted to answer all the questions associated with the themes they have taken up, much less solve all the related thorny problems. Sharpening the questions about each topic has always been a central goal, along with the hope of holding us Christian mission practitioners accountable for how we address that particular matter. The editors of this latest volume dealing with environmental dangers trust that more hope-based missional responses to the myriad calamitous realities confronting God's good creation will result.

Some previous volumes have included explanations about the "Korean" and "Global" aspects of "KGMLF," but the background and rationale bear repeating. While still unknown to some Western Christians, most active participants in Christian mission—including mission recipients throughout Asia and indeed worldwide—are quite familiar with the prominence of Korean missionaries over the past generation. By all accounts their numbers are well over twenty thousand, and their zealous spirituality and willingness, even eagerness, to go to the hardest contexts for gospel service have inspired many. Even so, for whatever reasons—perhaps language and cultural barriers, Western incapacity to hear Koreans as equals—it has only been much more recently that serious, intentional *missiological* interaction between Korean and other ("global") mission thinkers has begun to take place. Begun in 2011, KGMLF was born out of a desire to foster such interaction, so each biennial forum by design has had approximately half Korean and half non-Korean participants. Those who come together do so as friends and equals, expecting to learn from each other through the academic, spiritual, and informal interactions that take place.

Moreover, as in the present case all KGMLF books have been published in both English and in Korean. Making the same content available in both languages reinforces the KGMLF commitment to enable collaboration, mutuality, and much needed cross-pollination between Korean and non-Korean missionaries and agencies. William Carey Publishing has once again published the English volume; once again they have been nothing but pleasant, expert, and collaborative partners. For the Korean volume, Duranno will again serve as publisher.

It is also worth noting that the forums have been held in what might be called nondenominational settings. Many churches and agencies have wonderful facilities to house modest-sized groups like KGMLF, and it is not as though the forum organizers have stiff-armed away such venues. Even so, not meeting in any one church's location has enabled the KGMLF not to be bound to any particular Christian tradition's limits or wineskins. Such freedom has enabled the forums and books to address topics that might be too sensitive or risky for a single group to address, allowing the previous and present books to explore accountability issues pertinent to any sector of the worldwide mission movement.

Accountability in general, missionary families, megachurches, migration, missionary mental health, money, and now environmental calamities: all of these topics are challenging and ongoing. We participants in Christian mission are accountable for how we meet these challenges. Current plans are for the next forum and book to take up yet another vexing matter stirring among most sectors of the Christian movement, so readers can anticipate the ongoing KGMLF series to offer nourishing food for thought and for action.

"God saw all that he had made, and it was very good" (Gen. 1:31). Human rebellion and the resulting curse on creation have tarnished God's "very good" creation—and from the Industrial Revolution forward human beings seem to have found new and devasting ways to damage our earthly habitat to previously unimaginable extremes. In its descriptions and analyses, *Hope for Creation: Missional Responses to Environmental and Human Calamities* offers no manifesto or neat solutions. The book's contents do describe some missional responses that have been made. The book also suggests steps that you and others might consider taking. May our Creator and Redeemer guide us to respond urgently, wisely, and as those accountable for our missional responses.

Preface
From "What If?" to "Who Is!"

by Jonathan J. Bonk

"*What If?*" We live in an age of bad news … an age when globally interconnected communications technologies make news of distant calamity instantly local; an age when commercially driven algorithms multiply and amplify the frequency and volume of bad news in our smart phone news feeds; an age when human populations have never been more universally and simultaneously informed and misinformed. Ours is a seemingly hopeless world.

It is said that we live in the *Anthropocene* or *Human* Epoch,[1] the postindustrial period of our collective story when human capacity for both good or evil has been amplified by "advances" in technology, science, medicine, ravenously acquisitive, inequitable economic systems, and structurally dysfunctional governance yielding unprecedented climate-related disasters, insecurities, migrations, and wars. We are reaping what has been sown. No corner of our planet is spared. We live in an age of calamity and enervating fear. We have come to realize, Alas!, that of all of the species that comprise life on this planet, we are the number one invasive species, holding within our power the capacity to obliterate plant, marine, and animal life, including our own. Because history has no reverse gear, we can, apparently, only look forward in dread to an existentially grim future of our own making.

In fact all ages since the Fall have been "Anthropocene" or human centered, at least from the human point of view. It has been difficult for human beings to imagine themselves as anything less than the center of all that is around them, the ego hub of a circle radiating out across diminishingly worthy entities, including fellow humans who organize themselves differently socially, economically, linguistically, or religiously. In times of crisis, these "other humans" are reduced to subhuman creatures, worthy of degradation into servility or outright extermination.

---

1 "Anthropocene: The Human Epoch" is the title of a Canadian documentary film; see the resources section for the full reference and official trailer. See also "Anthropocene," National Geographic, last updated October 19, 2023, https://education. nationalgeographic.org/resource/anthropocene/.

What we are hearing, seeing, and experiencing may or may not be absolutely unprecedented. Nevertheless—because we are such short-lived creatures—the actual and looming existential disasters affecting entire populations, countries, oceans, civilizations, the atmosphere, and hence our planet *seem* unprecedented and are as devastating in actuality as they are dreadful in prospect.

"Who Is!" There is no doubt about it: we live in a perilous age of wars, rumors of wars, earthquakes, droughts, famines, floods, and environmental degradation. Some two thousand years ago Jesus, Very God in human flesh, predicted the kinds of terrifying events that have repeatedly inundated humankind before and since, and which traumatize us today (Matt. 24:1–14).

Isaiah, writing during the Babylonian exile some five hundred years before Matthew's account of the life of Jesus, reminded Cyrus that God is God in every situation, not just in pleasant times:[2]

> "I am the LORD, and there is no other; besides me there is no
> God. I strengthen you—though you don't know me—so all
> will know, from the rising of the sun to its setting, that there
> is nothing apart from me. I am the LORD; there's no other.
> I form light and create darkness, make prosperity and create
> doom; I am the LORD, who does all these things."
> —(Isaiah 45:5–7, CEB)

Writing at least seven hundred years before Matthew, the Psalmist provided a believer's framework within which to understand and respond to calamities overwhelming human populations of his day:

> God is our mighty fortress,
>   always ready to help in times of trouble.
> And so, we won't be afraid!
> Let the earth tremble
>   and the mountains tumble into the deepest sea.
> Let the ocean roar and foam,
>   and its raging waves shake the mountains.
> A river and its streams bring joy to the city,
>   which is the sacred home of God Most High.
> God is in that city, and it won't be shaken.
>   He will help it at dawn.
> Nations rage! Kingdoms fall!
>   But at the voice of God the earth itself melts.
> The LORD All-Powerful is with us.

---

2 Michel Distefano's "Toward a Biblical Theology of Calamity" in this book offers an excellent, more thorough overview of this crucial subject.

> The God of Jacob is our fortress.
> Come! See the fearsome things the LORD has done on earth.
>   God brings wars to an end all over the world.
> He breaks the arrows, shatters the spears,
>   and burns the shields.
> Our God says, "Calm down, and learn that I am God!
>   All nations on earth will honor me."
> The LORD All-Powerful is with us.
>   The God of Jacob is our fortress.
> —(Psalm 46, CEV)

What follows is offered in the conviction that faith in the Great "*Who Is!*" transcends dread of the existential "*What Ifs?*" of our time. Nondevilish faith always issues in practical action, in constructive missional response. Faith without action, James reminds us, is no more than a rotting carcass reeking of the stench of hypocrisy (James 2:14–26).

This book is the fruit of a modest forum of Christian leaders from Korea, Burkina Faso, Philippines, Vietnam, China, Singapore, Ireland, United Kingdom, Australia, New Zealand, United States, and Canada who gathered in Maiim Village, Korea from November 7–10, 2023. These leaders thought hard about the Gospel of Hope in this age of rightful despair, and they found—and trust you will find—hope and inspiration from missional responses to the environmental and human calamities that mark our time.

"Faith makes us sure of what we hope for and gives us proof of what we cannot see" (Heb. 11:1, CEV).

In Hope,
Jonathan Bonk
Outgoing President
Global Mission Leaders Forum 2023

Acknowledgments

by Jinbong Kim

The Bible declares that the world was created by God, "and it was very good" (Gen.1:31). Unfortunately, in an era where human beings, who are responsible for making the beautiful world better, are destroying it, I think the topic of KGMLF 2023 is very appropriate. Among the many Korean pastors I've encountered, very few address "the environment" in their Sunday sermons. Perhaps they underestimate its importance. Thus, I hope they will read this book and reconsider their perspectives.

In 2011, the inaugural KGMLF was launched, and now with the release of its seventh book, I find myself reflecting on the entire journey. Before extending my heartfelt gratitude, I would like to briefly touch on the beginnings of KGMLF.

KGMLF came about for two main reasons. First, when I began working with missionaries in the mission field, I faced various challenges due to a limited understanding of Korean culture and the Korean church among our multicultural team. I believed that providing accessible English resources on Korean missions and church dynamics could promote better collaboration and understanding. Second, while I was at OMSC, I was able to attend several Mission Leadership Forums (MLF). Twice a year, about forty to fifty mission scholars gathered for the forum; however, I was surprised to see that most of the attendees were Americans. There was a visible lack of attendance by Asian (and global) scholars, even though the topics discussed were related to China, Korea, and other international missions. Therefore, with the support of many, we set the goal of creating a different kind of international mission forum called the Korean Global Mission Leaders Forum.

I would like to acknowledge several individuals who have played integral roles from the beginning. First and foremost, I'd like to thank Dr. Jonathan Bonk. In 2008, he gladly accepted this newly proposed forum. He has played the most important role in creating and supporting KGMLF for more than fifteen years. In fact, in 2015 when I was laid off by OMSC, Dr. Bonk came to my house and encouraged me, saying, "Jinbong, I'm still healthy, so let's form a new organization and continue KGMLF," and with Dr. Nelson Jennings, Dr. Dwight Baker, Dr. Sam Keun Chung, Rev. Jae Hoon Lee, and Dr. Won Sang Lee as GMLF board and trustee members, we registered the new mission agency with the Connecticut state government. Last month

(November 2023), Dr. Bonk handed over the presidency of GMLF to Nelson Jennings. However, I believe that if God gives him good health, he will continue to work on KGMLF to make it better.

I'd also like to thank Reverend Jae Hoon Lee. Without Rev. Lee and his church's support, today's KGMLF would not have existed. In fact, since 2012, Rev. Lee has been serving the KGMLF as actively as if he were faithfully and humbly serving the Lord. I must mention Dr. Dwight Baker, who gave me unwavering encouragement, courage, and strength to endure the difficulties that arose during this journey. Also, with his help we were able to secure a contract with William Carey Publishing, where we have published the KGMLF books since the third installment in the series.

It is also my honor to acknowledge with thanks Dr. Christopher Wright, who was my principal and professor at All Nations Christian College in England more than twenty-seven years ago. Dr. Wright served as the Bible instructor at the first KGMLF, held in New Haven, Connecticut in 2011, and at the KGMLF 2017, 2019, 2021, and 2023 meetings, which were held in Korea. I pray that he will come to the KGMLF 2025 as well and make a great contribution. I am very grateful for his insightful and practical application of the Bible. I extend my sincere thanks to all the authors who prepared their papers during already busy schedules, and then traveled all the way to South Korea to participate in the forum. This book would not have been possible without them.

I also want to extend my sincere gratitude to Reverend Hong Joo Kim and all the staff and missionaries from Onnuri church who poured their heart into making KGMLF successful.

I also want to thank Rev. Dr. Do Hoon Kim, senior pastor of New Haven Korean Church in Hamden, CT, USA, where I have lived for about eighteen years. His church has supported KGMLF in countless ways for many years. I am so grateful to mention my family for their support as always. Finally, I would also like to express my sincere gratitude to Dr. Michel Distefano, Dr. Gihong Park, and Dr. Youngmi Shin for their work in ensuring the highest quality in the KGMLF books.

No matter how I think about it, I am foremost of sinners, who has no qualification or ability to serve the KGMLF. However, if we can find a reason why KGMLF has been able to continue so far, it is only by the grace of God. May his glorious name be praised!

Rev. Dr. Jinbong Kim
Managing Director of GMLF
Coordinator of KGMLF

Section A

Bible and Theology

CHAPTER 1

God's Word to a Nation in Denial and Rebellion
Jeremiah 1

by Christopher J. H. Wright

What's it like to be a preacher, or a pastor, or a missionary in times like these? In a world where, in some cultures, there is deep rooted skepticism about any claims or assumptions. There may be "your truth" and "my truth" and "his or her truth," but nobody can claim to have or know "the truth." That kind of relativism used to be confined to matters of opinion or religious faith, but now is rampant even in the so-called "real world" of "facts" and "alternative facts." Not even science is trusted by large swathes of people, as the anti-vax and conspiracy theories that flourished during the COVID-19 pandemic demonstrated.

And in some other cultures, of course, there is only one permitted truth—whatever the state dictates, whether in the form of extreme religious fundamentalism or of totalitarian tyranny by a single party or single strongman leader.

Meanwhile, we live with diabolically obscene inequality, between galactic-scale wealth and gutter-level destitution—a disparity that used to be mapped globally between wealthy countries and poverty-stricken ones, but is now devastating and shameful within the wealthiest countries as well. Corruption and greed stalk the land, adding to the pain and anger of mass poverty.

And all the while, the existential threat of climate chaos, whose deadly consequences are already making life unsustainable in some places, confronts the planet as a whole—"undeniable and irreversible" as the latest IPCC report told us. Undeniable, perhaps, now, but very deniable for the past half century by those whose vested interests were threatened by revealing the truth they already knew.

3

For at least forty years the warnings have been there from reputable and international climate scientists. But skepticism, confected confusion, and political inertia seem to be driving us headlong toward a global calamity. Forty years. That was approximately the length of time between the day when God called a young lad called Jeremiah to warn Judah of a coming calamity and the day it actually happened at the hands of Nebuchadnezzar's Babylonian army. By "hands" read "swords," "spears," "chains," "flames," and "rape and "pillage," as Jerusalem was destroyed in 587 BC and the people carried off in exile to an unclean land.

What was it like to be a preacher in times like that—for forty years! Forty years of warnings that went unheeded by most of the population—such was the depth of skepticism, denial, and rebellion in Judah by that late stage of their long history of unfaithfulness to their God. Well, Jeremiah tells us very bluntly what it was like. Here is a selective catalog of the culture of Judah in Jeremiah's day—it is only a sampling of the early chapters of the book. It doesn't take much imagination to see abundant echoes and parallels with what we still see in some of our societies today.

Marks of a Skeptical Society

They place a high value on things that are of no real value, but are instead utterly worthless and empty.

> This is what the LORD says:
> "What fault did your ancestors find in me,
>   that they strayed so far from me?
> They followed worthless idols
>   and became worthless themselves."
> —*Word of Yahweh, Jeremiah 2:5*

They have no sense of guilt—repeatedly protesting their innocence; theirs is a culture of moral denial.

> On your clothes is found
>   the lifeblood of the innocent poor … .
> Yet in spite of all this you say,
> "I am innocent;
>   he is not angry with me."
> But I will pass judgment on you
>   because you say, "I have not sinned."
> —*Word of Yahweh, Jeremiah 2:34–35*

They are skilled and practiced in evil, not in doing good.
> My people are fools;
>> they do not know me.
> They are senseless children;
>> they have no understanding.
> They are skilled in doing evil;
>> they know not how to do good.
> —*Word of Yahweh, Jeremiah 4:22*

And this has become so ingrained as to be incorrigible—they are unable to change.
> Can an Ethiopian change his skin
>> or a leopard its spots?
> Neither can you do good
>> who are accustomed to doing evil.
> —*Word of Yahweh, Jeremiah 13:23*

There is a complete loss of truth, honesty, and integrity.
> Go up and down the streets of Jerusalem,
>> look around and consider,
>> search through her squares.
> If you can find but one person
>> who deals honestly and seeks the truth,
>> I will forgive this city.
> Although they say,
> "As surely as the LORD lives,"
>> still they are swearing falsely.
> —*Word of Yahweh, Jeremiah 5:1–2*

They treat "God" as irrelevant and blind.
> They have lied about the LORD; they said,
>> "He will do nothing!
> No harm will come to us;
>> we will never see sword or famine."
> —*Word of Yahweh, Jeremiah 5:12*

The people are characterized as foolish, senseless, stubborn, and rebellious.
> Hear this, you foolish and senseless people,
>> who have eyes but do not see,
>> who have ears but do not hear … .
> But these people have stubborn and rebellious hearts;
>> they have turned aside and gone away.
> —*Word of Yahweh, Jeremiah 5:21, 23*

There is wealth for some, but no concern for the poor; injustice reigns.
> They have become rich and powerful
> > and have grown fat and sleek.
> Their evil deeds have no limit;
> > they do not seek justice.
> They do not promote the case of the fatherless;
> > they do not defend the just cause of the poor.
> —*Word of Yahweh, Jeremiah 5:27–28*

They hate and ridicule the Scriptures.
> Their ears are closed
> > so they cannot hear.
> The word of the LORD is offensive to them;
> > they find no pleasure in it.
> —*Word of Yahweh, Jeremiah 6:10*

The popular pundits and commentators peddle a superficial, shallow optimism.
> They dress the wound of my people
> > as though it were not serious.
> "Peace, peace," they say,
> > when there is no peace.
> —*Word of Yahweh, Jeremiah 6:14*

And they do it with shamelessness, advanced hardness that cannot even blush over wrongdoing.
> Are they ashamed of their detestable conduct?
> > No, they have no shame at all;
> > they do not even know how to blush.
> —*Word of Yahweh, Jeremiah 6:15*

There is a culture of self-deceiving intellectual arrogance, which is tantamount to lying.
> How can you say, "We are wise,
> > for we have the law of the LORD,"
> when actually the lying pen of the scribes
> > has handled it falsely?
> The wise will be put to shame;
> > they will be dismayed and trapped.
> Since they have rejected the word of the LORD,
> > what kind of wisdom do they have?
> —*Word of Yahweh, Jeremiah 8:8–9*

There is loss of social integrity. Deception is rife; trust nobody!

> Beware of your friends;
> > do not trust anyone in your clan.
> For every one of them is a deceiver,
> > and every friend a slanderer.
> Friend deceives friend,
> > and no one speaks the truth.
> They have taught their tongues to lie;
> > they weary themselves with sinning.
> You live in the midst of deception.
> —*Word of Yahweh, Jeremiah 9:4–6*

But ironically, they trust in any false gods that are around!

> You have forgotten me and trusted in false gods.
> —*Word of Yahweh, Jeremiah 13:25*

And there is an accumulating pile of wickedness from one generation to the next. Things are going from bad to worse.

> When you tell these people all this and they ask you,
> "Why has the LORD decreed such a great disaster against us?
> What wrong have we done?
> What sin have we committed against the LORD our God?"
> then say to them,
> "It is because your ancestors forsook me,"
> declares the LORD,
> "and followed other gods and served and worshiped them.
> They forsook me and did not keep my law.
> But you have behaved more wickedly than your ancestors.
> See how all of you are following the stubbornness of your evil hearts
> instead of obeying me."
> —*Word of Yahweh, Jeremiah 16:10–12*

And behind all of the above, and accounting for them, they had become a nation that no longer listened to the voice of God.

> Therefore say to them,
> "This is the nation that has not obeyed
> *[listened to the voice of]* the LORD its God
> or responded to correction.
> Truth has perished; it has vanished from their lips."
> —*Word of Yahweh, Jeremiah 7:28*

Indeed, the defining moment for Judah and Jeremiah was when the nation's government and king, representing the whole people, chose to burn the word of God—the scroll that Baruch so painstakingly had written with all Jeremiah's warnings for some twenty-three years. Not just to burn it, but to insist on listening to it read out aloud, and then systematically chopping it up and consigning it to the flames (the story is in Jer. 36). That was King Jehoiakim in 605 BC. It was all downhill after that—a downward vortex of denial and delusion until the catastrophe swamped the nation.

We may ask, Is it hermeneutically legitimate to compare OT Israel with the contemporary world? After all no nation—not even Korea!—stands in the same covenant relationship to God as Israel. No indeed. However, as I've argued in great depth elsewhere there was a paradigmatic aspect of Israel's social, economic, and political life, as revealed in the law-constitution that God gave them, precisely as a visible model to the nations of God's wider demand on human societies.[1] They were intended to be a "light to the nations." Tragically (but not surprisingly, for they were a nation of sinners as much as any other nation), the people who were to be the vehicle of God's blessing to all nations (as promised to Abraham) behaved as badly as the pagan nations around them, and even worse in some respects. So when we explore the symptoms of their social collapse, the causes of the calamity that befell them under God's judgment, along with the warnings that God so profusely gave them through the prophets, it is like looking in the mirror.

"They had become a nation that no longer listened to the voice of God," we read. Does that not describe the western culture that has come to dominate global realities, ever since it was decided some three hundred years ago in the so-called "Enlightenment" that it would be better for human flourishing if God were excluded from the public arena, other than in the lip service of religious rituals and incantations? God could be like a constitutional monarch—with all the trappings and splendor of those who like that sort of thing, but not a shred of actual power or relevance for all practical purposes.

And since we also need to see OT Israel as part of our story as the people of God—the church, is their failure to listen to the voice of God not also mirrored in the western church? We too stopped listening to the voice of God, certainly no longer hearing that voice within the pages of Holy Scripture. We reap the long-term fruit of the Enlightenment-inspired rise of liberal biblical criticism, with its claimed academic objectivity and secular presuppositions, which so infected the church's seminaries and teachers that "hearing the voice of God in the Bible" sank from the realm of any kind of

---

1   Christopher J. H. Wright, *Old Testament Ethics for the People of God* (Leicester: IVP, 2004).

authoritative preaching as public truth to the realm of private and smilingly naïve personal devotion.

We need to get back to Jeremiah.

For what was God's answer to the nation we have described above from his book? A very surprising one: a young lad who (rightly) felt himself utterly inadequate for the job God laid on his shoulders. But into a very skeptical world, God sent a skeptical preacher!

The Call of a Skeptical Preacher

God's opening words to Jeremiah are rich in theological and personal significance:

> The word of the LORD came to me, saying,
> "Before I formed you in the womb I knew you,
> before you were born I set you apart;
> I appointed you as a prophet to the nations." (Jer. 1:4–5)

None of us can claim that kind of precise prophetic calling or scriptural status, but the words can resonate with any who have discerned a calling from God to serve him in the task of sharing his Word among the nations of the world—whether in our own nation or to the ends of the earth. Our calling into pastoral or evangelistic ministry and mission, or into any of the wide range of missional tasks and professions through which God enables his people to serve the church and the world, has always had a certain prophetic dimension, since our works and our words go together (as Paul said), and both are rooted and shaped and centered in the biblical gospel.

We'll come back to those words of God in a moment, but first let's see Jeremiah's reaction in v. 6: "'Alas, Sovereign LORD,' I said, 'I do not know how to speak; I am too young.'" There's an irony in the fact that Jeremiah knows who he is talking to—"Sovereign LORD"—and yet he feels free to argue back, a habit that will persist throughout his long ministry. He is no puppet on a string or ventriloquist's dummy. His objection, in Hebrew format, combines *inability* ("I don't know this 'speaking' thing") with *inadequacy* ("a mere youth, that's me"). Both of those feelings are probably familiar to many of us, no matter what stage of our ministry and mission we may be in.

Who of us hasn't sometimes felt profound inability or lack of skill, unequal to the awesome challenge of communicating God's Word competently and effectively? There is such depth and power in the Scriptures, and who am I to match it with feeble words and phrases of my own? And inadequacy goes along with inability very naturally—just not feeling really up to the job at all. For Jeremiah (as for Timothy) it was feeling too young. For Moses and some of us, it was probably feeling too old. That's my feeling sometimes, at least.

Can I really still "cut it" when it comes to clear and powerful preaching? You listen to some dynamic younger preacher expounding the Bible with admirable creativity and eloquence while steeped in the text itself, and you wonder … Was that me once?

And for all of us, there is the temptation to disillusionment—Will it really make any difference? Has it actually made any difference after all these years so far? Is anybody really listening? It is easy to become skeptical about our calling and ministry—cynical, depressed, resentful. That was Jeremiah's temptation for a lifetime, judging from his painfully honest confessions and complaints to God. Is it yours?

So Jeremiah responds with acute skepticism to God's calling, expressing inability and inadequacy. And maybe that's not a bad posture for any of us, actually. For the opposite is surely not the best answer or what God actually wants. "Sure God! I can do this! I'm brilliant at it actually. I'm fully equipped, done the training, got the certificate. Here I am, I'm your man (or woman). Here I come, listen to me, folks!" That's never going to end well, is it?

The Assurance of the Sovereign God

Just as Jeremiah didn't respond in the way I've just caricatured, neither did God respond to Jeremiah's plea of inability and inadequacy with some kind of pep talk: "You'll be fine! You're a star! I can tell you've got what it takes! Just believe in yourself and this will be a great success." Rather, God's response focuses on four things for us to consider:

- the givenness of the preacher
- the givenness of the word
- the dual impact of God's word
- the assurance of God's presence

a) The Givenness of the Preacher (v. 5)

Verse 5 has four verbs with God as subject: I formed … I knew … I set apart … I gave …" The last word is usually translated "appointed." It is the Hebrew verb *nathan* (נָתַן) and it comes again in v. 9, translated as "put." Both the preacher and the word itself are "given" by God.

The life of Jeremiah the man and the book of Jeremiah the prophet didn't happen as the outworking of Jeremiah's career plan. They had been shaped by the mind and plan of God from eternity. Which means that the state of the nation at this point in their history, while it caused God great grief and pain and anger, had not caught God by surprise. In his sovereign providence, God had anticipated this situation and prepared his preacher for it—even before he existed as an unborn fetus.

And even that—his prenatal life—was no mere biological product of his father (Hilkiah) and mother's marital union. No.

i) "I formed you"—as a potter shapes clay into a pot, the same word is used as a metaphor for God's sovereign governance of the world. The God who shapes the destinies of nations had shaped Jeremiah as a prophet to the nations.

ii) "I knew you"—a word of intimate personal knowledge and relational commitment. It's usually and appropriately translated in this kind of context as "I chose you." So God's foreknowledge and choice of his preacher even before his conception and birth had nothing to do with his good qualities and abilities in life. There were no grounds for pride in such a calling.

iii) "I set you apart"—a word used frequently of Israel themselves. They were set apart from the nations, as God's priestly people in their midst. "Made holy"—different, distinct, separated from the rest. That would be literally true for Jeremiah, as he stood apart from his family and community, from the rest of the prophets, the priests, and even the king (or most of them). His was a lonely sanctification—as is still the lot of many faithful servants of God, pastors, preachers, and missionaries.

iv) "I gave you"—literally "a prophet to/for the nations, I have given you." That's what I mean by the "givenness of the preacher." It was not so much that God was giving a job to Jeremiah, as that God had already given Jeremiah to this job. Jeremiah was not so much *gifted* (like "a gifted speaker," as we say), as *given*. This accounts for the sense of inescapable compulsion that Jeremiah expresses throughout his ministry. He was not "forced" to preach God's word, but he was given no other option, for it was agony when he tried to stop. He was quite literally born for this—a fact that sometimes depressed and angered him so much that he wished he'd never been born at all.

What does all this say about our own ministry and mission as preachers and teachers of God's word and leaders of God's people? Of course, we are not inspired prophets like Jeremiah. But there is a sense in which we are "given" by God to his people. Certainly that's how Paul puts it in Ephesians 4:11–13:

> So Christ himself gave the apostles, the prophets, the evangelists, the pastors and teachers, to equip his people for works of service, so that the body of Christ may be built up until we all reach unity in the faith and in the knowledge of the Son of God and become mature, attaining to the whole measure of the fullness of Christ.

Those verses seem to me to be the reverse of the popular view of the clergy in our churches. God doesn't give a congregation to the pastor to support him in his ministry. It's exactly the other way round. God gives the pastor to the congregation to equip *them* for *their* ministry—which is out there in the world! Some young pastors straight out of seminary may think of themselves as "God's gift to the church." Well, they are! But not in the way they may think!

I wonder if this "givenness of the preacher" may be an effective antidote to that weariness or disillusionment that can engulf us when our preaching or other pastoral or missional tasks seem futile and fruitless—as Jeremiah undoubtedly experienced. It is to remind ourselves that "God has given me to this task—even before I was conscious of being called to it." Ministry and mission are not all about having gifts, but of being the gift as a person— God's gift.

I think it also gives a stronger foundation and integrity to our own self-dedication to our work. Have you ever said something like, "I've really given myself to this ministry"?—and of course we mean it! But in reality, that self-giving is a reflex of the fact that God has given me to this work first.

Indeed, there is something analogous to the Lord Jesus Christ himself in this combination. Paul can rejoice in knowing "The Son of God who loved me and gave himself for me" (Gal. 2:20). But at the same time, John affirms that "God so loved the world that he gave his only Son …" (John 3:16). God gave the Son, and the Son gave himself. And so it is for us. We give ourselves to God's service because God first has given us to his people and for his mission in the world.

So there is the givenness of the preacher, but just in case the idea of being "God's gift to the church" might stoke our pride or status, it is immediately qualified by the givenness of the word.

b) The Givenness of the Word (vv. 7, 9)

This is partly expressed by the specific scope and limits set around Jeremiah's ministry. Verse 7 is literally, "to everyone to whom I send you, you shall go" "and everything that I command you, you shall say."

Everyone, everything; wherever, whatever. Jeremiah had no free choice either of his audience or his message. There was no question of addressing only those who liked him or paid him well, telling what they wanted to hear. There were enough prophets doing that in Judah already (cf. 23:9–40).

The relentless pressure of this double mandate—this "wherever I send you, and whatever I command you"—would cause Jeremiah great unpopularity and suffering for year after year. It was like a "fire in his bones," he will say (20:9).

But even more explicit is what God says in v. 9:

> Then the LORD reached out his hand and touched my
> mouth and said to me,
> "I have put my words in your mouth." (1:9)

And that little word "put" is once again the Hebrew *nathan*—as in v. 5: literally "I have given my words in your mouth." There is an echo here, probably consciously, of Deuteronomy 18:18—when God had said he would raise up a prophet like Moses and put his words in his mouth.

So Jeremiah then is a given preacher, with a given word. The preacher and the word are *both* God's gift. Indeed, there is a very close identification between the "words of Jeremiah" (1:1) and "the word of the LORD" (1:2). Verse 2 starts with a relative pronoun—*'ăsher* (אֲשֶׁר)—sometimes translated "to whom." But in the syntax of the two verses it more naturally refers, not to Jeremiah the man, but to "the words of Jeremiah." That is, we could translate the two verses as: "The words of Jeremiah … *which were (or constituted)* the word of the LORD to him. …" And that opening is echoed in the closing of the book at 51:64 (since ch. 52 is a kind of appendix)—"The words of Jeremiah end here." In other words, the whole book containing everything in between is simultaneously the words of Jeremiah and the word of God.

Andrew Shead has argued, convincingly I think, that "The Word of the LORD" is in itself one of the chief characters in the book.[2] Some statistics make that plausible. Shead gives even more than the following examples:

- *dbr* (דבר, as noun and verbal forms) occurs more often in Jeremiah than any other OT book.

- *davar* (דָּבָר, sg.) occurs three times more in Jeremiah than in Isaiah.

- Jeremiah uses "word" formulas ("The word of the LORD came," "Thus says the LORD," "Oracle of Yahweh," etc.) more often than any other prophet.

Throughout the book there is a running battle between the word and will of God on the one hand, and the words and will of the people on the other—a constant, aggressive dialogue or confrontation. And in the end, we know that God's word wins! God himself puts it like this toward the end of the book's tortuous narrative, addressing those who chose to leave the land of Judah after the destruction of the city and take refuge in Egypt—against the advice of Jeremiah, who had been asked for a word from the LORD:

---

2 Andrew Shead, *A Mouth Full of Fire: The Word of God in the Words of Jeremiah* (Nottingham: Apollos, an imprint of IVP, 2012).

> Then the whole remnant of Judah who came to live in Egypt will know whose word will stand—mine or theirs (44:28).

And it wasn't theirs! God's word stands!

- One king burned the scroll (ch. 36)—but the word went on.
- Another king locked up the prophet (chs. 32–33)—but the word was free.
- The people were dragged into exile in an unclean land—the word could reach them even there (ch. 29).
- Babylon might rule the world for a while—but the word of God would sink Babylon in the Euphrates (ch. 50–51).

So then, God reassured Jeremiah with the givenness of his sovereign word. That reassurance was needed to sustain him through forty years of thankless, lonely ministry to a skeptical and rebellious nation.

Now, I repeat again, we are not prophets like Jeremiah. We cannot post the claim, "Thus saith the Lord" on our own sermons or lectures. God's word is now and forever "given" in Scripture. Nevertheless, amazingly God has entrusted his once-given word to our mouths, in the sense that when we speak and preach from the Bible, it is God's word that we take on our lips. That's what Peter means in 1 Peter 4:11: "If anyone speaks, they should do so as one who speaks the very words of God." And surely, taking God's word on our lips is

- an enormous privilege;
- a scary responsibility; and
- a strengthening reassurance—for God's Word will do its work, as surely as rain produces fertility and growth (Isa. 55:10–11).

Does this not offer you renewed strength and motivation?—if perchance you are experiencing frustration or weariness or disillusion in the midst of the chaos and foreboding of our world, the tumult of the nations, the groaning of the planet, and the apparent ineffectiveness and dysfunction of the church and so much of our missional endeavors. If God has called you into his service, then take seriously the double perspective from these texts (vv. 5, 7, 9):

- You are God's gift to his people, and through them to the world.
- The word you study, preach, and seek to obey is God's gift to his people, and through them to the world. It is not, as the world will try to tell you, a matter of your own opinions, views, and personal convictions; it is the given word of the living God.

But what will that word do? What will it accomplish? God spells that out in v. 10

c) The Dual Impact of God's Word (v. 10)

> See, today I appoint you over nations and kingdoms to
> uproot and tear down, to destroy and overthrow, to build and
> to plant. (1:10)

That probably came as a surprise to Jeremiah—"over nations and kingdoms," not just tiny little Judah. There would be some literal meaning to that, in the interesting fact that Jeremiah's messages were well-known in the outside world. The Babylonian intelligence experts certainly knew about him and how he had been urging Judah (and the surrounding tiny nations) to surrender to Nebuchadnezzar—for which he was branded a traitor in Jerusalem, but had his life spared by Babylon when they captured the city.

But in a far more profound sense, it is indeed the word of God, spoken through the prophets and recorded in Scripture, that governs human history. God has his plans and has articulated them in his word, and they overrule and override the plans and conspiracies of even the most powerful nations and empires, though they play their own part in the outworking of God's purposes.

That is the truth that Psalm 33 majestically affirms. After God's world-transforming word (in vv. 4–5, putting the world to rights by justice and unfailing love), and God's world-creating word (in vv. 6–9, speaking the whole universe into existence by the more breath of his mouth), comes God's world-governing word, in vv. 10–11:

> The LORD foils the plans of the nations;
> he thwarts the purposes of the peoples.
> But the plans of the LORD stand firm forever,
> the purposes of his heart through all generations. (Ps. 33:10–11)

And the OT itself is proof of that claim. Indeed, I would argue this is one major reason why God has given us this vast narrative we call the OT—namely to make us get this point. Earthly kingdoms and empires rise and fall, but God's word and God's mission continue. The sequence spans the history and prophetic books: Egypt, Canaan, Syria, Assyria, Babylon, Persia, Greece … Rome. Nations rise and fall. Empires come and go. But the word of God and the plans of God and the people of God—go on forever!

We could illustrate the same truth from the last two thousand years of history as well—or even just the last fifty. We need to lift our eyes sometimes from the immediate present crisis, or even from contemplating an imminent calamity of global proportions—and see all our preaching of God's Word in the light of God's mission. Paul has given us God's ultimate plan and purpose, for all creation and all nations:

> [God has] made known to us the mystery of his will according to his good pleasure, which he purposed in Christ, to be put into effect when the times reach their fulfillment—to bring unity to all things in heaven and on earth under Christ. (Eph. 1:9–10)

If our mission is aligned with God's mission, then we are "on the right side of history" (which we need to remember when we are accused of being on the wrong side). For history moves according to the plans of God and under the sovereignty of the reign of God. And it moves in surprising ways—as Jesus made clear in his parables about the kingdom of God. It is, for example, like a mustard seed—apparently so small and insignificant, yet producing enormous growth.

What about your church or your mission agency? It can seem so small in comparison to the "big world" (or if it seems pretty big to you, you may need to adjust your glasses). But together you are agents of the reign of God, and it is your privilege and responsibility to equip, teach, and lead God's people in "the truth that leads to godliness" (Ti. 1:1), which can transform even a den of iniquity like Crete when Paul wrote his instructions to Titus. So let your ministry in whatever form it takes be the mustard seed, and let God be God and his Word do its work. You will have Martin Luther as an ally. This was his tribute to the power of the preached word (and the comfort of good beer!) in the dangerous early days of the reformation in Wittenberg:

> I simply taught, preached, and wrote God's Word; otherwise I did nothing. And while I slept [cf. Mark 4:26–29], or drank Wittenberg beer with my friends Philip and Amsdorf, the Word so greatly weakened the papacy that no prince or emperor ever inflicted such losses upon it. I did nothing; the Word did everything.[3]

Notice also the dual impact of the word:
- uproot, tear down, destroy, and overthrow

- build and plant

The metaphors are striking. On the one hand, there is digging out wild or unfruitful trees in order to plant new ones. On the other hand, there is demolishing an old, unsafe building in order to build something new and

---

3 Martin Luther, "The Second Sermon, March 10, 1522, Monday after Invocavit" in *Luther's Works*, vol. 51, *Sermons I*, ed. and trans. John W. Doberstein (Philadelphia: Fortress Press, 1959), 77.

lasting. Jeremiah had more of the first to do, though he did get round to the positive side of his prophetic vision as well (especially in chs. 30–33). Again, without claiming the mantle of biblical prophets, our ministry ought to have elements of both. There is a destructive and a constructive dimension to our task in ministry and mission. It would be worth asking of any sermon we are planning, or any project we envisage:

- What falsehoods or evils will this uproot and demolish?

- What truths and kingdom blessings will this build up and plant?

It would be wise not to do one without the other.

Finally, for such a complex and demanding mission, Jeremiah needed God's final word in his call experience.

d) The Double Assurance of God's Presence (vv. 8, 19)

> "Do not be afraid of them, for I am with you and will
> rescue you," declares the LORD. (1:8)
> "They will fight against you but will not overcome you, for
> I am with you and will rescue you," declares the LORD.
> (1:19)

Jeremiah would surely have remembered that this was what God had said to Moses—in the face of the impossible task God was laying on him. Are you too old? Too young? Hear this: With you, am I"—says the living God.

Jeremiah would need that reassurance and reality for forty long years. And so do you and I. He faced massive public resistance. He was a miniscule minority (just him and Baruch and a very few friends at court), and he suffered from a combination of inferiority complex, almost suicidal depression, passionate longing for his own people and fear for their future, and a fraught relationship with God, at whose anger he shuddered, and whose tears of grief he shed.

But the fact that we have the book of Jeremiah in our Bibles is proof of who was right in the end:

- the lonely preaching of God's word by Jeremiah

- or the pervasive and deluded culture of lies and false optimism, and the tyrannically oppressive political culture of his nation

"I am with you," said God to Jeremiah, and to us.

Stick with the word of God.
And God will stick with you.

CHAPTER 2
God's Word in a Culture of Delusion and False Security
Jeremiah 7

by Christopher J. H. Wright

It all started like any other day in Jerusalem. You set off for the temple aiming to get through the gates into the outer courts in time for the morning sacrifice. You arrive there with crowds of others—a busy place just inside the gate where the crush was greatest, and that's where you heard that well-known voice again, raised in those familiar passionate tones—the unmistakable voice of that prophet from Anathoth, Jeremiah—"Hear the word of the LORD, all you people of Judah who come through these gates to worship the LORD. This is what the LORD Almighty, the God of Israel, says …" (Jer. 7:2–3).

It was familiar because you'd heard him preaching all over Jerusalem for the past eighteen years or more, ever since you were both teenagers. And it was getting ever more grating and unpopular. Especially with the authorities.

There's a new king on the throne now—Jehoiakim (the year is probably 609 BC by our reckoning, see 26:1), and the direction of his policies are quite at odds with the warnings of Jeremiah. For years Jeremiah has been warning about a terrible threatening danger "from the North"—describing it in graphic imagery as the most appalling calamity the country could face. And ever since Babylon ousted Assyria as the dominant power in the region, it is clear by now that he believes that "foe from the North" has Babylon's name written all over it. There is a small minority party in the corridors of power, and Jeremiah sympathizes with them, who advocate a friendly and submissive relationship with Babylon. But Jehoiakim and his government are determined to take a much more belligerent anti-Babylonian stance. Rebellion is in the air. But that way leads only to utter destruction, in Jeremiah's vision.

The political direction Judah was bent on, the international stance they were taking, was not only absurdly arrogant for such a tiny kingdom in the face of a resurgent Mesopotamian empire, but also, there was only one way such a road would end—calamity. And it would be a calamity of unimaginable proportions and mass suffering. A calamity not just for the king and his government but for all the inhabitants of the city, and indeed for the land itself.

So said Jeremiah. So he'd been saying for years (just read chs. 2–6).

But could that calamity be averted? Was there any likelihood of a change of mind and course? Well, Jeremiah thought so at first, from what we can tell of his early preaching: the warnings were precisely in the hope of repentance and change, so that the disaster might not fall, or at least need not be as all-encompassingly disastrous as his warnings portrayed. And that was God's longing too, for here's what God said as he sent Jeremiah to the temple courts that day with the message we are about to explore:

> This is what the LORD says: "Stand in the courtyard of the LORD's house and speak to all the people of the towns of Judah who come to worship in the house of the LORD. Tell them everything I command you; do not omit a word. *Perhaps they will listen and each will turn from their evil ways. Then I will relent and not inflict on them the disaster I was planning because of the evil they have done.*" (Jer. 26:2–3)

So that's what Jeremiah did. That's why you heard his familiar voice as you went to the temple that day—preaching, lecturing, warning, challenging, appealing …

But did you believe him? You and the rest of the crowds in the temple courts that morning? You'd heard it all before of course—warning after warning that seemed completely divorced from reality, exaggerated, "project fear," fake news … and anyway very much a "minority report" with plenty of other prophets saying the exact opposite. So no, you probably had got used to Jeremiah's gloomy predictions and were already blanking them out of mind as you pressed on through the crowd.

But this time it was different. What Jeremiah had to say that morning was so shocking, so scandalous, so treacherous, that it had got him arrested. And when he insisted that his message was what Yahweh, God of Israel, had told him to say, it was virtually blasphemous as well. The authorities had come very close to putting him to death on the spot. He'd only just escaped unharmed. Wow! What you were going to tell your wife and children when you got home! It was a day to remember.

So what did Jeremiah actually say? Like many expert preachers, Jeremiah states his two main points first—in verses 3 and 4, and then expands each of them in turn in the following verses. First comes a command (v. 3): "Change your ways." What he means by that is then explained in verses 5–7.

Then second comes a warning (v. 4): "Don't believe the lies ..." What he means by that is then explained in verses 8–11. And then he finishes with a lesson from their history that was as stark a threat as they'd ever heard.

Change Your Ways—Or Else (vv. 3, 5–7)

> This is what the LORD Almighty, the God of Israel, says:
> "Reform your ways and your actions, and I will let you live in
> this place." (7:3)

It begins, as I said, in a familiar way. God calls Israel to change their ways and behavior—to reform them, literally "to make them good" again. And as I said, you've heard that call before again and again from this prophet. Blah, blah, you're thinking. But what comes next is the shock. For it is an implied threat—if you *don't* change your ways, here's what will happen: I will *not* let you live in this place.

Now the exact meaning of the threat depends on what "this place" refers to. It could refer to the city of Jerusalem or the land of Judah. And that is how it is explained in verse 7, "the land I gave your ancestors for ever and ever." The threat then is this: if the people will not change, God will not allow them to go on living in the land. What?? The idea that God would throw his people out of the land he had promised them and given them centuries ago... unthinkable!

Or, "this place" could mean the very spot where Jeremiah and his hearers were standing—the temple (it is often referred to as "the place"). And the other words (with a tiny change in the vowel pointing to אֶתְכֶם) can be read as *"I will dwell with you in this place."* The threat, in that case, would be that if the people do not change for the better, then God himself would no longer dwell in the midst of his people—a threat Israel had first heard in the wilderness before the tabernacle was even built (Exod. 33). God would abandon his own temple!! What?? Again, the idea was unthinkable! In fact, the sheer shock of hearing such an unbelievable threat could well have been what sparked the response of the people that Jeremiah hears in v. 4, "This is the temple of the LORD, the temple of the LORD, the temple of the LORD!"— how dare you even suggest that God could ever abandon it? And we'll come to that in a moment.

Whether "this place" refers to the land or the temple does not really matter—and it might have been deliberately ambiguous, including both. For the point of the message was utterly unambiguous. It was a massive, blatant threat to everything the people held dear—their land, their city, their temple, and their relationship with Yahweh their God. "All doomed," cries Jeremiah, "unless you change your ways. And if you do not, what lies ahead is the utter calamity of exile, destruction, and abandonment: you will no longer live here and God will no longer live among you." What a shocking threat!

But what did he mean by "Reform your ways … ."? That's what vv. 5–7 spell out. Jeremiah was not talking about being more sincere in their worship, or just changing their attitudes, or showing greater piety, or praying harder. His demand, as always with God's prophets, focused on the practical, social, and ethical aspects of everyday life in the public arena. It was the classic demand of Israel's covenant law:

- do justice with one another in the community
- no oppression of the weak and vulnerable, the landless, homeless, and family-less
- no violence against the innocent
- no futile self-harm of going after the false gods of the surrounding cultures

Those had always been the conditions for secure and blessed residence in God's land—Deuteronomy had spelled them out persistently.

But then verse 7 injects a sharp tension. On the one hand, there is that clear condition—the "If" of verse 5. *If* the people would change *then* God would let them go on living in the land. *But if not, then not!* God would drive them out, just as he had done the Canaanites before, as God's earlier warning had very bluntly stated in Leviticus 18:27–28 and 20:22. So there is a clear conditional element here.

But then, on the other hand, verse 7 also includes the official theology of the land: according to countless texts since Abraham, it was "the land I gave your ancestors for ever and ever." But if the land had been given "for ever and ever," how could it be taken away? Was the gift of the land unconditional or conditional? The fact is it was both, in theologically important ways.

On the one hand, yes, the land had been promised to Abraham and then given to his descendants in divine faithfulness to that promise. The land was a monumental, tangible proof of the faithfulness of Yahweh. And it was unconditional in the sense that they had done nothing to deserve it. They owed it solely to God's redemptive grace and promise. But on the other hand, it remained Yahweh's land. "The land is mine," he said (Lev. 25:23). He was the divine landlord who reserved the right to determine the conditions under which his tenants should live in the land he owned and they now possessed. There had been no conditions for the original *gift* of the land, but there certainly were conditions for continued *enjoyment* of the land—

the conditions of obedience to the covenant law as a people of justice and compassion in every area of social, economic, and political life.

The land itself was an unconditional gift of grace; ongoing life and flourishing in the land was conditional on their grateful and obedient response to that grace. And failing that obedient response, the people forfeited their right to go on enjoying the gift itself. Not that God would abandon his promise, but that his people would exclude themselves from the covenantal privilege and blessing of enjoying it.

Now at this point I want us to step out of the courts of the temple in 609 BC, and transpose Jeremiah's words in scope and time. Remember that the triangle of *God, Israel,* and the *land* in the OT era functions as a "working model" or paradigmatic case for God's sovereignty over *all nations* and *all the earth.* And indeed, the OT applies similar concepts to *the earth as a whole and the human race upon it,* as to the land of Canaan and Israel's presence on it. One nation in one land, for the sake of all nations in the whole earth.

"The earth is the LORD's," sings the psalmist (Ps. 24:1). "To the LORD your God belong the heavens, even the highest heavens, the earth and everything in it," insists Moses (Deut. 10:14). God is the ultimate owner and landlord of all creation and especially the planet we live on. Nevertheless, "the earth he has *given* to mankind" (Ps. 115:16). The earth was given into the stewardship of humankind—male and female—to rule over as godly kings in the likeness of God himself (Gen. 1:26–28), and to serve and keep as priests (Gen. 2:15). In that sense, *the earth and its fullness is God's unconditional gift of grace to us all,* as he actually said to Noah:

> Then God blessed Noah and his sons, saying to them, "Be fruitful and increase in number and fill the earth. The fear and dread of you will fall on all the beasts of the earth, and on all the birds in the sky, on every creature that moves along the ground, and on all the fish in the sea; they are given into your hands. Everything that lives and moves about will be food for you. Just as I gave you the green plants, *I now give you everything.*" (Gen. 9:1–3)

And that gift came with a covenanted promise—the Noachian covenant with all creation, explicitly with "every living creature" (9:10, 12), with "all life on the earth" (9:17):

> As long as the earth endures,
> seedtime and harvest,
> cold and heat,

summer and winter,
day and night
will never cease. (Gen. 8:22)

That sounds like "for ever and ever," doesn't it? But is it? The opening line literally reads in Hebrew, "unto all the days of the earth." And that phrase *all the days of* is the repeated refrain in Genesis 5 for the long lifetimes of the great antediluvians from Adam to Lamech: "All the days of … were … years, *and he died.*" They were long days, but limited ones. None of them lived forever and ever, on this earth at least.

What am I saying? I am firmly committed to the foundational significance of God's covenant through Noah with all life on earth. God has promised to preserve the conditions of life on earth for all the days of the earth itself. But the number and length of those days is determined by God. God decided not only the days of the generations before Noah but also in each case when those days were over. What is the mind and decision of God about the days of the earth?

If, on the one hand, the gift of God's earth to humanity stands under his covenanted promise to Noah (just as the gift of God's land to Israel stood under his covenanted promise to Abraham), is it possible, on the other hand, that humanity's folly and rebellion could contrive to make the earth uninhabitable, such that we are no longer able to "dwell in this place"—just as Israel's folly and rebellion led to the desolation of their land, city, and temple?

I am not a prophet, but I feel it right at least to explore the analogy between Jeremiah's warning of the coming calamity, along with his (and God's) desire to avert that calamity or at least mitigate it through his passionate appeal that people should change their ways before it would be too late, and the warnings of the IPCC and the whole scientific community (warnings that have been there for longer than even Jeremiah's whole ministry) of the impending climate catastrophe for this planet, along with the possibility (that we are told still exists—only just) to at least avert the worst potential outcomes of global warming through the passionate appeals for urgent action by governments and nations before it is too late. And if there is any validity in that comparison, should not the church and its many mission agencies be joining the urgent warning, the passionate appeal for change, and changing our own ways too?

And again, without claiming any prophetic mantle, I simply ask, Could it be that "all the days of the earth" under God's sovereign preservation of the conditions for human life could end with God's "final whistle" when we—his fallen, sinful, rebellious, and foolish human creatures—so degrade, destroy, denude, and pollute the earth he entrusted into our hands, our bloodstained hands, that the final trumpet heralds the return of Christ? For then, we know, the old order of things will pass away and we look forward to the new heavens and earth, the new creation in which God will dwell with us—forever indeed. That is the ultimate end of this story—to which we must return a bit later.

For Jeremiah hasn't finished.

Challenge Your False Security (vv. 4, 8–11)

So there you are in the temple courts. Actually, you might admit that you do go to the temple these days with some foreboding. The news in Jerusalem can be disturbing—even if you discount the wild-eyed predictions of Jeremiah. Assyria was always the big beast in the whole region—had been for 150 years or more, but now the once all-powerful Assyrian Empire seemed to be falling apart, which might be good for little nations like Judah and her neighbors. But on the other hand there was this new rising power of Babylon. What were their ambitions? If one empire simply replaced another, how would the little nations fare? As the Africans say (though you hadn't heard this one yet), "When the elephants fight, the grass gets trampled."

So you go to the temple, because that, surely, is the one place you know you'll be safe. Indeed, the temple itself is the guarantee that the city and kingdom as a whole will be safe. For after all, it is the temple of the LORD! The temple of the LORD! And you join in with the chanting of the crowds, boosting your collective confidence and assurance. This is the place to be. We're safe here—whatever that Jeremiah is moaning on about. Until you suddenly hear him call out above the chants: "Lies! Lies! Stop trusting in false words! You're all deceiving yourselves!" (vv. 4, 8, my paraphrase).

Shock number two! And even worse than the first. What on earth could Jeremiah mean this time? "The temple of the LORD?" Of course, it was. That was the truth, wasn't it?

And indeed it was true. This building and its courts were the work of glorious King Solomon some four centuries ago, but its origins went back to God's promise to David, and indeed to the tabernacle of Moses in the wilderness. The whole place was saturated with the presence of God in Zion, in the city and temple that bore the name of Yahweh, God of Israel. They told stories about it and sang hymns about it. And who could forget that more than a hundred years earlier, under great King Hezekiah, the prophet Isaiah had seen off the terrifying threat of the Assyrian king, Sennacherib. Had God not said them, "I will defend this city and save it, for my sake and for the sake of David my servant" (Isa. 37:35; cf. 33–34)? Surely that was all the guarantee they needed—God will always defend his city and especially this temple. It's the safest place on earth!

Lies! insists Jeremiah! Why?

Well, yes indeed, God had defended Jerusalem and the temple back in the days of Isaiah—spectacularly so. The problem was that the people had turned that into a complacent and false sense of security. Jerusalem, they thought, would be inviolable forever. God simply would not, could not, ever let it be destroyed. God would always defend his temple, no matter what.

So, the words of the worshippers were true in themselves—it was indeed the LORD's temple—but that chant had become a deception; or rather—a self-deception (which is the worst kind, as the world of social media rife with conspiracy theories amply proves). God was not *bound* to these buildings per se. Yahweh's name tag on the temple was not some divine insurance policy against persistent disobedience and rebellion. The *truth* (that it *was* the temple of the LORD) had become a *lie* (if they imagined that God would never let it be destroyed, and them with it).

They thought that so long as they could get into the temple courts they were safe from any enemy. Well, you are, says Jeremiah—*unless God himself has become the enemy,* which is exactly what you have done by your persistent covenant breaking. And if God is your enemy, then the temple is the most dangerous place to be! It's like a den where robbers feel safe after their crimes, unaware that the pursuing forces of the law know exactly where you are hiding and are watching your every move:

> "Has this house, which bears my Name, become a den of robbers to you? But I have been watching!" declares the LORD. (7:11)

So what was it exactly that had turned their trust in the temple into a deception? That's what verses 8–11 spell out. Here's why their ritual chants were worthless lies. Their lives had become a daily round of breaking the ten commandments. Listen to the list:

> Will you steal and murder, commit adultery and perjury, burn incense to Baal and follow other gods you have not known, and then come and stand before me in this house, which bears my Name, and say, "We are safe"—safe to do all these detestable things? (vv. 9–10)

That includes the first, sixth, seventh, eighth, and ninth commandments—a swamp of violence, bloodshed, sexual promiscuity, economic oppression, judicial corruption, and outright idolatry. And yet, they would flock to the temple to claim the protection of Yahweh in a society that had ignored his basic demands week after week. Jeremiah ruthlessly exposes what Derek Kidner describes as "the nonsense—and the effrontery—of tearing up the ten commandments and then turning up in church, as though saved to sin."[1] Their worship was deluded, self-deceived, and divorced from morality. Their lives made a mockery of the words they spoke and the claims they made in God's presence.

They had turned a truth into a grotesque lie, and based a totally false sense of security on it. And what was worse, the whole direction of the government's national policy was based on the same self-deception. They seemed to believe that they could rebel against Babylon with impunity, because they had God on their side. They could wave their Judahite-nationalism flag, throw off the foreign yoke, and make Judah great again, like in David and Solomon's day. Babylon might come down from the north like Assyria. Let them. God would defend them. And they had Scriptures to prove it—from Isaiah no less. Nothing to worry about, folks. Peace, Peace …

And so their actions and choices (or rather, their *refusal* to act and choose in the way Jeremiah was urging) were based on *a false sense of security*, which in turn was based on the ironic *perversion of a biblical truth into a self-deceiving falsehood.*

Hmm!

I suspect we could break into small groups right now and come up with many different ways in which Christians, as individuals, churches, and whole Christian traditions and cultures have turned something valid and true in its own context (including scriptural texts) into a deception that gives false security or false hopes or false comfort. Biblical truths about God's desire for human flourishing and the rewards of faith are perverted into the cruel deceptions of the "prosperity gospel." Biblical injunctions to submit to earthly authorities are perverted into blind nationalisms and "evangelical" support for corrupt or tyrannical regimes. And so on.

However, in relation to the primary issue before this conference, are there false securities justifying refusal to take action in relation to climate change, which lurk within plausible biblical or doctrinal truths? The first one I would suggest is the one I affirmed just a moment ago. The Noachian covenant. God promised to preserve the conditions of life on earth. So it's

---

1 Derek Kidner, *The Message of Jeremiah: Against Wind and Tide*, The Bible Speaks Today (Leicester and Downers Grove, IL: IVP, 1987), 49.

really up to God, we are told. You need to trust that promise. The future of the planet is not in our hands. God will save the earth himself. It is even a form of hybris to think that it's our responsibility. You don't need to do anything in this whole ecological crisis thing. Sit down and let God be God.

Or there's something of an opposite to that, with those who take more literally than Peter intended his imagery in 2 Peter 3 about the earth and all the elements being consumed by fire. So, if it's all going to be burned up in the end, why bother to protect or care for it now? That has always seemed to me a ludicrous *non sequitur*. Even if God's intention for this earth in its present material form is some kind of fiery dissolution as the means by which he will bring about the new creation that Peter immediately refers to, it is no reason for not obeying his original mandate to rule and care for this creation now. That would turn a truth (or at least a possible one, depending on one's interpretation of the text) into a self-serving, self-deceptive abnegation of all responsibility in relation to God's earth. It would be like a doctor saying to a manifestly ill patient, "Well, you're going to die sometime [true] and probably be all burned up in a crematorium, so why should I bother caring for you now?" I think you'd get out of the surgery pretty fast!

Or then there are those who are passionately committed to mission as they understand it. "This is the mission of God, the mission of God," they chant, insisting that the Great Commission demands only evangelism and discipling. Now the Great Commission is a great truth—like all biblical truth, something to be "done" and obeyed, not just believed. But to use a limited interpretation of the Great Commission as a way of self-excusing oneself or the church from wider missional responsibilities drawn from the Bible as a whole seems to me deceptively dangerous in implication.

Let's take Jeremiah's point seriously and think it through. In the face of an impending calamity, Jeremiah confronted a people who refused to take action that might have averted or mitigated it. And one reason why they complacently did so was that they were turning a precious part of their heritage of faith—a truth that had saved the nation in generations past—into a false sense of guaranteed security, no matter how they lived, no matter what they did or didn't do in response to Jeremiah's warnings and appeals. In what ways might we, our churches or mission agencies be guilty, even unwittingly, of something comparable to that self-deception? May the Holy Spirit help us to discern his voice if he prods us into identifying such areas and waking up to their danger.

But Jeremiah isn't finished yet! He has one last arrow to fire. One last shocking thing to tell them.

Check Your History! (vv. 12–15)

> Go now to the place in Shiloh where I first made a dwelling for
> my Name, and see what I did to it because of the wickedness
> of my people Israel. (7:12)

Remember Shiloh? Of course they did. They knew it well. It was a few
miles north of Jerusalem in what had been the territory of the northern
kingdom of Israel, but was now just a province of the Assyrian Empire.
By Jeremiah's time, it would have been an overgrown ghost town, a future
archaeological site, a possible picnic place among the ruins. But it had once
been *"my place"* (מְקוֹמִי is what God actually calls it in v. 12). It had been the
place where the tabernacle and the ark of the covenant had been stationed
in a central sanctuary for the tribes of Israel, while Jerusalem was still a
Canaanite enclave. Samuel had grown up there. It had been God's address
on earth centuries before the temple was built in Jerusalem.

But now? Abandoned. Derelict. Most likely it had been destroyed by the
Philistines in the mid-eleventh century BC. So, go to Shiloh and have a good
look round, says Jeremiah. And what you'll be looking at is your own future.
For what God did to Shiloh he is planning to do to *this* place—this place in
which you feel so complacently safe:

> Therefore, what I did to Shiloh I will now do to the house that
> bears my Name, the temple you trust in, the place I gave to you
> and your ancestors. I will thrust you from my presence, just as I
> did all your fellow Israelites, the people of Ephraim. (7:14–15)

Well that was just too much! The people of Judah knew why God had
destroyed Shiloh and Samaria and scattered those northern tribes to the far
corners of the Assyrian Empire—the reasons are all there in 2 Kings 17.
They had been such apostates and idolaters up there, and hadn't even had
kings descended from David. Whereas *we,* on the contrary, stand under God's
favor and protection, with a son of David on the throne and the temple of
the LORD in our midst. What happened to Shiloh could simply *never happen*
to Jerusalem. They thought. But it will, insists Jeremiah, because you never
learned the lesson, you simply wouldn't listen. That terrible warning up north
didn't lead you to repentance but merely fed your pride and complacency:
"I spoke to you again and again, but you did not listen; I called you, but you
did not answer" (v. 13).

Along with the whole crowd in the temple courts, you've heard enough.
Haven't you? This is blasphemy. This deranged preacher from Anathoth is
demonstrably a false prophet—from his own mouth. So this was the point—

the mention of Shiloh—when they stepped in to silence him for good. Here's the account in chapter 26:

> The priests, the prophets and all the people heard Jeremiah speak these words in the house of the LORD. But as soon as Jeremiah finished telling all the people everything the LORD had commanded him to say, the priests, the prophets and all the people seized him and said, "You must die! Why do you prophesy in the LORD's name that this house will be like Shiloh and this city will be desolate and deserted?" And all the people crowded around Jeremiah in the house of the LORD. (26:7–9)

Well, we must leave Jeremiah there, and you can read the rest of the story of his narrow escape in that chapter. For, after all this very sobering journey, I do want to end on a positive note. For you see, while Jeremiah increasingly realized that his words would go on falling on deaf ears and the calamity he so much shuddered and wept to even think about would inevitably fall, he knew that that would not be the end of the story. It would be the end for that generation—nothing but death or exile faced them a few years hence. But it was not the end of God's plan and purpose for his people—or indeed for the land. The judgement to come would be horrific in scale and totality. The siege of Jerusalem would end in slaughter, pillaging, rape, torture, and enslavement, the temple would be pillaged and trashed, and then the whole city burned to the ground.

But in the midst of that siege, as darkness closed in and the end drew near, *Jeremiah bought a field—acting as its kinsman-redeemer*! The story is in chapter 32, and it is quite astonishing. It was an act of apparent futility (the land was worthless and probably wrecked by the Babylonian army, and Jeremiah being unmarried had no heir to pass it on to). But it was also an act of *vivid prophetic hope for the future*—as God explained to Jeremiah, who was baffled by his own obedient action. The land would be restored! The people would return! Beyond judgment lay the grace of God's future. The story of God would go on! There was hope, for the promises of God— whether to Noah, Abraham, David—or us—cannot be thwarted.

And this says to me, Who knows what lies ahead for this wonderful planet, God's earth, our earth? But even if it sits within God's sovereign permission that we succeed in reducing it to an overheating globe, inhospitable to a suffering human race and many of our fellow creatures, even if all that—still every act of caring for the earth now, *every equivalent to Jeremiah purchasing that field*, has its worth and value as a pointer to what lies beyond "the end of the world" (whatever that means). Is that what Martin Luther meant in the (possibly apocryphal) saying attributed to him, that if asked what he would do if he knew the world would end tomorrow, said that he would plant a tree? For even a tree can be a signpost of the new creation. As can anything done in Christ's name—the Lord of heaven and earth. For the earth is the Lord's and all its fullness, and we look forward with all creation itself to its liberation from God's curse and our fallen folly.

Maranatha. Come Lord Jesus.

CHAPTER 3

God's Word of Global Judgment and Salvation
Isaiah 24-25

by Christopher J. H. Wright

Mission agencies often refer to "unreached people groups." Meaning that *we* haven't reached them yet with the gospel; there are no known believers among them. It is an appropriate way to consider the extent and the limits of our own human mission efforts. However, just because a people is "unreached" by *us* does not mean that they are unknown to *God,* or that God is not already there, in his goodness, justice, wrath, and mercy. For there is nowhere outside the truth and reality of God's omnipresence. He may, as yet, be the unknown God, but he is not the absent God. For the God of the Bible is the God of all creation, all humanity, all nations, all history, and all the past, present, and future. He is Lord of heaven and earth and all its inhabitants.

So when *we* reach out in mission, we reach out in the name of the God who has not left himself without a witness in every place, the God whose existence and power is visible in creation to all humanity, and the God who has already reached down in Christ. He is, as Paul told his sophisticated audience in Athens, the God who "gives everyone life and breath and everything else … ." and does so "so that they would seek him and perhaps reach out for him and find him, though he is not far from any one of us. 'For in him we live and move and have our being'" (Acts 17:25, 27–28).

That's the kind of universal language that we find in these chapters of Isaiah. And it is surprising in its context. For this whole section of the book comes from a time of intense danger for the tiny kingdom of Judah. It was in fact a time of great international turmoil and national political and spiritual turbulence as well. The massive war machine of Assyria was virtually battering on the door. They had "global" ambitions to conquer all the way to the Mediterranean and down to Egypt—and Judah was simply a miniscule kingdom that stood in the way of their imperial intentions. From an Assyrian point of view, Judah was a mosquito to be squashed.

But from God's point of view, Assyria was merely a stick in his hand, the agent of Yahweh's own global sovereignty. Both Judah and Assyria—and all other nations—had more to fear from the reality of Yahweh's judgment than from each other.

So it is in this context—a world of war and potential devastating invasion, a world of impending danger, threat, and fear—that Yahweh the God of little Judah makes these massive affirmations about the global reach of his sovereignty in both judgment and salvation. We need to get our minds around both.

The Global Reach of God's Judgment (Isaiah 24)

This is a truly awesome chapter. It is hard to read without a shudder. It portrays God's universal judgment on humanity as a whole—a prophetic future vision of final judgment couched in graphic apocalyptic imagery.

Verse 1 simply states the fact, in bald summary. The earth as the place of sinful human habitation is destined for devastating judgment by God:

> See, the LORD is going to lay waste the earth and devastate it;
> he will ruin its face and scatter its inhabitants. (24:1)

Following that startling announcement, the rest of the chapter says four enormous things about this judgment (the last of which will be quite a surprise).

a) God's Judgment Will Be Comprehensive—No Exemptions (v. 2)

One of the things in life that causes us so much frustration and anger is when people "get off with it." That is, when they escape any kind of accountability and punishment for wrongdoing, simply because of some privilege or corruption, or an "escape clause" that applies to them. In the UK in recent years we have seen politicians—even prime ministers—getting away unaccountably for behavior that for any ordinary citizen would have meant dismissal or a heavy fine. "It's one rule for them and another rule for the rest of us!" is the cry from the disgusted public.

But it will not be so in God's judgment, says verse 2. No different "rules." "It will be the same for …"—just look at the list:

> for priest as for people,
> for the master as for his servant,
> for the mistress as for her servant,
> for seller as for buyer,
> for borrower as for lender,
> for debtor as for creditor. (24:2)

So there will be:

- no impunity for elite religious status;
- no impunity for social status, or wealthy employers treating staff as expendable; and
- no impunity for the economically powerful, able to buy their way out of accountability.

And there is some relief in that, isn't there? *God's* justice, unlike flawed and corruptible *human* justice, cannot be bought, or evaded. God's justice will be truly impartial because it will be ruthlessly universal. No exemptions. No free passes. No immunity clauses.

b) God's Judgment Will Fall on the Guilt of Human Violence (vv. 4–6)

> The earth dries up and withers, the world languishes and withers, the heavens languish with the earth. The earth is defiled by its people; they have disobeyed the laws, violated the statutes and broken the everlasting covenant. Therefore a curse consumes the earth; its people must bear their guilt. Therefore earth's inhabitants are burned up, and very few are left. (24:4–6)

"The everlasting covenant" in v. 5b almost certainly refers to God's covenant through Noah with "all life on the earth" (Gen. 9:17) after the flood. Genesis tells us emphatically that the flood was God's response to two specific marks of human fallen sinfulness—*corruption and violence*:

> Now the earth was corrupt in God's sight and was full of violence. God saw how corrupt the earth had become, for all the people on earth had corrupted their ways. So God said to Noah, "I am going to put an end to all people, for the earth is filled with violence because of them. I am surely going to destroy both them and the earth." (Gen. 6:11–13)

And after the flood, God demands accountability for human life—in a world from which, sadly, violence had not been washed away:

> And for your lifeblood I will surely demand an accounting. I will demand an accounting from every animal. And from each human being, too, I will demand an accounting for the life of another human being. Whoever sheds human blood, by humans shall their blood be shed; for in the image of God has God made mankind. (Gen. 9:5–6)

The shedding of blood is consistently depicted as one of the worst of human evils condemned in the Bible—in the Law, Prophets, Psalms, and Wisdom Literature. It is abhorrent to God and calls down his judgment. And we live in a world that is awash with human blood. There is the obvious present reality of conflict and wars and atrocities on every continent, some of them massively costly in human lives. But there is also the long-term legacy of the centuries of bloody violence associated with racism, slavery, and historic genocides. In the USA there is the ghastly and almost daily bloodletting of gun violence and mass shootings. And for all of us, in western nations at least, there is the inescapable fact that our cheap, consumerist lifestyle, in terms of food, clothing, and gadgets, comes stained with the blood of cruelty, oppression, and violence against workers, some still enslaved, in the supply chains.

Notice also how our verses point out, with stark prophetic foresight, that these various forms of human violence (war, ethnic "cleansing," consumerist greed, etc.), all take their toll on the earth itself (see 24:4, 6a). How devastatingly true and blazingly apparent in these alarming days for our planet. God's judgment will deal not only with humanity's collective guilt, but also with its dire impact on God's own created earth.

c) God's Judgment Will Be Cosmic in Scale and Scope (vv. 18–23)

> The floodgates of the heavens are opened, the foundations of the earth shake. The earth is broken up, the earth is split asunder, the earth is violently shaken. The earth reels like a drunkard, it sways like a hut in the wind; so heavy upon it is the guilt of its rebellion that it falls—never to rise again. In that day the LORD will punish the powers in the heavens above and the kings on the earth below. They will be herded together like prisoners bound in a dungeon; they will be shut up in prison and be punished after many days. The moon will be dismayed, the sun ashamed; for the LORD Almighty will reign on Mount Zion and in Jerusalem, and before its elders—with great glory. (24:18b–23)

An earthquake must be an utterly terrifying thing (I can't speak from experience). Who can forget the apocalyptic images of the massive destruction and human suffering of the recent earthquakes in Turkey and Syria, Ecuador, Haiti, Pakistan, Japan … and more. What did those poor people endure? What unimaginable trauma and fear! No wonder the Bible uses earthquakes as imagery for the severity and terror of God's judgment—

here and elsewhere. And climactically in Revelation's picture of the ultimate judgment of God—the greatest and terminal earthquake of Revelation 16:

> The seventh angel poured out his bowl into the air, and out of the temple came a loud voice from the throne, saying, "It is done!" Then there came flashes of lightning, rumblings, peals of thunder and a severe earthquake. No earthquake like it has ever occurred since mankind has been on earth, so tremendous was the quake. The great city split into three parts, and the cities of the nations collapsed. God remembered Babylon the Great and gave her the cup filled with the wine of the fury of his wrath. (Rev. 16:17–19)

Significantly, however, Isaiah's words (anticipating the beasts and dragon of Revelation) remind us that the guilt of the earth's rebellion is not merely human. Note in 24:21, "the powers in the heavens above," meaning the *spiritual powers* of evil in rebellion against God—the same evil forces that Paul describes as "principalities and powers."

From the beginning the Bible makes clear that the essence of the Fall, that is the entry of sin and evil into human history, was a matter of our human *collusion* with "the serpent"—the mysterious and unexplained source of satanic temptation and evil. And today, it is more than ever apparent that there is demonic evil at work in and through and behind the atrocities of human brutality and violence. What else can explain the overwhelming wanton destructiveness and madness of wars that are devastating human life, human civilizations and cultures, and God's creation itself?

But we also see the fingerprints of "the father of lies" in the escalation of naked and blatant lying in high places—not only in the traditional propaganda machines of warring nations, but in the almost routine falsehoods and normalized deceit of political leaders. The cry of Psalm 12 describes the mendacity and arrogance of our politics with agonizing, if somewhat hyperbolic, perception:

> Help, LORD, for no one is faithful anymore;
> those who are loyal have vanished from the human race.
> Everyone lies to their neighbor;
> they flatter with their lips but harbor deception in their hearts.
> May the LORD silence all flattering lips and every boastful
> tongue—those who say,
> "By our tongues we will prevail;
> our own lips will defend us—who is lord over us?"
> (Ps. 12:1–4)

"The powers in the heavens above and the kings on the earth below" (v. 21)—what a potent, toxic, destructive collusion of satanic evil and government power! And what a succinct portrayal of phenomena we can observe in multiple forms across the whole international order (or disorder). Isaiah's vision is as globally relevant today as in the ancient Near East of his day. But his claim is that God Almighty sees, God knows, God is not fooled, and God will ultimately call the whole dismal "herd" to account and to retribution.

d) God's Judgment Is Good News! (vv. 14–16)

Here comes the surprise, in the middle of the chapter:

> They raise their voices, they shout for joy; from the west they acclaim the LORD's majesty. Therefore in the east give glory to the LORD; exalt the name of the LORD, the God of Israel, in the islands of the sea. From the ends of the earth we hear singing: "Glory to the Righteous One." (24:14–16a)

Rejoicing?? Really? In the midst of such a chapter of cosmic judgment?

Yes, for this is rejoicing in the triumph of the justice of God—which is one of the biggest themes of biblical faith. It was first expressed unambiguously in the rhetorical question of Abraham, "Will not the Judge of all the earth do right?" (Gen. 18:25). Indeed he will, thank God. For Yahweh is the God who loves justice, the God for whom righteousness and justice are the foundation of his throne. And that is good news to be celebrated.

For it is indeed good news that evil will not have the last word in God's universe. It is good news that unrestrained and unrepentant evil doers will not escape accountability and justice forever. It is good news that Satan and all evil powers will finally be destroyed as Revelation assures us. In other words, the expectation and certainty of God's ultimate judgment here and elsewhere in the Bible, including its climax in Revelation, is part of the gospel itself. Wrongs will be righted. Evil will be destroyed. God will put all things right before he makes all things new—the message of Revelation itself. There is a great, total, cosmic rectification coming. And in Revelation also, as here in Isaiah, it is something to be greeted with rejoicing—as the multiple "Hallelujahs" of Revelation 19 testify when the news goes out that "Babylon has fallen!"

But we should notice very carefully that this is not the rejoicing of vindictive schadenfreude. This is rejoicing in the triumph of God's justice, not gloating at the suffering of the wicked under God's wrath. The quotation above was not complete. Here is Isaiah's groaning response to the vision he is delivering:

> But I said, "I waste away, I waste away! Woe to me! The treacherous betray! With treachery the treacherous betray!" (24:16b)

God is very clear that he takes no pleasure in the death of the wicked. Judgment is his "alien work," his necessary but unwelcome (to himself) response to evil and sin. God inflicting judgment is very real but does not come "from his heart" (Lam. 3:33; NIV's "not willingly" is lit. "not from his heart"). On the contrary, what God longs for is repentance, forgiveness, and life:

> Son of man, say to the Israelites, "This is what you are saying: 'Our offenses and sins weigh us down, and we are wasting away because of them.How then can we live?'"Say to them, "As surely as I live,declares the Sovereign LORD, I take no pleasure in the death of the wicked,but rather that they turn from their ways and live. Turn! Turn from your evil ways! Why will you die, people of Israel?" (Ezek. 33:10–11)

God takes no pleasure in the death of the wicked, and neither should we. On the contrary, God sheds tears over those who suffer under his judgment— as Jeremiah's remarkable oracle of condemnation against Moab reveals. After horrendous descriptions of Moab's humiliating defeat and devastation, God himself expresses these astonishing emotions:

> Therefore I wail over Moab, for all Moab I cry out, I moan for the people of Kir Hareseth. I weep for you, as Jazer weeps, you vines of Sibmah ... . So my heart laments for Moab like the music of a pipe; it laments like a pipe for the people of Kir Hareseth. (Jer. 48:31–32, 36)

There is an ancient Jewish rabbinic tradition commenting on Exodus 15, the song of Moses, and Miriam justifiably celebrating God's triumph over the tyrant Pharaoh and his liberation of the Israelites from genocidal slavery, that when some of the angels wanted to sing along too, God rebuked them saying, "The work of my hands is perishing in the sea, and do you sing songs?" (b. Sanh. 39b).

The visionary wailing and weeping of God, heard by Isaiah and Jeremiah—God sobbing for the suffering of those who bear the ultimate cost of their own folly, recalcitrance, rebellion, and refusal to change—becomes literal and physical when God incarnate in Jesus of Nazareth weeps over the fate of Jerusalem, as he foresees its coming destruction and the suffering it will cause:

> As he approached Jerusalem and saw the city, he wept over it and said, "If you, even you, had only known on this day what would bring you peace—but now it is hidden from your eyes. The days will come upon you when your enemies will build an embankment against you and encircle you and hem you in on every side. They will dash you to the ground, you and the children within your walls. They will not leave one stone on another, because you did not recognize the time of God's coming to you." (Luke 19:41–44)

"Do not weep for me," he said to the women as he stumbled to Calvary, but "weep for yourselves" and for what is coming … . (Luke 23:27–31).

So the ultimate judgment of God will be comprehensive and cosmic—nothing and nobody will be hidden from his final audit or escape his perfect justice. But the fact that this is good news (a matter of simultaneous gladness and grief) leads us to our second main point, as we turn to Isaiah's next chapter.

The Global Reach of God's Salvation (Isaiah 25)

The God who judges is also the God who saves—and there is only one God! Later in the book of Isaiah, the very nations who stand condemned, defeated, and disabused of their impotent gods are summoned to turn for salvation to the same God who has so dismantled them:

> There is no God apart from me, a righteous God and a Savior;
> there is none but me. Turn to me and be saved, all you ends of
> the earth; for I am God, and there is no other. (Isa. 45:21–22)

Isaiah 25 is an incredible contrast to chapter 24. From cosmic judgment we are suddenly uplifted to eternal salvation. Verse 1 is again a summary statement, here of personal praise for God's faithfulness and sovereignty, which will then be filled out in what follows:

> LORD, you are my God; I will exalt you and praise your name,
> for in perfect faithfulness you have done wonderful things,
> things planned long ago. (Isa. 25:1)

The pictures that follow show us three major points about God's salvation:

a) God's Salvation Reaches Even God's Enemies (vv. 2–3)

> You have made the city a heap of rubble, the fortified town a ruin, the foreigners' stronghold a city no more; it will never be rebuilt. Therefore strong peoples will honor you; cities of ruthless nations will revere you. (Isa. 25:2–3)

"The city" in verse 2 probably refers to Babylon, or Tyre, or their symbolizing the accumulated human arrogance, greed, and violence that eventually gets portrayed as the great prostitute "Babylon" in Revelation. This is the "city of man" in rebellion against God, sinful, corrupt, destructive, consumptive, oppressive—and headed for doom.

But, amazingly verse 3 pictures what the Bible in various other places affirms, namely that there will be people from even those enemy nations and cities who will turn to God to honor and fear him, and thereby ultimately to be saved. Isaiah 25:3 is a small instance of that persistent hope—but a real one nevertheless. A much fuller and breathtaking vision comes in Isaiah 19. In the first half of the chapter, contemporary Egypt is placed relentlessly under the judgment of God in every aspect of its social, political, agricultural, economic, and spiritual life. But then in the second half, in an eschatological reversal, "in that day"—God will intervene in "Egypt" with an "exodus" reloaded—they will cry out to him and he will send a savior. And in the climax, along with Assyria, they will become part of the very people of God with Israel. Archenemies turned into God's own people!

This motif finds its pinnacle in the book of Revelation. Throughout the book, the nations and the kings are "the bad guys." They are in rebellion against God, persecuting and slaying God's people, and in league with the dragon and the beasts. They are unmistakably "enemies," targets of God's acts of judgment. But, in almost inconceivable redemptive reversal, John's vision of the new creation envisages nations and kings, in transformed humility, bringing all their glory and splendor no longer to the city of the great prostitute but into the city of God. These verses in Revelation 21 are like an expanded commentary on the tantalizing brevity of Isaiah 25:3:

> The city does not need the sun or the moon to shine on it, for the glory of God gives it light, and the Lamb is its lamp. The nations will walk by its light, and the kings of the earth will bring their splendor into it. On no day will its gates ever be shut, for there will be no night there. The glory and honor of the nations will be brought into it. Nothing impure will ever enter it, nor will anyone who does what is shameful or deceitful, but only those whose names are written in the Lamb's book of life. (Rev. 21:23–27)

So our future hope is that, yes, God will indeed judge the earth with his justice, but God will also save, even from among his enemies, those who turn to him in repentance. Hallelujah! For that, of course, includes all of us. For it was while we were still enemies that God loved us and Christ died for us (Rom. 5:8–10).

b) God's Salvation Reaches the Poor and Needy (v. 4)

We have seen that God's judgment is comprehensive and impartial (24:2). But it is also discriminating. God hears the cry of the oppressed and exploited, the poor and needy, the violated and victimized. And God offers refuge for them:

> You have been a refuge for the poor, a refuge for the needy in their distress, a shelter from the storm and a shade from the heat. (25:4)

What is this "storm"? In the following verse it is a metaphor for the invading enemy, but in the wider context it almost certainly also carries the sense of God's judgment—since the human enemies in Israel's story were in any case the agents of God's historical temporary acts of judgment. But as we've seen, the "storm" of chapter 24 is of ultimate and cosmic proportions.

And where is this refuge? In God himself! "*You* have been a refuge for the poor … ." Here then is the astonishing paradox: God himself is the shelter from the storm of God's own wrath and judgment! God in mercy provides protection from God acting in justice. Mysterious indeed. But not unprecedented in Israel's history and faith. In that last terrible plague on Egypt—the death of their firstborn—God provided the Israelites a "shelter" from the "Destroyer"—the angel of death as he is called in the narrative. God himself provided the refuge, through the daubed blood of the Passover lamb, from his own agent of judgment.

Ultimately, of course, the rest of the Bible explains that God could himself be the shelter from the storm of his own judgment only by choosing to bear that judgment in himself, in the person of his Son, Jesus Christ. God the just judge chose to become the unjustly judged—in our place and for our sake—on the cross. Which is why we can truly join the psalmist in gratitude and assurance that "God is our refuge and strength," and all that follows in Psalm 46.

> Beneath the Cross of Jesus, I fain would take my stand,
> The shadow of a mighty Rock, within a weary land … ."[1]

---

1 Elizabeth Cecilia Clephane, *Beneath the Cross of Jesus.*

c) *God's Salvation Reaches Even Beyond Death Itself (vv. 6–8, cf. 26:19)*

This is one of the most jaw-dropping visions of any prophet. It is well known that the ancient Israelites, unlike surrounding ANE cultures, especially Egypt, did not show great curiosity or engage in much speculation about life after death. Which does not mean that they had no faith beyond the boundaries of this life. Yahweh, after all, is indeed the Lord of life and death, as Hannah could sing fairly early in Israel's journey of faith (1 Sam. 2:6). And psalmists could occasionally glimpse a death-defying future for the faithful righteous (e.g. Pss. 16:9–11; 49:15; 73:23–26). But here, Isaiah goes beyond that simple truth to a glorious vision of Yahweh taking death out of the picture altogether:

> On this mountain the LORD Almighty will prepare a
> feast of rich food for all peoples, a banquet of aged wine—
> the best of meats and the finest of wines. On this mountain
> he will destroy the shroud that enfolds all peoples, the sheet
> that covers all nations; he will swallow up death forever.
> The Sovereign LORD will wipe away the tears from all
> faces; he will remove his people's disgrace from all the earth.
> The LORD has spoken. (25:6–8)

Two wonderfully graphic pictures are combined here:

i) A banquet for all peoples (v. 6). One of the horrible portrayals of God's judgement in 24:7–11 is the loss of food and wine and the ensuing starvation, hunger, and thirst—powerful imagery of suffering and death. But here, in this glorious opposite, God is preparing a banquet, a massive feast of the very best food and drink one could imagine, and not just for Judah, but for an infinite guest list—"all peoples"!

In the New Testament, this turns into the great messianic banquet, the wedding feast of the Lamb as Revelation will describe it. Indeed, Jesus himself—astonished by the faith of a Gentile centurion—echoes Isaiah in envisaging people from all over the world coming to the feast—a wonderful anticipation of the gentile mission and its now global extent:

> When Jesus heard this, he was amazed and said to those
> following him, "Truly I tell you, I have not found anyone in
> Israel with such great faith. I say to you that many will come
> from the east and the west, and will take their places at the
> feast with Abraham, Isaac and Jacob in the kingdom of heaven.
> But the subjects of the kingdom will be thrown outside, into
> the darkness, where there will be weeping and gnashing of
> teeth." (Matt. 8:10–12)

ii) Death swallowed up forever (vv. 7–8). There's not much point being a guest at the most fantastic meal if you're going to die soon anyway (unless your life's Epicurean philosophy actually is, "Eat, drink and be merry for tomorrow we die"). So God's promise here is extraordinary and—I was going to say "breathtaking," but actually "breath-giving" would be better! Here at last is the reversal of the curse of Genesis 3, when, as Paul said, death entered the world through sin. But when God's judgment has dealt with sin forever, then death itself—as the consequence of sin—will be destroyed too:

- the shroud that covers every prostrate human corpse—gone! Destroyed!
- the Great Swallower—the black hole of death—itself swallowed up forever!
- the tears that have soaked human faces at every bereavement— wiped away!

Those tears will be wiped away personally by the Lord God himself, what tenderness! And this is the gloriously comforting promise that John hears repeated in person from the very throne of God when heaven comes to earth and the bridegroom embraces his bride:

> He will wipe every tear from their eyes. There will be no more death or mourning or crying or pain, for the old order of things has passed away. (Rev. 21:4)

And where will God do all this? "On this mountain. ..." (v. 7). By which Isaiah meant Zion, the mountain of the Lord. And indeed, it would be exactly there, at the hill of Calvary, that God swallowed up death, by taking it into himself in the death of his own Son, made sin for us, crucified, died, and buried, so that through his death we might share his risen and eternal life, and have assurance of the undergirding truth of Isaiah 25:7–8.

"How great the Father's love for us, how vast beyond all measure ... ."[2]

And so, the global reach of God's salvation fully covers the global reach of God's judgment.

So what?

Our response must surely be what Isaiah himself calls for in the immediately following verse 9, and then in chapter 26:

> In that day they will say, "Surely this is our God; we trusted in him, and he saved us. This is the LORD, we trusted in him; let us rejoice and be glad in his salvation." (Isa. 25:9)

---

2 Stuart Townend, *How Deep the Father's Love for Us.*

You will keep in perfect peace those whose minds are steadfast, because they trust in you. Trust in the LORD forever, for the LORD himself, is the Rock eternal. (Isa. 26:3–4)

CHAPTER 4

Toward a Biblical Theology of Calamity

by Michel G. Distefano

I am the LORD, and there is no other.
I form the light and create darkness, I bring prosperity
and create disaster; I, the LORD, do all these things.
—Isaiah 45:6–7

Calamities in the Bible are described with general terms, in various lists, and as specific events. God is the cause of calamities; there are thousands of verses that confirm this, not just Isaiah 45:7! But he still holds humans morally responsible for the calamities he brings. Calamity plays a major role in salvation and judgment in the Bible, that is, how, when, and why God deals retributive justice. Calamity is so pervasive in the Scriptures that I only list and discuss representative verses. At the end I will discuss living in the midst of calamities and weathering these storms.

Definition, Scale, and Lists and Catalogs

Merriam-Webster defines calamity as "a disastrous event marked by great loss and lasting distress and suffering.[1] In this paper, "calamity," "disaster," and "catastrophe" are used interchangeably for the underlying Hebrew words, in the body of the text and in the translations. I quote from different English versions to preserve the nuances of the originals.

Large-Scale Calamitous Events

Small-scale calamities affect individuals, houses, and clans, which the Bible describes as the result of personal enmities and injuries and as God's judgment. This paper will focus on large-scale calamities that affect larger populations. In the Bible, such population groups inhabit unwalled settlements, walled cities, tribal territories, and nations. At times of greatest distress, the entire globe and the cosmos will be affected.

---

1 Merriam-Webster, s.v. "calamity (n.)," accessed January 14, 2023, https://www.merriam-webster.com/dictionary/calamity.

Lists and Catalogs

> You have not obeyed me; you have not proclaimed freedom to your own people. So I now proclaim "freedom" for you, declares the LORD—"freedom" to fall by the sword, plague and famine. (Jer. 34:17)

This verse includes the standard three-part list of calamities—famine, sword, and plague. The two-part list drops "plague" and the four-part list adds "wild animals." The two and three-part lists occur together in Jeremiah 44:12–13, as disasters that God is determined to bring on Judah (v. 11). The four-part list occurs in Ezekiel 14:21, as "four dreadful judgments," also called disasters (v. 22), that God is sending against Jerusalem—"sword and famine and wild beasts and plague—to kill its men and their animals." These four calamities were also mentioned in the previous verses (vv. 13, 15, 17, 19). While wild animals do not make the list very often, they are mentioned frequently in the catalogs, for example, "a lion from the forest will attack them, a wolf from the desert will ravage them, a leopard will lie in wait near their towns" (Jer. 5:6). The four-part list is also taken up in the New Testament, for example: "I looked, and there before me was a pale horse! Its rider was named Death, and Hades was following close behind him. They were given power over a fourth of the earth to kill by sword, famine and plague, and by the wild beasts of the earth" (Rev. 6:8).[2]

In addition to these standard lists, there are catalogs that describe a variety of calamitous events in much more detail, for example, the plagues of Egypt (Ps. 78:44–51; 105:28–36), the covenant curses (Lev. 26:14–39; Deut. 28:15–68), and numerous prophetic discourses that vividly describe awful disasters and their devastating effects on the land and its people, including the calamities in the contexts of the lists I just mentioned, and the book of Lamentations. I will briefly describe some of these disasters.

Calamitous Events

Natural Disasters

A natural disaster is "a sudden and terrible event in nature (such as a hurricane, tornado, or flood) that usually results in serious damage and many deaths."[3] The Bible describes many such weather events: a storm in

---

2 For other examples of these lists, see: the two-part lists in Jeremiah 5:12; 11:22; 14:13, 15–16, 18; 42:16; 44:12, 27; the three-part lists in Jeremiah 14:12; 21:7, 9; 24:10; 27:8, 13; 29:17–18; 32:24, 36; 34:17; 42:17, 22; Ezekiel 5:12; 6:11–12; 7:15; and the four-part lists in Deuteronomy 32:24–25 and Ezekiel 5:16–17. In each case, it is specifically mentioned in the immediate context that the items are calamities sent by God.

3 Merriam-Webster, s.v. "natural disaster (n.)," accessed January 14, 2023, https://www. merriam-webster.com/dictionary/natural%20disaster.

general, rain, lightning, hail, whirlwind, flood, and earthquake. In the Bible, God controls nature and causes all these calamities. Calamities interact as systems. God controls rain, so withholding it or sending too much can be equally devastating. Drought causes famine; too much rain causes flooding. This simple mechanism is mentioned in Job 12:15: "If he holds back the [rain]waters, there is drought; if he lets them loose, they devastate the land." Rainstorms also hold other calamities within—lightning/fire, wind, hail, thunder, and darkness.

Flood. The first natural disaster was the Genesis flood. God promised to not send such a devastating flood again (Gen. 8:21; 9:11, 15; Isa. 54:9). But the power and devastation of local flooding was well known. For example, "a flood will carry off his house, rushing waters on the day of God's wrath" (Job 20:28). The ancients were also aware of the power of flooding rivers (e.g., of the Euphrates [Isa. 8:7–8]) and of flash floods of wadis.

Forest fire. Forest fires advanced like storms (Ps. 83:14–15) and "consumed everything around" (Jer. 21:14 ; cf. Ps. 83:14). God warns that his wrath "will break out and burn like fire because of the evil you have done—burn with no one to quench it" (Jer. 21:12; cf. Nah. 1:6). Just as the ancient world was destroyed by the flood, "the present heavens and earth are reserved for fire, being kept for the day of judgment and destruction of the ungodly" (2 Pet. 3:7).

Rainstorm. A rainstorm is a whole system of calamities. A downpour of rain causes flooding. Storm wind causes destruction. The sound of thunder can be terrifying. Lightning causes fires. And hail intensifies the devastation. An excellent example of the power of the storm is: "The Lord has one [Assyria] who is powerful and strong. Like a hailstorm and a destructive wind, like a driving rain and a flooding downpour, he will throw it forcefully to the ground" (Isa. 28:2). On the sea, violent storms can cause shipwrecks and loss of life (Jon. 1; Acts 27).

Drought and famine. God controls the rain, drought, and famine, "when the heavens are shut up and there is no rain because your people have sinned against you" (1 Kgs. 8:35). For instance, God offers David a choice of calamity, one of which is three years of famine in the land (2 Sam. 24:13). The Bible records many famines caused by drought, some of which lasted several years: in Canaan (Gen. 12:10; 26:1); Egypt and the surrounding region, including Canaan (Gen. 41:54; 47:13, for seven years); Judah (Ruth 1:1; 2 Sam. 21:1, for three years; Neh. 5:3); Samaria (1 Kgs. 17:1; 18:1–2, for three years); Gilgal (2 Kgs. 4:38); Shunem (2 Kgs. 8:1, for seven years); and the entire Roman world (Acts 11:28 [for several years according to extrabiblical sources]).

Plague. The three-part list in Jeremiah 16:4 substitutes "deadly diseases" for expected "plague" (*deber*). Plague as a disease has a high mortality rate, thought to be bubonic plague. One example is the plague on the Philistines in 1 Samuel: God (whose hand was heavy on the people, 5:6) sent a plague (6:4–5) that caused suffering and death (5:11–12) against the Philistine cities of Ashdod (5:6), Gath (5:9), Ekron (5:10–11), and eventually Gaza and Ashkelon, the five fortified cities and their unwalled villages, extending it to the whole country (6:4–5, 17). The Philistine's later acknowledged that God sent the plague; it wasn't just a coincidence: "Send it [the ark] on its way, but keep watching it. If it goes up to its own territory, toward Beth Shemesh, then the LORD has brought this great disaster on us. But if it does not, then we will know that it was not his hand that struck us but that it happened to us by chance" (6:8–9, and see v. 12).

Earthquake. There is an earthquake mentioned in Zechariah 14:5: "You will flee as you fled from the earthquake in the days of Uzziah" (cf. Amos 1:1). Earthquakes are also mentioned as part of "birth pangs" (Matt. 24:7–8), and in connection with theophany and accompanying judgment, especially in the apocalypse.

Man-Made Disasters

War and its effects. A marching army easily conquers unwalled villages and the open fields around them, devastating the land, crops, and forests, and slaughtering animals and people. As an army approaches, many flee to walled, fortified cities. A siege cuts off food supplies, and sometimes water. When food runs out, there is a siege famine. Starvation is accompanied by plague and disease. "Those in the city will be devoured by famine and plague" (Ezek. 7:15). For those who would venture outside the city walls, only the sword awaits. Yet "those killed by the sword are better off than those who die of famine; racked with hunger, they waste away for lack of food from the field" (Lam. 4:9). When an army finally breaches a city wall there is more slaughter, followed by looting, burning, and further destruction of temples, palaces, buildings, fortifications, and city walls. Some survivors are exiled. After an army retreats, the very poorest who remain continue to suffer starvation, as the invaders have eaten (and/or destroyed) all the food and disrupted the whole agricultural system; there is no harvest, no seed to sow, and no animals left to plow. It takes time to replenish the food supply.

Natural disasters serve as metaphors for marching armies and the devastation they cause. Armies are described as a flood, torrent, and raging waters (Ps. 124:4–5) that sweep through like a flood (Dan. 9:26; 11:10, 40), river floodwaters (Isa. 8:7–8), and an approaching storm (Ezek. 38:9; Isa. 28:2).

Genocide. If we define genocide as "the deliberate and systematic destruction of a racial, political, or cultural group,"[4] without requiring the absolute precision of no survivors, as in the ancient Near Eastern context, there were a few attempted ones in the Bible. Two of them were at God's command: the seven nations occupying the promised land (Deut. 7:2) and the Amalekites (Exod. 17:14; Deut. 25:19; 1 Sam. 15:2–3). Both groups were initially almost wiped out, with surviving remnants (the Canaanites in Josh. 16:10 and other places, and the Amorites in 2 Sam. 21:2–3; the Amalekites in 1 Chron. 4:43). These genocides were punishment for the "abominable practices of those nations" (Deut. 18:9, ESV) that reached "full measure" (Gen. 15:16), and for Amalek's attack on Israel's stragglers (Deut. 25:17–18). There was also Saul's attempted genocide of the Gibeonites (2 Sam. 21:1–2), which God punished with a three-year famine (v. 1).

God threatened to destroy Israel for worshipping the calf idol and to start afresh with Moses (Exod. 32:10). But after Moses interceded, "the LORD relented and did not bring on his people the disaster he had threatened" (Exod. 32:14; cf. the incident in Num. 14:12–20). The nations also attempted to destroy Israel at several turns, but God prevented them. The first of these was Pharaoh's plan to kill all the Israelite males, which would have led to intermarriage of the females, assimilation, and the disappearance of Israel (Exod. 1:15–22). The second and third happened while Israel was in exile: "'Come,' they say, 'let us destroy them as a nation, so that Israel's name is remembered no more'" (Ps. 83:4), and the officially sanctioned genocide throughout the Persian empire (Est. 3:12–14; 8:5–6).

Uncreation

All large-scale calamities that devastate the land can be viewed as retroversions of creation, with the absence of the things created on day six, five, four, etc. In a few cases, the landscape returns to its original uncreated state—a dark desert wasteland covered with water. The most systematic retroversion is described in the Genesis flood.[5] The account also describes the renewal of creation in the same order as Genesis 1. After God promised to not flood the earth again, the undoing of creation can only reach the point of original darkness, for example, in the plagues of Egypt[6] and in Jeremiah's

---

4 Merriam-Webster, s.v. "genocide (n.)," accessed January 14, 2023, https://www.merriam-webster.com/dictionary/genocide.

5 Peter described this reversal as, "The earth was formed out of water and by water. By these waters also the world of that time was deluged and destroyed" (2 Pet. 3:5–6).

6 That is, the darkness in Exod. 10:21–23. From the ancient Egyptian perspective, the plagues represented disorder and the movement toward the original undifferentiated state, without forms and in darkness.

vision of "disaster from the north" and "disaster [that] follows disaster" (Jer. 4:6, 20), referring to Babylon's destruction of Judah:

> I looked at the earth, and it was formless and empty; and at the heavens, and their light was gone. I looked at the mountains, and they were quaking; all the hills were swaying. I looked, and there were no people; every bird in the sky had flown away. I looked, and the fruitful land was a desert; all its towns lay in ruins before the LORD, before his fierce anger. (Jer. 4:23–26)

The ultimate uncreation is in 2 Peter and Revelation, in which "the present heavens and earth are reserved for fire, being kept for the day of judgment and destruction of the ungodly" (2 Pet. 3:7), and "the first heaven and the first earth had passed away, and there was no longer any sea" (Rev. 21:1). God's judgments at the end devastate the earth before he makes everything new, including "a new heaven and a new earth" (Rev. 21:1, 5).

Divine Sovereignty and Human Responsibility for Calamity

Divine Causality

> Ask the animals, and they will teach you, or the birds in the sky, and they will tell you; or speak to the earth, and it will teach you, or let the fish in the sea inform you. Which of all these does not know that the hand of the LORD has done this?
> —Job 12:7–9

In Isaiah 40–48, God declares he is incomparable (Isa. 40:18, 25; 44:7; 46:5, 9). He alone is God, there is no other, there was no other, and there will be no other (Isa. 43:10; 44:8; 45:5–6, 14, 18, 21–22; 46:9). He is the only one who announces calamity before it happens (Isa. 43:9; 44:7; 45:21; 46:10; 48:3, 5, 14–15), and he is the one who does/brings it (41:4; 46:11; 48:3, 16). He was the one who sent calamity against Israel (42:24–25, i.e., "the violence of war" [v. 25], destruction [43:28], desecration [47:6], and many other references to the destruction of Jerusalem and the exile); he was about to send calamity against Babylon (emphatically in 47:11—disaster, calamity, and catastrophe); and he was about to gather Israel from exile and prosper them again, that is, reverse their calamity.

God also challenges idols to do good or bad, that is, to cause prosperity or bring calamity, and to announce it beforehand:

> Tell us, you idols, what is going to happen. Tell us what the former things were, so that we may consider them and know their final outcome. Or declare to us the things to come, tell us

what the future holds, so we may know that you are gods. Do something, whether good or bad so that we will be dismayed and filled with fear. But you are less than nothing and your works are utterly worthless. (Isa. 41:22–24)

In contrast, God says that he is going stir up a king and his army, Cyrus and the Persian army, against Babylon, which would also be good news for Jerusalem (Isa. 41:25–28; cf. vv. 2–4; 45:1, 13).

As these themes continue to develop and intertwine, God reiterates that he is the cause of the calamity that will soon befall Babylon (45:1–6) and the cause of the restored fortunes of Jerusalem (45:13–17). And in between these two claims, he states unequivocally, in a kind of tailor-made theological statement, that he causes calamity and prosperity:

> I am the LORD, and there is no other. I form the light and create darkness, *I bring prosperity and create disaster*; I, the LORD, do all these things. (Isa. 45:6–7)

There are also other similar statements: "Is it not from the mouth of the Most High that both calamities and good things come?" (Lam. 3:38; cf. Job 2:10; Eccl. 7:14), and "when disaster comes to a city, has not the LORD caused it?" (Amos 3:6). And there are thousands of verses that say God causes specific calamities, including prophetic warnings and predictions of calamities, which only God can announce beforehand and bring to pass (e.g., in the immediate context of Isaiah 45:7), war calamities wrought by oppressors and armies that God sent as his instruments, and God as the affecter of curses.

Human Responsibility and Retributive Justice

God sends calamity as punishment for sin. Simply put, "retributive justice [is] punishment proportionate to sin."[7] God dealing retributive justice is one of the main themes of Scripture, beginning with punishment for the breach of the first commandment (Gen. 2:17; 3:16–19, 23–24) and culminating in the punishment of sinners in Revelation. In between are the covenant curses, prophetic discourse on breaching the covenant, the wisdom tradition of rewards and punishments, the argument in Romans that "the wages of sin

---

7 D. A. Carson, *How Long, O Lord? Reflections on Suffering and Evil*, 2nd ed. (Nottingham: IVP, 2006), 148, Kindle for PC. The Bible writers were aware that "a simple theory of retributive justice—punishment proportionate to sin"—"the link between suffering and retribution found in, say, Deuteronomy, Proverbs, and Romans" does not hold true in every case (Carson, 148, 140). Some books and passages questioned the limits of mechanistic retribution (Job, Ecclesiastes, and parts of the Psalms). As Carson puts it, they "disown simplistic, mathematically precise, and instant applications of the doctrine of retribution" (155). In our case, large-scale calamities are indiscriminate in nature and can affect the innocent. There is also suffering disproportionate to sin.

is death" (6:23), and most importantly, the death of Jesus for our sins, "the righteous for the unrighteous" (1 Pet. 3:18). This is so because God created a moral universe, with wisdom at his side "like a master workman" (Prov. 8:30, RSV) walking in righteousness and justice (v. 20).

Ezekiel 7 is a good example of retribution theology, in which "disaster! unheard-of disaster!" (v. 5) and "calamity upon calamity" (v. 26), with sword, famine, and plague (v. 15) are repayment for sinful conduct and judgment for detestable practices (with slight variation, vv. 3–4, 8–9, 27), "to punish the wicked" (v. 11) "because of their sins" (v. 13), including trusting in wealth (19–21), idolatry (20), bloodshed and violence (v. 23), and pride (v. 24). A summary of the prophetic catalogs of sins would include idolatry, adultery, bloodshed, violence, greed, theft, bribery and injustice, oppression of the vulnerable in society, and arrogance and pride, all based on a lack of knowledge of God and his commandments and the defilement of his moral creation order with structural injustice that promotes insatiable power and greed.

Interchangeable Causalities

Divine sovereignty and human moral responsibility are so intertwined that both causalities are used interchangeably. Jeremiah says, "*Your own conduct and actions have brought this on you. This is your punishment*" (Jer. 4:18), referring to God "*bringing disaster* [the Babylonian army] from the north" (v. 6; cf. "disaster follows disaster, the whole land lies in ruins," v. 20). Another example of this is: "*I [the LORD Almighty] scattered them* with a whirlwind among all the nations, where they were strangers. The land they left behind them was so desolate that no one traveled through it. This is how *they made* the pleasant land desolate" (Zech. 7:14). Before the exile, "Jerusalem and its surrounding towns were at rest and prosperous, and the Negev and the western foothills were settled" (v. 7); now it lay desolate. Even though *God* scattered them, the final catastrophe in a calamitous chain of events that he caused, he says that "*they* made the pleasant land desolate."[8]

Moral Corruption Causes Earth Devastation

These passages make the crucial point that moral decay is ultimately responsible for calamities that devastate the earth. This has always been the case and always will be. Before God sent the flood, he "saw how great

---

8 These interchanges are not meant to absolve God of moral responsibility by placing the blame on others; he is a righteous judge. "God stands behind evil in such a way that not even evil takes place outside the bounds of his sovereignty, yet the evil is not morally chargeable to him: it is always chargeable to secondary agents, to secondary causes" (Carson, *How Long?*, 189).

the wickedness of the human race had become on the earth, and that every inclination of the thoughts of the human heart was only evil all the time" (Gen. 6:5). "The earth was corrupt in God's sight and was full of violence. God saw how corrupt the earth had become, for all the people on earth had corrupted their ways" (Gen. 6:11–12). "Corrupt" refers to moral corruption.[9] "So God said to Noah, 'I am going to put an end to all people, for the earth is filled with violence because of them. I am surely going to destroy both them *and the earth*'" (Gen. 6:13). God destroyed the earth and its people in the flood because of moral corruption. This destruction was the undoing of creation on land—every living creature on the land with the breath of life perished, all vegetation was destroyed, and the land reverted to its original state, a desert wasteland covered with water. We can also fill in that clouds and rain blocked the sun and it was dark.

Similarly, when the time comes for "destroying those who destroy the earth" (Rev. 11:18), God will pour calamities upon the ungodly in an intense buildup to the final judgment. In the process, he will destroy the earth. Koester gives an excellent summary of how the verb *diaphtheirein*, "to destroy," is used in this verse, which "can mean to destroy physically and to ruin morally. When used of the opponents of God, both ideas are operative." He then identifies the "agents of destruction" in Revelation that "ruin the earth morally" as Satan who "fosters idolatry," the beast that "makes itself an object of worship," the false prophet who "ruins people by deceiving and coercing them into participation in the ruler cult," and Babylon, "a corrupting whore, [who] entwines the nations through the allure of profit and luxury" and is "morally ruinous."[10] Just like in Old Testament passages above, God will destroy physically those who ruin the earth morally. As he pours out judgments in the last seal, trumpets, and bowls, the ungodly will be killed and in the process the land will be devastated, to the point that some of it will revert to its uncreated state.

How and When God Sends Calamity

- God is patient, long-suffering, and "slow to anger" (Exod. 34:6).
- God does not want "anyone to perish, but everyone to come to repentance" (2 Pet. 3:9).
- "He does not enjoy bringing affliction or suffering on mankind" (Lam. 3:33, HCSB).

---

9 It is also one of the definitions in David J. A. Clines, ed., *The Dictionary of Classical Hebrew* (Sheffield, Eng.: Sheffield Academic Press; Sheffield Phoenix Press, 1993–2011), s.v. "שׁחת."

10 Craig R. Koester, *Revelation: A New Translation with Introduction and Commentary*, The Anchor Yale Bible (New Haven: Yale Univ. Press, 2014), 516–17.

- In his patience, God warns through his prophets (2 Kgs. 17:23), sending them again and again (Jer. 44:4).

- In his patience, God sends calamities of ever-increasing intensity (e.g., after God sends ever-intensifying calamities he repeatedly says, "Yet you have not returned to me" [Amos 4]).

- Finally, when sin saturates a large, unrepentant group, he sends awful, intensive, destructive calamities (e.g., the flood, and the destructions of Sodom and Gomorrah, the nations occupying the promised land, Nineveh, and Babylon).

- There are other mysteries at play, including how the unseen world with its divine councils, wars, and enmities affect life on earth.

Jesus's Teaching on Calamities in the Present Age: The Beginning of Birth Pains

Jesus addressed underlying assumptions about retributive justice and calamities in his day:

> Now there were some present at that time who told Jesus about the Galileans whose blood Pilate had mixed with their sacrifices. Jesus answered, "Do you think that these Galileans were worse sinners than all the other Galileans because they suffered this way? I tell you, no! But unless you repent, you too will all perish. Or those eighteen who died when the tower in Siloam fell on them—do you think they were more guilty than all the others living in Jerusalem? I tell you, no! But unless you repent, you too will all perish." (Luke 13:1–5)

Jesus did not deny that retribution theology played a role in these calamities. The Galileans and Jerusalemites were sinners, but not necessarily worse sinners than their fellows. The first lesson he drew was that the living should not judge the dead. The second lesson was that the living should repent.

In another episode, Jesus regarded calamities as normally occurring events before the end:

> You will hear of wars and rumors of wars, but see to it that you are not alarmed. Such things must happen, but the end is still to come. Nation will rise against nation, and kingdom against kingdom. There will be famines and earthquakes in various places. All these are the beginning of birth pains. (Matt 24:6–8)

War, famine, and earthquakes will continue in various places in the present age, and intensify at the end. The first four seals in Revelation 6 follow the same prophetic timeline. Before the cataclysmic, apocalyptic judgments of the sixth seal, there will be conquering (v. 2), sword (v. 4), famine (v. 6), and an outburst of sword, famine, plague, and wild beasts "given power over a fourth of the earth to kill" (v. 8). These words are also the words of Jesus (Rev. 1:1; 22:16). In short, the judgment of the nations predicted in the prophets (e.g., Jer. 25:32) in "the days that are coming" (Jer. 9:25–26) blended with visions of the "day of the Lord" and judgment during the "last days," which began with Jesus's appearance. All calamities in various places are types and warnings of the most intense and final calamities of the apocalypse. Today Jesus would say, "Repent, or you too will perish." It was in the context of teaching about present and future calamities that he said, "Heaven and earth will pass away, but my words will never pass away" (Matt. 24:35).

Living in the midst of Calamity

When Calamity Strikes at a Distance:

- We the living must not callously judge those who died in calamities.
- We also must not rejoice in destruction—"One who rejoices over calamity will not go unpunished" (Prov. 17:5, HCSB; cf. Job 31:29).
- We must examine ourselves to see whether there is something we should repent of.
- We must let calamity do its work in others, as a call to repentance.
- We must refocus on God's moral creation order.
- We must refrain from discussing the mysteries of God's sovereignty in salvation and judgment, which we simply cannot know.
- Finally, we must help: "The disciples, as each one was able, decided to provide help [famine relief]" (Acts 11:29).

When Calamity Strikes at Home

Since natural disasters are indiscriminate by nature and can affect anyone, we may find ourselves suffering for Christ in God's larger plan of salvation and judgment. But we know that he does warn, single out, and rescue his people from calamities. He also promises to care for his people during disasters.

We may not know how God will care for us until calamity strikes or future events unfold, but we can read about how he cared for his people in the past and how he will in the future. A short list of verses will suffice:

- "The blameless spend their days under the LORD's care, and their inheritance will endure forever. In times of disaster they will not wither; in days of famine they will enjoy plenty" (Ps. 37:18–19).

- "If he did not spare the ancient world when he brought the flood on its ungodly people, but protected Noah … and seven others; if he condemned the cities of Sodom and Gomorrah … and made them an example of what is going to happen to the ungodly; and if he rescued Lot … if this is so, then the Lord knows how to rescue the godly from trials and to hold the unrighteous for punishment on the day of judgment" (2 Pet. 2:5–7, 9).

- "The LORD makes a distinction between Egypt and Israel" (Exod. 11:7; cf. 9:4; 9:26; 10:23).

- "Come out of her, my people, so that you will not share in her sins, so that you will not receive any of her plagues" (Rev. 18:4).

- It is true that some of his people fill the sufferings of Christ with their deaths. But even in this, there is a constant hope and comfort.

Conclusion

The greatest promise to believers who anticipate or live through calamities is:

> Who shall separate us from the love of Christ? Shall trouble or hardship or persecution or *famine* or nakedness or danger or *sword*? (Rom. 8:35)
> Neither death nor life, neither angels nor demons, neither the present nor the future, nor any powers, neither height nor depth, nor anything else in all creation, will be able to separate us from the love of God that is in Christ Jesus our Lord. (Rom. 8:38–39)

Discussion Questions

1. Carson says "God uses disaster as a megaphone ... [to] call to repentance."[11] If so, who is God speaking to in his message?

2. What does idolatry and greed, which is idolatry, look like today? What do we need to repent of?

3. How does God's sovereignty mitigate fears about current calamities and disasters? Is he in control or not? What parts of his character also mitigate such fears?

4. How does your belief about whether calamities can separate us from the love of God in Christ affect your mission?

---

11 Carson, *How Long?*, 61.

Response

by Han Young Lee

I feel very much honored for having been invited as one of the respondents. However, I have to confess I have no previous expertise in theology of calamity, which put me in a great quandary when I was first contacted by Dr. Jonathan J. Bonk regarding my participation. Nevertheless, in light of current global calamities, such as COVID-19, the Russian invasion of Ukraine, global warming, etc., and provided the subject was presumably within the parameters of biblical theology, I decided to take this opportunity to learn about the subject, to come up with some complementary questions, if any, and to share some of my personal thoughts on Dr. Michel G. Distefano's article. So, it's with a humble spirit of apprentice that here I venture to present my brief response.

Article's Summary

Dr. Michel Distefano's research focuses mainly on biblical "large-scale calamities" that affect not only the population groups in different habitational and geographic spheres but as well the entire globe and the cosmos.

Having mentioned a variety of calamity lists and catalogs within the biblical texts (Jer. 34:17; Ezek. 14:21; Ps. 78:44–51; Rev. 6:8), Dr. Distefano describes some of them under three major categories:

a. Natural disasters
Flood (Gen. 8:21; Job 20:28; Isa. 8:7–8)
Forest fire (Ps. 83:14–15; Jer. 21:14; Nah. 1:6; 2 Pet. 3:7)
Rainstorm (Isa. 28:2; Jon. 1; Acts 27)
Drought and famine, some lasting several years (1 Kgs. 8:35; 2 Sam. 24:13; Gen. 12:10; 26:1; Ruth 1:1; 2 Sam. 21:1, Neh. 5:3; 1 Kgs. 17:1; 18:1–2)
Plague (Jer. 16:4)
Earthquake (Zech. 14:5; Amos 1:1; Matt. 24:7–8)
b. Man-made disasters
War and its effects (Ezek. 7:15)
Genocide (Exod. 17:14; Deut. 7:2, 25:19; 1 Sam. 15:2–3)

c. Uncreation
   Genesis flood (Gen. 6–7)
   Egypt's plagues (Exod. 7:14–12:30)
   Jeremiah's vision (Jer. 4:6, 20)
   Eschatological (2 Peter and Revelation)

Regarding causality as a biblical motif of calamity narratives, Dr. Distefano selectively exposes the following ones:

a. Divine causality (Job 12:7–9)

b. Human responsibility and retributive justice (Gen. 2:17; 3:16–19, 23–24; Ezek. 7; Rom. 6:23)

c. Interchangeable causalities (Jer. 4:6–20)

d. Moral corruption causes earth devastation (Gen. 6:5–13)

On how and when God sends calamity, Dr. Distefano underlies God's patience and long-suffering. Calamity as judgment is the last divine resort and gradual in proportion to intensity and saturation of sin (Exod. 34:6; 2 Pet. 3:9; 2 Kgs. 17:23; Jer. 44:4).

After an exposition of major biblical calamities, mostly from Old Testament texts, a short discussion on Jesus's teaching on calamities in the present age is briefly presented. The author interprets Luke 13:1–5 as a case for retributive justice and Matthew 24:6–8, 35 and Revelation 6:2–8 as the beginning of eschatological birth pain, that is, end phenomena.

Finally, Dr. Distefano proposes some practical ways, drawn from selective biblical texts, on how to deal with calamity. Accordingly, when calamity strikes at a distance, the keyword is empathy, self-reflection, divine mystery, sovereignty, and relief and help. When calamity strikes at home, the keywords are hope and comfort, trusting in God's ultimate care (Ps. 37:18–19; 2 Pet. 2:5–7, 9; Exod. 11:7; Rev. 18:4).

Dr. Distefano concludes that calamity is inevitable even for believers. However, believers are not overcome by it but assured, for "nothing can separate us from the love of Christ" (Rom. 8:35–39).

Some Questions and Thoughts

Dr. Distefano's article was very much informative and thought provoking, especially more vis-à-vis the present time when large calamities of various categories are taking place around the globe. Personally, on my close reading of the article, I recalled my sister who died after being bedridden for twenty-seven years with unbearable excruciating cancer pain. All these led me to ponder some critical issues and questions as follow:

1. This article is meticulous in exposing as many issues as possible that are related to biblical calamities. However, it seems to be covering too many topics, so that towards the end of second half of its discourse one may feel the details are in want.

2. A selective list of biblical calamities was given as natural disasters, man-made disasters, and uncreation. In our modern time of scientific and social development, we understand that they overlap each other and often may find no distinction. In light of scientific advances in disciplines such as medicine, geology, physics, and astronomy, some of the theological reflection on calamity may lose it meaning, significance, and logical persuasion. Should we still consider birth pain as God's punishment when today we have epidurals for the relief of labor pain? Should we consider astronomic phenomena such as entropy, expansion of the universe, death of stars, etc. as uncreation or natural disaster? Though it's clear Dr. Distefano was mainly addressing biblical theological questions, not systematic theology.

3. As to causality as a biblical theme in calamity narratives, whether it's divine, human, or interchangeable, what underlies them all seems mostly to be either divine judgment or retribution. For instance, in a lament and call to repentance in Amos 5:1–17, the prudent reacts in shock and anguish before the calamity that consists of war destruction and natural disasters because they reflect God's judgment on evil.[12] And this nuance, judgment and retribution, is quite consistent throughout calamities in the prophetic books. Unfortunately, this theological reflection faces fierce challenges in our postmodern society as *politically incorrect*. Also, some of the biblical statements, for example, the promise to never again curse the ground because of man's evil (Gen. 8:21), are subject to controversial interpretations. How should we respond to "the ethical revolt against Christian orthodoxy"[13] that is so preponderant in our modern society?

4. Though this article is more of an exposition or description of biblical calamities, an attempt toward a biblical theology of calamity, critical questions regarding divine retribution permeate the whole discourse. This raises many vital theological and contemporary pastoral concerns, especially about theodicy. How can one vindicate a just God who causes calamities?

12 Matthew Goff, "Awe, Wordlessness and Calamity," *Vetus Testamentum* 58 (2008): 642.

13 Andrew Atherstone, "Divine Retribution: A Forgotten Doctrine," *Themelios* 34, no.1 (2009): 59.

5. According to this article, calamity as judgment is the last divine resort and gradual in proportion to intensity and saturation of sin (Exod. 34:6; 2 Pet. 3:9; 2 Kgs. 17:23; Jer. 44:4). I think overall this is true. However, gradation or proportionality is not always consistent in the biblical narratives. In Genesis, the calamity of death came at once, soon after Adam committed the sin. In the book of Numbers, all sorts of calamities as judgment occur every time the Israelites complain against Moses or God (11:1–3; 11:4–34; 12:1–16; 13:1–14:45; 16:1–50; 21:4–9), though intensity seems to have played a role in the event of the Canaanite exploration (Num. 13–14).

6. Finally, this article briefly mentions some of the practical and deeply thought-out ways to deal with calamities, whether they are distant or at home, which I found very positive and helpful. It also lists four critical questions for further discussion. However, I understand it was beyond the scope of this article to further elaborate the prescriptions, especially because of its limited space.

Postlude

Personally, Dr. Distefano's article was very much awakening and laid a groundwork for my future studies on the subject. I realized calamity per se may transcend our reasoning and theological accountability. That in light of current postmodern worldviews and scientific advances, one should not only be faithful to biblical texts but at the same time be much more careful in delivering apologetic discourses in terms of Christian orthodoxy, especially in the matters of divine judgment and retribution.

Charles R. Blaisdell voiced that "there is a crucial difference between saying, on the one hand, that God wills and causes everything, and, on the other hand, saying that God is in the midst of everything working in love to bring the good that is possible."[14] But how such an insight works out practically in our real circumstances is an ongoing challenge. Charles R. Swindoll writes, "When we shift our focus from why to what, we can begin to face the inevitable troubles of life as opportunities for growth and great joy."[15] This sounds like Ecclesiastes 7:14—"When times are good, be happy, but when times are bad, consider this: God has made the one as well as the other." So, though we may still hold on to our traditional doctrine of

---

14 Charles R. Blaisdell, "The Hope That Is Within You: Luke 11:11–13, 1 Peter 3:13–17," *Encounter* 74, no. 3 (2014): 69.

15 Charles R. Swindoll, *Never Lose Hope: Biblical Promises for Times of Trouble, Chaos, and Calamity* (Carol Stream, IL: Tyndale Momentum, an imprint of Tyndale House, 2023), 7.

biblical judgment and retribution in light of calamities, Dr. Distefano seems to implicitly emphasize that the prioritization of theological humility and pastoral care should seriously be considered in any of our efforts "toward a biblical theology of calamity."

CHAPTER 5

Biblical Foundations for Creation Care

by Dave Bookless

"Creation care" is a relatively recent term. It came to prominence in the US during the 1990s, gradually displacing other terms for Christian environmental engagement such as "earthcare," "creation stewardship," and "missionary earthkeeping." As a modern term, creation care is obviously not found in the Bible. That is not in itself a problem. After all, the term "Great Commission" is not in the Bible either! The important issue is whether creation care accurately describes a biblical understanding of humanity's responsibility towards God's world, and to explore biblical foundations for creation care. That is the aim of this paper.

Careful definition is important. In most countries, "creation care" is unproblematic and uncontested, a straightforward description of our God-given responsibility toward creation. However, to some in the US the term is divisively politicized. In an essay entitled, "'Creation Care': Origins and Definition," posted in 2020 on the conservative Capital Research Center website, Hayden Ludwig describes creation care as "a 'gospel' of global warming, junk science, and radical anti-human ideology in place of biblical teaching."[1] That is why this subject is critical for contemporary missiology. If creation care simply mimics secular environmentalism or co-opts contemporary economic or political agendas, then Ludwig's critique is valid. If, however, we can demonstrate that the Bible calls God's people to care for creation as part of mission and discipleship, then the implications are unavoidable and enormous.

This paper seeks to avoid proof texts or favorite passages, instead presenting a biblical overview of God's overarching purposes from creation to new creation. It presupposes that if creation care is part of our mission—the *missio ecclesia*—then it must originate in God's purposes—the *missio Dei*. We can discover God's priorities by examining five decisive divine interventions within the biblical accounts:

---

1   Hayden Ludwig, "'Creation Care': Origins and Definition," Capital Research Center, accessed Dec. 14, 2022, https://capitalresearch.org/article/creation-care-part-1/.

- the Creation
- covenant
- Jesus Christ
- Pentecost and the church
- the new creation

I developed this structure during my doctoral studies at the University of Cambridge. I was addressing the question, Why and how should wild nature be preserved?, examining a biblical understanding of the value of nonhuman creatures: the living beings with which we share this planet. As I reread the Bible with this question in mind, it became clear that these five central biblical themes summarize the *missio Dei*, God's mission within the world. The outline owes much to generations of theologians, from Irenaeus to N. T. Wright, who have presented a thematic overview of the Christian Scriptures with a similar categorization:

- the Creation
- the Fall
- Israel
- Jesus Christ
- the new creation

I used this outline in my book, *Planetwise*, published fifteen years ago and now translated into several languages, including Korean. However, as my thinking developed, I became aware of two things. Firstly, "the Fall," the entry of human sin into the world, differs from the other four themes in that it is a result of human action, whereas the others are divine initiatives. Secondly, moving directly from Jesus Christ to new creation results in an inadequate ecclesiology. While new creation begins with the risen Christ, most eschatology is so future-oriented that it relegates the mission of the church to a footnote.

If instead we ask, What is God's overarching mission? we find the five divine initiatives that I propose. Firstly, "creation," whereby the love between Father, Son, and Holy Spirit existing eternally in loving relationship speaks material creation into being. Secondly, "covenant," in which God responds to sin's catastrophic effects by offering a new start based on response to divine initiative. Thirdly, as the old covenant fails under the weight of human lawbreaking, God comes personally in Jesus Christ to be born, live, die, rise, and ascend to glory offering a new covenant of grace and redemption.

Fourthly, God pours out the Holy Spirit to turn confused disciples into the church, the body of Christ. Finally, Christ will return to judge and save, and to establish God's eternal reign on earth as in heaven. Each of these represent a divine missional initiative with eternal consequences not only for humanity but—crucially—for all creation. We will see each of these provides biblical impetus for creation care as an expression of our calling to participate in God's mission in God's world.

1. Creation

In the beginning, God spoke time and matter into existence. Creation itself is the first missional act: the centrifugal force of divine love moving ever outwards to create our ever-expanding cosmos. The perichoretic dance of eternal love at the heart of the Trinity could not be contained but took material form in planets and galaxies, oceans and mountains, plants, birds, animals, and humans. God's delight in creation is captured in Genesis 1's repeated chorus, "And God saw that it was good," culminating in the final, "God saw all that he had made, and it was very good." The emphasis here is upon the "all." Creation in its entirety and diversity is very good. Importantly, it is not only Genesis that affirms creation's goodness. The Psalms repeatedly express God's delight in creation, and creation's response in worship. Psalm 104 is the most detailed example. Here, humanity is but one of multiple creatures inhabiting different ecological niches. Birds occupy riverside trees, while high mountains belong to wild goats. The night belongs to lions and forest creatures, but daylight allows humans to go out to their fields. Each species is described in loving detail, sustained and cared for by God. Similarly, in Proverbs 8:30–31, wisdom is constantly at God's side, "filled with delight day after day, rejoicing always in his presence, rejoicing in his whole world and delighting in mankind."

Western Christianity has often underplayed the importance of material creation. It has been influenced in turn by Greek philosophy's "great chain of being," where the spiritual is seen as higher than the material, later by the Enlightenment's separation of humanity from the rest of nature—creating a subject/object dualism, and more recently by a fear of worshipping creation rather than the Creator. Yet, as the early church fathers from Augustine to Maximus the Confessor knew, God has given us two books: nature and Scripture. They illustrate and interpret each other, and we need both to know God.

If the mission of creation is to reveal, glorify, and worship God, what about our human vocation towards the natural world? In Genesis we see humanity described as the image of God, a phrase used rarely in Scripture yet the source of vast theological conjecture. Whatever else *imago Dei* may mean, in its context in Genesis 1:26 it chiefly concerns the human mission towards creation. God says, "Let us make mankind in our image, in our likeness, *so that* they may rule over the fish in the sea and the birds in the sky, over the livestock and all the wild animals, and over all the creatures that move along the ground."

Those two words "so that" are key to our mission. We are made in God's image so that we might rule over our fellow creatures. This is our job description. It is the first Great Commission, given to all humanity irrespective of ability, location, or belief. The terms "rule over" or "have dominion" have often been misinterpreted as giving humanity license to exploit creation, but such interpretations abuse Scripture. To bear God's image means to reflect the character and purpose of the God who describes creation as very good. Rule and dominion are related to the biblical ideal of kingship: the shepherd King who nurtures and cares for his flock.

Genesis 2:15 provides a helpful commentary on 1:26–28. Here God calls Adam to "work" and "take care of" the garden. The Hebrew terms ʿabad and šamar can be translated as "serve and "preserve." They permit the shaping and developing of the natural world, but only with the purpose of the sustainable flourishing of the whole. It is a stupid and selfish gardener who overexploits their garden, turning it into a barren wasteland, and yet that is exactly what humanity has done to planet earth. In less than my lifetime, we have allowed 69 percent of the world's wildlife populations to disappear.[2] If God's first missional act creates a flourishing, biodiverse creation, and our first Great Commission is to participate in God's care for that world, then we need to repent, lament, and rethink our missional priorities.

2. Covenant

Today's multiple ecological crises, from biodiversity collapse to climate chaos, are a vivid illustration of how sin has affected every part of God's world. From Genesis 3 onwards, the Bible is clear that sin destroys every relationship. The intimacy Adam and Eve shared with God was shattered as they hid and were expelled from their garden home. They mistrusted each other as interhuman relationships were infected. There was also an ecological impact as Adam, whose name is linked to ʾădamah—soil or earth—was told the soil would be cursed because of him. Throughout the Old Testament, we

---

2 R. E. A. Almond et al., eds., *Living Planet Report 2022—Building a Nature-Positive Society* (Gland, Switzerland: WWF, 2022), 4, https://wwfint.awsassets.panda.org/downloads/embargo_13_10_2022_lpr_2022_full_report_single_page_1.pdf.

see human sin destroying relationships between God, people, and nature. Hosea 4:1–3 vividly overturns the Genesis creation account by describing how "the beasts of the field, the birds in the sky and the fish in the sea are swept away" and the land "dries up" or "mourns" (ESV) because God's people are unfaithful and sinful.

Within this context of distorted and broken relationships God offers the hope of covenant, first through Noah and later through Abraham and Moses. It is often assumed that the biblical covenants focus exclusively on God's chosen people. Yet from the start, and throughout, they also include land and creatures. Of forty-six promises God makes to the patriarchs, only six have no reference to "land," and twenty-nine are largely or exclusively about land.[3]

The Noachian covenant is foundational to later covenants and reveals the scope of God's missional purposes. Noah's ark has often been seen as paradigmatic of the salvation brought about by Christ in the New Covenant. The ark is the ship of salvation, the church. Yet, two simple questions force us to revisit God's missional strategy through the ark and ensuing covenant. First, who gets saved? Second, who is God's covenant with?

The math is very simple! We read of eight human beings saved on the ark: Noah, Ham, Shem, Japheth, and each of their wives. Alongside them were seven pairs of every clean animal and bird, and a single pair of those species that were unclean (Gen. 7:1–3). God's reason is simply "to keep their various kinds alive throughout the earth" (v. 3), implying they have value to God independently of their usefulness to Noah. The biblical account suggests the God who declared creation very good has an enduring interest in all life on earth, not only human life. To put it another way, God's mission— and the mission of the human he calls, Noah—is that the earth should be cleansed of sin so that all life on earth should flourish. To use contemporary language, God's mission includes biodiversity conservation.

Turning to the second question, God's covenant confirms his missional purpose. It is a covenant not only with Noah and his descendants but with "every living creature on earth" (Gen. 9:10, 15–16). The Hebrew text states repeatedly that God's covenant includes nonhuman creatures and the earth itself. The implications for both missiology and soteriology are immense. The earth and its creatures do not exist for humanity's sake. They matter to God in and of themselves. Moreover, our human role—exemplified by Noah—is not only to provide for our own species but includes a vocational mission towards biodiversity conservation. Each species was created by God

---

3 Gerhard von Rad, *The Problem of the Hexateuch and Other Essays* (London: SCM, 1966), 79–80.

according to its kind, was included on the ark of salvation, and is the subject of a covenant relationship with God. Who are we to ignore God's purpose and allow avoidable extinctions?

3. Jesus Christ

The popular understanding of mission among many evangelicals might be summarized as "telling people about Jesus." Yet, to limit God's mission in Christ to humanity is to dilute the biblical vision. The extraordinary fact is that the New Testament's human authors discerned that Jesus's incarnation, life, death, resurrection, and ascension had cosmic implications. In a culture dominated by individualism and anthropocentrism we have tended to dwell only on the personal, but the gospel is both personal and cosmic.

The incarnation is the beginning of recovering the gospel's full scope. John's Gospel begins by quoting Genesis, "In the beginning," before turning the attention to Christ, God's Word, immediately identified as co-creator: "through him all things were made; without him nothing was made that has been made" (John 1:3). A few verses later, we read "the Word became flesh and made his dwelling among us" (v. 14). What is significant is the term "flesh," *sarx* in Greek. Our familiarity with this passage means we fail to notice the importance of this. The obvious term is *anthrōpos*—human— but John chooses *sarx*. Like Hebrew *baśar, sarx* includes both human and animal flesh. John is claiming that in Christ God has chosen to identify with creaturely life. The Creator becomes a creature. It is a radical and, to Jewish ears, deeply shocking claim. Yet, it is not a mistake. Two chapters later John says, "For God so loved the world [*kosmos* in Greek] that he gave his one and only Son" (3:16). John is highly intentional in his vocabulary. While we should not construct our theology on single verses, the cumulative impact of John 1–3 is very clear. The coming of Jesus Christ into the world was both particular and universal. He was born as a male Jewish human baby, a second Adam to rid humanity of Adam's curse. Yet he was also the Creator entering into material creation in order to restore broken relationships throughout the created order.

Turning from John to Paul, Colossians 1:15–20 is a dense theological summary of Christ's significance. As in John 1, Jesus is the creator of all things "visible and invisible," but Paul goes further in stating that all things are created *for* him (v. 16). In other words, the *telos* or purpose of the whole created order is found in Jesus Christ. Rainforests, fossil-fuel reserves, oceans, and every individual species were created for Christ, not for humanity. Paul then goes further in placing Christ at the centre of the cosmos, stating that "in him all things hold together" (v. 17). This is a staggeringly bold claim. The carpenter of Nazareth is the one in whom the whole universe coheres. Distant galaxies, the biogeochemical flows in earth's ecosystems, the bloodstream in a human body all hold together in Christ. Yet, Paul still hasn't finished! He continues that it was God's pleasure "through him [Christ] to reconcile to himself all things, whether things on earth or things in heaven, by making peace through his blood, shed on the cross" (v. 20). The very heart of the gospel, the good news of Jesus's redemptive death, brings reconciliation to "all things." Therefore, if the *missio Dei,* God's mission in Christ, addresses the whole created order, then surely our mission as God's people should also do so? Creation care is an inescapable consequence of the lordship of Christ.

4. Pentecost and the Church

Ecological ecclesiology is still a fledgling subject as theologians grapple with the implications of Christ's saving work for the church's mission in the world. Yet, in the book of Acts and the pastoral Epistles we see theological principles confirming that to proclaim Jesus as Lord necessarily involves proclaiming his lordship over all creation.

Perhaps the clearest text concerning the church's ecological responsibility is Romans 8:19. Paul states, "For the creation waits in eager expectation for the children of God to be revealed." "Children of God" is Pauline language for the redeemed community, so this passage effectively claims, "creation is waiting for the church." Let those words sink in. In our age of ecological crisis when the worldwide church has often appeared irrelevant or uninterested, creation is waiting for the church. Yet, theologically, this makes absolute sense. If Christ is creator, sustainer, and saviour of all creation, and if the church is Christ's body, then the future of creation and the work of the church are deeply intertwined. Both Ephesians and Colossians speak of the connection between Christ as head of the body and as supreme in creation. Ephesians 1:22–23 states "God placed all things under his feet and appointed him to be head over everything for the church, which is his body, the fullness of him who fills everything in every way." Similarly, Colossians 1:18, "He is the head of the body, the church; he is the beginning and the firstborn from among the dead, so that in everything he might have the supremacy."

This connection between Christ's lordship in the church and in creation is, perhaps, a mystery to be contemplated as much as a mechanism to be comprehended, but its implication is clear. Stating "Jesus is Lord" is not only a matter of personal allegiance. Jesus's lordship in the lives of believers and in the church will one day be seen throughout the whole universe. Creation waits eagerly for that day, and the church in the power of the Spirit is tasked and equipped to proclaim Christ's lordship in word and action. Like Adam and Eve in Eden, like Noah with the ark, the *missio ecclesia* must include creation care.

5. New Creation

Evangelical eschatology has been the bugbear of creation care. Dispensationalism has often led to an escapist missiology, with the task restricted to rescuing people from a doomed planet. Yet, to those (like me) reared on visions of believers floating to glory while earth is incinerated, three points should cause us to pause and consider. First, earth's complete destruction goes against the whole sweep of God's missional purposes in creation, covenant, Christ, and the church. Why would the God who commands us to serve and preserve creation, who rescues creatures of every kind in the ark, who sends Jesus so that "all things" might be reconciled, and who reminds us that creation is waiting for the church, decide to destroy his precious creation? Secondly, eschatologies teaching earth's destruction are largely absent in Christian history until the eighteenth century. Is it coincidental that the rise of extractive industrial technologies allowing humanity to destroy the earth arose at the same time as theologies arguing that creation does not ultimately matter? Thirdly, the "proof texts" used to argue for earth's destruction rely on poor exegesis and are outweighed by the witness of Scripture as a whole.

There is not space here to attempt a detailed exegesis of every eschatological passage, but key principles and examples will suffice. In many cases we are dealing with apocalyptic literature's dramatically symbolic language, so caution is needed regarding specific and literal application. What is clear from numerous passages is that there will be both judgment and redemption, discontinuity and continuity. There will be cosmic disruption: nature reacting as mountains, oceans, and heavenly bodies are dislocated. Yet, the emphasis is on being prepared and alert for Christ's return rather than on what exactly will occur.

What we can say with certainty is that the risen Christ provides the hermeneutical key to the future. Jesus's risen body shows both discontinuity and continuity. It is sufficiently different that his disciples struggle to recognize him, and he appears and disappears. Yet, it is a physical body that can eat, be touched, and crucially retains the wounds from his crucifixion. These are important clues to the new creation inaugurated by Christ's resurrection. Significantly, the Greek word always used in Scripture for "new" creation and "new" heavens and earth is *kainos*, not *neos*. *Kainos* is about radical renewal and transformation rather than total replacement. It recognizes change may be radical and fundamental, but what is "new" always has continuity with what has gone before. This is the hermeneutical key.

If we turn to 2 Peter 3, the only passage explicitly referring to earth's destruction by fire, this principle of discontinuity and continuity unlocks its meaning. The passage compares final judgment by fire to the destruction caused by water with Noah's flood. Yet, of course, the flood was a cleansing judgment, not the total replacement of the earth. Similarly, the language of fire would have taken first century Jewish readers to Malachi 3:2 where judgment is pictured as a refiner's fire or launderer's soap—cleansing, not destroying. In 2 Peter 3, the "elements" that are destroyed are not the physical elements of creation but the evil principalities and powers that damage and destroy.

In the end, the only interpretation that makes sense of both those passages that use strong destructive imagery and also those that speak of hope for creation is that final judgment will remove sin, death, and evil in order that what is good and pure might be renewed. Romans 8 speaks of creation groaning in expectation but affirms clearly that "the creation itself will be liberated from its bondage to decay and brought into the freedom and glory of the children of God" (v. 21). Likewise, Peter speaks about Christ's ascension and return: "Heaven must receive him until the time comes for God to restore everything" (Acts 3:21).

God's final plan is not to destroy and replace the creation he calls us to care for, but to renew, refine, and restore it. This paper has demonstrated that each of God's major initiatives in the biblical drama place the care of creation at the center of God's missional purposes. Furthermore, humanity's first task in bearing God's image relates to the conservation and protection of the natural world and its creatures. Thus, creation care is at the heart of both the *missio Dei* and the *missio ecclesia*—it is fundamental to mission.

2024 will see the Lausanne 4 Congress take place in South Korea, building on the 2010 Lausanne 3 Cape Town Congress, the largest global gathering of evangelical leaders in history. Lausanne 4 aims to set the global missions agenda from now until 2050. Currently, creation care is somewhat marginal to an agenda dominated by multiple competing concerns. However, the Lausanne movement needs to study its own Cape Town Commitment:

> If Jesus is Lord of all the earth, we cannot separate our relationship to Christ from how we act in relation to the earth. For to proclaim the gospel that says "Jesus is Lord" is to proclaim the gospel that includes the earth, since Christ's Lordship is over all creation. Creation care is thus a gospel issue within the Lordship of Christ.[4]

Positioning creation care as a gospel issue means it cannot be avoided in framing our missiology. This paper has demonstrated that creation care is neither novel nor incidental to biblical mission. It stems from the *missio*

---

4 Rose Dowsett, *The Cape Town Commitment: Study Edition* (Peabody, MA: Hendrickson, 2012), 28.

Dei, the missional heart of the Godhead. It is central to God's purposes in creation, in covenant, in the saving work of Christ, in the role of the church, and in God's final purposes to make all things new (Rev. 21:5). As we face an era of unprecedented ecological crisis, the Bible gives us clear foundations and a compelling mission regarding Christ-centred creation care.

Questions for Discussion

1. What factors (cultural, historical, theological) have led to creation care being marginalized in much evangelical mission thinking and practice?

2. If our starting point in mission is God's purposes (the *missio Dei*) rather than human need, what difference does that make to the place of creation in mission?

3. How can creation care enhance and combine with other aspects of mission, including apologetics and evangelism, disciple making, church planting, and seeking justice and peace?

4. What practical changes to mission strategy and practice are needed in the light of the biblical call to care for creation?

Response

by Regina Ryu

Key Points

In his paper, "Biblical Foundations for Creation Care," Dave Bookless presents biblical foundations for creation care grounded in *missio Dei*. Bookless begins by asking what God's purpose is for his created world, and in response points to a framework grounded in God's overarching mission, comprising five divine initiatives: the Creation, covenant, Jesus Christ, Pentecost and the church, and new creation. By explaining how each of these has eternal consequences not only for humanity but for *all* creation, Bookless shows that creation care lies at the center of God's missional purposes.

As God's ultimate plan is to renew, refine, and restore his creation in its entirety, Bookless argues that creation care is our God-given responsibility to care for God's whole world. More specifically, since we are primarily charged with the task of protecting and conserving the natural world, creation care must take center stage not only as *missio Dei* but also in terms of *missio ecclesia*. Finally, reminding readers of the Cape Town Commitment proclaiming Christ's lordship over *all* creation and declaring creation care a *gospel issue* within the lordship of Christ, Bookless calls for a firm stance against the continued marginalization of creation care. Specific reference is made to the upcoming Lausanne 4 Congress in South Korea, where the global missions agenda through 2050 will be set, challenging all to be mindful of the task of creation care.

Questions for Thought and Discussion

This section sets forth some comments and questions for thought and discussion in response to Bookless's essay, specifically within the context of the South Korean church.

The subject of creation care has been largely neglected throughout the history of the Korean church. The church's understanding of Scripture is generally anthropocentric in nature, and issues such as creation care are deemed secondary to the presumably more urgent task of saving souls. Only in recent years has there been some effort or movement within the Korean church to better understand creation care as a matter of faith. Slowly, questions are being raised as to whether and how creation care might be included in the scope of the church's mission.

Notwithstanding the foregoing, the prevailing perspective in the Korean church is still one that posits creation care as a perhaps important, yet nonetheless ancillary matter. In this regard, Bookless's essay provides a solid point of departure for the Korean church's discussions regarding how creation care is indeed a gospel issue. As such, Bookless's effort to avoid prooftexting in his presentation of biblical foundations for creation care is particularly welcome. Given that proof texts and thematic selection of biblical passages have hitherto been the most common way for relatively inexperienced Korean churches to address the topic of creation care, Bookless's holistic approach offers a most sound, not to mention hermeneutically persuasive, alternative framework.

A concern remains, however, that even this approach may fall short of explaining how creation care is in fact a gospel mandate, especially for those who persist in their more traditional, limited understanding of the gospel. Arguing that creation care falls within the scope of *missio Dei* and that the church must therefore embrace it as *missio ecclesia*, does not solve the underlying problem of how the church, the members of the church are to understand creation care in relation to the gospel as they know it. In other words, what do we actually mean when we say that creation care is, to borrow the language of the Cape Town Commitment, a "gospel issue"? Would it be possible, perhaps, to elaborate further on the precise meaning of the gospel, so as to explain the place of creation care within the context of the gospel Jesus preached, namely the gospel of the kingdom of God?

With respect to each of the five divine interventions, the Creation, covenant, Jesus Christ, Pentecost and the church, and new creation, Bookless does an excellent job of explaining how God's purpose extends to the *entirety* of his created world, in *all* of its *diversity*, and that the gospel of our Lord Jesus Christ has clear *cosmic* implications, that he will bring reconciliation to *all* things. Accordingly, the church must also proclaim Christ's lordship over the *entire* created order, remembering that God's plan for his creation is renewal and restoration. After all, the kingdom of God is, as we all pray, to be established here on earth as it is in heaven. Again, however, Bookless does not expressly state whether creation care is (or is not) an integral part of the gospel, which raises the question of whether such an attempt to present biblical foundations for creation care must necessarily address this point head-on. Based on the overarching framework provided by Bookless, it seems possible to go beyond the claim that creation care must be included in the scope of mission and explicitly state that creation care is an integral part of the gospel itself, and that therefore, the church's missional mandate cannot but include it. It is not entirely clear, however, whether this is in fact the author's intent.

In preparation for the upcoming Lausanne 4 Congress, Onnuri Church, which has been firmly dedicated to overseas missions for the past three decades, has begun to explore in earnest the issue of whether and why and how creation care ought to be included in the scope of the church's mission. At present, however, it remains on the margins, as an important yet somewhat collateral issue. The greatest barrier to missions embracing creation care as a primary gospel issue appears to be the concern that somehow doing so would alter the meaning, and thus the integrity, of the gospel as the church has hitherto understood it. The prevailing understanding within the evangelical Korean church is still that the church is in the business of saving human souls, no more, no less. In this connection, our hope is that Bookless's paper will serve as a useful baseline for some constructive discussions regarding creation care within the church and especially in the missions setting.

One noteworthy point here is that the Korean church's hesitation regarding creation care as a gospel issue stems not only from church history and culture, but also involves a political element. Interestingly, much of the evangelical Korean church has historically been aligned with the political right, whereas the environmental agenda has largely belonged to the political left. While the church stands firm in its belief that politics ought not dictate its mission, broaching the subject of creation care is often met by suspicion or even outright aversion. This invisible yet very real cultural barrier must be overcome in order to advance our discussions regarding creation care, and Bookless's paper will hopefully serve as a politically neutral but strong theological foundation for creation care as a scriptural imperative.

It is also significant that Bookless's essay does not lean on the general issue of climate crisis to establish the significance of the issue at hand, which is to regard creation care as a biblical mandate. Although it is tempting to note the unprecedented ecological crisis facing us today and threatening our future, doing so could actually detract from the argument that creation care is first and foremost a God-given mission. Too often, the church's emphasis on the climate crisis inadvertently results in congregation members taking a passive position that is merely reactive to what is happening in the world (e.g., the threat to humanity's existence), rather than a proactive response to God's call. In this regard, Bookless provides a clear argument for how creation care as a gospel issue is a primary mandate that predates the climate crisis today.

Finally, it is important to consider the pervasiveness of materialism and consumerism (i.e., basic human greed) in the world today, which also serve to explain the general resistance against and dismissive attitude toward calls for creation care. Here, Bookless's biblical overview and arguments against an escapist missiology that supports the notion of earth's complete destruction are particularly well appreciated. Although Korean theologians and pastors will need to further explain the renewal and restoration understanding regarding the end times, Bookless's framework will greatly assist the positioning of creation care as a gospel mandate.

Section B

History and Culture

CHAPTER 6

Learning from the Past and Finding Hope for the Future

by Allison Howell

This paper presents case studies of two significant, historically disparate environmental and human calamities. The first event began around 536 CE. It triggered climatic change that impacted the environment, society, and beliefs in the Mediterranean area, Europe, the Middle East, and even in the Far East, for nearly a century. The second occurred in China between 1876 and 1879. Despite its devastating impact on society, it gave new directions for Christian mission. Both case studies underscore the importance of identifying the historical setting of environmental events and the theological and missiological issues, and they provide insights for Christian mission response to catastrophes and crises in our contemporary world.

Climate Change and Catastrophe in the Sixth Century

Prior to 536 CE, numerous catastrophes occurred in the northern hemisphere, including earthquakes, locust invasions, droughts, carnage of war, and environmental degradation.[1] The volatile time compounded heightening human need, as problems in the environment do not usually occur in isolation from other issues. In 536 CE, a veil of dust darkened the sky for at least eighteen months. The historian Procopius described it as "a most dread portent" for "the sun gave forth its light without brightness, like the moon ... and it seemed exceedingly like the sun in eclipse."[2]

Recent scientific studies reveal that an enormous volcanic eruption occurred in March 536 CE in Iceland, followed by two other substantial eruptions in 540 and 547,[3] which injected huge amounts of ash into the

---

1 *Pseudo-Dionysius of Tel-Mahre: Chronicle of Zuqnin, Part III*, trans. W. Witakowski, Translated Texts for Historians 22 (Liverpool: Liverpool Univ. Press, 1996), 83.

2 Procopius, *History of the Wars, Vol. II, Books 3–4: Vandalic War*, trans. H. B. Dewing, Loeb Classical Library 81 (Cambridge, MA: Harvard Univ. Press, 1916), 329 (4:14.5–6).

3 Ulf Büntgen, Vladimir S. Myglan, Fredrik Charpentier Ljungqvist et al., "Cooling and Societal Change during the Late Antique Little Ice Age from 536 to Around 660 AD," *Nature Geoscience* 9 (2016): 231–36; and Christopher P. Loveluck, Michael McCormick, Nicole E. Spaulding et al., "Alpine Ice-Core Evidence for the Transformation of the European Monetary System, AD 640–670," *Antiquity* 92, no. 366 (2018): 1571–85.

stratosphere. For Michael McCormick, 536 in Europe "was the beginning of one of the worst periods to be alive, if not the worst year."[4] Dropping temperatures resulted in very severe winters, food shortages, and famine.

To make matters worse, rat populations increased in Alexandria, Egypt, and spread disease through their disease-carrying fleas,[5] first across the Mediterranean and subsequently into Europe along the trade routes.[6] Between 540 and 543, a series of "Justinian" plagues devastated both rural areas and cities. As a result, there was extraordinary loss of life and economic stagnation in Europe that lasted nearly a century. The 536 event impacted multiple areas of life, as witnesses who experienced the plagues testified.[7] People responded in divers ways to the plague and its impacts.

In a major *physical* impact, the plague spread rapidly, striking people with fever at first. Within twenty-four hours swelling occurred, followed quickly by various symptoms, including delirium, before the person fell into a coma and soon died. As the plague spread, large numbers of people perished. In many houses, everyone died. In some places, the ground was covered with corpses and there was no one to bury the dead.[8] In Constantinople, initially people buried the dead. Then their number increased exponentially. John of Ephesus reported that between five thousand and sixteen thousand died in a day.[9] Without enough people to bury the dead, the city came to a standstill.

Cultural practices were also totally disrupted and people abandoned burial practices. Chaos reigned until the emperor Justinian, who had left the city, intervened and provided litters and paid people to bury the dead. Corpses were thrown into the sea or into large pits containing sometimes seventy thousand people. Finally, people set aside quarrels, unified, and began to help bury the dead. An estimated 35 to 55 percent of the population died.

The plagues devastated the *economy* and the *environment*. Although there was plenty of food growing in the fields around Constantinople, those

4 Reported in Ann Gibbons, "Eruption Made 536 'The Worst Year to Be Alive,'" *Science* 362, no. 6416 (Nov. 2018): 733.

5 William Rosen, *Justinian's Flea: The First Great Plague and the End of the Roman Empire* (London: Penguin, 2007), 189; and David Keys, *Catastrophe: An Investigation into the Origins of the Modern World* (London: Arrow Books, 2000), 9–20.

6 Rosen, *Justinian's Flea*, 201.

7 John of Ephesus in *Pseudo-Dionysius: Chronicle of Zuqnin*, 74–98; the lawyer, Evagrius, who lost family members and survived the plague himself, in Evagrius, *The Ecclesiastical History of Evagrius Scholasticus*, trans. Michael Whitby (Liverpool: Liverpool Univ. Press, 2000), 229–32, 237, 241, 246; Procopius, *History of the Wars*, 329 (4.14.5–6); and Gregory of Tours, *The History of the Franks*, trans. Lewis Thorpe (London: Penguin, 1974).

8 *Pseudo-Dionysius: Chronicle of Zuqnin*, 80–81.

9 *Pseudo-Dionysius*, 86.

living in the city could not access it. Farmers could not tend their animals or harvest crops, and they rotted in the fields. The plague attacked both cattle and deer. Animals ran wild. The system of transport broke down.

Issues arose over people's property, possessions. and wealth, especially when everyone in a family died. There were problems related to wills and inheritances. People needed to provide resources to deal with both the dead and the sick. They were forced to rebuild the economy.

Multiple *social* problems arose because whole families were wiped out and looters stole from houses and the dead. Rumors spread rapidly that a person could chase away death by throwing water pitchers from the upper floors of story buildings on to the streets, so people lost all their water storage containers. Many also fled to other towns to escape the plague.[10]

The *psychological* and *emotional* impact was significant. Some people wanted to die. John of Ephesus captured the sense of trauma thus: "It would be much better for us who saw [it] to be mingled with those who drank the cup of wrath, who ended their journey and did not experience that destruction; or with those whose heart is darkened together with their eyes, mind and thought."[11] Others walked about stunned as if drunk. Some "became demented and put aside life."[12] Some in Alexandria wore name tags when they went out so that if they died people could identify them. People experienced uncontrollable grief and terrible fear. John of Ephesus fled "in terror" from Syria to Constantinople, utterly traumatized by the way people treated the dead. For him, what "was painful was that corpses should be dragged out and thrown down, people dealing with other people—with [their] dead—as with dead beasts: they dragged and threw, dazed and upset, [fulfilling] thus what was called in the Scripture 'the burial of an ass' [Jer. 22:19]."[13]

Spiritually and religiously, there was a variety of reactions. For instance, John of Ephesus likened their experience to the afflictions and lamentations of the Jews in Jerusalem in the prophet Jeremiah's time. He frequently referred to "God's wrath" and to "a wine-press" and to people's bodies pitilessly trampled like beasts irrespective of their age, status, or rank. In a reference to Isaiah, he described Constantinople as being under "God's sentence."[14] He interpreted the actions of some in Constantinople as similar to Noah's, who knew the flood was coming. In this case, however, they tried to build ships of "almsgiving" by distributing possessions to the poor.

---

10 *Pseudo-Dionysius*, 97–98.

11 *Pseudo-Dionysius*, 96.

12 Evagrius, *The Ecclesiastical History*, 231–32.

13 *Pseudo-Dionysius: Chronicle of Zuqnin*, 92.

14 *Pseudo-Dionysius*, 74, 87–90, 96.

People held vigils calling woefully on God.[15] They fasted, prayed, repented, lamented humbly, and petitioned God to save them. Gregory of Tours observed a similar response when people were dying from plague in Tours and Nantes.[16]

People who saw apparitions of supernatural beings would utter holy names and try to exorcise them. Some locked themselves in rooms. Others built and worshipped deities of bronze, claiming angels had told them to do so. Some fled to sanctuaries and sought pardon from pillar saints. Evagrius suffered deep distress after the plague killed his wife, daughter, grandson, and other relatives.[17] He visited Saint Symeon on a pillar located on a mountain between Antioch and Seleucia to receive a pardon.[18]

Many people attributed the plague to the devil. In some areas people fled from monks, whom they believed personified death because of either their habits or shorn heads. John of Ephesus regarded this as demons leading people astray. He interpreted the plagues and people's mental illness as chastisement from God for sin. He wanted people to become wise, stop angering God, repent, and continually ask for mercy to avert the punishment. He included himself as one of the "fools and provokers" of God.[19]

For Evagrius, the disasters were either a sign of God's anger and punishment or the work of the devil or demons.[20] Gregory of Tours also interpreted the plagues as the "scourges of God".[21] He wished that people's sorrow would lead to their conversion, citing Jeremiah 4:10. He likened the experience to the one Jesus spoke about in the Gospels (Matt. 24:7; Mark 13:22).[22]

In summary, at the end of the sixth century there was an estimated twenty-five million fewer people in Justinian's empire.[23] Scientists identify the period from 536 to about 660 CE as the "Late Antique Little Ice Age," which spanned most of the Northern Hemisphere. They suggest that "this cold phase be considered as an additional environmental factor contributing to the establishment of the Justinian plague, transformation of the eastern Roman Empire and collapse of the Sasanian Empire, movements out of the

---

15 *Pseudo-Dionysius*, 86.

16 Gregory of Tours, *History of the Franks*, 468.

17 Evagrius, *The Ecclesiastical History*, xiv.

18 Glanville Downey, *A History of Antioch in Syria: From Seleucus to the Arab Conquest* (Princeton: Princeton Univ. Press, 1961), xiv, 553–57.

19 *Pseudo-Dionysius: Chronicle of Zuqnin*, 98.

20 Evagrius, *The Ecclesiastical History*, iv, 1, 156.

21 Gregory of Tours, *History of the Franks*, x, 1.

22 Gregory of Tours, 584.

23 Rosen, *Justinian's Flea*, 309.

Asian steppe and Arabian Peninsula, spread of Slavic-speaking peoples and political upheavals in China."[24]

What emerges from this case study is a paradigm of response in crisis. Understanding the areas of impact and response in the physical, social, cultural, economic/environmental, psychological, and spiritual/religious spheres provides a model for assessing impact and response in other catastrophes. This was demonstrated in the response of Sierra Leonean Wesleyan Church minister Kelvin Koroma to the Ebola outbreak in West Africa in 2014. His study of the 536 CE event and its aftermath provided him with helpful categories that he and other Christian leaders used to examine the impact of and to respond to the Ebola outbreak and its widespread devastation in Liberia, Guinea, and Sierra Leone.[25]

China and Timothy Richard

An event now known as an El Niño-Southern Oscillation (ENSO) occurred between 1876 and 1879, with considerable impact in many parts of the world. Some countries experienced extensive flooding, while in China, India, and Brazil, there were droughts and catastrophic famines. Millions died even though in all three countries grain surpluses existed that could have alleviated the suffering.[26] Missionaries reported on all these droughts to their constituents, but missiologists are yet to study the significance of these events.

The second case study is drawn from the response of Timothy Richard, a Baptist missionary from Wales, who served in China from 1870 to 1914.[27] Richard initially focused on learning the Chinese language and culture, preaching at street chapels, and giving people Christian literature. He realized the significance of using culturally appropriate methods in evangelizing the Chinese. He focused on the Bible's interpretation of the Chinese religious heritage and on reaching the literati. When typhus broke out in Shandong in 1876, he distributed quinine water, which helped save lives. This increased his credibility with the Chinese.[28] Between 1876 and 1879, rains failed in

---

24 Büntgen et al, "Cooling and Societal Change," 1.

25 Allison M. Howell and Karim Kelvin Koroma, "The West African Ebola Virus Outbreak: Context, Response and Christian Responsibility—The Experience of the Wesleyan Church of Sierra Leone," *Journal of African Christian Thought* 18, no.1 (June 2015): 4–17.

26 Mike Davis, *Late Victorian Holocausts: El Niño Famines and the Making of the Third World* (London: Verso, 2001), loc. 21–22, 137–38 of 519, Kindle.

27 Timothy Richard, *Forty-five Years in China: Reminiscences* (New York: Frederick A. Stokes, 1916), 29.

28 Paul Richard Bohr, *Famine in China and the Missionary: Timothy Richard as Relief Administrator and Advocate of National Reform, 1876–1884* (Cambridge, MA: Harvard Univ. Press, 1972), 11.

northern China, affecting five provinces. By the eighteenth century, China already had in place a well-structured famine relief response, which was more effective at mobilizing relief than any European polity.[29] Yet in spite of this, between eight and twenty million people are estimated to have died from the famine.[30] So what went wrong? Attributing the horrifyingly high death toll to the ENSO event and resultant drought fails to consider the contributive background issues, including political and economic problems that compounded the climatic event. The background factors that contributed to the severity of the famine in the five affected provinces included the following:

1. Large population growth between 1775 and 1850

2. Food resources unable to keep up with population growth[31]

3. Deforestation in mountainous areas and wet lowlands for the cultivation of nontraditional crops on largely infertile, unsuitable soils

4. Significant erosion of bedrock sediment and sand blocking rivers, which destroyed fertile farmland

5. Decrease in the level of water tables and wells running dry. Farmers lacked resources to access the water below their fields in the drought.[32]

6. Government neglect in conserving water, clearing navigation canals, and in maintaining the irrigations systems and flood control works[33]

7. Ethnic and social conflicts. Two opium wars (1839–42 and 1856–58), followed by the Taiping uprising (1850–64) and two subsequent civil wars, depleted China's revenues. Both sides deliberately destroyed forests, thus exacerbating deforestation. Rich agricultural land was destroyed, tax revenues were cut off, and huge funds went into maintaining the armies' depleting food reserves in granaries.[34] The earlier population growth was offset by large human loss related to the Taiping revolution.[35]

8. Decline of the granary system. In previous droughts, these granaries had mitigated the impact of drought.

---

29 Davis, *Late Victorian Holocausts*, 413 of 519.

30 Davis, 14, 79, 87, 138 of 519. See Andrew T. Kaiser, *Encountering China: The Evolution of Timothy Richard's Missionary Thought (1870–1891)* (Eugene, OR: Pickwick Publications, 2019), 2833–43 of 8176, Kindle.

31 Bohr, *Famine in China*, 74.

32 Davis, *Late Victorian Holocausts*, 414–16; 420–21 of 519.

33 Davis, 30, 349, 425–26 of 519.

34 Bohr, *Famine in China*, 24, 75.

35 Davis, *Late Victorian Holocausts*, 355 of 519.

9. Failure to invest in roads, railways, or telegraph services
10. Fraud by both merchants and magistrates depleting stocks in the granaries, which even honest officials could not overturn[36]

The interaction of all these issues had major repercussions when the rains ceased.

Impact of the Famine

Richard's approach to mission, his evangelical faith, and desire to empathize culturally with the Chinese informed his response to the famine in North China. Although the famine impacted five provinces, Richard was based initially in Shandong (with an estimated population of twenty-seven million) and later moved to Shanxi (with an estimated population of fifteen million prior to the famine). Richard observed the horrific impact of the famine. Crops failed and grain prices soared, forcing people to forage for whatever they could find in the fields. They dismantled their houses, sold the timber, and ate rotting sorghum stalks that were stored on their roofs. There was no fuel to burn for warmth so they dug underground pits to avoid the cold. Within six weeks, about a third of the population died. People sold their clothes as well as their children and women into slavery. Land values tumbled, farmland was left unplowed, and many people committed suicide. Millions of people fled to other areas where there was food.[37] The death rate was so high that people were buried in mass graves.

In 1877, the famine spread to Shanxi, a deforested, landlocked area with roads in disrepair. Timothy Richard was shocked at what he witnessed there. It was worse than Shandong. Crops failed and locusts devoured whatever remained in the fields. There was extensive robbery and evidence of cannibalism, with human flesh being sold in markets. An estimated 80 percent of the population of Shanxi suffered the impact of the famine.

Government Response

The Qing government had a deep concern for people's welfare, but their response to famine was slow. There were inadequate preparations and assistance as well as problems with communication. Their initial responses included prayers and banning people from having excessive banquets in the capital. They asked advisors to design a relief program, but nearly a year passed before small amounts of grain and silver began to be distributed.

---

36 Davis, 411 of 519.

37 Bohr, *Famine in China*, 14–15.

The government encouraged private giving. They transferred grain from imperial treasuries and formed local committees. They taxed areas unaffected by famine and stopped collecting land and grain taxes in the affected provinces.[38] They also supplied seed and tools to farmers. They established centers to administer relief. They attempted to distribute grain, and where no grain was available, they gave people cash.

The failure to repair roads caused *organizational* and *structural* difficulties. Ports were disorganized and transport on waterways was impossible. Costs of moving grain were prohibitively high and transport animals in short supply because they had either died or been eaten. Similarly, *administrative* and *institutional* difficulties mounted due to corruption and mismanaged aid.[39] Chinese private donations were impressive, and the gentry criticized the inadequate government relief.

Richard's Relief Efforts

Richard quickly realized the need to respond in culturally appropriate ways. He developed placards urging people who wanted rain "to turn from dead idols to the living God and pray unto Him and obey His laws and conditions of life."[40] He rode to eleven county towns, posted placards on the city gates, and stayed to talk with those who expressed interest in praying.

In mid-1876, Richard chose to stay, even though he realized he was in a dangerous situation.[41] Initially working in Shandong Province, he along with Chinese assistants moved to the Shanxi area in August 1877 to assess the situation and develop a response to the catastrophe. His method was similar to the one he had developed in Shandong. Richard had little funds, almost no savings, and no prior experience of relief distribution. He was aware that if he did give, it might arouse anger from government officials. However, he ultimately devised a method of relief that was to have long lasting consequences, in which he:

1. Organized small surveys to assess the situation. Richard surveyed villages to determine the resources available to the living, and the numbers of deaths. In Shanxi, local officials and Catholic priests assisted and reported on the deaths.[42] In one county, 95 percent of the people died. Overall, in Shanxi an estimated nine and a half million died.

---

38 Bohr, 30–34.

39 Bohr, 77.

40 Richard, *Forty-five Years in China*, 97–98.

41 Richard, 100–102.

42 Davis, *Late Victorian Holocausts*, 84, 138–39 of 519.

2. Distributed personal funds. Richard shared what he had until it ran out.

3. Requested help within China from Chinese government officials and from wealthy expatriates in China, who then formed a relief committee

4. Publicized his observations. Richard, traumatized by what he witnessed, published his observations, within China and then in the West.[43] People then began to donate money.

5. Developed appropriate distribution methods through trial and error. He also learned from the inadequate distribution methods of government and merchants.[44] He confined his efforts to one area and focused on distributing cash and not grain. His inspiration came from the story of Jesus feeding the multitudes where he made the people sit down. Richard realized that "a sitting crowd cannot crush."[45] The magistrate was astonished by Richard's effectiveness.

6. Cooperated with Chinese officials. Richard did not compete with the government but followed their relief distribution instructions, which provided him further opportunities to give assistance.[46] He gave officials advice about more effective ways of distribution. When he raised foreign funds, he gave them to the magistrate to distribute through his officials. When additional funds came in, he sought and obtained permission from the magistrate to distribute them himself in highly needy villages. Richard believed that "effective mission required a deep respect for the Chinese context wherein he and his colleagues were serving—a serious commitment to a form and method of mission that was sensitive to Chinese realities."[47]

7. Cooperated with fellow Christians and missionaries. Richard found honest Chinese men to assist him, and he compensated them. Other missionaries joined him in distributing relief. The China Famine Relief Fund raised relief funds locally and through committees in the UK and US. They used Richard's distribution methods and followed through on his suggestion to stop raising funds for distribution in remote areas, where the government could provide relief.

8. Founded temporary orphanages. Richard founded five orphanages for abandoned or disadvantaged children across the worst-impacted counties. They received food and training in employable skills. When

---

43 Kaiser, *Encountering China*, 2896 of 8176.

44 Kaiser, 2953–54 of 8176.

45 Richard, *Forty-five Years in China*, 102.

46 Kaiser, *Encountering China*, 2968 of 8176.

47 Kaiser, 2913–2915 of 8176.

the famine was over, Richard closed the orphanages since the Chinese Christians did not support them and could not manage them.[48]

9. Understood the causes of the famine. Richard realized that nature could not be solely blamed for the impact of the drought. Historical, political, economic, and structural issues needed to be addressed in order to prevent a similar disaster occurring. He advocated structural reform and held discussions with the governor. He published his thoughts in 1876[49] and proposed the study of meteorology and new agricultural techniques as well as initiating industry and mining, improvements in transport and communication, teaching in scientific subjects, and training of Chinese experts.

10. Advocated Christian mission and ministry-integrated relief work. Richard neither viewed the relief work as a distraction to his evangelism nor resented being involved with it. He interpreted the famine spiritually and prayed with those who received funds. He urged people to thank God for the food they received and integrated relief distribution with the gospel message. As Kaiser points out, "Richard's personal participation in alleviating the physical suffering that accompanied famine was an 'organic' development of his empathetic identification with the people around him as well as of his convictions as an evangelical missionary: this was compassionate, evangelical activism in practice."[50] He ran Bible classes with men and women leaders. Richard and his Chinese coworkers continued to work with the growing church. After the famine ended, more than two thousand inquirers regularly met at many worship places.[51] Richard also believed that famine relief should be integrated with teaching practical knowledge and skills related to the situation and teaching "spiritual truths." He saw it as part of the relationship between material progress and Christianity. His view was informed by his belief that material improvement and spiritual rebirth were highly interconnected. He also expanded his biblical teaching to include God's sovereign operation in nature.

---

48 Kaiser, 2968 of 8176.

49 Bohr states, "In September 1876 Richard elaborated on his recommendations to Governor Ting in an article published in the *Wan-kuo kung-pao*." The reference given is, Timothy Richard, "Tsai i she-fa tsao chiu" [Methods should be devised early to prevent disaster], *WKKP* (September 9, 1876): 55–55b. This was a Chinese-language journal "to promote Christian scientific and general knowledge among the Chinese." See Bohr, *Famine in China*, 141, 256, 272.

50 Kaiser, 3032–34 of 8176.

51 Richard, *Forty-five Years in China*, 106.

Conclusion

Timothy Richard has been recognized as the pioneer of famine relief in China.[52] Although his own contribution as a foreigner was small, he became engaged from the outset in his response to the famine and assumed a pioneering role. His publicity of the famine created public awareness of the tragedy, and people in turn responded with financial assistance. He developed new approaches to famine relief which others copied. The ways and techniques that he developed profoundly influenced the way famine relief was undertaken for many years. Richard's experience during those famine years enlarged his vision of Christian mission. As a missionary myself who encountered and had to respond to famine, it would have been quite helpful to know about Richard's method at the time rather than learning of it later.

---

52 Bohr, *Famine in China*, 126–28; Kaiser, *Encountering China*, 2998 of 8176,

Discussion Questions

1. What have you learned from the impact of and responses to the 536 CE event and the following plagues that is critical for guiding you and your church or mission in responding to a largely expected catastrophe?

2. How do the various categories of response relate to the gospel of Jesus Christ?

3. Which features of Timothy Richard's response to the China famine would you consider to be the most important that would guide you or your mission in facing a similar situation?

4. Through most of 2022, much of eastern Africa has faced drought and famine conditions. Many Christian missionaries work in this area, yet the voice of missions has been largely silent. What should and could be the work of missions in seeking to alleviate the suffering?

Response

by Jung-Sook Lee

Dr. Howell's paper, which describes two historical events from the late antique West and the modern East, captures the essence of the topic for KGMLF 2023, environmental and human calamities, by showing that they are inherently interrelated in their origin, progress, and inevitable results. She also explained that environmental disasters can affect human life on various levels—physical, cultural, social, psychological, emotional, spiritual, and religious, and her study sketched the cruel and devastating experiences of the people who suffered through these events. Her paper further suggests there are ways for humans to minimize or at least alleviate suffering during such calamities, whether through government intervention or by individual efforts, such as those by missionaries. It was also true that Christians took decisive action with spiritual wisdom to help alleviate suffering. They are now part of the great cloud of witnesses (Heb. 12:1), who are cheering for us to become beacons of hope for those who suffer through such events in our time.

A Sixth-Century Late Antique Case Study

Dr. Howell began with a case study from the Late Antique Ice Age, which began in 536 CE and ended in 660 CE in the West. The age began with a volcanic eruption in Iceland in 536, followed by two others in 540 and 547. The effect of the first eruption was so severe and extensive that it has been called "the beginning of one of the worst periods to be alive, if not the worst year." Unusually low temperatures and ensuing conditions, such as famine and food shortage, made it difficult for the people in Europe to survive. Further, a series of the plagues in 540 and 543, during the reign of emperor Justinian I (527–565), exacerbated the cruelty of life not just for the people who lived then but also for the following generations.

Even as a church historian, this case was not well known to me. I was astonished to learn about the importance of climate changes in history and their immediate impacts on human life. Descriptions about climate change in 536 to 537 are quite vivid: "a veil of dust darkened the sky for at least eighteen months," as "a most dread portent" for "the sun gave forth its light without brightness, like the moon … and it seemed exceedingly like the sun in eclipse." This case is intriguing because church history has been relatively silent regarding the sixth through to the eighth century in the West, the time after the fall of Rome (476) and before the coronation of Charlemagne (800).

This period was a time of retreat due to the fall of Rome, barbarian invasions and expansions, and the rise of Islam.

However, it seems that climate change during the Late Antique Little Ice Age may have been another reason for the standstill in Christian evangelism and other activities. The history of world Christianity (or church history) has focused its attention on theological, ecclesiastical, and worship developments, mission movements, and so on. As a result, unfortunately, natural disasters, climate changes, disease, and migrations did not receive their proper due. In this regard, church history has overlooked some important theological discussions regarding the possible causes of the disasters that occurred during and following the volcanic eruptions. Notable theologians like John of Ephesus (507–588) and Gregory of Tours (538–594) freely expressed their views to draw people's attention to God, through and to whom all things are (Rom. 11:36).

Nineteenth-Century Modern Case Studies

China

Dr. Howell's other case study is drawn from modern history. An El Niño-Southern Oscillation (ENSO) event took place from 1876 to 1879 in Northern China, which caused widespread drought, famine, distress, and mass migrations. Howell clearly demonstrated that this environmental disaster was exacerbated by at least ten human factors, whether at the individual or government level.

The English Baptist missionary Timothy Richard (1845–1919), who served in China from 1870 to 1914, spent much time taking care of and supporting the famine victims and displaced persons, and it is through his writings that this case is so well known to us. Richard's relief work among the Chinese people had a long-lasting impact as a model of Christian love and service. Howell summarizes Richard's famine relief model in ten points. To summarize, Richard (1) researched the causes and situations, (2) cooperated with Chinese government officials, and (3) collaborated with Christians within and outside of China. He also publicized the case to bring it to the world's attention. I am sure he was busy writing reports and letters every possible minute he found amid his busy relief work. As I was writing this response, I happened to hear that South Asia, especially Vietnam, will most likely experience an El Niño event this year, and I hope that missionaries and Christians there respond in mature and intelligent ways modeled after Richard's relief work.

Korea

Since it was mentioned that the 1876–1879 ENSO event affected not only China but also India and Brazil, I wondered if there were also records of climate change in Korea during those years. Since there are no missionary records during that time,[53] I checked the *Veritable Records of the Joseon Dynasty* (조선왕조실록)[54] from 1876 to 1879. It was an eye-opening experience for me because I had never read history to understand weather and its effects. Incredibly, the records show that Korea had unusual weather for all of 1876, the first year ENSO appeared in China! Between April and May (lunar calendar), severe drought and low water levels (measured by a rain gauge, 측우기) were recorded, so the desperate king (Gojong) ordered special prayer rituals asking for rain (기우제), twelve times in April and May and six more times in June. With a sincere heart and desire, the king himself led the rituals several times to appeal to heaven. One record highlighted the seriousness and importance of the prayer ritual—high officials who were absent without clear evidence of illness were dismissed from office.[55]

The king also ordered a reduction in the number of his dishes, and prohibited music, making alcohol, including rice wine, and rice syrup. At the end of the last (eighteenth) ritual, it rained and there was a thanksgiving ceremony. However, other extreme weather events immediately followed the June rain—a flood in July and August, an early frost on August 2, and thunder and lightning with hailstones at harvesttime on October 7. All of these events led to a severe famine that year, which had a long-lasting impact of three years. On September 22, the government released its funds and rice to all who were affected by the famine and reduced or deferred their taxes. Many individuals also participated in the relief efforts. In 1877, the government recognized and awarded those who had helped their suffering neighbors.

---

53   Some Koreans embraced Catholic teaching and faith in the late eighteenth century, before missionary evangelism (which officially began in 1784), and also the Protestant teaching and faith before the first Protestant missionary came to Korea in 1884.

54   "The Veritable Records of the Joseon Dynasty," National Institute of Korean History, accessed May 10, 2023, https://sillok.history.go.kr/main/main.do. These include the records of twenty-seven kings of the Joseon Dynasty from 1392–1928. Since they were written in Chinese characters and not accessible to lay people, they were translated into modern Korean from 1968 to 1993 and digitized.

55   "Annals of King Gojong, Volume 13, 1st Article on Byeongsul on May 25 in the 13th Year of King Gojong, 1876, Year 485 of the Founding of Joseon," The Veritable Records of the Joseon Dynasty, National Institute of Korean History, accessed May 10, 2023, https://sillok.history.go.kr/id/kza_11305125_001. Although we cannot rule out the possibility of using this occasion to rid the government of political opponents, it is clear that they held the belief that heaven and human sincerity are closely interrelated and affect good and bad in the cosmos, including human life.

Relief records continue for the following years. On November 28, 1878, the record states that "the famine of 1876 was so severe … " and two towns could not pay for the last two-year taxes, with discussions about alternative solutions.[56] Climate calamities, including floods and two earthquakes (March 12, 17), were reported in 1879. However, the floods mentioned in the records could have occurred the previous year because they were mentioned in the context of relief work, and these dates are too early to see floods in Korea.[57]

In my reading of these records, two things particularly stand out: first, king Gojong's lament and penitence over drought and famine, and second, the seriousness of prayer rituals and relief efforts by both the government and individuals. In fact, king Gojong's lament and repentance, albeit a non-Christian response, is a counterpart to Western theologians' reflections on famine or plagues. The king's remorse appeared several times in these records during those years. He repeatedly says two things: that there is a reason for this disaster,[58] and all has to do with his lack of virtue.[59]

Conclusion

Although, ironically, there have been windfalls from climate calamities in history, such as the wood used to make Stradivarius violins,[60] the events mentioned above demonstrate the cruel hardship of human life and casualty loss that follow climate catastrophes. These sorts of hardships were antecedently attested in the Romans 8:22, which reads "… . *the whole creation has been groaning together* in the pains of childbirth until now"

---

56 "Annals of King Gojong, Volume 15, November 20, 15th Year of King Gojong, Eulchuk, 1st Article, 1878, Year 487 of the Founding of Joseon," The Veritable Records of the Joseon Dynasty, National Institute of Korean History, accessed May 10, 2023, https://sillok.history.go.kr/id/kza_11511020_001.

57 The records state that relief was given to the victims of floods in specific areas, on Jan. 24, Feb. 17, and March 9 and 22.

58 Disaster often relates to the dissatisfaction of heaven, in other words, to the dissatisfaction of the supreme being in ancient Korean religious expression.

59 In reckoning the heaven's (or Christian God's) intention during disaster, it is noteworthy that the non-Christian king saved his breath instead of offering futile discussion. Often Christians have no scruples about surmising God's intention or the cause of bad things. In this regard, I cannot forget a Chinese student who came up to me crying over fellow students' open conjectures and claims during a prayer meeting at school that the earthquakes in Southwest China (where she originated) that year (2010) were caused by the sins of Chinese people.

60 Stradivarius violins were made "mostly from spruce and maple trees, [which] grew during the Little Ice Age, a period of widespread cooling and a drop in average global temperatures from around 1300 to 1850, in which Europe was hit particularly hard" ("Stradivarius Violins," Climate in Arts & History, Smith College, accessed May 20, 2023, https://www.science.smith.edu/climatelit/stradivarius-violins/).

(ESV, emphasis mine). It is our belief and confession that human beings were the ultimate cause of all these troubles, and we need to learn how to take full responsibility for these troubles by taking care of our environment and our neighbors in suffering. In this sense, history has a wisdom to share for all of us Christian workers, whether positively or negatively.

CHAPTER 7

Indigenous Epistemologies
Connecting with Christ and Creation

by Jay Mātenga

Prelude

Kia ora (a greeting of life blessing)! Māori custom compels me to locate myself as an indigenous[1] person … *Kō Takitimu te waka* (my tribal canoe is the Takitimu). *Kō Te Waka o Kupe me Tuhirangi ngā maunga* (my mountains are known as the canoes of high chief Kupe and Tuhirangi, the sea serpent that Kupe chased along the Pacific in his discovery of Aotearoa New Zealand). *Kō Ruamahanga te awa* (my river is the Ruamahanga—it was in this river that I was baptized as a new believer in Christ in 1984). *Kō Ngāti Kahungunu ki Wairarapa, kō Ngāti Porou, kō Kai Tahu ōku iwi* (I have birth heritage connections to these three tribes, which span the East Coast of the North Island and the South Island of Aotearoa New Zealand). *Kō Ngāti Rākaiwhakairi tōku hapū* (my primary clan or family group name means "to lift up or hang in adornment"). *Kō Kohunui tōku marae* (my clan's customary meeting place is called Kohunui—a physical piece of land on the outskirts of the village of Pirinoa, with buildings for meeting/sleeping, cooking/eating, and keeping tools and supplies). *Ko Jay Matenga tōku ingoa* (my name is Jay Mātenga), *kō Aperahama Kuhukuhu Tui Mātenga tōku tupuna* (descendent of Abraham Kuhukuhu Tui Mātenga). *Nō reira*, and therefore … *raranga katoa* (it is all woven together).

---

1 In this chapter I will be using "indigenous" in two ways. First, the United Nations definition of an indigenous person (see "Indigenous Peoples, Indigenous Voices: Factsheet," United Nations Permanent Forum on Indigenous Issues, accessed Dec. 24, 2022, https://www.un.org/esa/socdev/unpfii/documents/5session_factsheet1.pdf) and then a broader application that includes people from collectivist cultural backgrounds, for which I capitalize "Indigenous." I contrast "Indigenous" with "Industrial," referring to people from individualist cultural backgrounds, usually, but not exclusively, Westerners. In this way I prefer a values-based to economic or geographic categorizations. Individualist/Collectivist (Industrial/Indigenous) are two of the most dominant value determiners for the people of the world today, sitting at opposite poles of a spectrum.

The Emergence of Difference

The intellectual movement that emerged in Western Europe in the seventeenth century, commonly known as the Enlightenment, had a defining influence on Protestant Christianity. It changed the rules of the game, especially regarding how theological thought was structured, what was chosen for theological investigation, and what was determined to be normative and nonnegotiable. *The Oxford Companion to Philosophy* explains that the term "'Enlightenment' contrasts with the darkness of *irrationality and superstition* ... Kant ... said that enlightenment is the 'emergence of man from his self-imposed *infancy* ... .'"[2] Alternative rationalities or integrated epistemologies (systematic ways of knowing) unfamiliar to Western Europeans were considered inferior. As suggested by Kant's comment, anything that was not normative for the West was perceived to be "less-than," and this sense of superiority, soon to be backed by the technology and power of the Industrial Revolution, went unquestioned by Western European explorers, traders, colonizers, academics, theologians, and missionaries—until recently.

It is easy to underestimate the influence of philosophical thinking on our lived reality, but it is impossible to overstate it. Over time, what Thomas Kuhn identified as a revolutionary restructuring of ideas, or "paradigm shift,"[3] permeates a culture, and a new understanding of lived reality is normalized such that it ceases to be questioned. That is, until circumstances prompt new questions—prompting the next revolution of ideas. We are living on the cusp of a shift away from the Enlightenment towards something new, generated by questions arising out of the very globalized reality that the spread of the European diaspora and global trade created. From early in the twentieth century, amplified by the second world war, the central question that emerged among those concerned about international relationships and global stability was something like, How can we all get along? The efficacy of geopolitics, economics, science, and religion are rightly assessed by the degree to which they can provide solutions to this question, or at least some interim stability. We are living in an era where former solutions are failing, with divisions increasing—a threshold between times.

Exposure to difference had a reverse effect on European realities. The development of evangelicalism over the past two centuries was defined in a large part by global, more than local, realities. Information about new

---

2 Ted Honderich, ed., *The Oxford Companion to Philosophy* (Oxford: Oxford Univ. Press, 1995), 236.

3 Thomas S. Kuhn, *The Structure of Scientific Revolutions*, 4th ed. (Chicago: Univ. of Chicago Press, 2012), 66.

worlds and people from those new worlds exposed Europeans to ways of living that differed markedly from that of the tribes of the European continent and British Isles. Explorers and traders were initial sources of such information, but from the late 1700s, colonizers and missionaries became the major influencers. As colonies were established, missionaries followed. Where missionaries went, the gospel was seeded into new soil. While local theological interpretations were sternly resisted by missionary and denominational authorities, the expression of Christian faith that flourished in new places was a highly indigenized one, rooted in and affected by the context. As Sebastian and Kirsteen Kim attest, "socio-politically, the worldwide presence of Christianity today is not primarily the result of attempts by powerful churches to replicate themselves worldwide but the result of indigenous response and grassroots movements."[4]

The Emancipation of Theology

Theological thought cannot be easily constrained. Denominational leaders may try to dictate what is considered theologically orthodox for their congregants, but biblically faithful expressions of our faith that endure emerge from lived realities of Jesus's followers, and questions resulting from their experiences—current and historic. To borrow the framework of Bevans and Schroeder, valid Christian theology develops around core thematic constants in dialogue with a context. They identify six thematic theological constants: christology, ecclesiology, eschatology, soteriology, anthropology, and culture.[5]

As local churches mature, confidence grows generation by generation. Much older Christian movements, such as the historic Eastern and Western orthodoxies and their spin-offs, hold to theological thought developed over centuries. In the face of Enlightenment critique, Western theologies became more systematized, with passionate concern for defending the faith against scientific critique. This context shaped its articulation of the constants. Together with strengthening theological developments in the United States of America, this context nurtured the modern missionary movement. Theological developments became dogma. Biblical interpretations became doctrine. But theology imposed upon another context, regardless of dogma, doctrine, edict, or decree, will not flourish if it does not address the ancient

---

4 Sebastian Kim and Kirsteen Kim, *Christianity as a World Religion: An Introduction*, 2nd ed. (New York: Bloomsbury Academic, 2016), 3.

5 Stephen B. Bevans and Roger Schroeder, *Constants in Context: A Theology of Mission for Today* (Maryknoll, NY: Orbis Books, 2004).

and new questions relevant to each context. This holds true as much in the shifting contexts of Western Christendom (where the faith is rapidly waning) as it does in the contexts of cross-cultural missions. Crises and questions in context must be addressed in biblically faithful ways according to the assumptions of a given context—in conversation with historic Christian perspectives and the global church but guided and governed locally.

The relatively recent discipline of world Christianity reveals how a truly global Christianity is maturing, with indigenous theologies gaining validity. As more work is published, theologies from the Majority World are reaching a broader audience and their credibility is growing. A strengthening confidence from Majority World theologians, attuned to the questions of their own contexts, and the inability of Western theology to stem attrition from the faith within its own contexts, are among the reasons why the Eurocentric theological consensus is losing its authority as the arbiter of orthodoxy for the Protestant world. Theology is becoming emancipated from Western constraints. Commentators observe that we are living in an increasingly polycentric global reality but, as Sebastian and Kirsteen Kim are careful to point out,[6] this has been the reality of Christianity since the first century.

My reason for noting this shift from Western dominance to a more decentralized, diverse, and dispersed World Christianity is to establish legitimacy for the theological reality I will present. It is a sad academic fact that we are forced to paint Indigenous theologies onto the canvas of established Industrial[7] norms, but this is a relationship Indigenous theologians must accept while Industrial theology remains dominant in evangelical thought. However, while Indigenous theologies need to dialogue with the Industrial theological establishment, they need not be defined by or restricted to those norms. Our contexts are different, our ancient questions are different, our reading of the unchangeable and authoritative Scripture is different. Our conclusions will be different—more relevant for our contexts. We do not intend to diminish Industrial theological axioms. Rather, we leave it to their theologians to critically assess their assumptions for their own context. We only ask that Western theological propositions not be imposed upon our experience of God in Christ, and how we interpret those experiences by what we find in the Bible.

---

6 Kim, *Christianity as a World Religion*, 3.

7 See n. 1 for explanation of my use of Industrial and Indigenous.

Seeing through Different Eyes

The emancipation of theology from Eurocentric constraints is gaining momentum, supported by books exploring alternative hermeneutics or ways of reading Scripture, while remaining faithful to the narrative of the holy text. Many are written by Westerners trained in Western theology seeking to defend alternative interpretations discovered during their intercultural encounters in cultures foreign to them. As helpful as this is, the "outsider" perspective must be treated cautiously. There is a dimension to interpretation within Indigenous cultures that can only be accessed by blood—by genetic heritage.

In his treatment of *Reading Romans with Eastern Eyes*, the Western author who uses the pseudonym "Jackson Wu" claims:

> To say Westerners cannot have an Eastern perspective effectively nullifies all biblical interpretation... . People are not born with cultural perspectives. They are learned and adjusted over a lifetime. Various experiences and relationships shape one's view of the world.[8]

It is indeed legitimate for "outsiders" to learn to interpret well, so long as they humbly recognize their limitations. But to defend his claim, Wu appeals to the contested "nurture over nature" thesis, which recent scientific research finds wanting. Instead, researchers are finding that our genetic code carries cultural information. Innate cultural preferences can be altered by life in a very different context from our heritage, but we too easily underestimate how much of our interpretation of lived experience is intuited from inherited coding. Therefore, Wu cannot provide a fully Eastern perspective since he was not born Asian, he will never be Asian, and his perspective will only at best approximate an Asian one. To suggest otherwise is cultural appropriation. This is evident in my Indigenous reading of his work.

For example, he makes much of the term "honor and shame." This reveals the dependence of Industrial intercultural commentators on Industrial assumptions. The term, its derivatives, and the psychology built around them is rooted in largely dismissed early twentieth century North American anthropology, yet intercultural academics and missions practitioners persist with its use. For the Indigenous, building honor is a great motivator, and defense of honor is as paramount as the protection of one's financial wealth is for Industrials. Shame is a different category altogether. One must inherit

---

8 Jackson Wu, *Reading Romans with Eastern Eyes: Honor and Shame in Paul's Message and Mission* (Downers Grove, IL: IVP Academic, 2019), 9.

the ability to understand cultural concepts like this at a deep, visceral level. Contrary to popular belief, it is not something that can simply be acquired through purely cognitive means over time.

Another anthropological concept misappropriated by theologians, missionaries, and intercultural researchers, is that categorized as "animism," the belief in a vital life force permeating and sustaining the material world. Use of the term infers the rejection of life force as a legitimate prime assumption, with those who hold to this belief being treated as underdeveloped humans. Disparagingly, CMS Missionary William Gairdner characterized animism as "the religious beliefs of more or less backward or degraded peoples all over the world."[9] Yet, when one considers how pervasive a belief in a vital life force is around the world,[10] the Industrial perspective is the aberrant one. Industrial arrogance places itself in the superior position, and the dismissal of life force is proving a significant downfall. We only need to look at the damage industrialization has done to our environments or the mental health crises confronting Industrial societies to perceive correlated effects.

Philosopher Charles Taylor[11] addresses the diminishing sense of a spiritual essence to life, which I describe here as life force, as the disenchantment of Industrial[12] society and suggests a need for reenchantment. Taylor observes that Industrials experience the world as individuals buffered, or closed off, to outside influence. In contrast, he suggests, we are better off experiencing life as porous, allowing and engaging with outside influences, including spiritual ones. The functional deism of Industrial Christianity has done the world a great disservice.

Making the Creation Connections

An Indigenous perspective in contrast, is porous. It invites and engages in relationships with reality outside of itself. There are many commonalities in the value systems of the collectivist cultures I group together as Indigenous, even if they are not technically classifiable as indigenous peoples. I cannot

---

9   David Chidester, *Empire of Religion: Imperialism and Comparative Religion* (Chicago: Univ. of Chicago Press, 2014), 53.

10 This reality is described in many ways, such as *Qi* (Chinese), *Ki* (Japanese), *Prāna* (Hindu), *Vijñāna* (Buddhist), *rûaḥ/Spirit* (Judeo-Christian), *Barakah* (Islam), *Ntu* (Bantu), *Manitou* (Algonquian), *Ni* (Lakota), *Nilch'I* (Navajo), *Bio-Plasmic Energy* (Euro-Russian), *Mana* (Melanesian); in New Zealand Māori, we call it *Mauri Ora*.

11 Charles Taylor, *A Secular Age* (Cambridge, MA: Belknap Press, 2007), 25ff.

12 Again, Industrial is my way of describing people from individualistic/Western cultural backgrounds; it is not Taylor's.

authoritatively speak on behalf of all, but I can fairly represent my people for illustrative purposes, as an example of how indigenous views interpret reality and the impact that has on our theology of creation—and our missions.

Māori Anglican theologian and *tohunga* (traditional spiritual expert) Rev. Māori Marsden introduces our "first principles" this way:

> Ultimate reality is wairua or spirit. The universe is process. The Creator or first cause, Io Taketake (the ancient one) is the genesis of the cosmic process. Spirit is ubiquitous, immanent in the total process; upholding, sustaining, replenishing, regenerating all things by its hau or mauri—the Breath of Life principle (or vital life force). As a corollary of (all of this, therefore), All is One and interlocked together.

(Humanity) is both human and divine, an integral part, both of the cosmic process and the natural order. The Māori approach to life is holistic. There is no sharp division between culture, society and their institutions.[13]

From *mauri* (vital life force) comes *mauri ora* (activated life force) that animates all living things. This manifests as *mana* (personality, character, power, authority), which is honored as it is recognized by others. *Mana* is relational currency and highly prized. It is increased by giving it away. *Mana* grows when invested in relationships, through generosity, use of skill, application of wisdom, and contributions to society. *Mana* is also an attribute of the nonhuman world, both spiritual and physical. Created order has *mana* according to its kind.[14] It is to be respected, honored for its contribution to life and wellbeing, and related to with care.

For biblically faithful Christ followers, this perspective opens up a world of understanding about God and creation, connecting Christ with creation as "supreme over all creation," through whom "God created everything" and who "holds all creation together" (Col. 1:15–17, NLT). This passage is too easily interpreted metaphorically when, for indigenous cultures like mine, they are quite literal. A biblically faithful reinterpretation of my culture's first principles sees *Io* the uncreated One as the God of the Bible, and *hau/mauri* in the Genesis account of creation, especially in Genesis 2:7 where *mauri ora*, the breath of God, activates life in humankind. For those with eyes to see, evidence of God's vital life force in all of creation permeates the whole of Scripture. When we read passages like Job 12:7–10, we do not doubt the interconnected, interactive relationship expressed there. Again, it is not

---

13 Māori Marsden and Te Ahukaramu Charles Royal, *The Woven Universe: Selected Writings of Rev. Māori Marsden* (Otaki, NZ: Estate of Rev. Māori Marsden, 2003), 33.

14 A deliberate allusion to Genesis 1.

metaphorical. We enjoy a deeply intimate relationship with our habitats. We are connected to creation and perceive our transcendent God as immanent, not absent from it. Any theology that thinks sin can separate God from creation fails to appreciate the sovereignty of God and the overwhelming evidence to the contrary in Scripture.

When Industrial Christians repudiate animism, they associate it with pantheism (worship of terrestrial-inhabiting spiritual beings), but an intimate relationship with creation need not infer worship. Worship requires a level of allegiance where the worshipper becomes subordinate to and in some ways controlled (constrained or compelled) by the object being worshipped, seeking that object to work supernaturally on the worshipper's behalf. All Christ followers must renounce idolatry and witchcraft and find such things reprehensible. But spiritual beings do not just cease to be. Rather, because we follow Christ, we no longer need to fear, nor try to manipulate, spiritual beings for our own gain. They are to be acknowledged, respected, and mostly ignored, unless terrestrial spirits interfere with human well-being.

For Māori, humans are subordinate to creation in the sense that we are heavily dependent upon it for our survival. We carry a responsibility to care for creation, not because we inherit it from our forebears but because we are borrowing it from our children's children. A popular way for Māori to encapsulate our innate sense of responsibility for creation is the term *kaitiakitanga* (guardianship, protection, security, nurture). Selby et al. explain that "Kaitiakitanga is not an obligation which we choose to adopt or ignore; it is an inherited commitment that links ... the spiritual realm with the human world and both of those with the earth and all that is on it."[15] With animist fears firmly set aside, this could be deemed an act of worship of the Creator in the sense that we are serving God by ensuring we nurture that which God determined to be "good" and actively sustains. The alternative is damning. The last stanza of the twenty-four elders' song in Revelation 11:18 should shake us all to the core.

---

15 Rachael Selby et al., *Māori and the Environment: Kaitiaki* (Wellington, NZ: Huia Publishers, 2010), 1.

Conclusion

Whenua, the Māori word for our environment, is the same word we use for the placenta. The concept is identical—a place that sustains us, feeds us, and provides oxygen and nutrients for our bodies. *Whenua* is a gift from the Creator—Parent,[16] Son, and Holy Spirit. Our habitat is our context, which has been torn apart by the influence of sin, evidenced by broken relationships. Through Christ's redeeming work on the cross, those of us who follow him have Holy Spirit power that enables us to overcome sin's influence and live in perpetually reconciled relationships, saving the rent universe one relationship at a time, including our relationship with creation. We are saved into a covenantal community in Christ, to live in Holy Spirit-enabled shalom harmony, transformed by learning to live and love in relationships that prioritize kenotic mutuality and reciprocity. All the while, we long for the day when sin will be no more, relationships will be fully repaired, and creation will cease its groaning and reveal the full glory of God unveiled. These are theological constants worked out in our context, and they resonate with many other decolonized indigenous Christ-following theologies.

Raranga katoa (it is all woven together). Until we accept once more the immanence of God—Parent, Son, and Spirit—with creation (which includes all humanity), indivisibly interconnected, we will continue to apply utilitarian values to our treatment of creation. No ecotheology, decolonized or otherwise, can be theologically and practically effectual unless we acknowledge God's involvement. If we truly understood God's grace in sustaining the world with vital life force, we would treat the material world with much more care. May our merciful and loving Lord enlighten us all.

---

16 Most Māori proper nouns are nongendered, especially for elder relations (parents, uncles/ aunts, etc.).

Discussion Questions

1. "The Eurocentric theological consensus is losing its authority as the arbiter of orthodoxy for the Protestant world" means that Western theologies are not as universally orthodox as we might think. How does this cause you to react? What implications might this have for your ministry and future theological development?

2. Take some time to consider your first-principle or worldview assumptions. In cross-cultural contexts it does not take long to discover our assumptions are not as universal as we thought. In what ways does exposure to Māori cosmology confirm or challenge your understanding of reality?

3. Do you tend to be "buffered" or "porous," closed off or open to spiritual and supernatural phenomena? How might becoming more porous, more open and connected, but also more vulnerable to the spiritual dimensions of reality, change your relationship with our Lord and Savior Jesus Christ?

4. What are some key hurdles that keep you from accepting the immanence of God in creation? How might accepting it change your relationship with creation?

5. Discuss your thoughts about worshipping God amid creation (in open nature) and the possibility of worshipping God by caring for creation.

Response

by Seung-hyun (Nathan) Chung

Prelude

The International Association for Mission Studies (IAMS) 15th International Assembly was held in Australia on July 7–11, 2022. There was an interesting ritual at the opening. Instead of the usual way of starting with a worship service or opening speech in a lecture hall, all attendees followed a guide and went out into the open air. Three Aborigine Christians smoked and invited all attendees to enter the smoke individually. This was their traditional ritual of inviting guests—Aborigines welcome outsiders, but first they must be purified of their sins through the smoke before entering the Aborigine land. Even after converting to Christianity, the lives of the Aborigines were found to be intricately tied to their ancestral land.

Korean traditional lives and rituals have been deeply rooted in Korea's beautiful seasons, mountains, and oceans. For example, Korean farmers determine the sowing and harvesting days by the four seasons and the lunar calendar. In addition, mountaineers do not climb any day to gather wild ginseng and herbs for a living but start work on a day specially designated by a shaman. Furthermore, fishermen perform a ritual with a pig's head before fishing at sea, to pray that the sea gods will not be angry and allow good weather while fishing. This kind of religious spirit of Koreans can also be seen in Christians. For example, Christian fishermen worship before setting sail, and Christian captains give tithes of their fishing profits to the church.

Biblical Discussion

In fact, creation is significant in the Bible, particularly in the Old Testament. Within creation, Christopher Wright insists that the land is profoundly related to God's covenant, and this appears throughout the Old Testament:

> The anticipation of the promised land in Deuteronomy, however, is but the culmination of a major theme running through the whole Pentateuch. The promise of land is a constituent part of God's covenant with Abraham; the Exodus is presented as God's first act in preparing to fulfill that promise; the law and covenant are given with a view to life in the land ... . Beyond the Pentateuch, the land remains a primary theme: its capture and division in Joshua; the struggle to survive on it in Judges; the eventual complete control of

the whole territory under David and Solomon; the prophetic protest at injustices perpetrated on the land; the Exile as divine judgment and the people's eventual restoration to the land as a token of a renewed relationship with God. And beside all this there are all kinds of laws, institutions, and cultic practices concerned with the use of the land.[17]

Wright shows that in the Old Testament, the land is at the center of God's amazing salvation plan, beyond the simple care of man. In a similar discussion, Ja-yong Ku, a professor of the Old Testament at Juan International University, informs us how theological zoology is developing. He defines theological zoology as an interest in and studying the relationship between God, humans, and animals. This zoology adheres to the idea that God is the "Lord of the animals" and that humans and animals compete in a hierarchical relationship as rivals, rulers, and subjects. In the prophetic messages of judgment, animals often replace humans whom God's judgment has cast out (e.g., Isa. 13:20–22). In addition, Isaiah's vision of the future, in which all animals will enjoy happiness and peace in the kingdom of God, is certainly enough to awaken interest in studying the relationship between humans and animals.[18]

In such a sense, Mātenga's argument is very appropriate. The relationship between God and creation recorded in the Bible (Col. 1:15–17; Gen. 2:7; Job 12:7–10) should be taken literally rather than interpreted metaphorically. "We are connected to creation and perceive our transcendent God as immanent, not absent from it." Mātenga does not simply praise creation but insists on God's mastery over his creation. In addition, Mātenga challenges us that if God is not separate from his creation, how are humans supposed to relate to creation?

Kong3al Community

In South Korea, there is *Kong3al* (Three Beans) community that works with a deep connection to God's creations, including the land. Kong3al, located on Gang-hwa Island, Incheon, South Korea, was established in 2005. It is said that Korean ancestors planted three seeds when planting beans: one bean was to be eaten by insects or birds, one was to be shared with neighbors, and the last was to be eaten by the planter himself. As such, *Kong3al* began

---

17 Christopher Wright, *God's People in God's Land. Family, Land, and Property in the Old Testament* (Grand Rapids: Eerdmans, 1990), 4.

18 Ja-yong Ku, "야웨, 동물의 주: 신학적 동물학에 대한 소고" [Yahweh, the ruler of animals: A study on a theological zoology], 구약논단 [*The Korean Journal of Old Testament Studies*] 56 (2015): 205–6.

with the spirit of a farmer who plants three seeds to bear fruit: one for the community to form a mutually life-giving fellowship, another to share with others out of the joyful overflow, and the last to be harmoniously integrated to sustain the ecological cycle.

Jung-hoon Suh, who leads *Kong3al*, was born into a long line of farmers. His life experience sparked his interest in rural missions and pastoral work after his seminary days. While studying ecological theology, he searched for an agriculture-based ministry and communal life. *Kong3al* aims for the self-reliance of the community and its members by planting and harvesting beans to make and sell organic tofu products. The community practices sharing while working with the socially underprivileged. Sixty percent of its employees are people with disabilities in the local area. *Kong3al* takes care of the mentally ill and the disabled as well. In addition, *Kong3al* helps elderly farmers and returning villagers to resume farming. Furthermore, it allows people tired of city life to gain alternative experiences by forming a social agricultural network.

Through these processes, *Kong3al* considers humans and nature to be mutually dependent in a harmonious and sustained interaction. Nature provides people with a place to live. The disabled and nondisabled live together while planting, cultivating, harvesting, and making tofu. They participate in God's ongoing creation in places that could quickly become wastelands. Through creation, God wants the perfect fellowship seen in perichoresis (the relationship of the three persons of the triune God) to be realized on earth. For this, God sent his only begotten Son, and he broke down all human barriers. Men and women, Hebrews and Greeks, poor and rich, the nondisabled and the disabled, and people of other faiths, can now all experience fellowship with the God of creation. And human beings who have experienced that fellowship extend it to all creatures, ultimately giving glory, praise, and worship to God who allowed that fellowship.

Conclusion

Mātenga shares with us several beautiful Māori words. One is *whenua*, which is "our environment … the same word we use for the placenta." Environment and life are inseparable for the Māori. Jesus Christ is the God of creation as well as the God of salvation. These two characteristics of Jesus are inseparable. If we believe in Jesus Christ as our only savior, then we must develop a proper relationship with his creation. Most of all, creation should be the center of Christian theology, like salvation. Creation cannot be treated as an option or fringe of Christian theology. In addition, the church needs to take concrete and practical actions for God's creation, such as worshiping and evangelizing for the salvation of souls. Mātenga deals with a critical topic for today's Christians living amid the climate change crisis, and makes an essential proposal for Korean Christianity, which focuses only on salvation rather than the creation of Jesus Christ.

CHAPTER 8
Creation Care
The Gospel's Third Dimension[1]

by Ed Brown

The missionary movement to carry the message of Jesus Christ's death and resurrection is arguably based primarily on the Great Commission as presented by Matthew. We find it both in Jesus's teaching on the Mount of Olives during his final week and just before he ascended:

> *And this gospel of the kingdom will be* preached in the whole world as a testimony to all nations, and then the end will come. (Matt. 24:14)

Then Jesus came to them and said, "All authority in heaven and on earth has been given to me. *Therefore go and make disciples of all nations*, baptizing them in the name of the Father and of the Son and of the Holy Spirit, and teaching them to obey everything I have commanded you. And surely I am with you always, to the very end of the age" (Matt. 28:18–20).

The *command* to go and make disciples is not in question. That command is clear. It has generally been accepted by Christians everywhere and, with a few exceptions, throughout most of church history. It is the *content* of the "gospel of the kingdom" that has kept church leaders, missiologists, and a few ordinary Christians up at night.

Is the essential content of the gospel limited to the message of personal salvation? Or does it also extend to such "kingdom" concerns as poverty and justice? This debate is familiar to all of us and is what led in the 1960s and '70s to the integral mission movement. This two-dimensional gospel is generally accepted as the standard for missions today. As articulated by the Micah Declaration in 2001,

> integral mission or holistic transformation is the proclamation and demonstration of the gospel. It is not simply that evangelism and social involvement are to be done alongside

---

1 This chapter is adapted from my article, "Is Creation Care Really a Gospel Issue?," *Evangelical Missions Quarterly* 59, no. 2 (April 2023): 8–12. Note that all italics in block quotes are added (i.e., emphasis mine).

each other. Rather, in integral mission our proclamation has social consequences as we call people to love and repentance in all areas of life. And our social involvement has evangelistic consequences as we bear witness to the transforming grace of Jesus Christ. If we ignore the world, we betray the word of God which sends us out to serve the world. If we ignore the word of God, we have nothing to bring to the world.[2]

The problem with this two-dimensional gospel is that it has no place for the rest of God's creation. It is a gospel for humans alone. In the following paragraphs, we will show that such a gospel is less than biblical in that it ignores some significant biblical material speaking of the role of creation in God's redemptive plan.

It is true that one can make a strong pragmatic case for including creation care as part of missions. In every direction we look today, mission goals are affected and often blocked by concerns related to the environment. Those who work with the world's poor have to prepare for the effects of degraded agricultural land and ongoing weather disasters. Health-care missionaries must reckon daily with environmental diseases. Even traditional mission agencies focused on evangelism and church planting can grind to a halt when major disasters occur, like the floods in Pakistan. We cannot be successful in our mission efforts without taking the crisis in God's creation into account.

But there is another reason why we ought to include creation care in our mission strategies. The command to care for God's creation is rooted in our identity as human beings, and even more so as the people of God. When we view creation care this way, it cannot just be a pragmatic issue. It is a *gospel issue* that we can closely connect to the movement in the late twentieth century known as integral mission.

The Cape Town Commitment and the Jamaica Call to Action

The assertion that "Creation care is a gospel issue" is found in the following paragraph in the Cape Town Commitment (CTC), first presented at Lausanne's Congress on World Evangelization in Cape Town, South Africa in November 2010:

---

2 Melba Maggay, *Integral Mission: Biblical Foundations*, M-Series: Integral Foundations (im:press, an imprint of Micah Global, 2007), 12, https://d1c2gz5q23tkk0.cloudfront.net/assets/uploads/3390300/asset/1._Integral_Mission_Biblical_Foundations.pdf?1662647840.

The earth is created, sustained and redeemed by Christ. We cannot claim to love God while abusing what belongs to Christ by right of creation, redemption and inheritance. We care for the earth and responsibly use its abundant resources, not according to the rationale of the secular world, but for the Lord's sake. If Jesus is Lord of all the earth, we cannot separate our relationship to Christ from how we act in relation to the earth. For to proclaim the gospel that says "Jesus is Lord" is to proclaim the gospel that includes the earth, since Christ's Lordship is over all creation. Creation care is thus a gospel issue within the Lordship of Christ.[3]

This historically important statement comes not from a fringe environmentalist faction or a creation care organization, but from the largest gathering of Christian leaders in history. It is rooted in the evangelical movement, which defines itself by its commitment to the gospel. Through this declaration, the movement says (to itself and others) that because creation care is part of the gospel, it is an essential part of the evangelical identity.

This statement has received remarkably little pushback, considering the historic ambivalence toward environmental issues within the church and the radical implications it suggests. Even so, knowing some members of the evangelical family may view this as a novel, dangerous, or potentially heretical idea, the senior leadership of the Lausanne movement asked me to convene the Global Consultation on Creation Care and the Gospel. This event was held in November 2012—two years after the Cape Town Congress—and produced the Jamaica Call to Action (CTA).

CTA affirms two convictions. Firstly, creation care is indeed a gospel issue, and secondly, creation is in an urgent crisis that "must be resolved in our generation." Let's look in more detail at the first conviction. Here it is quoted in full:

> Creation care is indeed a "gospel issue within the lordship of Christ" (CTC I-7-A). Informed and inspired by our study of the Scripture—the original intent, plan, and command to care for creation, the resurrection narratives, and the profound truth that in Christ all things have been reconciled to God—we reaffirm that creation care is an issue that must be included in our response to the gospel, proclaiming and acting upon

---

3 Lausanne Movement, "The Cape Town Commitment" (Peabody, MA: Hendrickson, 2011, by arrangement with Didasko Publishers), pt. I, sec. 7, par. A, https://lausanne. org/wp-content/uploads/2021/10/The-Cape-Town-Commitment-%E2%80%93-Pages-20-09-2021.pdf.

the good news of what God has done and will complete for the salvation of the world. This is not only biblically justified, but an integral part of our mission and an expression of our worship to God for his wonderful plan of redemption through Jesus Christ. Therefore, our ministry of reconciliation is a matter of great joy and hope and we would care for creation even if it were not in crisis.[4]

The CTA thus makes the implications in the CTC paragraph explicit: our identity as Christians is bound up in God's plan of reconciliation, which extends to all of his creation. We can trace the initial development of this paragraph to a meeting in Lebanon in February 2010.

Lebanon 2010: Peter Harris and Chris Wright

The CTC was written by Chris Wright, but it was based on several years of work by Lausanne's Theology Working Group (TWG), of which he was the chair. Since Lausanne's slogan for many years has been "the whole church taking the whole gospel to the whole world," the TWG gave itself the task of examining each of these ideas in preparation for the upcoming third Lausanne Congress in Cape Town. By February 2010, they were ready to consider the final section, *the whole world*, at a meeting in Beirut.[5]

I have had several conversations with Chris Wright about the origins of the section of the CTC we are considering here. In one of them he said, "Oh, it wasn't me, Ed. That came from Peter Harris."[6]

Harris is cofounder of A Rocha International (arocha.org), the largest Christian conservation organization. It turns out his participation in the Beirut meeting was critically important, though unplanned. This is how Harris remembers it:

> It seemed very strategic to ask Chris if I might join that theological commission meeting in Beirut, although it was a bit of a nerve as I do not count myself as a theologian in any sense. He graciously agreed, but what became obvious during the meetings ... was that I was pushing on an open door.[7]

4 "Creation Care and the Gospel: The Jamaica Call to Action," Lausanne Movement, 2012, https://www.lausanne.org/content/statement/creation-care-call-to-action.

5 "The Whole Church Taking the Whole Gospel to the Whole World," Lausanne Movement, 2010, pt. 3, https://lausanne.org/content/twg-three-wholes.

6 Chris Wright, email to author, August 12, 2021.

7 Peter Harris, email to author, June 12, 2021.

Harris did attend and gave a paper entitled, "Towards a Missiology of Caring for Creation."[8] In it, he addresses evangelical church leaders and missionaries who might be afraid that the creation care movement represents a different gospel or an alternative mission for the church. He indicates that creation care as a part of mission is already implied in commonly accepted mission frameworks:

> I would argue that entirely adequate justification for considering creation care as a normal element of an authentically biblical mission agenda can be found in either of two well-known missiological frameworks. The first is that which stresses the proclamation of the Kingdom of God, and the second sees mission as the church's proclamation of the Lordship of Christ. Either of these current evangelical missiologies quite naturally provides a foundation for the urgently needed integration of the care of creation into our thinking, and more importantly, gives us a solid basis for action.[9]

In other words, Harris says anyone teaching, preaching, or practicing missions already has the theological framework for a vision of mission that includes God's wider creation, whether their approach is from social action (the kingdom of God) or evangelism (the lordship of Christ).

Incidentally, Harris makes another point that supports the pragmatic case for engaging in creation care, which we addressed briefly at the beginning. Quoting philosopher Max Oelschlager, he explains that the church may be the last, best, and perhaps only hope for God's suffering creation. Here's Harris again:

> If the Christian church world-wide understands that its relationship with God's creation is an integral part of its worship, work and witness, then there will be immediate hope for some of the most environmentally vulnerable and important areas on earth. If, however, we continue to be as damaging a presence as the rest of human society, then, as I will explain more fully below, there is probably little we can do to arrest the rapid degradation that is proving so devastating for them all.[10]

---

8   "Lausanne Occasional Paper: Towards a Missiology of Caring for Creation," Lausanne Movement, 2010, https://lausanne.org/content/lop/towards-a-missiology-of-caring-for-creation-lop-63-c.

9   Peter Harris, "Towards a Missiology of Caring for Creation," *Evangelical Review of Theology* 34, no. 3 (2010): 224, https://lausanne.org/wp-content/uploads/2007/06/LOP65-2010Beirut-Lebanon.pdf.

10 Harris, 231.

Harris's paper and the discussion that followed had a direct impact on Chris Wright, and it became the source of the *gospel issue* phrase that appears in the CTC. Here's Wright from an email:

If you look at the Cape Town Commitment Part 1.7.A—and the sentences beginning "If Jesus is Lord of all the earth, we cannot separate … within the Lordship of Christ," I wrote that all down furiously straight from Peter saying it during one of our discussion sessions. The words are pretty much his *ipsa verba*. It just sounded so true and logical and irrefutable to me, that I thought it had to go into our TWG report, and eventually into the CTC.[11]

Latin America, 1960s and '70s: Integral Mission

The open door for creation care within the TWG, to which Harris referred, was somewhat unexpected. However, I believe the ground had been prepared by a prior development that we now know as integral mission.

For most of its history, the evangelical church has struggled with what we described in the introduction as the two dimensions of the gospel. Too often these have been presented as an either-or choice. On the one hand, there is *evangelism*, the need for personal salvation, and the obligation to make this salvation known "to the ends of the earth;" on the other, social action, the call to feed the hungry, clothe those in need, heal the sick, and bring justice to the earth.

This either-or is a false choice. Choosing one will always be wrong. Jesus clearly calls us to do both. In spite of this, for many years Christians in North America and in other countries in the Global South that derived their theology from there, understood missions to be primarily evangelism. Social action, when considered at all, was simply a way to support the saving of souls.

In the 1960s and '70s, a group of young theologians in Latin America looked at their world, rife with poverty, injustice, and political corruption and said, "No, we don't have to choose." They argued that both evangelism and social concern must be and are part of the gospel. The main leaders of this movement were René Padilla (who passed away in 2021) and Samuel Escobar. Their movement to integrate these two calls into one gospel became known as *mission integrale* or integral mission.

Padilla made the case for integral mission at the first Lausanne Congress in 1974:

> My purpose is to show that according to Scriptures the Gospel is addressed not to man as an isolated being called to respond to God with no reference to his life context, but rather to man in relation to the world. The Gospel always comes to man

---

11 Chris Wright, email to author, August 12, 2021.

in relation to the world of creation, the world that was made through Jesus Christ and that is to be re-created through him. It comes to man within the present order of existence, immersed in the transient world of material possessions. It comes to man as a member of humanity—the world for which Christ died, but, at the same time, the world hostile to God and enslaved to the powers of darkness. The aim of evangelization is, therefore, to lead man, not merely to a subjective experience of the future salvation of his soul, but to a radical reorientation of his life ...[12]

Padilla later said of the Lausanne Covenant that "despite its shortcomings—especially its failure to point to the inextricable relation between evangelism and social responsibility—the covenant was a death blow to the traditional reduction of the Christian mission to the multiplication of Christians and churches."[13] Though tension between the two—evangelism and social engagement—continues to this day in some quarters, most evangelicals now accept that the integral mission vision of a comprehensive gospel is biblical and necessary.

The Micah Declaration (2001) gives perhaps the best summary and definition of integral mission. Let's quote it again:

Integral mission or holistic transformation is the proclamation and demonstration of the gospel. It is not simply that evangelism and social involvement are to be done alongside each other. Rather, in integral mission our proclamation has social consequences as we call people to love and repentance in all areas of life. And our social involvement has evangelistic consequences as we bear witness to the transforming grace of Jesus Christ. If we ignore the world, we betray the word of God which sends us out to serve the world. If we ignore the word of God, we have nothing to bring to the world.[14]

A Three-Dimensional Gospel

When we come to the Cape Town Commitment in 2010, we discover something new. Here we find the assertion that there really are not just two dimensions of the gospel that need to be integrated. The gospel must include

12 René Padilla, "Evangelism and the World," in *Let the Earth Hear His Voice: International Congress on World Evangelization, Lausanne, Switzerland. Official Reference Volume, Papers and Responses*, ed. J. D. Douglas (Minneapolis: World Wide Publications, ©1975), 134, https://lausanne.org/wp-content/uploads/2007/06/0134.pdf.

13 C. René Padilla, *Mission between the Times: Essays on the Kingdom*, rev. ed. (Carlisle: Langham Monographs, 2010), 3.

14 Maggay, *Integral Mission*, 12.

evangelism, social action, *and* care for God's wider creation. This is how this was expressed in the CTC:

> Integral mission means discerning, proclaiming, and living out, the biblical truth that the gospel is God's good news, through the cross and resurrection of Jesus Christ, for individual persons, and for society, and for creation. All three are broken and suffering because of sin; all three are included in the redeeming love and mission of God; all three must be part of the comprehensive mission of God's people.[15]

To put it another way, the gospel stool doesn't have two legs, it has three. Unless we are preaching and practicing evangelism, social action, *and* care for God's wider creation, we are presenting an incomplete and less than biblical gospel. The world's unreached desperately need the whole gospel, including the third stool leg.

Conclusion: Why It Matters

Seeing creation care as a gospel issue has significant strategic and practical implications for global missions. This brief historical survey primarily reminds us of two things.

First, our own recent evangelical history reminds us that through the Cape Town Commitment our global church family has broadly agreed that the gospel of Jesus Christ is comprehensive. It is, in fact, a three-dimensional gospel. It impacts individuals, human society, and the wider nonhuman creation. If we are to be true followers of Jesus in his mission vision, we must embrace a gospel that begins in the human heart but extends to all of creation.

Second, creation care is not optional. It is part of our identity as Christians and involves the very core of the gospel. It cannot be assigned to a few specialists; rather it is an obligation for every Christian, whatever their specific ministry calling might be. Missions cannot be exempt. It is an obligation we all need to take up. All creation is waiting.

> For the creation was subjected to frustration, not by its own choice, but by the will of the one who subjected it, in hope that the creation itself will be liberated from its bondage to decay and brought into the freedom and glory of the children of God. (Rom. 8:20–21)

---

15 Lausanne Movement, "The Cape Town Commitment," pt. I, sec. 7, par. A.

Discussion Questions

1. If the "global church family has broadly agreed" with the three-dimensional view of the gospel, how should local churches proclaim the truth of the gospel?

2. If creation care is not optional for a Christian, what changes do we need to make in our personal and family lives to be obedient in this area?

3. To what extent should our own mission family (agency, congregation, etc.) reflect a three-dimensional gospel in its strategic planning and implementation?

Response

by Youngmi Shin

Biblical and Theological Support

Ed Brown's paper helped me understand God's biblical plan and purpose for us more widely and deeply. Rather than a two-dimensional explanation of the gospel that is limited to/for human beings, a three-dimensional explanation and interpretation of the gospel that encompasses the entire universe, the earth, and all the creatures within the righteousness and will of God's kingdom is more creatively advanced than any previous interpretation of the gospel. In the three-dimensional reinterpretation of Jesus's command in Matthew 28:18–20, the Great Commission, along with Genesis 1:28, the first commandment of God to humans, God sends us not only to humans to make disciples but also to all living organisms and their environments everywhere in the world to steward them—to be fruitful, multiple, and fill the earth to expand the kingdom of God. To follow his command to govern, reign, and care for the creation, the kingdom of God must be expanded beyond two dimensions to a third, evangelizing not only humans but sharing the good news of creation care on the earth. This is the right way to go—make disciples, baptize, and teach them to obey the commands in the entire Bible.

For example, if we are called by God as missionaries to go from our comfortable and familiar places to certain mission fields to spread the gospel, we would relocate to a new environment, weather, people, culture, and languages. This means that we do not go there only for the people but for all creatures God made in an entirely different ecosystem. This is three-dimensional missional commitment based on the Bible. When we consider the entire elements of the mission field, the contents of ministry can expand in the various ways, and we can prepare for missional ministry more effectively. Therefore, in order to build/expand the kingdom of God with the gospel, we should consider the people, environment, weather, culture, and languages concurrently to evangelize for the righteousness of God.

According to Old Testament scholar John H. Walton's temple theology, the entire universe in which all things were created is a place of worship for the kingdom of God, and Genesis 1 describes a blessed and holy miraculous feast in which the temple of God's presence is born, preceded by the miracle of the creation. He also asserts that these feasts are a key link between science and theology since each day has an important functional element for the creation of the world.[16] If worship is the purpose and reason for God's creation and all the creations are the temple of God to worship and praise the Lord, then the two-dimensional idea that limits the object of the gospel to humans is a complete failure to understand God's words because the entire world, including the environment and all living things, will be part of the kingdom of God.

Identity as the Image of God

The author also mentions that understanding and interpreting the gospel in its third dimension is a way for us to discover our created essence and find ourselves. This perspective is a way to look forward and wait for our King, Jesus Christ, not only in our lives but also in the entire Christian community, with a more complete identity of ourselves. According to John Wesley's theology, when we were created we were made in the image of God in three different images—the natural, the political, and the moral image. Among these, the political image is closely related to the stewardship—creation care—we have been given by God.[17] In Genesis 1–2, God commands to us to name, rule, and care for all creatures. These commands are directed to God's political image embedded in us, and we should obey God's commands in the likeness of his character. Otherwise, the more we sin, the more we move away from God's disposition and assume the characteristics of Satan, who wants to have the lordship to govern the world by himself and to ruin God's creation, including humans, the environment, and living organisms on the earth. This means that our continued sins have resulted in the reality of our current spiritual and environmental crisis.

If we had maintained a static image as good stewards who obeyed God's commands and did not sin and, we would not be in this crisis. Genesis 1:2 says that there was darkness, chaos, and emptiness. This is what the world looked like before God created the world. If, as John Walton said, all of God's creation is a temple of worship to God, and the Creator's act of creation is the ritual and feast of the temple's building, then returning the temple to its former form (darkness, chaos, and emptiness) is Satan's strategy to

---

16 John H. Walton, *The Lost World of Genesis One: Ancient Cosmology and the Origins Debate* (Downers Grove, IL: IVP Academic, 2009), 24-45; Martin Hanna, "It Takes a Miracle: An Analysis of John H. Walton's View of Cosmic Temple Inauguration," *Andrews University Seminary Studies* 49, no. 1 (2011): 177-89, https://digitalcommons. andrews.edu/cgi/viewcontent.cgi?article=3134&context=auss.

17 James Pedlar, "John Wesley and the Mission of God, Part 1: The Image of God," James Pedlar: Theologian and Pastor, July 28, 2011, https://jamespedlar.ca/2011/07/28/john-wesley-and-the-mission-of-god-part-1–the-image-of-god/.

prevent worship of God. This means that when we recover God's political image, being completely free from the sin to care for the creation—which encompasses all three dimensions of the gospel—we can worship God in the completed form of ourselves. This also becomes a great weapon of the Word against Satan's hidden strategy.

In Romans 8:18–22, the creation is looking forward to the children of God to glorify the Lord:

> I consider that our present sufferings are not worth comparing with the glory that will be revealed in us. For the creation waits in eager expectation for the children of God to be revealed. For the creation was subjected to frustration, not by its own choice, but by the will of the one who subjected it, in hope that the creation itself will be liberated from its bondage to decay and brought into the freedom and glory of the children of God. We know that the whole creation has been groaning as in the pains of childbirth right up to the present time.

When we recover from the sinful nature to the image of God that we were originally created in by the Holy Spirit, all creations can start to recover with three-dimensional evangelization. Then, when Jesus Christ returns, we—all creation, including humans, living, and nonliving things on the earth—can completely be saved, and be recovered to glorify God forever.

Scientific View

Advances in science have made it clear that we can no longer ignore the health of the earth. As UN reports and various environmental papers indicate, the increase of global temperature is accelerating, and in fact, we are facing the reality that the sea level is rising due to the increase in global temperature, and many coastal facilities and settlements have been destroyed by extreme weather events, typhoons, and hurricanes.[18] In the US, a huge amount of funds is paid out annually by government agencies, local companies, and insurance agencies, and one of the big challenges is how to deal with climate and environmental change and find suitable alternatives. As a researcher at the Connecticut Institute for Resilience & Climate Adaptation (CIRCA) for the past few years, I have learned a lot about how important and urgent these things are. According to a paper published in 2020, hurricanes are

---

18 Jonathan A. Moo and Robert S. White, *Let Creation Rejoice: Biblical Hope and Ecological Crisis* (Downers Grove, IL: IVP, 2014), 21–52; "How Is Climate Change Impacting the World's Ocean," United Nations, accessed Aug. 10, 2023, https://www.un.org/en/climatechange/science/climate-issues/ocean-impacts; Katherine Hayhoe, "Challenges of Climate Change," *Journal of the Texas Tech University Ethics Center* 1, no. 1 (2017): 22–28.

accompanied by high waves, and when combined with the tide, they cause great damage to coastal areas in the form of storm surges, and as a result of modeling the return interval of a hurricane with high waves through the last fourteen years of observational data, it was found that the return interval and wave height were proportional, and the future wave height was always higher than the predicted results of existing models. In other words, reliable long-term observations suggest that as sea levels rise, coastal damage caused by extreme weather will increase faster than previously expected.[19]

Glorify the Gospel

In the future, climate change and environmental issues will become even bigger challenges that will raise the following questions: Are we recovering the precious and essential creatures we have been gifted by the Creator, the true owner of all things, through the image of God? On the day of Jesus's return, will we be proclaiming the gospel in the midst of the groaning, waiting, ruling, and cultivating, and looking forward to the true king, our Lord Jesus Christ? Before it is too late, we must move on from two-dimensional evangelization to a three-dimensional or multidimensional gospel for our personal lives, families, communities, churches, nations, and all creatures in order to worship the Lord together. This will take the form of giving back the glory that pleases the Lord, which God's children should have in this time of the end.

---

19 Y. Shin et al., "Waves in Western Long Island Sound: A Fetch-Limited Coastal Basin," *Journal of Geophysical Research: Oceans* 126, no. 2 (2021): e2020JC016468, https://agupubs.onlinelibrary.wiley.com/doi/10.1029/2020JC016468.

CHAPTER 9

Environmental and Human Calamities in Korea and Implications for Mission

by Bright Myeong-Seok Lee

Introduction: Tsunami Stones and Modern Technology

As Mark Willacy,[1] Tokyo correspondent for ABC[2] from 2008 to 2013 covered Japan's 2011 tsunami and Fukushima meltdowns, he described the "hundreds of years old" tsunami stones[3] dotted along the northeast coastline of the island of Honshu as "biblical stone tablets, promising salvation to those who heed their commandments."[4] Willacy observed that the tiny village of Aneyoshi on an isolated peninsula survived unscathed the magnitude 9 earthquake and subsequent tsunami that resulted in more than eighteen thousand deaths in Japan. The residents had listened to their ancestors warning, "Do not build your homes below this point!," carved on a stone tablet erected just below the mountainous village. Regrettably, Willacy observed that "these days, cell phones have replaced stone tablets as Japan's early warning system" and the Japanese "pay special attention to these phone alerts."[5] Japan today heavily relies on technology to manage natural disasters such as earthquakes. This is evident in Japan's "most sophisticated earthquake detection network in the world—a system of 4,235 seismometers can detect the very first waves from a quake, before estimating its focus, magnitude and seismic intensity."[6] But the modern detection system could not prevent the destruction of major

---

1 Mark Willacy won a Walkley Award for his coverage of Japan's 2011 tsunami and Fukushima meltdowns (Mark Willacy, "Japan Earthquake: Fukushima Nuclear Plant Remains the Gap in a Wall of Disaster Defences," *ABC News*, updated Nov. 22, https://www.abc.net.au/news/2016-11–22/fukushima-nuclear-plant-gap-in-japans-wall-of-disaster-defences/8045894).

2 Australian Broadcasting Corporation.

3 I first heard about the tsunami stones episode in Prof. Allison M. Howell's lecture, "Theology, Human Needs and Environment," while a PhD candidate at Akrofi-Chistaller Institute, Ghana in 2013.

4 Willacy, "Japan Earthquake."

5 Willacy.

6 Willacy.

national infrastructure, including Fukushima Nuclear Plant, with deadly consequences. Willacy is right in saying that the Japanese experience is reminding us that "warnings—whether they be inscribed in stone, or sounding from cell phones—should never be ignored."[7]

This paper aims to explore such warnings on climate change, and social unrest in the premodern history of Korea. There are correlations between abnormal climate change and the competition for limited common forest resources worsening social inequality, frequent plagues and how they contributed to the emergence of an indigenous religious movement, and the progress of Protestant mission. To this end, the researcher will analyze the Chosŏn people's responses to the ecological challenges of the late Chosŏn Dynasty and subsequent political and religious changes. Against this backdrop, the researcher will engage with implications for mission in the twenty-first century.

Climate Change and Responses in Premodern Korea

Various ecological changes related to climate anomaly have significantly impacted human societies worldwide since the seventeenth century. In the seventeenth century, people observed a prolonged abnormal temperature drop worldwide. People have called this period the Little Ice Age.[8]

Based on the vast volume of weather event records in the Annals of the Chosŏn Dynasty, the Korean historian Tae-Jin Yi suggests that the cause of the Little Ice Age was a meteor shower that generated dust clouds (recorded in the Annals as "colored vapors"). Among those records, Yi discovered that 1,052 weather events during 1501–1750 AD were related to the meteor shower.[9]

7 Willacy.

8 In 1939, F. Matthes coined the term "Little Ice Age" to indicate the Neoglacial period, which occurred during the Late Holocene period at about four thousand-year climatic intervals. Instead of that original usage, the term Little Ice Age is now conventionally used to describe the most extensive, recent mountain glacier expansion period during the mid-sixteenth to the nineteenth century, which impacted the climate on a global scale (Michael E. Mann, "Little Ice Age," in *The Earth System: Physical and Chemical Dimensions of Global Environmental Change*, Michael C. MacCracken and John S. Perry, eds., vol. 1 of *Encyclopedia of Global Environmental Change*, ed. Ted Munn (Chichester: John Wiley and Sons, 2002), 504-09.

9 Tae-Jin Yi, "Meteor Fallings and Other Natural Phenomena between 1500-1750 as Recorded in the Annals of the Chosŏn [Chosŏn] Dynasty (Korea)," *Celestial Mechanics and Dynamical Astronomy* 69, no. 1 (1998): 199-220.

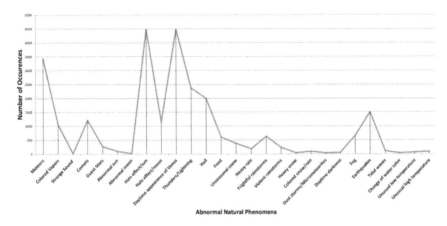

Figure 9.1: Abnormal natural phenomena recorded in the annals of the Chosŏn Dynasty[10]

The reason for leaving detailed observations and records on disasters related to abnormal weather in the Chosŏn Dynasty was not purely scientific interest in the modern sense. Archival records of the Chosŏn Dynasty (1392–1910 AD) show that Koreans paid particular attention to climate anomalies mainly related to celestial events.[11] In addition to solar eclipse, premodern Koreans saw drought, frost, flood, and hail as punishments from the heavens. This means that for premodern Koreans, abnormal climate events were interpreted as more than natural phenomena, carrying a message from heaven.[12] In particular, the events also served to check the absolute power of the rulers, ensuring accountability and justice in the process. This was a positive function inherited from the Koryŏ Dynasty (936–1392 AD).[13]

When abnormal weather events occurred related to abnormal celestial activities, the king humbled himself and granted amnesty to the people,

---

10 The graph is modified from the study of Tae-Jin Yi ("Meteor Fallings").

11 Yi argued that 1,052 weather events occurred between 1501–1750 AD that were related to meteor showers (Yi, "Meteor Fallings").

12 Yo-han Bae, *The Divine-Human Relationship in Korean Religious Traditions: The Presence and Transformation of the Themes from the T'angun Myth in the Chosŏn Chujahak Tradition and Korean Protestant Christianity* (Saarbrüken: VDM Verlag Dr. Müller, 2010), 64-78.

13 During the Koryŏ Dynasty, there were cases in which national finances and resources were wasted by relying too much on apocalyptic prophecies for political gain. The Chosŏn Dynasty adopted Confucianism and its principles as the systematic pillar of society to rationalize a stratified order. In principle, Confucianism establishes harmonious interaction and coexistence of heaven, human institutions, and nature (Y. S. Tzu, trans. J. K. Choi, 북송유가의 천일합일에서 본 환경윤리의 문제 [A justification of holistic unity of man and nature from Song Confucians and its implications for environmental ethics], *Studies on Life and Culture* 20 (2011): 117-18.

seeking forgiveness from heaven.[14] Thus, the hidden purpose of astronomical observation records on abnormal weather events in premodern Korea was to secure good governance in politics. Until the mid-Chosŏn Dynasty, the peasant relief system continued to function, even during times of various natural disasters thanks to adequately functioning governance. However, the governance that functioned between the ruling elites and the king excluded the participation of common people.

Political Changes in East Asia Brought About by the Abnormal Climate Events

The late Chosŏn Dynasty faced significant internal and external challenges. In addition, the government's ability to overcome those challenges diminished drastically for the following reasons: (1) the depletion of national resources after the wars; (2) the dissolution of functioning governance due to changes in the power structure within the central government; and (3) the country's disaster relief system did not work appropriately due to rampant corruption among government officials.

Wars and Technological Development

The climate anomalies profoundly impacted entire Northeast Asia and led to military conflicts for hegemony in the region. Seven years of war between Korea and Japan (Imjin War, 1592–1598 AD), followed by the Jurchen Invasion (1627, 1636), depleted vast forest resources, destabilizing ecosystems. Consequently, a series of droughts, floods, and famines swept through the entire Chosŏn from the late eighteenth century onward. The two wars in Chosŏn led to industrial development, further increasing demand for forest resources. The continued temperature drops of the Little Ice Age boosted the nationwide spread of *ondol*, a home-heating system using forest resources. In addition, new agricultural technology to meet the demand of population growth and industry development further contributed to rapid reduction of common forest resources.

Lack of Good Governance in the Central Government

In the beginning of the Chosŏn Dynasty, the central government enacted a regulation called *Sanlimcheontaek*[15] to control common resources in forests and rivers, which in principle prevented powerful individuals from

---

14 Tae-Jin Yi, "An Interim Report of the Study on the Little Ice Age (1500-1750) Phenomena Based on the Records of the Annals of the Dynasty of Chosŏn," *The Korean Historical Review* 149 (1996): 227-28.

15 *Sanlimcheontaek* literally means "the benefits of mountains, rivers, and reservoirs should be shared among the people."

privatizing common resources.[16] In the late Chosŏn Dynasty, however, as the demand for limited common resources increased, the ruling Confucian elites privatized forest resources, barring commoners and peasants from access, and thereby deepened social inequality.

In contrast, the political leadership that should have distributed limited resources fairly throughout society did not function. The economic difficulties and social unrest in the seventeenth and eighteenth centuries that followed abnormal weather events were not inevitable. In late Chosŏn society however, corruption was rampant among clans of queen mothers.[17] At that time, the ruling power centered on the Queen Mother Sun-won and her family's corrupt relatives who bought and sold government posts.[18] The absence of well-functioning governance aggravated the suffering and poverty of the peasants. Along with the faulty tax system and privatization of land and forest resources by the Confucian elites,[19] the social inequalities and injustices forced the peasants to turn to slash-and-burn farming.[20] As a result, the lives of common people were ruined.

Frequent Outbreaks of Epidemics

Another distinctive feature of this period was the frequent outbreak of plagues, such as cholera, dysentery, and typhoid, threatening the lives of the peasants. Massive migration that occurred during the wars contributed to the spread of epidemics. The peasants who lost their livelihood went into the mountains to avoid tax collection and engaged in slash-and-burn farming. The increase in slash-and-burn populations further accelerated depletion of forest resources. The destruction of forests encroached on animal habitats, which also contributed to frequent outbreaks.[21] In this regard, the two wars that swept through premodern Korea and the extreme inequalities in the late Chosŏn Dynasty were deeply related to frequent outbreaks of epidemics. These epidemics devastated the living conditions of the peasants, whose

---

16 Sung-kyung Kim, "A Study of the Sajŏm of Sanlimchontack in the Late Chosŏn Dynasty," (PhD diss., Kyunghee University, 1999), 14-61.

17 Susan Shin, "The Social Structure of Kŭmhwa County in the Late Seventeenth Century," *Occasional Papers on Korea* 1 (April 1974): 9-35.

18 Won-lim Pyŏn, 순원왕후 독재와 19세기 조선사회의 동요 [Queen Mother Sunwon's dictatorship and the agitation of nineteenth century Chosŏn society] (Seoul: Iljisa, 2012), 243-68.

19 Ho-cheol Shin, "A Study on the Expansion of the Slash-and-Burn Agriculture in the Late Chosŏn," *Yŏksahakpo* 91 (1986): 57-108.

20 James B. Palais, *Politics and Policy in Traditional Korea* (Cambridge, MA: Harvard Univ. Press, 1975), 58-61.

21 George Kallander, *Salvation through Dissent: Tonghak Heterodoxy and Early Modern Korea* (Hawaii: Univ. of Hawaii Press, 2013), 34.

discent was already on the verge of explosion. As a result, many small and large riots and revolts occurred in the provinces in the nineteenth century. The central government exhausted state resources to quell these revolts. Won-lim Pyŏn rightly argues that the cause of frequent revolts should be "found in the imbalance of power and wealth."[22]

Conversion to Catholicism and Emergence of New Religious Imaginations

Some local Confucian scholars dismayed by the prevailing corruption in the government withdrew themselves and emersed themselves in "Western Learning" or *Sŏhak* with Catholic texts imported from China.[23] This was before the arrival of Father Zhou Wenmo, the first Chinese Catholic missionary to Korea in 1795.[24] The Chosŏn government saw the presence of Catholics "as a precursor to Western subjugation and colonization."[25] The government banned all Catholic religious practices in public and further embarked on widespread persecution of Catholic Christians.[26] Despite the relentless suppression of the Catholic faith in Chosŏn, the religion survived in small groups of converts scattered in the mountainous regions, where they practiced their beliefs in secret throughout the nineteenth century.

It was against this socio-politico-religious backdrop that the *Tonghak* movement emerged in the latter part of the nineteenth century.[27] *Tonghak* adherents demanded the abolition of corruption among local officials and the reformation of forest regulations.[28] In 1894, the peasants, particularly from the southern part of the granary provinces, rebelled under the leadership of Bong-jun Chun. This uprising was known as the *Tonghak Rebellion*. Bong-jun Chun cited the *Bongsan*,[29] the forest regulations, and *Hwangok*[30] (granary taxation) as their major motivations behind the rebellion. *Tonghak* arose in

22 Pyŏn, 순원왕후 독재와 19세기 조선사회의 동요 [Queen Mother], 302.

23 Sung-jun Kim, 한국기독교사 [The history of Korean Christianity] (Seoul: Korean Christian Education Institute, 1980), 31.

24 James H. Grayson, "A Quarter-Millennium of Christianity in Korea," in Robert E. Buswell and Timothy S. Lee, eds., *Christianity in Korea* (Honolulu: Univ. of Hawaii Press, 2006), 9.

25 Kallander, *Salvation through Dissent*, 9.

26 Kallander, 3.

27 *Tonghak* was an indigenous religious movement established by Ch'oe Cheu'. Ch'oe advocated equality of all beings as opposed to social stratification. He insisted on the coexistence of heaven, humanity, and the rest of the living things (Kallander, *Salvation through Dissent*, 3).

28 Palais, *Politics and Policy*, 18.

29 Sun-Kyoung Kim, "A Study on the Forest Land Ownership in the Late Chosŏn Dynasty," *The Tong Bang Hak Chi* 79 (1993): 534–35.

30 Palais, *Politics and Policy*, 18.

a period of socio-political turmoil and essentially served to bridge Catholic missionary efforts of the eighteenth century and Protestant missionary endeavors in the nineteenth century.

Protestant Mission in Korea

Protestant Christianity was introduced to Korea during the nineteenth and early twentieth century Chosŏn Dynasty. When the first Protestant clergy missionaries arrived in Korea in 1885, disintegration of the political and religious system in Chosŏn had already begun. Protestant missionaries provided access to education regardless of gender and used the indigenous Korean language system *Hangul*, rather than the Chinese characters of the elites, contributing to the leveling of knowledge and alleviation of inequalities. Missionaries recorded observations of frequent epidemics threatening the peasants[31] and taking the lives of missionaries.[32] The missionaries' sacrificial medical work opened up opportunities for Protestant missions. This is consistent with Rodney Stark's analysis that one of the most significant factors in the expansion of Christianity in the early church community was Christians' sacrificial love expressed in ancient Roman society swept by epidemics.[33] Clearly, the decline of Confucian Chosŏn society in the face of integrated crises and the failure to give appropriate meaning to social disorder provided conditions in which Protestant Christianity could function as an alternative.

Implications for Mission in Twenty-First Century Post-Pandemic Times

The situation of the late Chosŏn Dynasty in response to climate change and the history of Protestant Christian missions in Korea suggest the following missionary measures for twenty-first century post-pandemic times:

Lessons from the Past: The Indispensable Role of Good Governance

In the late Chosŏn Dynasty, unequal distribution of common resources and climate change-related disasters intensified interclass tensions and worsened social instability. The crisis of late Chosŏn society was heightened when the ruling class neglected their social responsibilities and clung to their personal interests. Ordinary people were exploited when the ruling powers rushed to satisfy private interests or pursue policies only for the sake of their own clans. This again became unbearable for the vulnerable, and many of them

---

31 Lillias H. Underwood, *Fifteen Years among the Top-Knots: Or, Life in Korea* (New York: Young People's Missionary Movement of the United States and Canada, 1908), 123–83, 293.

32 Underwood, 98–99.

33 Rodney Stark, *The Rise of Christianity* (Princeton: Princeton Univ., 1996), 76–94.

became refugees. As a result, this became a factor behind social unrest, and as the socially vulnerable class collapsed, the entire Chosŏn society eventually came under Japanese rule. The collapse of well-functioning governance in the late Chosŏn dynasty weakened its potential to overcome national calamities and led to an irreversible national crisis. From this past, we can learn the indispensable role of good governance to check political power, whether in the form of religion or otherwise.

Environmental Justice

As in the case of forest resources in the Chosŏn Dynasty, electric energy is now an essential resource for society. Infrastructure to supply electricity is also a contested social issue. In 2021, Korea's nuclear power plant utilization rate was 74.5 percent. Contrary to the global trend, the new presidential administration in 2022 announced plans to increase the nuclear power plant utilization rate to 82 percent.[34]

The government's decision contrasts with the local residents' concerns about safety. Yet local governments with little financial resources and local commercial and industrial stakeholders actually welcome the construction of dangerous facilities in expectation that they may revitalize the local economy. There is an injustice in placing the social burden of risk on the vulnerable.[35] This collaboration between local regimes and potentates that brings ecological disasters to the locals and the next generations in exchange for private gain is not unique to Korea. For example, illegal gold mining by Chinese companies is one of the significant problems in Ghana, resulting in severe environmental destruction.[36] Also, a Peruvian mining company developed a

---

34 Ji-Hoon Lee, 한수원, 올 원전 이용률 82%까지 올린다 [Korea Hydro & Nuclear Power (KHNP) raises nuclear power plant utilization rate to 82%], *Hankyung News Paper Online*, May 5, 2022, https://www.hankyung.com/economy/article/2022050557721. The unit capacity factor, also known as the utilization rate, is a significant performance metric for nuclear power plants (NPPs) in addition to measuring nuclear power use. During the 2023 KGMLF forum in Maiim Vision Village, Yeo-ju, South Korea, Prof. Jong Ho Hong, a plenary speaker, kindly informed me that South Korea's present nuclear power use is around 30 percent. For more information, refer to the World Nuclear Association website (https://world-nuclear.org). President Yoon Suk-yeol, elected in March 2022, set a goal for nuclear power to contribute at least 30 percent of the total energy generation by 2030 ("Nuclear Power in South Korea," World Nuclear Association, updated Oct. 2023, https://world-nuclear.org/information-library/country-profiles/countries-o-s/south-korea.aspx).

35 Sang-jin Hahn, 핵발전소 입지를 둘러싼 지방 레짐의 형성과 시민사회 거버넌스의 대응 [The formation of a local nuclear power plant regime and the confrontation of the civic governance: Focusing the case of Sin-Gori nuclear power plant in Ulsan], *ECO* 16, no. 1 (2012): 45–68.

36 James Boafo, Sebastian Angzoorokuu Paalo, and Senyo Dotsey, "Illicit Chinese Small-Scale Mining in Ghana: Beyond Institutional Weakness?," *Sustainability* 11, no. 5943 (2019): 1–18.

mine with a water resource license obtained from the government, prevented local farmers from using the water, and polluted the common resource.[37]

These instances require consideration of what Julian Agyeman calls distributive justice for the "equitable distribution of environmental benefits." In addition, as Agyeman mentioned, environmental justice should also include procedural justice for the "meaningful involvement of all people" and substantive justice for the "right to live in and enjoy a clean and healthy environment."[38] Thus, environmental justice requires equitable sharing of both project benefits and environmental risks.

The Church's Missionary Function

In order to deliver electricity produced by power generation facilities to densely populated cities or factory areas, extra-high voltage transmission towers must be installed at intervals of about two hundred meters. On December 5, 1978, the Korean government enacted the "Electric Power Development Promotion Act (hereafter EPDPA)"[39] to construct extra-high voltage transmission towers. Under the authority of EPDPA, the owners of the land where the towers were to be installed were forced to leave the land they occupied for several generations. EPDPA is a compulsory state enforcement similar to the notorious forest policy implemented in the late Chosŏn Dynasty. Local residents complain of post-traumatic stress disorder (PTSD)[40] due to being expelled from the land where they have lived for generations. In addition, they suffer from diseases caused by the magnetic field generated by the high-voltage transmission towers.[41] On the other hand, solar power generation facilities, considered pollution-free renewable energy, are not without issues. They seriously damage the landscaping rights enjoyed by residents. In the interests of local governments and power

---

37 Ji-hyun Seo, 자원 거버넌스와 자원의 신자유주의화: 페루 북부 안데스의 경험을 중심으로 [Common-Pool Resources (CPRs) Governance and neoliberalising nature: The experience from the Peruvian Northern Highlands], *Journal of Asia-Pacific Studies* 27, no. 2 (2020): 94-98.

38 Julian Agyeman, *Sustainable Communities and the Challenge of Environmental Justice* (New York: New York Univ. Press, 2005), 26.

39 전원개발촉진법.

40 Naomi Breslau et al., "Trauma and Posttraumatic Stress Disorder in the Community: The 1996 Detroit Area Survey of Trauma," *Arch Gen Psychiatry* 55 (1988): 626–32.

41 Sang-yun Lee, 밀양 송전탑 건설문제, 주민들이 왜, 얼마나 아파야 하는지 알아야 해법이 보인다 [The Miryang transmission tower construction problem can only be solved by knowing why and how much the residents are suffering], 월간복지동향 [*Monthly welfare trend*] (2013): 29–33.

companies, residents are deprived of their freedom to enjoy an ecologically healthy environment.[42]

The Korean church should play a role in these issues. Churches must lead in helping vulnerable community members protect themselves and defend their rights to live peacefully in the land of their ancestors. The church's missionary function should be strengthened to ensure civil society governance. This is one of the areas to which the missional church responds.

Concluding Remarks

In a global pandemic beyond the scope of national control, the vulnerable suffer the most. The collapse of the vulnerable class, as Rodney Stark argued in the case of ancient Roman society, resulted in the collapse of the empire.[43] In the same way, despite the environmentally friendly Confucian principles embedded in the Chosŏn Dynasty's socio-politico-religious system, intensifying social inequality, inadequate common resource management, and the absence of good governance shortened the life of the dynasty and led to the demise of the dominance of Confucianism.

Religious change occurs when the values and practices of religion fail to save society from disaster. Amid the current pandemic, under the endorsement of their governments, intellectual and medical resources meant for disaster relief are misappropriated to serve multinational medical corporations' bottom lines. Meanwhile, the vulnerable are pushed to the brink of death. In this context, the church should sound a bold, prophetic voice against that selfish collaboration of bad governance, and fulfill its missionary function in a moment of global crisis. Otherwise, as we have learned from the fate of the late Chosŏn Dynasty and its official religion of Confucianism, the Christian church may also be weeded out.

---

42 Seona Park and Sun-Jin Yun, 장소애착 맥락으로 본 태양광 발전시설 입지 갈등과 수용성 [Opposition to and acceptance of siting solar power facilities from the place attachment viewpoint], *ECO* 22, no. 2 (2018): 294-99.

43 Stark, *The Rise of Christianity,* 76-94.

Discussion Questions

1. What past lessons, even from before Christianity's advent in Korea with its different religious heritages, can we apply to our time?

2. As a responsible Christian community, in what practical ways can we promote good governance to be in place in various parts of our society?

3. What is your opinion about Korean government initiatives to privatize public services, such as power generation, mass transportation, and health services?

4. To serve as a local missional church community, are there any practical approaches to implementing environmental justice to prevent local regimes and potentates from depriving vulnerable local residents of their right to live in peace?

Response

by Jay Mātenga

Manaaki whenua, manaaki tangata, haere whakamua
Care for the habitat, care for people, go forward

Dr. Lee has provided an insightful case study illustrating the connections between power and poverty, the impact it has on our habitats, and how our habitats respond. The *whakataukī* (Māori proverb) quoted above captures the heart of the matter from one indigenous people's perspective. The proverb provides an ideal summation of Dr. Lee's thesis.

Māori have a strong connection to our *whenua* (ground, land, habitat, and ... placenta or afterbirth). Upon our *whenua* is written the history and mythology of our people. The way we associate the material world around us with our mother's womb reveals the intimacy of our relationship with our environments. With the reminiscence of our gestation in mind, Māori are compelled to treat our habitats with the greatest respect, even to the point of lobbying for their legal status as persons (not to be confused with worshipping nature as divine in itself).[44]

The land remembers and, *raranga katoa,* everything is woven together with the land. In the Māori world, our terrain serves as a guide to ancient knowledge. Hidden though the meaning may be in mythic narratives told by storyteller priests, our topographies contain histories of natural cataclysms and calamities, warning us to be wary of dwelling in places not safe. Often the warning involves tales of monsters or curses, which serve to keep people away. Such places, whose stories were ignorantly swept aside by European settlers, continue to be sites of great calamity (and huge insurance claims) as floods and tides, erosions, earthquakes, and volcanic eruptions make a mockery of human invention.

Ancient knowledge is far too easily dismissed, denied, and dishonored in today's industrialized world. The Industrial[45] drive to disenchant our

---

44 For example, the Whanganui River, the longest navigable river in Aotearoa New Zealand, was the first river in the world to be awarded the same legal rights as a person; see "Change-maker—the Whanganui River," *He Tohu*, accessed May 27, 2023, https://natlib.govt. nz/he-tohu/learning/social-inquiry-resources/cultural-interaction/cultural-interaction-supporting-activities-and-resources/change-maker-whanganui-river. Similarly, the Urewera Forest; see "Te Urewera Act," Environment Foundation, last updated Nov. 17, 2017, https://www.environmentguide.org.nz/regional/te-urewera-act/.

45 I prefer the terms *Industrial* and *Indigenous* (capitalization intended) to describe two

realities has underestimated the intelligence to be found in the ancient paths.[46] To the Industrial, this intelligence is an inconvenience, a speed bump on the road of progress for modern moguls. By demystifying or desacralizing our material world, the powerful among Industrialized humanity are then free to utilize every part of it as resource for profit and power, for their gain and the gain of those who would support them. This beastly tendency[47] among the elite in human history is as universal as sin. Dr. Lee's portrayal of injustice committed by the Chosŏn Dynasty of the early industrial era provides us with a classic example. An unchecked lust for power is a freeway to failure for any civilization, and it should not escape the reader's notice that the first step in neutralizing that which would hold power in check was to diminish the portents of prophets and priests.

The land responds to human activity in an interconnected way. Indigenous people have long recognized this. When our tribes went to war, for example, the former battleground was *tapu* (taboo, sacred, off limits from commoners) until a satisfactory period had passed for the land and its non-human inhabitants to recover from the trauma. After such a period, the priests would conduct a rite to lift the ban and allow profane (normal) activity to resume once more. This also allowed those most impacted by the war time to reflect on the conflict, learn from it, and (ideally) mature in peace. Similarly, a significant motivator for some of our rivers and forests to be awarded the legal rights of a person is to acknowledge that our habitats need nurture. Where there is damage, it needs repair. Where something is taken, it needs replacing. It is not about sustainability, the Industrial telos of which is to enable continued consumption, but about vitality, the promotion of life and growth.

So, when the elites of the Chosŏn Dynasty began to control, hoard, and consume disproportionate to the needs of their fellow human inhabitants, one can imagine all of creation groaning as it awaited more righteous treatment (cf. Rom. 8:18–22). In Romans 8, the apostle Paul speaks of creation being "subjected to God's curse" (Rom. 8:20, NLT, 2nd ed.) against its will. The NIV refers to this curse as "frustration," the KJV as "vanity." The Greek

---

ends of a spectrum of values, similar to *individualist* and *collectivist*. These terms avoid numerous complications that occur when speaking of Western/First/Global North world influence over against Developing/Third/Global South/Majority worlds.

46 Cf. Jeremiah 6:16: "This is what the LORD says: 'Stand at the crossroads and look; ask for the ancient paths, ask where the good way is, and walk in it, and you will find rest for your souls.' But you said, 'We will not walk in it.'"

47 "Beastly" is a deliberate allusion to power(s) described by John in Revelation as beasts, agents of Babylon, the counterfeit kingdom.

ματαιότης (*mataiotēs*) is strong, carrying the sense of moral depravity—not at the initiative of God but as a consequence of human agency. Such actions are void of any lasting fruit or benefit. They are pointless. The purpose for which God created the world is not being fulfilled. This is the very epitome of sin—it is relationally destructive. Seen through Indigenous eyes,[48] it is no mystery that corrupt governance was the source of such suffering; imperially, economically, environmentally, and epidemiologically—war, poverty, famine, and plague—all consequences of empire building.

Paul's assumption in Romans 8 is that all creation has volition, it has a will, and corrupt human activity is oppressive to the created order. Creation has a sense of time, it is waiting for Christ's followers to work for the good of creation, to reconcile and restore right relationships with our waters, land, air, and everything that lives there; to free it from decay. This is not simply an eschatological hope, it is a Genesis mandate for us all to fulfill in the here and now. As we are restored to right relationships through adherence to the gospel, so we are to undertake prophetic action in resistance to the powers that are destroying the earth, declaring that their end is destruction (cf. Rev. 11:18d). This perspective must become integral to the church's understanding of, and participation in, God's mission.

The neo-Confucian *Tonghak* movement is instructive. It shows how a religious narrative can generate effective resistance to abusive power. Rebellion and revolution are not the way of Jesus, but living in prophetic resistance certainly is. Demonstrating care for the illiterate and infirm prophetically reinforces how far the social elite's behavior is from God's righteousness, the righteousness of heaven, while also working to close the gap between the disadvantaged and the privileged. Protestant missionary engagement in Korea is to be praised for doing this. As Dr. Lee points out, they perceptively chose to educate using an indigenous language system, and met felt needs of the common people, bravely, at the cost of some of their lives. We can learn much from their care of the suffering during epidemics, and the esteem that this compassionate response generated for Protestant missions among the people—still evident in South Korea's fifty years of enthusiasm for missionary sending, albeit something that is apparently waning.[49]

If the Korean experience was anything like elsewhere during the high-colonial era missions of the late-nineteenth century, the Christian message that arrived with Protestant missionaries was deeply influenced

---

48 See n. 45.

49 This is the sense I get from conversing with some South Korean missions leaders and researchers (e.g., through the Korean World Mission Association and Korean Research Institute for Mission).

by the industrial revolution and colonial expansion, synchronous with the emergence of modernism. Eurocentric evangelical theologies emerging from this period (still dominant today in global missions) presented a largely segmented, individualistic gospel. Coming from contexts where Christianity still enjoyed privilege, they neglected to establish a robust theological foundation for the resistance of abusive power, support of masses impoverished by the wealthy's resource hoarding and legal control, and the need to proactively care for creation as a relative. In effect, such theologies separated the spiritual from the sociopolitical, despite engaging in medical and educational work (embraced for its spiritual impact). Therefore, the lust for power continues throughout the world today, especially from former Christendom. As Dr. Lee points out, seeking power is now quite literal—harnessing and controlling energy, which is the life force of industrialization and essential to processes of progress. All the while, the underprivileged continue to bear the greatest cost.

Where is the South Korean Church's resistance to the ecological and economic abuse created by this unfettered elitist thirst? Could it be that over the past one hundred years or more of "redemption and lift,"[50] South Korean Christians have become part of the powerful? Has the cost of resisting industrial progress become too high because of the accommodation of affluence? Has a concern for the underprivileged diminished? These are questions only our South Korean brothers and sisters can answer, but such questions must be taken seriously if a prophetic response to the abuse of people and their habitats by the powerful is to be effective. In his conclusion, Dr. Lee notes that "religious change occurs when the values and practices of religion fail to save society from disaster." He rightly calls the church to a "a bold, prophetic voice against that selfish collaboration of bad governance," yet fears that "the Christian church may also be weeded out" by the people as previously ineffective religions were. This is a stern warning for the church in any context. When we collaborate with the type of power that puts people and provinces at risk, we do so at our peril. Hear the warning of the Prophet-Priest—there are monsters lurking in these contexts:

> I will spit you out of my mouth!
> You say, "I am rich. I have everything I want. I don't need
> a thing!" And you don't realize that you are wretched and
> miserable and poor and blind and naked.
> —Revelation 3:16–17

---

50 A principle identified by missiologist Donald McGavran; see Donald A. McGavran, *Understanding Church Growth*, 3rd rev. ed., ed. C. Peter Wagner (Grand Rapid: Eerdmans, 1990), 209–20.

Section C

Economics, Sufficiency, Justice, Perceptions of Christian Leaders and Missionaries

CHAPTER 10
Climate Crisis and Stewardship
A Christian Economist's Perspective

by Jong Ho Hong

The Status of Global Climate Crisis

The world changed in 2020. A pandemic struck the earth. A new virus named COVID-19 brought disease and death with unpredictable transmission power. Movement and contact restrictions to prevent the spread of the virus froze economic activity in an instant. At the same time, accumulating greenhouse gases caused heat waves, forest fires, floods, and droughts. Europeans suffered from a heatwave of over 40°C, and Australia had to endure a disaster during which an area more than twice the size of South Korea was burned. In Pakistan, more than sixteen hundred people died after one-third of the country was submerged by a devastating flood in 2022. The case of Pakistan, which accounts for 2.8 percent of the world's population but is responsible for only 0.5 percent of global greenhouse gas emissions, shows the inequality in damage caused by climate change. These ongoing crises—the triple threat of pandemic, economic downturn, and extreme weather events—have driven humanity to the edge.

What is even more frightening is that these crises are in a cyclical relationship that affect each other. The rise in global temperature has increased the survival rate of wild animals and expanded their range of movement, resulting in the spread of zoonotic diseases. The pandemic paralyzed tourism, restaurant, airline, and logistics industries, and took away jobs. When the economy suffers, there is a high probability that economic activities that exacerbate climate crisis, such as coal use and logging, will increase in developing countries. At the bottom of this vicious cycle is the "carbon-based economy."

Korea is no exception. In the summer of 2018, the Korean Peninsula experienced its worst heat wave on record. On August 1, Seoul recorded a temperature of 39.6°C and Hongcheon, Gangwon-do, 41°C. Each was the highest temperature ever recorded in the given region. Two years later in the summer of 2020, South Korea had to endure the pain of the longest monsoon season ever. Downtown Busan was flooded, and the local market in Gurye, Jeollanam-do turned into a sea of water. The fifty-four-day rainy season reminded the Korean people that climate change is not just a remote story of a distant country, but a harsh reality that anyone can experience here and now.

The disease crisis of COVID-19 and the climate crisis of heat waves and floods were intertwined and shook our lives. As if confirming the climate crisis, a huge forest fire spread around Gangwon-do in early 2022. The winter drought caused the forest fire to spread out of control. Korea Forest Service had to do everything possible to keep the flames from spreading to the nearby nuclear power plant and LNG storage tanks.

The most authoritative body on the scientific research on climate change is the Intergovernmental Panel on Climate Change (IPCC) under the United Nations. It is an international organization jointly established by the United Nations Environment Program (UNEP) and the World Meteorological Organization (WMO) in 1988 to address climate change issues. IPCC's mission is to perform academic review of climate change, to address the impact and damage of climate change on the ecosystem and socio-economic environment, and to present alternative solutions to mitigate climate change. Since the publication of the "First Assessment Report (AR1)" in 1990, IPCC has been publishing the report every five to six years.

In the Fifth Assessment Report published in 2015, important facts about the relationship between climate change and humans are listed. The report concluded that it is "extremely likely" that anthropogenic activity is the dominant cause of climate change since the mid-twentieth century; "extremely likely" implies more than 95 percent probability.[1] Greenhouse gases, such as carbon dioxide from fossil fuel consumption and methane from livestock manure, are heating up the earth. Natural resources, forests, and livestock are indispensable elements in human-led production and consumption processes. There is no denying that human economic activities are causing global climate change, which is the biggest challenge facing humanity in the twenty-first century.

What will our future look like? Has the prelude to human catastrophe due to climate crisis and biodiversity loss already begun, or can we overcome the threat of climate change through revolutionary changes in our economic activities? In this paper I will investigate the biblical understanding of the

---

1 Core Writing Team, R. K. Pachauri and Leo Meyer, eds., *IPCC, 2014: Climate Change 2014: Synthesis Report. Contribution of Working Groups I, II and III to the Fifth Assessment Report of the Intergovernmental Panel on Climate Change* (Geneva: IPCC, 2015), 37, 47.

Christian stewardship of creation, and the possibility of reconciliation of humans with nature through the lens of the half-century growth path that Korea pursued.

Biblical Understanding of the Stewardship of Creation

The Bible clearly states God's purpose embedded in the creation, especially the relationship between humans and nature, There are two aspects to human creation. First, humans, just like light, water, land, trees, and animals, are part of creation. On the sixth day of creation, God created wild animals, livestock, and creatures that move along the ground (Gen. 1:24–25). And then on the same day, God created man from "the dust of the ground" (Gen. 2:7). Humans came from the earth, which was also created by God. Therefore, humanity essentially has commonality with the rest of creation.

Second, humans are unique in the sense that "God created mankind in his own image" (Gen. 1:27). Human beings were created fundamentally different than other creatures. As the Bible states, "Let us make mankind in our image, in our likeness" (Gen. 1:26). What do these two notions imply? Humans, as part of God's creation, are no different from the rest of creation, but at the same time, they are particularly granted the image of God, unlike other creatures.

There have been many theological arguments about what is meant by "the image of God." From the Bible, it is evident is that God gave a special mandate only to humans. Man, as he is created in the image of God, is blessed with a mission given directly from the Creator. What is the divine mandate to humanity from God? The answer lies in two verses from Scripture: Genesis 1:28 and 2:15.

"God blessed them and said to them, 'Be fruitful and increase in number; fill the earth and subdue it. Rule over the fish in the sea and the birds in the sky and over every living creature that moves on the ground'" (Gen. 1: 28). There are two commands in this verse that can be applied only to humans: "subdue" and "rule." In Hebrew, "subdue" implies "to bring into bondage," while "rule" means "to trample."[2] These are indeed very strong words. Genesis 1:28 clearly testifies that God created man and woman to be positioned as superior to the other creatures.

---

2 Peter De Vos et al., *Earthkeeping in the Nineties: Stewardship of Creation*, rev. ed (Grand Rapids: Eerdmans, 1991), 287.

"The LORD God took the man and put him in the Garden of Eden to work it and take care of it" (Gen. 2:15). Here, we need to focus on the two terms "work" and "take care of." "Work" in Hebrew means "till," "cultivate," and "serve," while "take care of" is a Hebrew word for "keep," "watch," and "preserve." In an older version of the Korean Bible, "rule over" in Gen. 1:28 and "work" in Gen. 2:15 were both translated by a common Korean word, daseurida, meaning "to govern." The Hebrew meanings, however, show emphatically that the two words have different implications for the creation mandate given to humanity. Genesis 1:28 is balanced by Genesis 2:15, and vice versa.

God did not allow humans to take advantage of their dominant status to exploit the rest of the creation, but to work and serve responsibly in the environment that God created. This is the biblical perspective on the relationship between humans and nature. Man and woman are created in the image of God, only to carry out their God-given mission of the stewardship of creation.

"Theocentricism" plays a critical role in the biblical view of the relationship of humanity to nature. Theocentricism states that God is at the center of all existence, including human beings and nature, as opposed to either anthropocentrism or ecocentrism. God gave humanity a holy mandate to take good care of all creation. It is our fundamental responsibility to look after the world as faithful stewards because "God saw that it was good" (Gen. 1: 4, 10, 12, 18, 21, 25).

Conflict and Harmony between Growth and Conservation: The Case of Korea[3]

The Age of Black Smoke (1962–1991)

Over the past sixty years, Korea rose out of the depths of poverty and became the tenth largest economy in the world in 2021. According to the World Bank, per capita gross national income (GNI) of Korea in 1962 was only $110. Throughout the 1960s and 1970s, however, the Korean government adopted a series of growth-oriented economic policies, including establishing industrial complexes and promoting heavy and chemical industries. Over the thirty-year span from 1962 to 1991, the Korean government initiated six five-year economic development plans. During this period, Korea enjoyed

---

3 This section is a revised and updated version of Jong Ho Hong, "Green Growth Strategy of Korea: Past and Future," in *Green Growth: Issues and Policies*, ed. Jisoon Lee (National Research Council for Economics, Humanities, and Social Sciences, Random House, Korea, 2011), 44–70. The subsection below, *The Age of No Smoke: 2012–present*, is newly added.

on average a 9.6 percent annual GDP growth rate, which was by far the highest in the world.

From 1960 to 1980, Korean industry increased its share of overall economic activity from approximately 12 percent to more than 30 percent. This was accompanied by a rapid rate of urbanization from 28 percent in 1960 to more than 70 percent by the mid-1980s.[4] As a result, a country whose per capita income level was 119th out of 120 UN countries in 1962 has risen out of poverty at an unprecedented pace in the history of economic development.

The success of the Korean economy, however, entailed heavy cost. Rapid industrialization, urbanization, and mass production gave rise to large-scale environmental degradation, with ambient air and water quality standards being repeatedly violated. Until the early 1990s however, the Korean government did not place a high priority on environmental conservation policy. Environmental problems, which were already becoming prevalent in many parts of Korea, were still something the government did not want to talk about, not to mention to act upon. As a result, the *compressed growth* that the Korean government pursued since the 1960s has brought about *compressed environmental degradation* on a grand scale.

President Park Chung Hee, who had demonstrated strong leadership in the industrialization of the Korean economy, declared that "when we witness industry-produced *black smoke* dissipating into the air … the hope and development of our homeland will be realized."[5] At that time, pollution-heavy black smoke symbolized Korea's exodus from hunger and poverty into economic growth and modernization. With a majority of people suffering from subsistence-level living standards, Korea might have had no other choice but to sacrifice the environment for economic growth. In vivid contrast, in the early 1990s Korea entered the *age of white smoke,* and is now trying to transform quickly and embrace the new *age of no smoke* in the face of the global climate crisis.

The development path Korea decided to follow at the earliest stage, which can be summarized as a government-driven, growth-oriented economic strategy without environmental consideration, cannot be regarded as sustainable. Several limits and constraints made it extremely difficult for Korea in its early developmental stage to pursue a sustainable development strategy. Not only Korea lacked knowledge, technological development,

---

4 Byung-Nak Song, *The Rise of the Korean Economy*, 2nd ed. (Hong Kong: Oxford Univ. Press, 1997), 34.

5 A congratulatory remark by acting president Park Chung Hee at the construction of Ulsan Industrial Center in 1962, which was inscribed on the Ulsan Industrial Tower built in 1967.

and financial resources to harmonize economic growth and environmental preservation, but the world economy in general.

There was one exception to the economic policies the Korean government adopted during the age of black smoke: reforestation. In the 1950s, for several years immediately after the Korean War, forests were left in a state of extreme devastation, a result of excessive cutting during Japanese occupation and the war. In less than fifty years however, a miracle occurred. The 2005 forest statistics show that the Republic of Korea has 6.39 million hectares of forest covering about 64.2 percent of the total land area. International organizations such as the Food and Agriculture Organization (FAO) highly recognize the forest greenification policy of Korea and showcase Korea as a model country.

Lester Brown, a famous American environmentalist, introduced Korea as a successful model of international forest land greenification. Brown said, "South Korea is in many ways a reforestation model for the rest of the world. When the Korean War ended, half a century ago, the mountainous country was largely deforested. Beginning around 1960, under the dedicated leadership of President Park Chung Hee, the South Korean government launched a national reforestation effort. Relying on the formation of village cooperatives, hundreds of thousands of people were mobilized to dig trenches and to create terraces for supporting trees on barren mountains."[6]

Forest greenification in Korea contributed important economic benefits, including flood control, preservation of agricultural land, and creation of hundreds and thousands of jobs when the unemployment rate was over 30 percent in the late 1950s and early 1960s. In today's perspective, reforestation is a prototypical example of sustainable development, where both ecosystem improvement and job supply with GDP growth are achieved at the same time.

Korean experience shows that the age of black smoke cannot last. More than thirty years of rapid economic growth allowed the Korean people to understand the importance of quality of life, such as a better environment. In 1980, the Environment Administration was established by expanding and reorganizing the Environmental Affairs Bureau within the Ministry of Health and Social Affairs. Korean people have started to express opinions that a clean environment is as important as economic development and that it will contribute to long-term economic development. This led to the next stage, the age of white smoke, which began in the early 1990s.

---

6 Lester Brown, *Plan B 3.0: Mobilizing to Save Civilization* (New York: W. W. Norton, 2009), 157.

The Age of White Smoke (1992–2011)

Korea enjoyed one of the fastest growing economies in the latter half of the twentieth century. Without proper environmental regulatory measures, however, there was a trade-off between economic growth and environmental degradation. The environmental regulatory body in the government did not have the power to enforce appropriate policy measures over polluting behaviors of economic agents. The natural environment was considered dispensable in the pursuit of continuing economic growth.

Since the early 1990s, however, there have been visible changes in the environmental policies of Korea. The National Assembly passed several environmental laws that maintain higher environmental standards and broader regulatory measures. In 1990, the Environment Administration was upgraded to the cabinet level as the Ministry of the Environment, thereby allowing it to take greater charge over environmental policies and affairs within the government. In 1994, the Ministry of Environment was granted greater authority following a major structural overhaul in the Korean government.

Among the reasons for this visible change of direction in environmental policies were severe environmental accidents in the 1990s, which had a major impact on the general awareness of the importance of environmental quality. The "Phenol Leakage" accident, which occurred in 1991, forever changed Korean people's general perception of environmental accidents and their devastating consequences. It had much influence on realizing the importance of effective environmental measures and policy implementation both at the national and local levels. The civil environmental movement has gained popularity and influence in Korean society. One of the major conglomerates in Korea, Doosan, which was responsible for the leakage, suffered from massive civilian protests all over the country, which turned out to be a massive public relations disaster for the company.

On March 14, 1991, thirty tons of phenol, a toxic chemical, was leaked into the upper Naktong River of Kumi. Five days later, after a thorough investigation, the local police announced that Doosan Electro-Materials Co. in Kumi, Kyongsang-pukdo, a subsidiary of the Doosan Group, was responsible for polluting the tap water source by discharging wastewater containing phenol into a tributary of the Naktong River. Police also announced that since November 1990, Doosan Electro-Materials Co. had illegally dumped a total amount of 325 tons of phenol into the Naktong River. This river is the source of piped water in Taegu, Pusan, and other cities, with a combined population of over 5 million at that time.[7]

---

7 Jong Ho Hong and Jin Soo Whang, "Korean Major Environmental Accidents and Capital Market Responses," *Journal of Economic Research* 6, no. 1 (2001): 79–80.

The phenol accident had an enormous impact on many aspects of Korean society as far as environmental issues are concerned. That is why I would call this period the age of white smoke in contrast to the previous period of black smoke. People recalled vividly the devastating consequences of an environmental accident. The company realized how severe public resistance and protests could be against such polluting behavior. The government realized the importance of tighter environmental policies and stricter monitoring to reduce the risk of such a devastating accident ever happening again.

Stricter regulatory measures followed in the Water Quality Conservation Act. By the mid-1990s, incentive-based environmental regulatory policies were further introduced, including a deposit refund system and volume-based fee system (VBF) for domestic waste. The VBF was introduced country-wide in January 1995 to achieve a cleaner environment by producing less waste. This policy measure was unique in the sense that Korea was the first country in the world to introduce VBF on a national level. The VBF is a policy measure that imposes a charge for domestic waste by applying the polluter pays principle, which provides economic disincentive to the person who discharges waste by charging proper disposal costs based on the quantity of waste produced. It is intended to reduce waste at the stage of its production. The system also provides incentive to recycle as much waste as possible, since the VBF is not applied to recyclable waste.

In the beginning of the 1990s, the world began to focus on the threat of climate change. At the "Rio Earth Summit" in Brazil in 1992, heads of state addressed the issue of carbon emission as a major agenda. It was a historic event that highlighted global warming as an imminent issue. After the Rio meeting, countries began in earnest to develop domestic policies and to embark on international negotiations to regulate fossil fuel use and reduce carbon emissions. The Rio summit had a huge impact on Korean society in terms of understanding that environmental issues are not confined to local pollution but can be extended on a global scale.

During the age of white smoke, the Korean people started making efforts to balance economic growth and environmental quality, which is exactly the goal of sustainable development strategy. The fact that during this period there had been many cases of severe social conflict over government-driven development projects and conservation efforts is concrete evidence that Koreans slowly realized the importance of environmental preservation and quality of life.

The Age of No Smoke (2012–present)

Climate crisis has led the world to enter the age of no smoke, and Korea is no exception. The question, however, is whether the Korean people are ready for this challenge. Unlike the previous periods in Korea where environmental issues were largely disregarded or they were confined to local areas, we are now facing a global environmental issue.

Environmental problems such as local pollution tend to improve as the general public's awareness of clean air and water grows, and thus policy priorities change. Understanding that only the coexistence of the economy and the environment can create a sustainable society leads to concrete actions. Climate change, however, is inherently different from local environmental problems. Greenhouse gases that cause climate change, such as carbon and methane, are global pollutants. It does not matter which economic agent emits greenhouse gases. They contribute equally to global warming once they are emitted and spatially distributed.

As a result, any greenhouse gas emitter is tempted to expect others to reduce emissions without changing its own behavior. The intention of this "selfishness" is to enjoy the benefits provided by others without bearing its cost. Imagine what would happen if every consumer, every company, and every country in the world possessed the same attitude that they would only seek their own selfish interests at the expense of others. Earth will continuously become hotter as more and more carbon dioxide is released. In the literature, this tragic situation is called "race to the bottom."[8] Humanity will fail to respond to the climate crisis, and in the end, environmental catastrophe and human casualty will be waiting to happen.

The energy situation in Korea is bleak. Korea's primary energy consumption ranks tenth in the world. Korea relies on imports for virtually all of its fossil fuel consumption. As a result, the dependence on energy imports was 92.8 percent in 2020, one of the highest in the world. Carbon dioxide emissions ranked seventh in the world in 2020. The fact that Korea ranks tenth in energy consumption and seventh in carbon dioxide emissions from fuel combustion means that the proportion of fossil fuel use is high.

There are other gloomy statistics. The concentration level of fine dust in Korea ranks first among the thirty-eight OECD countries. Fine dust comes from the combustion of fossil fuels such as coal and oil. In density of nuclear power capacity, which indicates the proportion of nuclear power plant facilities compared to the land area, Korea ranks first in the world.

---

8 Jong Ho Hong, 기후위기 부의 대전환 [Climate crisis: The great shift of wealth] (Paju: Dasan Books, 2023).

Even more shocking is the fact that the share of renewable energy in Korea's electricity generation is ranked in last place among all the OECD countries.

Despite all this, none of the key members of our society, including politicians, civil servants, experts, industries, the media, and even churches, seem to make conscientious efforts to change their thoughts and actions to tackle climate crisis. I believe that overall, Korea has successfully overcome the challenges of the ages of black smoke and white smoke. However, the biggest challenge for the sustainable future of Korea still lies ahead.

Prospects for Reconciliation of Humanity and Nature

Korea never achieved lowering carbon dioxide emissions in the last half-century, except during the period of negative economic growth in 1998 when the currency crisis was in full swing. Carbon emissions decreased that year, not because of mitigation efforts but because economic activity plummeted. However, in the era of the climate crisis, the Korean people will have to go on a "road not taken" to ensure a sustainable economy while reducing carbon emissions.

Climate change is a vivid example where fallen humanity has failed to obey the creation mandate, which is to cultivate and responsibly look after the environment that God created. Christians need to step up. Churches have to remind and educate people about the importance of practicing stewardship of creation to reconcile humans with nature. I believe it is the mission every child of God should have in facing the global climate crisis.

Discussion Questions

1. How can we understand the climate crisis that humanity is currently facing from the perspective of the creation mandate in Genesis 1:28 and 2:15?

2. How can we understand the "blessings" of Korea's remarkable economic growth in the last half-century from the perspective of stewardship of creation?

3. What should be the mission of the Korean church in reconciling humanity with nature? How much emphasis does the Korean church put on the importance of environmental issues in facing the climate crisis?

Response

by Dave Bookless

As somebody who is neither an economist, nor a climate scientist, nor an expert on South Korean economic history, it was with trepidation that I accepted an invitation to respond to Dr. Jong Ho Hong's paper, "Climate Crisis and Stewardship: A Christian Economist's Perspective." Consequently, these reflections are offered tentatively and humbly, as the views of a western-educated theologian working with a global Christian conservation organization, A Rocha International.

First, I would like to complement Dr. Hong on the clarity of explanation of South Korea's "economic miracle" since the 1950s, and the subsequent environmental consequences. Few nations have accomplished national rebuilding, the almost complete eradication of poverty, and the development of a sophisticated modern society with the speed and success of South Korea. Nevertheless, as Dr. Hong points out, these achievements have come at considerable environmental cost. I particularly appreciated the typology of the three eras of "black smoke" with little or no environmental restraint, "white smoke" after the Doosan phenol disaster and other issues led to calls for regulation and protection, and the current era of "no smoke" as South Korea responds to the global climate crisis.

There are two areas in the paper that I would like to explore further: firstly, the multifaceted nature of the global ecological crisis, and secondly, some theological reflections on our human role, particularly regarding the use of "stewardship" and "theocentrism."

The Nature of the Crisis in Nature

Dr. Hong provides an accurate and helpful summary of the IPCC's Fifth Assessment Report (2015), with its authoritative conclusion that human economic activity is the main driver of current global climate change. Due to the timetable of submission of papers, this has now been superseded by the Sixth Assessment Report (2023),[9] which states that "human activities, principally through emissions of greenhouse gases, have unequivocally

---

9 "AR6 Synthesis Report: Climate Change 2023," Intergovernmental Panel on Climate Change, accessed May 16, 2023, https://www.ipcc.ch/report/ar6/syr/. Note that at the time of writing, "the approved Summary for Policymakers and adopted Longer Report remain subject to final copy editing and layout."

To grasp the complexity and severity of the threats human activity is causing, it is worth summarizing these nine planetary boundaries:

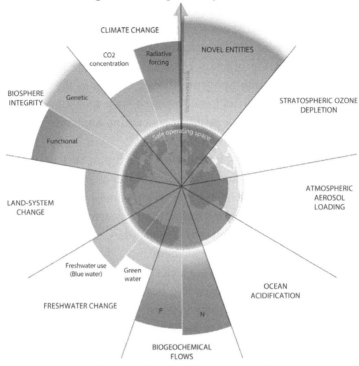

Figure 10.1: The nine planetary boundaries[10]

HIGH RISK
Loss of biosphere integrity (biodiversity loss and extinctions): Assessed as high risk, with enormous potential impacts on pollination, oxygen, food and water supply, and the stability of earth's life-support systems.

Biogeochemical nitrogen and phosphorus flows: Assessed as high risk, caused by fertilizer overuse, which impacts on soil and water quality globally.

INCREASING RISK
Land system change: Assessed as increasing risk, caused by conversion of forests, wetlands, and grasslands for human use.

Climate change: Assessed as increasing risk, with concern that large, irreversible changes may become inevitable.

SAFE
Ocean acidification: Currently safe but changing rapidly, affecting, for example, coral reefs

Freshwater consumption and the global hydrological cycle: Currently safe but by 2050, five hundred million people will be subject to severe water stress.

Stratospheric ozone depletion: largely addressed through the 1987 Montreal Protocol.

Chemical pollution and the release of novel entities: Not yet quantified, but including chemical, heavy metal, and radioactive impacts upon organisms and fertility.

Atmospheric aerosol loading: Not yet quantified, but pollutants currently cause eight hundred thousand deaths per year.

---

10 "The Nine Planetary Boundaries," Stockholm Resilience Centre, University of Stockholm, accessed May 16, 2023, bit.ly/42MWHRH. The planetary boundaries framework. Licenced under CC BY-NC-ND 3.0. Credit: J. Lokrantz/Azote based on Steffen et al., 2015. This URL "has been superseded," with a new title, "Planetary boundaries," and three figures—2009, 2015, and 2023—to compare the "evolution of the planetary boundaries framework," i.e., the increasing number of boundaries assessed and crossed.

caused global warming."[11] The report further states the need for "deep, rapid and sustained global greenhouse gas emissions reduction" in order to avoid "abrupt and/or irreversible changes"[12] to earth's ability to sustain human and other life. In other words, the consensus of climate scientists has moved yet further toward the urgency of tackling the climate crisis.

However, despite the urgency of addressing emissions reductions, it would be wrong to see anthropogenic climate change as the only issue that the global economy needs to address. Rather, it is the most obvious symptom of a deeper and more extensive problem concerning humanity's relationship with nature.

The concept of "planetary boundaries" (see figure 10.1 on the previous page) has been developed[13] and refined,[14] and has received broad scientific support in terms of describing nine areas of human impact upon natural systems.[15] The boundaries use a "traffic light" system to indicate for each area whether current human impact is "green" (dark gray in the center of the graphic)—a SAFE operating area for humanity, "amber" (the lighter gray extending beyond the dashed line)—a zone of uncertainty and INCREASING RISK, or "red" (darker grays extending beyond the lighter gray)—beyond uncertainty and HIGH RISK to human thriving.

Because climate change is not the only global crisis, simplistic attempts to "fix the climate" by increasing green energy or tax carbon without addressing an economic model predicated on ever-increasing pressure on natural systems, are a dangerous fantasy. We need alternative models for a sustainable economy. This brief response can only touch on these, but perhaps the two most promising are the "circular economy" and "doughnut economics." The circular economy overcomes the critical problems of continual destruction of nature and increasing waste and pollution by seeking to recirculate products, eliminate waste, and regenerate nature. Tearfund's

11 "AR6 Synthesis Report: Headline Statements," Intergovernmental Panel on Climate Change (sec. A.1), accessed May 16, 2023, https://www.ipcc.ch/report/ar6/syr/resources/spm-headline-statements/.

12 "AR6 Synthesis Report: Headline Statements" (sec. B.3), accessed May 16, 2023.

13 Johan Rockström et al., "A Safe Operating Space for Humanity," *Nature* 461, no. 7263 (2009): 472–75.

14 Will Steffen et al., "Planetary Boundaries: Guiding Human Development on a Changing Planet," *Science* 347, no. 6223 (2015): 736-46.

15 "The Nine Planetary Boundaries," Stockholm Resilience Centre, University of Stockholm, accessed May 16, 2023, https://www.stockholmresilience.org/research/planetary-boundaries/the-nine-planetary-boundaries.html.

Closing the Loop report[16] provides a Christian rationale for the circular economy, addressing social and environmental issues together.

Doughnut economics[17] is the brainchild of Prof. Kate Raworth of Oxford University. It suggests humanity needs to exist within a "doughnut" of safe economic activity, avoiding people falling into the "hole in the middle" by keeping above the "social foundations" of adequate food, water, health, education, housing, work, and equity for all, while also avoiding transgressing the "outer ring" consisting of the nine planetary boundaries referred to above.

Theological Reflection on "Stewardship" and "Theocentrism"

The Bible does not offer a single divinely sanctioned economic model, but it does provide a vision of God's plan for all creation and of humanity's role within it. This vision, summarized most simply by the prophetic messianic dreams of *shalom* throughout the created order, and by Jesus's summary of the gospel as "the kingdom of God" (God's rule of justice and peace on earth as in heaven), provides a clear sense that God's intention is for humanity to thrive within a world of flourishing biodiversity, where all creatures worship God as they were created to. This vision provides a stark critique of our current economic and ecological reality, where inequality, resource depletion, biodiversity loss, and pollution continue to escalate.

The conventional Christian response is to speak of humanity's role as "stewards" of creation. However, the language of stewardship has been critiqued extensively. David Horrell points out that the Bible never explicitly uses it to describe humanity's role in nature,[18] Clare Palmer accuses it of making God an absentee landlord and giving humans a feudal, exploitative relationship with nature,[19] and Richard Bauckham says stewardship is "too freighted with the baggage of the modern project of technological domination of nature."[20] Perhaps the biggest issue is that we steward

---

16 Alexandre Gobbo Fernandes, *Closing the Loop: The Benefits of the Circular Economy for Developing Countries and Emerging Economies* (Tearfund: London, 2016), https://res.cloudinary.com/tearfund/image/fetch/https://learn.tearfund.org/-/media/learn/resources/reports/2016-tearfund-closing-the-loop-en.pdf.

17 Kate Raworth, *Doughnut Economics: Seven Ways to Think Like a 21st-Century Economist* (Random House: London, 2017).

18 David Horrell, *Ecological Hermeneutics: Biblical, Historical and Theological Perspectives* (T. & T. Clark: London, 2010), 6.

19 Clare Palmer, "Stewardship: A Case Study in Environmental Ethics," in *Environmental Stewardship*, ed. R. J. Berry (T. & T. Clark: London, 2006), 63-75.

20 Richard Bauckham, *Living with Other Creatures: Green Exegesis and Theology* (Waco: Baylor Univ. Press, 2011), 62.

"objects"—inanimate things—whereas the Bible envisages all creation as "subjects," in relationship with God, each other, and humanity. From the start, Adam is tasked with naming the creatures—fostering an attentive, empathic relationship. Maybe the language of "guardianship" is a better descriptor of the Genesis mandate to have dominion, and to "tend and keep" the garden. If we are entrusted with another's children as their guardian, our power and authority is constrained by our loving responsibility.

Finally, Hong helpfully uses the language of "theocentrism," contrasting it with anthropocentrism and ecocentrism, and comments that "God is at the center of all existence" rather than humanity or nature. In my doctoral thesis,[21] I explore theocentrism and identify that it can be abused to give divine sanction to humanity's destructive tendencies (theo-anthropo-centrism), whereas the overwhelming biblical vision "might be called 'theo-eco-centrism' in that what God values most is not the thriving of one species, but the thriving of the whole of creation together within a theocentric universe."[22]

If we are to tackle the enormous challenges of our multiple ecological crises, we need a coherent and convincing vision of humanity's place in nature, as creation's guardians within a theo-eco-centric universe, and we need sustainable economic models that allow people and nature to thrive.

---

21 David Bookless, "Why Should Wild Nature Be Preserved? A Dialogue between Biblical Theology and Biodiversity Conservation" (PhD diss., University of Cambridge, 2019), https://doi.org/10.17863/CAM.40844.

22 Bookless, 47.

CHAPTER 11

The Transformation of Korean Missionaries' Epistemological Beliefs on Environmental and Human Calamities
A Critical Analysis

by Jooyun Eum

Since the 1990s, a sense of the enormity of the environmental crisis, including pollution and global warming, has been spreading. It was only upon entering the twenty-first century that various countermeasures were taken at the individual, corporate, community, national, and global levels. This paper focuses on the transformation of Korean missionaries' epistemological beliefs and practices related to environmental and human disasters. For this study, constructivist grounded theory, one of the methodologies of qualitative research, was used, which is based on the philosophical view that humans construct knowledge and meaning from their own experiences. Specifically, this study analyzed data obtained through in-depth interviews with twenty-eight Korean missionaries selected according to the principle of theoretical sampling. First, missionaries show reactions such as indifference, avoidance, or denial regarding the issues of environment and human calamities due to stakeholders' expectations, theological resistance, and eschatological beliefs. Second, missionaries critically evaluate their existing epistemology, taking into account direct observations and experiences of this destructive phenomenon, which appears continuously and repeatedly in mission contexts. Third, missionaries expand missionary practices based on new epistemological beliefs. These three points can be summarized as "reestablishing epistemological beliefs through reflection on phenomenological discoveries." Considering the trend of increasing environmental and human disasters, joint efforts such as establishing an evangelical mission theology of environmental and human disasters, strengthening missional education and training on environmental problems, and working collaboratively with the global mission community are urgently required to help alleviate these crises.

Research Background

Each new era presents issues and challenges that require new mission theologies, strategies, and practices. Today, environmental and human calamities are trending toward fundamental, profound, and irreversible changes on a global scale. These existential issues that we are all facing require critical reevaluation of and creative alternatives to epistemological beliefs[1] and missional responses by Christians and churches. In fact, over the past decades new theories, strategies, and practices have been advanced through active theological investigations related to environmental and human calamities. Ecological spirituality,[2] creation theology,[3] eco-theology,[4] ecology and Christian mission,[5] missionary earthkeeping,[6] and eco-justice[7] are just some of the ongoing prophetic discussions in this area. And it is very encouraging that Korean theologians, scientists, and practitioners have been among those discussing these issues in seminars and writings.

It is noteworthy that epistemology, which has traditionally been dealt with in philosophy on the premise of the universality and generality of knowledge,[8] is being adapted to epistemological belief or individual

---

1 Epistemology is a philosophical discipline that explores the nature, limits, and acquisition methods of knowledge. Epistemological beliefs are personal philosophies related to the acquisition of knowledge that changes based on an individual's life experience. In this paper, these terms are used for the purpose of exploring how missionaries change their existing epistemological beliefs through observations and experiences related to individual and social changes in environmental and human calamities in their mission contexts.

2 Ian Carter, "An Ecological Spirituality: Insights from Teilhard De Chardin," in *The Earth Beneath: A Critical Guide to Green Theology*, ed. Ian Ball et al. (London: SPCK, 1992), 87-103.

3 Neil Darragh, "Creation Theology: How Well Are We Coping with Ecological Issues?," *Compass* 27 (Spring 1993): 22–28.

4 Celia Deane-Drummond, *A Handbook in Theology and Ecology* (London: SCM Press, 1996); Peter Scott, "Types of Ecotheology," *Ecotheology* 4 (Jan. 1998): 8-19; Joseph Sittler, "Ecological Commitment as Theological Responsibility," *Zygon* 5 (1970): 172–81; and David G. Hallman, ed., *Ecotheology: Voices from the North and South* (Maryknoll, NY: Orbis Books, 1994).

5 J. A. Loader, "Life, Wonder and Responsibility: Some Thoughts on Ecology and Christian Mission," *Missionalia* 19 (1991): 44-56; and Myeong-Seok Lee, "A Study of the Development of Ecotheological Thought and Its Implications for Christian Missions," *JKEMS* 50, no. 2 (2020): 245-73.

6 Dennis E. Testerman, "Missionary Earthkeeping: Glimpses of the Past, Visions of the Future," in *Missionary Earthkeeping*, ed. Calvin B. DeWitt and Ghillean T. Prance (Macon, GA: Mercer Univ. Press, 1992).

7 Walter Wink, "Ecobible: The Bible and Ecojustice," *Theology Today* 49 (1993): 465-77.

8 Stephen Hetherington, *Epistemology: The Key Thinkers*, 2nd ed. (Bloomsbury Academic, 2019), Kindle; Matthias Steup and Ram Neta, "Epistemology," in *The Stanford Encyclopedia of Philosophy*, Fall 2020 ed., edited by Edward N. Zalta, https://plato. stanford.edu/archives/fall2020/entries/epistemology/; and Jason Stanley and Timothy Williamson, "Knowing How," *Journal of Philosophy* 98, no. 8 (2001): 411–44.

epistemology, centering on education, psychology, and other academic fields of study.[9] A multifaceted study of epistemological belief or personal epistemology could also apply to missiology. Although there are differences in terminology and academic approaches, missiologists also deal with epistemological beliefs from their own points of view. For example, Paul Hiebert has suggested the concept of "self-theologizing," whereby locals themselves become an interpretive community that engages in theological inquiry.[10] This study implies that environmental and human calamites can be one of the major subjects that significantly impacts missionaries' epistemological transformation or self-theologizing. Since these calamities affect all mankind, it would be appropriate for missionaries to also be involved in local, contextual self-theologizing.

In this context, the goal of this study is not to list missionaries' activities related to environmental and human calamities, or to measure how actively they engage in these issues. This study focuses more on critically analyzing the relationship between missionaries' traditional epistemology and the transformation of their theological and missiological perspectives based on current realities on the ground.

The Purpose of the Study

The purpose of this study is to present a relationship model of Korean missionaries' epistemological beliefs and missional practices regarding environmental and human calamities. Grounded theory, one of the qualitative research methodologies, was adopted to achieve this goal.[11]

Subjects for the study were selected according to Charmaz's theoretical sampling method.[12] For open sampling, a total of twenty-eight Korean

---

9 Matthew Kelly, "Epistemology, Epistemic Belief, Personal Epistemology, and Epistemics: A Review of Concepts as They Impact Information Behavior Research," *JASIST* 72, no. 4 (April 2021): 507-19; Mikyeong Yang, "A Critical and Comprehensive Review of Research on Learner's Epistemological Belief," *The Journal of Yeolin Education* 14, no. 3 (2006): 1–25; and B. K. Hofer and Paul R. Pintrich, eds., *Personal Epistemology: The Psychology of Beliefs about Knowledge and Knowing* (Mahwah, NJ: Lawrence Erlbaum Associates, 2002).

10 Paul Hiebert and Eloise Hiebert Meneses, *Incarnational Ministry: Planting Churches in Band, Tribal, Peasant, and Urban Societies* (Grand Rapids: Baker Academic, 1995).

11 This theory was chosen because a conceptual framework suitable for explaining the relationship between environmental and human calamities and Korean missionaries' epistemological beliefs and missional practices has not yet been clearly identified, and an understanding of the relationship between concepts and categories is lacking. In addition, there have been no studies related to the topic to determine suitable and unsuitable variables.

12 K. Charmaz, "'Discovering' Chronic Illness: Using Grounded Theory," *in More Grounded Theory Methodology: A Reader,* ed. B. G. Glaser (Mill Valley, CA: Sociology Press, 1994), 65-94; and K. Charmaz, "Grounded Theory: Objectivist and Constructivist Methods," in *Handbook of Qualitative Research,* 2nd ed., ed. N. K. Denzin and Y. S. Lincoln (Thousand Oaks, CA: Sage Publications, 2000).

missionaries were selected based on observations and interviews related to the research topic. These informants included missionaries of various ages in different stages of their careers, from new missionaries to those about to retire. The reason for including subjects with broad, rich missionary experience was to obtain research materials for hermeneutic discussions about changes in beliefs and practices regarding environmental and human calamities. These interviews centered on questions about the missionaries' theological perspectives on these calamities and how they affected their daily lives and ministries.

Later, discriminate sampling was conducted to complement the less structured categories, and supplementary questions and answers tested the validity of the core categories and theories tentatively derived.

Research Procedure

Due to the nature of qualitative research aimed at logical generalization, applying appropriate criteria in selecting research subjects plays an important role in ensuring the validity of this study. The preliminary research was conducted from March to May 2022 with eight missionary subjects belonging to evangelical mission organizations in Korea.

After establishing the research question based on the preliminary research data, a full-scale questionnaire was developed and interviews were conducted. However, during the course of the main interviews, the questions were continuously modified through data analysis. Full-scale interviews lasted from June to November 2022. When the number of informants reached twenty-eight, the researcher judged that the data had reached a saturation point and further interviews were deemed unnecessary. Interviews took an average of one and a half hours, and the transcribed data amounted to 402 pages. Informants were each assigned a number to protect their identities and the transcription data will be completely destroyed after being strictly managed for two years.[13]

Research Questions

Research Question

To what extent do issues of environmental and human calamities affect missionaries' epistemological beliefs and missional activities?

---

13 Prior to the in-depth interviews, the researcher obtained consent from the informants regarding ethical standards, video recording, and transcribing the data.

Research Subquestions:

1. How do missionaries respond to phenomena related to environmental and human calamities that they face in their mission contexts?

2. How do missionaries justify their beliefs when their intuitive analysis of the environmental human calamities they face in mission contexts conflicts with their existing epistemology?

3. What factors promote or hinder the transformation of missionaries' epistemological beliefs?

4. How do we overcome the factors that hinder the transformation of missionaries' epistemological beliefs?

5. In what ways can missionaries effectively deal with the threats of environmental and human calamities?

Centering on the series of research questions mentioned above, the researcher analyzed the different responses and compared and contrasted them. In addition, in order to obtain specific and practical research data related to these research questions, the following items were keenly observed:

- the subjects' ministry philosophy and theological beliefs

- the process of formation of epistemological beliefs related to theological perspectives recognized as universal truths

- examples of human and natural calamities contributing to changes in epistemological beliefs

- different perspectives and policies of stakeholders and mission agencies regarding the relevance of human and natural disaster issues to missions

- criteria for judging which claim is valid when different viewpoints present themselves

- criteria for judging the validity of missionary work in human and natural calamities

- epistemological beliefs and practices that missionaries must adopt in order to effectively deal with the problems of human and natural calamities

- seeking ways churches, mission agencies, and missionary training communities can better motivate missionaries to participate in mitigating human and natural calamities

The videotaped interviews were transcribed and coded. The coded categories were analyzed precisely according to frequencies and semantic relationships, as were repeated keywords. Specifically, the following steps were taken according to the constructivist grounded theory research methodology presented by Kathy Charmaz. However, some of her procedures were simplified according to the purpose and needs of the study.

Initial Coding

In the first step, categories and subcategories were derived through the process of primary coding using the line-by-line method. A total of 101 codes were derived in this initial coding process. Fifteen of these were general observations not directly related to any particular research question. The remaining eighty-six codes related to research questions, twenty-one of which related to existing epistemology, thirty-three to acceptance of new epistemological beliefs, and thirty-two to transformation of mission strategy based on new epistemological beliefs.

In particular, missionaries living in areas highly dependent on agriculture are paying more attention to climate change. They argue that the increase in droughts, floods, and typhoons caused by climate change is affecting crop yields, resulting in food shortages and loss of income. Therefore, missionaries in these contexts generally agree that a missionary response is needed to solve or alleviate these problems. Informants who are carrying out missionary work in cities also testify that increases in heat-related diseases are affecting the working and living conditions of more and more people.

Overall, there appears to be no significant differences in the degree of awareness of the impact of climate change, but there are substantial differences in theological perspectives on this issue. Some missionaries recognize that climate change should be one of the major issues of theology and missiology. They generally agree with McFague's claim that climate change is the greatest crisis of the twenty-first century and also our most pressing theological problem.[14] She defined climate change as the most heinous sin that destroys the body of God through our daily lifestyles, and on the premise that Christians are responsible for environmental destruction she proposed an urban ecology. Since theology is a study that deals not only with God but also with human beings and their living contexts, environmental issues including climate change and natural calamities that directly affect human life should be one of its main topics of inquiry.

---

14 Sallie McFague, *A New Climate for Theology: God, the World, and Global Warming* (Minneapolis: Fortress Press, 2008).

The missional practice of informants who agree with this point of view is largely divided into two categories. One is to practice various measures to cope with climate change by directly reflecting this theological perspective in their mission work. These include shifting awareness toward environmentally friendly consumption patterns, recycling waste, and planting trees. The other is to agree with theological inquiry into climate change but not with particular missional actions. Informants in this category prefer to deal with the issue of climate change primarily on a personal level, and tend to prefer individual and voluntary participation rather than public responsibility.

A significant number of informants emphasized that theological discussions on climate change and environmental calamities should include ecological justice, eco-theology, eco-missiology, and missional implications from an evangelical perspective. Theological and missiological discussions on these topics are not something new. But today's urgent environmental situation calls for new reflections in these areas. Most informants who make these statements have in common that these epistemological beliefs have been strengthened after discovering an urgent need that cannot be ignored or avoided.

Another very clear and powerful voice that emerged through this study is the interpretation of climate change and natural calamities through the lens of eschatological judgment, which tends to understand climate change and natural calamities on a global scale in terms of God's eschatological providence. Specifically, it understands this global phenomenon as a sign of the end times and divine judgment on the sinful world. Informants who fall into this category believe that signs of the end times include not only climate change and natural calamities but also devastating worldwide pandemics and unjust wars. They believe that the end times will be chaotic and filled with various calamities, during which the chosen ones will be saved and the fallen world will be left behind and perish. According to this study, they tend to think that human efforts to mitigate climate change and natural calamities cannot be the priority task of missions; rather, the more the severity of natural and human calamities intensifies, the more urgent the task of evangelism becomes. However, none of them denies the necessity of human effort to mitigate the impacts of various calamities and alleviate suffering. As responsible global citizens, they are also taking various measures at the individual and family level to address this enormous problem.

An important central concept raised at this stage of the research is the need to better understand various epistemological beliefs about environmental and human calamities. Although missionaries are currently experiencing the same types of calamities, understanding the different interpretations of these events and resultant practices can be an important foundation for moving to the next step.

Focused Coding and Structural Analysis

The three main categories derived in the focused coding stage can be summarized as identifying limited beliefs, finding integrated beliefs that are more empowering, and missional implications.

Identifying Epistemological Beliefs

The first research subquestion of this study attempts to identify epistemological beliefs. There were twenty-one codes related to this question. Twelve of them were repeatedly featured by seven or more informants. A significant number stated that the challenges posed by natural and human calamities provided an opportunity to recognize the limitations of existing epistemological beliefs. This raises the question of whether their epistemological convictions can adequately address the theological and missiological implications of these events.

Furthermore, the majority of informants stated that they had not addressed the issue of environmental and human calamities in their sermons and teachings over the past year. There are various reasons why missionaries are apprehensive about dealing with this issue officially at the church level. First, as mentioned above, there is a fundamental belief in apocalyptic eschatology based on the fall of man and God's judgment. In other words, the increasing number of environmental and human calamities is evidence that the end is imminent, at which time the chosen ones will be saved and the fallen world that remains will perish. Whether explicitly or implicitly, there is general agreement that if natural and human calamities are part of God's eschatological plan, then the best way to resolve this situation is to evangelize the lost with eschatological urgency.

Second, missionaries' efforts to address environmental and human calamities are generally personal, passive, and defensive, rather than community-oriented with integrative strategies for long-term sustainability. For example, due to climate change local communities are experiencing food shortages, increases in pests, respiratory diseases caused by sandstorms and fine dust, droughts and floods, lack of drinking water, and forced migrations as climate refugees. However, some informants respond to climate change by separating garbage and recycling, sharing food occasionally, conserving household energy, and occasionally using public transportation.

Although the importance of such personal practices cannot be overlooked, there is an urgent need for missionaries to devise feasible, effective, and sustainable long-term strategies that mitigate the effects of climate change and alleviate the suffering of individuals, families, churches, local communities, and nations.

Finding Integrated Beliefs That Are More Empowering

Most of the informants who indicated the need for theological investigations and missionary responses to current environmental and human calamities said that their direct observations and experiences in their missions have strengthened this belief. Specifically, missionaries living in relatively poor or underdeveloped countries tend to show more interest in topics such as ecological justice, human dignity, and social equality than missionaries in other regions. These trends in changed perception and behavior do not imply the abandonment of past epistemological beliefs. While they are still committed to missionary activities based on traditional beliefs, such as evangelism, discipleship, and church planting, their interests have widened to include theological and missiological explorations of how to respond to the realities they face on the ground.

Environmental and human calamities have influenced missionary's epistemological beliefs in continuity with general beliefs held in the past. This means that the fields of theology and missiology, like philosophy and education, provide the preexisting context in which to discuss personal epistemology conceptualized as a matter of specific personal beliefs. As mentioned earlier, informants who further strengthened their traditional epistemology faced the challenges of environmental and human calamities. They did not devalue or become indifferent to the issue, but rather reinterpreted it within their existing epistemological framework.

A significant number of informants are well aware of the limitations of human efforts to overcome environmental and human calamities. Nevertheless, they also believed that such efforts at the individual and community level could bring about positive change. All informants recognize their calling and responsibility to preserve the world created by God. Nevertheless, they generally were reluctant to use terms such as eco-theology, eco-justice, and creation spirituality as hermeneutic frameworks to interpret anew the problems occurring in the world created by God.

Missional Implications

In order to effectively address global problems, including environmental and human calamities, mature interdependence and cooperation as a global life community are required of all people. Missionaries need to take responsibility for and model such mature interdependence and cooperation as global citizens, transcending differences in values and worldviews, religion and politics, and culture and ideology.

This study reveals there is a wide gap between missionaries' epistemological beliefs and missional responses. In general, missionaries are not only aware of the seriousness of natural and human calamities, but are also suffering from them alongside their neighbors in their mission contexts. However, due to reasons such as lack of professional knowledge and experience, missionary priorities, and a wide range of expectations from missionary organizations, churches, and supporters, they respond passively to this issue rather than with integrity. It appeared that a significant number of missionaries hoped that individuals with specialized knowledge, professional organizations, corporations, and countries would take the lead in solving this problem. However, none of the missionaries participating in this study sponsored the activities of professional individuals and organizations working to address the challenges of environmental and human calamities.

The majority of informants were seeking an answer to the question, Should the preservation of creation be included in mission? Missionaries who have long insisted that only humans are the object of missions are also reevaluating their view. The immediate impact of climate change on the quality of life of human beings, the target of mission, is causing them to rethink this issue. In this way, a change in epistemological values is taking place in missionaries based on the close relationship between humans and their natural environment. For example, the increasing number of people moving to other regions in search of new jobs after agricultural lands have been destroyed by severe drought or floods requires significant changes in missionary goals and strategies.

In addition, climate change has become a major focus of missionaries because they work among people who remain in their hometowns and suffer physically and mentally from air pollution, desertification, and water and food shortages. In fact, it is also true that many of the main prayer requests of believers' communities to which missionaries belong are directly or indirectly related to suffering from natural and human calamities. When missionaries continuously face such situations, they experience a significant change in their epistemological beliefs about holistic mission compared to before they became missionaries. In this context, the change in epistemological beliefs that missionaries strive for is related to the eternal and complete recovery that human beings must pursue, the total recovery from human sinfulness and destroyed nature.

Theoretical Coding

This includes items such as phenomenological discoveries concerning environmental and human calamities, reassessing existing epistemological beliefs, embracing new epistemological beliefs, and transforming mission strategies based on these new beliefs. This work requires "reestablishing epistemological beliefs through reflection on phenomenological discoveries." The core concept is the transformation of epistemological beliefs and missional practice that occurs through voluntary or involuntary theological or missiological reflections related to environmental and human calamities, a phenomenon that is continuously and repeatedly raised in their mission contexts.

Missionaries need to be interested in the relationship between the environment and God the creator, the environment and the church, the environment and theology, the environment and religion, and the environment and missions, and also need to exercise self-restraint and self-control. Furthermore, missionaries have a prophetic mission to call for transformation of the epistemological beliefs and practices of others, wherever they are located and minister. The prophetic responsibility for natural and human calamities given to missionaries should complement and enrich traditional missionary activities, not replace them with others or add new ones.

Missionaries have a responsibility to bring the biblical message to people living in specific social or environmental contexts. Therefore, the missionary must derive a message from the biblical text and deliver it in a way suitable for a particular social situation. In this process, they must deal with the problems of human sinfulness, greed, and injustice that intensify destruction and amplify poverty. Here, the missionary's epistemological belief about the relationship between existing epistemology and phenomenological discoveries requires transformation. The overall results of the data analysis are summarized in the table below.

Table 11.1: Summary of data analysis

Coding process	Categories	Codes (Repetition)	Core concepts
Initial coding	General	15 (12)	Phenomenological discoveries
Focused coding	Identifying limited beliefs	21 (14)	Reevaluating preexisting epistemological beliefs
	Discovering integrated beliefs that are more empowering	33 (18)	Accepting new epistemological beliefs
	Missional implications	32 (20)	Transforming mission strategies based on new epistemological beliefs
Theoretical coding	Overall	101 (44)	Reestablishing epistemological beliefs by reflecting on phenomenological discoveries

Discussion

The dominant epistemological belief of Korean evangelical missionaries in this era is dichotomous soteriology. Missionaries' work styles are more diverse than ever, but their ultimate focus is on the spiritual dimension. The reason is that many stakeholders, including churches, mission organizations, and supporters, explicitly or implicitly demand that missionaries devote themselves only to evangelism, discipleship, and church planting, rather than focusing on issues such as the environment and human calamities.

If missionaries actively participate in activities to mitigate and prevent climate change and natural calamities, they may be questioned by their stakeholders about the validity of their theological perspectives and mission strategies. The informants who were well aware of these sentiments responded passively by using defense mechanisms such as separation, denial, ignoring, avoidance, and justification, even as environmental problems became more and more serious. Some of them even condemned fellow missionaries who are actively working to address environmental issues. However, missionaries who are obsessed with dichotomous soteriology are also participating in activities such as resource recycling and energy conservation at the individual and family levels.

Sentiments about environmental and human calamities have changed significantly in recent years. At the same time, missionaries' awareness of the seriousness of this issue and their participation in countermeasures have increased. This is generally not the result of missionaries accepting relatively new ideas such as eco-theology, eco-justice, ecological spirituality, and/or creation theology. It is more the result of participation in the traditional practices of evangelism and church planting and meeting local people who are suffering from poverty and the right to life, poor health, and housing shortages due to heat waves, heavy rain, drought, sea level rise, and acidification caused by climate change. This suggests that the reason for the increased involvement of missionaries in this issue is a transformation of their beliefs based on the direct impact of climate change on individuals and societies in mission contexts, not on the pursuit of their own epistemological beliefs. The inevitability of this transformation of epistemological beliefs provides a powerful reason for their stakeholders to become more receptive to this issue as part of their missions.

For a while now, the global evangelical missionary community has recognized the issue of social engagement as a major Christian agenda.[15]

---

15 "The Manila Manifesto," Lausanne Movement, 1989, (pt. A, sec. 4), https://lausanne.org/content/manifesto/the-manila-manifesto.

In this context, all Christians, including missionaries, have the responsibility of evangelism and social participation. Evangelical Christians and missionaries do not necessarily have to embrace the cutting edge of controversial theology to address environmental and human catastrophe. Nor does it help to slander missionaries who, in varying degrees and ways, are seeking solutions to this critical issue based on different epistemological beliefs. The mutual cooperation of Christian missionary communities to mitigate and in some cases prevent environmental and human calamities does not compromise the priority of evangelism and church planting in any respect.

Many of the informants had no experience engaging in theological or missiological discussions on climate change, global warming, and human catastrophe prior to becoming missionaries. In order to redress this situation, supporting Korean churches, seminaries, and mission training institutions must redefine the relationship between environmental and human calamities and evangelical missions and teach it to missionaries before they go to the field. In order to broaden and deepen this discussion, a collaborative, multidisciplinary approach is required that includes the natural sciences, social sciences, biblical theology, and missiology. The unique challenges facing each mission situation call for mutual cooperation between local, Korean, and global communities of experts and practitioners to solve the unique problems of a specific region rather than applying a uniform policy.

This study dealt with the transformation of Korean missionaries' epistemological beliefs about natural and human calamities, among the major crises presently impacting all mankind. Given the limited time and research materials, the researcher asks the evangelical missionary community to supplement and update the study through more in-depth, integrated, and multifaceted research on the subject. As a result, it is hoped that evangelical missiologists and community practitioners will be further empowered to present the gospel of hope to all those suffering from these crises.

Discussion Questions

1. What are your theological beliefs related to environmental and human calamities? How do these beliefs affect your daily life and ministry?

2. What are your suggestions for helping missionaries to balance traditional missionary work, such as evangelism, discipleship, and church planting, with efforts to mitigate environmental and human calamities in their mission contexts?

3. As a responsible Christian of this age, how can you witness the gospel of hope to your neighbors and communities suffering from climate change and environmental destruction?

Response

by J. Nelson Jennings

Jooyun Eum's qualitative research project, entitled "The Transformation of Korean Missionaries' Epistemological Beliefs on Environmental and Human Calamities: A Critical Analysis," provides groundbreaking insights into Korean missionaries' relationships to environmental matters. Eum's project combines scholarly expertise, spiritual sensitivity, and targeted outcomes to produce a clear if varied picture of how, and more importantly why, Korean missionaries' environmental involvements have developed over the past generation. Along with KGMLF 2023 forum participants, book readers, and their various communities, the wider Christian mission community and indeed all those concerned about human involvement in environmental care are indebted to Jooyun Eum for this constructive and pointed research project.

Eum's Research Project Summary

Eum first clearly states the project's research methodology: "constructivist grounded theory ... based on the philosophical view that humans construct knowledge and meaning from their own experiences." In particular, Eum conducted "in-depth interviews with twenty-eight Korean missionaries ... ."

Eum notes that the study did not attempt simply to compile a descriptive list of how Korean missionaries engaged "environmental and human calamities." Rather, "This study focuses more on critically analyzing the relationship between missionaries' traditional epistemology and the transformation of their theological and missiological perspectives based on current realities on the ground." In probing missionaries' assumptions, attitudes, and changes therein, Eum's study aims "to present a relationship model of Korean missionaries' epistemological beliefs and missional practices regarding environmental and human calamities."

One of Eum's important summary observations is that "missionaries living in areas highly dependent on agriculture are paying more attention to climate change." These missionaries also "generally agree that a missionary response is needed" to address the problem of decreased "crop yields, resulting in food shortages and loss of income," which have been affected by "the increase in droughts, floods, and typhoons caused by climate change." In addition, missionaries working in cities "also testify that increases in heat-related diseases are affecting the working and living conditions" of urban dwellers.

Even so, Eum's analysis "reveals there is a wide gap between missionaries' epistemological beliefs and missional responses." While missionaries are aware of "the seriousness of natural and human calamities" and indeed "are also suffering from them alongside their neighbors in their mission contexts," Eum concludes that "due to reasons such as lack of professional knowledge and experience, missionary priorities, and a wide range of expectations from missionary organizations, churches, and supporters, they respond passively to this issue rather than with integrity."

Eum further notes, "The dominant epistemological belief of Korean evangelical missionaries … is dichotomous soteriology… . Their ultimate focus is on the spiritual dimension." They focus on the spiritual because "many stakeholders, including churches, mission organizations, and supporters, explicitly or implicitly demand that missionaries devote themselves only to evangelism, discipleship, and church planting, rather than focusing on issues such as the environment and human calamities." Missionaries thus live within the tension between both stakeholders' and missionaries' own spiritual emphasis and "the direct impact of climate change on individuals and societies in mission contexts" where they serve.

Four Maxims

In response to Eum's careful and insightful study, I wish to offer four maxims that the study exemplifies.

Practical Experience and Concrete Contexts Drive Theological and Missiological Developments

We Christians might imagine that our theologies of God, salvation, and the world were formulated in a pristine spiritual vacuum, unstained by worldly realities. Similarly, we might imagine our missiological understandings and strategies to have been inspired through prayerful contemplation and, if not revealed directly from heaven, at least inspired by the Spirit's direct leading. We evangelicals are particularly prone to such imaginations, birthed as Evangelicalism was out the of the European Enlightenment and its penchant for allegedly decontextualized, rational, and universally true claims.

In reality, however, the world's Creator and Redeemer deals with humankind in our contextual concreteness of particular languages, struggles, relationships, and challenges. We know God and understand his world within our concrete finitude—and our knowledge and understandings grow, change, and develop within the rough and tumble of life's experiences and situations. Hence the old covenant people of God knew him by such Hebrew terms as *Yahweh* and *Elohim*, new covenant people of God called him *Kurios* and

Theos, and those of us here today use the Korean label *Hananim*, the English term *God*, and other indigenous terms by which the world's Creator and Redeemer is happy for us to use.

Jesus's followers who were Greek-speaking Hellenists had to deal with new questions to which their inherited cosmogonies, cosmologies, and philosophical worldviews demanded answers, hence they had to hammer out new Christological and trinitarian formulations. Across the generations all sorts of Christian communities have had to wrestle with how to deal with ancestors and religious traditions. William Carey responded to Captain James Cook's travel reports by interweaving the examples of stock companies, religious communities, and voluntary societies to spark the formation of mission societies. The influential nineteenth-century English mission leader Henry Venn needed to motivate missionaries to move to new contexts and help pay for indigenous pastors—hence the three-self church-planting formula.

All these and countless other examples are akin to what Eum has called Korean missionaries "reestablishing epistemological beliefs through reflection on phenomenological discoveries" about environmental and human calamities. More than conceptual arguments or specifically religious motivations per se, Christians' practical experiences and concrete contexts are what epistemologically shape our theological and missiological formulations.

A Variety of Responses to Climate Change and Natural Calamities in Theological Perspectives and in Missional Practices Is Consistent with Christianity's Inherent Diversity

Eum's interviews revealed different convictions and attitudes among Korean missionaries about environmental concerns and how missionaries might involve themselves accordingly. Some missionaries focused on personal environmentally friendly practices, for example recycling or planting trees. Some thought that theological energy should be spent on ecological topics. Some brushed aside the urgency and importance of dealing with environmental calamities out of eschatological convictions about Christ's imminent return and a corresponding need to focus on evangelism.

Various observers of Eum's research results will judge variously the various postures among the missionaries interviewed. Such varieties—among missionaries and among their observers—are consistent with the diversity that marks the Christian faith. To be sure, Christian unity is true insofar as "there is one body and one Spirit ... one hope ... one Lord, one faith, one baptism, one God and Father of all" (Eph. 4:4–6). But alongside the different gifts that Christ gives to his people (Eph. 4:7–11) are the multitude of contexts, backgrounds, and circumstances into which the faith is translated and lived. By divine design Christian unity is characterized by diversity rather than by uniformity.

Of note from a religious studies perspective is how Christianity's various traditions, practices, beliefs, and postures bear a strong resemblance to varieties within Buddhism—also a translatable (at least in large part) religious tradition. Grouping Christianity with Judaism and Islam as the so-called "Abrahamic religions" can obscure Christianity's inherent diversity due to its translatable traits alongside Buddhism.

People—Perhaps Especially Christians—Tend to Respond Conservatively to New Challenges

The worldwide environmental movement has gained traction as ramifications of the Industrial Revolution have become increasingly evident. While stark political disagreements reflect the economics related to heavy industries connected to environmental destruction, there is widespread concurrence with such environmentally friendly measures as recycling and reducing carbon emissions.

South Korea's economic "Miracle on the Hangang River" began only in the post-Korean War 1960s,[16] later than most developed economies. Korea's environmental movement has thus grown significantly only since the 1990s. It is thus understandable that today's Korean missionaries, particularly those born and raised before the 1990s,[17] would not be as instinctively attuned to environmental concerns as missionaries of other nationalities.

South Korea's relatively late modern industrial development adds to the human proclivity to respond conservatively to new challenges. In the New Testament, for example, Jewish Christians were reticent to accept Gentile Christians on equal terms. More generally, risk avoidance is a self-protective instinct. For missionaries, actively embarking on ecological involvements could jeopardize their support base, who may not share those same values.

Spirit-Cultivated Love Drives Christians to Meet Needs and to Face Reality—Even When Existing Frameworks Resist

Eum's research shows the epistemological barriers that Korean missionaries face in considering involvement with environmental concerns. Priorities of

16 "The Korean Economy—the Miracle on the Hangang River," KOREA.net, Ministry of Culture, Sports and Tourism and Korean Culture and Information Service, accessed June 2, 2023, https://www.korea.net/AboutKorea/Economy/The-Miracle-on-The-Hangang.

17 It would thus be helpful to know the ages of the missionaries whom Eum interviewed.

spiritual and church-centered matters, both within their own psyches and among Korea-based supporters, push ecological crises into the background.

Even so, Korean missionaries who undeniably see fellow human beings suffering—and who suffer themselves—the adverse effects of environmental destruction and natural calamities cannot help but respond to those needs in love. God's Spirit stirs the hearts of his people to serve others, including seeking solutions to crises that human beings can work to alleviate.

CHAPTER 12

Who Will Feed the World in the Twenty-First Century?

Lessons and Questions from a Brief Comparison of China's, India's, and Africa's Food Systems and Food Sovereignty

by Zhou Li

In his 1994 article "Who Will Feed China?," Lester Brown framed China's food security problem as a global issue.[1] Now that nearly a quarter of the new century has passed the question has become, Who will feed China in the twenty-first century?[2] And who will feed India and Africa in the twenty-first century? These questions call for urgent attention. Newly emerging challenges in the field of global food security require new solutions.

Climate change, economic recession, and regional conflicts, all exacerbated by the COVID-19 pandemic, have threatened food security for many developing countries and their poor. In 2020, 720 to 810 million people worldwide faced hunger; the number in India alone reached 210 million, accounting for about a quarter of that number. There were 46 million more hungry people in Africa and nearly 57 million more in Asia in 2020 compared to 2019. In contrast, the incidence of hunger in China fell below 2.5 percent.[3]

This chapter will analyze the world food security situation and then briefly discuss how faith relates to real-world hunger challenges.

---

1 Lester R. Brown, "Who Will Feed China?," *World Watch* 7 (1994): 10–19; his book, *Who Will Feed China? Wake-Up Call for a Small Planet* followed the next year (Washington, DC: Worldwatch Institute, 1995).

2 L. Zhou, J. Luo, and P. Fang, 谁来养活21世纪的中国—疫情危机、全球本土化与有组织地负起责任 [Who will feed twenty-first century China?—Pandemic crisis, glocalization and organized responsibility] *International Economic Review* 155 (2021): 53–80.

3 FAO et al., *The State of Food Security and Nutrition in the World 2021* (Rome: FAO, 2021), 12–14, https://doi.org/10.4060/cb4474en.

Who Will Feed China in the Twenty-First Century?

China has moved from famine to feast (吃不饱 [starvation] to 吃饱了 [well-fed], see figure 12.1, left). In the 1960s, China's annual grain output per capita surpassed the average levels of developing countries. Influenced by Brown's analysis, China returned to a moderate agricultural policy after 2000, with grain production its key component. The policy proved successful as grain was harvested every year from 2004 to 2021.[4] Furthermore, since 2010 the annual grain output has exceeded the standard level of 400 kg per person. Hence, China is not likely to experience a systemic food crisis because it has already surpassed the global average in terms of total and per capita output. The constant emphasis on national food security has enabled China to become self-sufficient.

The ability of China to feed its own people has directly contributed to achieving some of the UN sustainable development goals for 2030. In 2020, the Food and Agricultural Organization revised the incidence of hunger in thirteen countries, including China, whose incidence was lowered to less than 2.5 percent. The scale effect of the country's large population decreased the global incidence of hunger in 2019 from an original estimate of more than 800 million people to 690 million.[5] In July 2021, China announced winning the battle against poverty, with peasant households reaching the annual net income per capita standard for national poverty alleviation, and rural poor people free from worries over food and clothing and having access to compulsory education, basic medical services, and safe housing.[6] "Free from worry over food" refers to adequate food for low-income groups so that almost no one faces hunger in China today.

Despite these achievements, China has been claiming that its supply and demand for food have been in a tight balance for nearly twenty years. Constrained by limited resources, China has found it difficult to reach the stage of "feast." Its arable land accounts for only 6.9 percent of the world's total, but its people account for 18.5 percent. Under current technical conditions, the country requires at least 230 million hectares of crop planting area to ensure a balance between food supply and demand, but the actual

---

4 国家统计局关于2021年粮食产量数据的公告 [Announcement of the National Bureau of Statistics on 2021 grain output data], National Bureau of Statistics of China, 2021, http://www.stats.gov.cn/tjsj/zxfb.

5 FAO et al., *The State of Food Security and Nutrition in the World 2020* (Rome: FAO, 2020), https://doi.org/10.4060/ca9692en.

6 人类减贫的中国实践白皮书 [Poverty alleviation: China's experience and contribution], The State Council Information Office of the People's Republic of China, 2021), http://www.xinhuanet.com/.

planting area is only about 170 million hectares. The remaining crop shortage has to be filled by imports.[7]

Since the beginning of the twenty-first century, China has been self-sufficient in rice and wheat, but imports of corn and soybeans have increased significantly (figure 12.1). Imports in 2020 were 122.684 million tonnes, about 8.2 times more than in 2001.[8] Grain imports in 2018 and 2020 remained at high levels of more than 97 million tonnes. China used to be almost self-sufficient, but now a fifth of its food supply derives from imports.

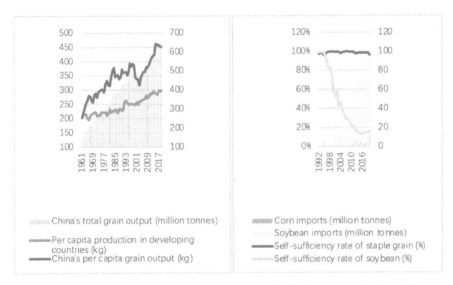

Figure 12.1: China's total grain output, output per capita, and self-sufficiency rate of main varieties

Note: The developing countries on the left were selected according to the country group published by UNDP, which includes data from 147 countries. The blue horizontal axis represents the standard of 400 kg per capita per year. The staple food self-sufficiency ratio on the right refers to the combined average quantity of rice, wheat, and corn. The combined figures take into account that China's food consumption habits, production policies, and statistical caliber set the staple foods as rice, wheat, and corn. In fact, China's rice and wheat self-sufficiency rates are both close to 100 percent, with fluctuations in corn at a minimum of 95.6 percent. When we considered the import volume of corn separately and compared it with soybean, we found the increase in corn import volume in recent years only amounted to 11.3 percent.

---

7 Y. Du, "China's Food Security Strategy (Part 2)," *Rural Work Communication* 22 (2020): 17–21.

8 "UN Comtrade Database," Trade Statistics Branch, UN Statistics Division, 2021, https://comtrade.un.org/data/.

How should we understand this change? We must go beyond Brown's initial framing of the problem as "famine" and deeply examine China's transition from "feast" to a "healthy and balanced" diet.

China's grain imports are mainly used for livestock feed, so grain imports do not directly affect self-sufficiency in the staple crops. Self-sufficiency rates for rice, wheat, and corn have remained above 95 percent. The change in corn imports during 2020 was only a short-term deviation. To combat African swine fever[9] and accelerate the recovery of live pig production, corn imports reached a record high of 11.2942 million tonnes in 2020. In contrast, policy makers employed an import substitution strategy for soybean after 2001, which resulted in a self-sufficiency rate that has been hovering below 20 percent since 2012.

Increased imports of feed grains have been directly related to increased demand for meat, eggs, and milk. Soybean oil serves the food processing industry, whereas soybean meal serves as feed for meat, egg, and dairy industries. These increases reflect changes in animal consumption patterns during the last forty years of China's economic development. However, we do not expect this trend to continue to grow linearly because China's dietary structure, as in other East Asian countries, has been based mainly on plant protein for thousands of years.

China's dietary structure has shown an unhealthy trend with major meat and fat intakes higher than recommended levels.[10] The changes in China's consumption patterns have been approximating those in Europe and the US, resulting in higher incidences of cardiovascular and cerebrovascular diseases, which are more common in developed countries.[11] Hyperlipidemia (34.0 percent), hypertension (25.2 percent), hyperglycemia (9.7 percent), and obesity (30.1 percent) have become serious health problems.[12] This situation not only requires a rebalancing of dietary structures, but also requires that

9   S. You et al., "African Swine Fever Outbreaks in China Led to Gross Domestic Product and Economic Losses," *Nature Food* 2 (2021): 802–808, https://doi.org/10.1038/s43016-021–00362-1.

10 L. Huang et al., "Nutrition Transition and Related Health Challenges over Decades in China," *European Journal of Clinical Nutrition* 75 (2021): 247-52, https://doi: 10.1038/s41430-020-0674-8.

11 A. D. Lopez and T. Adair, "Is the Long-Term Decline in Cardiovascular-Disease Mortality in High-Income Countries Over? Evidence from National Vital Statistics," *International Journal of Epidemiology* 48 (2019): 1815-1823, https:// doi: 10.1093/ije/dyz143.

12 Bureau of Disease Prevention and Control, National Health Commission of China, *Report on Nutrition and Chronic Diseases of Chinese Residents* (Beijing: People's Medical Publishing House, 2021), 100-147.

soybean imports be used to meet flexible rather than rigid consumption patterns, because self-sufficiency in plant protein is more critical than an increased supply of animal protein.

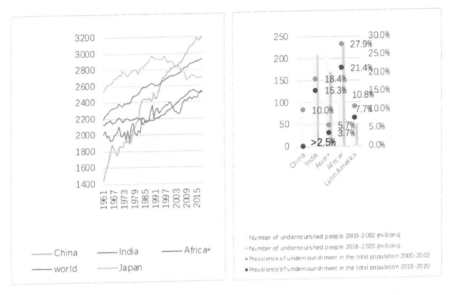

Figure 12.2: China's caloric intake level and the number of hungry people in the total population

Note: Africa* refers to sub-Saharan Africa, and Asia** refers to Asia excluding China and India. The unit of country and region comparison on the left is kcal/capita/day. The right presents two features. First, since 2005 China's per capita calorie intake has not only surpassed the world's level but even surpassed Japan's level, which has a similar dietary structure. Second, India's caloric intake per capita is close to that of sub-Saharan Africa. It is worth noting that India's population is about to surpass China's, and the number of hungry people in India has exceeded the sum of the hungry people in Asia. These figures clearly present new challenges to global food security.

The challenge of feeding China in the twenty-first century has more to do with changes in the supply of feed grains for nutritional upgrading rather than food security. "Feast" and a "healthy and balanced" diet have different meanings and represent a two-phase, progressive relationship. The first phase involved the problem of feeding China, which has been solved. The second phase emphasizes nutritional upgrading and rebalancing as the key factors affecting the country's demand for food. Reasonable consumption patterns of meat and oil would help reduce the demand for feed grain, and thus imports of soybeans and corn. Under technologically optimized conditions, China will be able to produce enough to meet 45 percent and 100 percent of its respective demands for soybeans and corn by 2035.[13] Moreover, waste reduction could lead to more efficient use of about 27 percent of the total food production.[14]

Who Will Feed India and Africa in the Twenty-First Century?

As the world's population continues to grow, the problem of food security becomes increasingly important. It soared from 3.03 billion people in 1960 to 7.79 billion people in 2020. Population growth in Africa (373.1 percent), Latin America (196.6 percent), and Asia (172.2 percent) was particularly notable.[15] The global number of people unable to afford nutritionally adequate diets is projected to increase by 220 million in 2022.[16] From 1960 to 2020, future productivity losses due to excessive stunting and child mortality amounted to $29.7 billion.[17] With climate change considered, total global food demand will increase by as much as 62 percent between 2010 and 2050, while the population at risk of hunger will increase by 30 percent.[18]

The Challenge of Feeding India and Africa in the Twenty-First Century

Food security issues in India are particularly prominent. Since the late 1980s, India's caloric intake per capita has been close to that of sub-Saharan Africa. In 2020, its population reached 1.38 billion people, which accounted for 17.7 percent of the global population. Soon, India will become the most populous country. However, its number of people facing hunger has reached 208 million, which exceeds the combined total of those in other Asian countries, excluding China and India. High levels of hunger also exist in nearby Pakistan, Bangladesh, and Indonesia. A similar situation exists

---

13 Z. Liu et al., "Optimization of China's Maize and Soy Production Can Ensure Feed Sufficiency at Lower Nitrogen and Carbon Footprints," *Nature Food* 2 (2021): 426–33, https://doi.org/10.1038/s43016-021-00300-1.

14 S. Wang et al., "Urbanization Can Benefit Agricultural Production with Large-Scale Farming in China," *Nature Food* 2 (2021): 183-91, https://doi.org/10.1038/s43016-021-00228-6.

15 "World Population Prospects," Department of Economic and Social Affairs, Population Division, UN 2019, https://population.un.org/wpp/.

16 D. Laborde et al., "COVID-19 Pandemic Leads to Greater Depth of Unaffordability of Healthy and Nutrient-Adequate Diets in Low- and Middle-Income Countries," *Nature Food* 2 (2021): 473-75, https://doi.org/10.1038/s43016-021-00323-8.

17 S. Osendarp et al., "The COVID-19 Crisis Will Exacerbate Maternal and Child Undernutrition and Child Mortality in Low- and Middle-Income Countries," *Nature Food* 2 (2021): 476-84, https://doi.org/10.1038/s43016-021-00319-4.

18 M. van Dijk et al., "A Meta-analysis of Projected Global Food Demand and Population at Risk of Hunger for the Period 2010–2050," *Nature Food* 2 (2021): 494-501, https://doi.org/10.1038/s43016-021-00322-9.

in Africa, with 21.4 percent of the sub-Saharan population facing hunger. These worrisome data not only highlight the long-term and arduous nature of the "famine" problem in India and Africa but also present a more serious challenge: how to improve food security and self-sufficiency in developing countries and regions.

China's Model for the World

As the world strives to achieve the UN sustainable development goals for 2030, China's creative solutions to continuously provide enough food for its own people can serve as a reference and model for the rest of the world. China's experience can also inspire confidence in other developing countries affected by climate change and COVID-19.

The key lesson of China's food security self-sufficiency is that the government takes full responsibility for feeding its own citizens. Even with a relatively high self-sufficiency rate in the country, the Chinese government still emphasizes the national policy of "Chinese bowl for Chinese rice," which reflects its belief that administering food security is one of the most basic functions of government. Consequently, we can leave behind the "organized irresponsibility"[19] in the risk society described by Beck and move toward "organized responsibility"[20] for food security.

China's policy of "the land to the tiller" ensures self-sufficiency for peasants and effectively enhances the food security of low-income groups. The policy is essentially a land equalization program in which everyone is provided a field for cultivating crops. China has been able to restore and consolidate the fundamental position of its peasants as the most basic unit for the production and management of food supplies. The inseparability of production and consumption in peasant households proposed by Chayanov[21] and of production and management in peasant households as the most basic units proposed by Schultz[22] suggest that widespread land ownership ensures self-sufficiency. Peasants, who comprise 98 percent of China's agricultural operations, can sustain their livelihoods with a variety of nutritional food sources, without relying on markets. Currently, 580 million peasants are

19 Ulrich Beck, *Counter-Poisons: Organized Irresponsibility* (Cambridge: Cambridge Univ. Press, 1992).

20 Zhou, Luo, and Fang, 谁来养活21世纪的中国？[Who will feed twenty-first century China?].

21 A. Chayanov, *The Theory of Peasant Economy* [1925 ed.] (Manchester: Manchester Univ. Press, 1966).

22 T. W. Schultz, *Transforming Traditional Agriculture* (New Haven: Yale Univ. Press, 1964).

able to feed themselves.[23] By forming social organizations, peasants can also participate in and contribute up to 80 percent of the food supply chain.[24]

China's example of a government-led food sovereignty system should be established and developed. Under the national conditions of "big country with small holders," China's policy of moving the food system in the direction of "improving autonomy and realizing independence" has been implemented as a long-term strategy. Public policies address issues such as increased investment in water conservancy projects, farmland infrastructure, etc., with continued support for the use of improved varieties, chemical fertilizers and pesticides with low toxicity and high efficiency, and mechanization and informatization in production. In addition, the domestic food distribution system must address underdeveloped food production in some regions and unbalanced product structures.

Finally, the versatility of the food system should be improved to facilitate the transition from "feast" to "healthy and balanced." The Chinese government first emphasized the development of multiple functions in agriculture in 2007, as stipulated in Document No. 1. After 2013, policies such as "food crop production strategy based on farmland management and technological application," zero growth of chemical fertilizers and pesticides use, and crop rotation and fallow system were successively introduced to ensure sustainable food security. These polices were implemented by upgrading agricultural infrastructure, formulating innovative technologies and programs, guiding sustainable food production, promoting nutritional upgrading, and rebalancing consumption patterns. As in the developed countries, China has begun to emphasize versatility and to move toward the stage of "healthy and balanced."

Faith and Real-World Hunger

The above is only an analysis of secular knowledge and world reality. The Lord God says, "Behold, the days come ... that I will send a famine in the land, not a famine of bread, nor a thirst for water, but of hearing the words of the LORD" (Amos 8:11, KJV). There is a famine of the word of God in the debate about how to feed the world. But there is wisdom in his word that can be applied to our current situation.

---

23 Z. Si and L. Zhou et al., "'One Family, Two Systems': Food Safety Crisis as a Catalyst for Agrarian Changes in Rural China," *Journal of Rural Studies* 69 (2019): 87-96, https://doi.org/10.1016/j.jrurstud.2019.04.011.

24 S. K. Lowder, M. V. Sánchez, and R. Bertini, "Farms, Family Farms, Farmland Distribution and Farm Labour: What Do We Know Today?" FAO Agricultural Development Economics Working Paper 19-08, Rome, FAO, November 2019.

The Bible records a large-scale, long-term famine in ancient Egypt and neighboring countries. Joseph interpreted Pharaoh's dreams that God sent to show him there would be seven years of plenty followed by seven years of famine. As ruler of Egypt, second only to Pharaoh, and with the "Spirit of God" (Gen. 41:38, KJV), Joseph wisely prepared for the coming famine by collecting and storing food during the abundant years. "God meant it unto good, to bring to pass, as it is this day, to save much people alive" (Gen. 50:20, KJV). Today we are facing many difficult food security issues, including famine. Will it be necessary for someone like Joseph to prepare for famines in the good years?

Another passage states that "Agabus stood up and through the Spirit predicted that a severe famine would spread over the entire Roman world. (This happened during the reign of Claudius.) The disciples, as each one was able, decided to provide help for the brothers and sisters living in Judea. This they did, sending their gift to the elders by Barnabas and Saul" (Acts 11:28–30). Applying this to our time, should those who live in areas of abundance send relief to those who live in famine areas?

Finally, God's word says, "And when he had fasted forty days and forty nights, he was afterward an hungred. And when the tempter came to him, he said, 'If thou be the Son of God, command that these stones be made bread.' But he answered and said, 'It is written, "Man shall not live by bread alone, but by every word that proceedeth out of the mouth of God"'" (Matt. 4:2–4, KJV). Jesus said that God's words are as important to life as the food we eat. By applying God's word with all wisdom, we will walk with God in these challenges. Let us return to the sovereign God and the Origin of all things. We will find the fundamental answers in him and work them out in our world!

Discussion Questions

1. Who is the One who ultimately feeds the world and every single person? Who gives sunshine, air, water, land and seeds, as well as a people's ability to work? What is the significance of your answer in considering the massive practical challenges of feeding the world's population?

2. If the word of the Lord is relevant to our world, how should we interpret the experience of China feeding itself without the Christian faith? How should we interpret the reality that India (Hindu, Muslim, and Christian), Africa (Christian and Muslim) and some Latin American (Christian) countries are unable to feed themselves?

3. With the ongoing threat of COVID-19 and the prospect of a world war, what bearing does the word of the Lord (the gospel) have on the immense and complex challenges of feeding more than 800 million hungry people?

Acknowledgment

This study was written in consultation with Dr. Fang Ping and PhD Candidate Luo Jianzhang, and supported by the Fundamental Research Funds of Renmin University of China, "On Cross-Sector Collaboration and Holisitic Governance" (20XNL012).

Response

by Anna lisa Mudahy

Are We Equipped to Feed the World?

Who will feed the world in the twenty-first century? This striking question is the epitomic theme in Dr. Zhou Li's chapter of the same title, subtitled "Lessons and Questions from a Brief Comparison of China's, India's, and Africa's Food Systems and Food Sovereignty." In this thought-provoking chapter, Dr. Li tackles one of the fundamental aspects of human society, food security. Using China as a case study, he highlights the possibilities of moving toward global food security through the enaction of targeted efforts that incorporate sustainability and self-sufficiency. The chapter analyzes China's transformation from being at the center of an extensive food crisis in the 1990s to a state of well-curated food self-sufficiency in 2020 and suggests that efforts by China's government be used as a blueprint in addressing the global hunger crisis.

Dr. Li's analysis of China's food system and its global application is valuable. The alarm of a climate crisis coupled with a continuously rising global population and extensive growth in various regions, such as the Indian subcontinent and Latin America, raises the questions of how and from where the food needs of these growing populations will be supplemented.

China's success story of food security seemingly gives hope for a potential global solution to the food crisis. Nonetheless, though the concept is endearing, accomplishing global food security through established efforts similar to China's presents daunting challenges. Questions of how, who, where, and when, overlaid by a minefield of geosocial and political realities, complicate the task of addressing the global food crisis. Dr. Li describes the food system in China as a "government-led food sovereignty system," suggesting that similar efforts would require other countries to enact strategies from a top-down perspective to curb food poverty. However, considering the political structure of China in comparison to other regions and countries faced with severe food crisis, the ability to enact similar programs may present an insuperable obstacle. Extensive governmental input of this nature may be seen as an overreach of political power and may not receive the same support as in China. In addition, maintaining such a system until its desired outcome is achieved poses another severe challenge. China's food policy extended over two decades, which may not be feasible in developing countries that experience political change more frequently. Fundamentally, though this policy was successful in China, thorough, region-specific analyses would be needed to determine feasibility in other countries.

The Gospel and Global Hunger

Considering these limitations, it may be impossible to implement a global version of China's food system in every region experiencing food insecurity. However, valuable insights can be gained and applied to the gospel effort globally through missionary projects on smaller but more targeted scales. The United Nations estimated that 828 million people were affected by hunger in 2021,[25] but as Christians we are direly aware of a greater crisis impacting all of humanity, a hunger for the word of God. With the ultimate fate of our world opened before our eyes, there is a burden in our hearts to share the good news of salvation with the world so that souls may be saved for the kingdom of heaven. Spiritual starvation has left billions craving for a fulfillment that only Christ, the Bread of Life, can satisfy. During his ministry on earth, Jesus sought to point Israel to its need for spiritual fulfillment but did not ignore the physical ailments that plagued them as well. Through the miracles he wrought he demonstrated the connection between the practical and the spiritual aspects of the gospel. The love of God is shown not just in words and fancy sounding philosophies but by our actions.

The methods employed by the Chinese government of empowering the poorest of its citizens to achieve independence and food security can be valuable to us in our global ministry efforts. Facilitating holistic and relevant projects that can help build the communities we minister to and address crucial issues such as hunger can have lasting impacts, beyond what we can imagine. Combined with sharing the good news of the gospel, we can help to provide both physical and spiritual food in places that need it the most.

God Will Provide What We Need to Fulfill His Work

From the onset of creation, the necessity of food to human survival and God's role as its ultimate provider is stated explicitly: "And God said, 'See, I have given you every herb that yields seed which is on the face of all the earth, and every tree whose fruit yields seed; to you it shall be for food'" (Gen. 1:29, NKJV). Millenia later in his sermon on the mount, Jesus sought to remind us of the same principle of God as our provider. Jesus says, "Therefore I say to you, do not worry about your life, what you will eat or

---

25 "UN Report: Global Hunger Numbers Rose to as Many as 828 Million in 2021," World Health Organization, July 6, 2022, https://www.who.int/news/item/06-07-2022–un-report--global-hunger-numbers-rose-to-as-many-as-828-million-in-2021.

what you will drink … . Look at the birds of the air, for they neither sow nor reap nor gather into barns; yet your heavenly Father feeds them. Are you not of more value than they?" (Matt. 6:25–26, NKJV). Our Creator in his infinite wisdom created a world with exactly what is needed to feed humanity and gives care and thought to supplying our needs and those we minister to.

God wants us to share bread with the hungry (Isa. 58:7), yet we must remember that it is not from us that these blessings will flow. Job reminds us that the Lord giveth and taketh away (Job 1:21), and the psalmist tells us that the "the earth is the LORD's, and the fulness thereof" (Ps. 24:1, KJV). Just as he sent his disciples out to minister with the promise to keep and provide for them, just as he fed the children of Israel as they sojourned through the wilderness, and just as he fed the over five thousand by the sea of Galilee, the Lord will supply our needs "according to his riches in glory" (Phil. 4:19, KJV) to complete the mission he has given to us. We simply need to present ourselves as willing vessels, ready to go wherever he leads.

The global food crisis is a medium through which we can fulfill our duties as Christians in these final moments of earth's history. As children of God, we are commissioned to bear each other's burdens and by so fulfill the law of Christ (Gal. 6:2). In working to mitigate the hungering needs of 800 million people, we can fulfill a greater desire, one that reaches beyond this life and extends to eternity.

CHAPTER 13

Gold Mining in the Southwest of Burkina Faso and Christian Mission
The Great Commission and Structural Evil

by Ini Dorcas Dah

I have lived in Gaoua, the capital of the Southwest Region of Burkina Faso, since 1990. In this region, mainly called Lobi land, 1 there are many artisanal mining sites including gold mines. I have witnessed many changes over the years that have inspired me to do research on gold mining in the region. In this chapter I will give a brief account of the traditional view of gold in the area, which limited its small-scale extraction. Then I will examine how breaking from tradition led to large-scale gold mining and many associated calamities. Finally, I will look at how Christian mission through the Great Commission can address structural evil, in southwestern Burkina Faso in particular and in the world in general.

Traditional Attitude to Gold in the Southwest of Burkina Faso

Traditionally, the people in the Southwest of Burkina Faso believed that gold was sacred. This sacredness was maintained through the observance of taboos and other related traditional laws for the protection of the environment. The earth is still regarded as sacred by most of the people in Lobi land. The presence of *tĩgan* (the earth shrine) among the Birifor (one of the major ethnic groups in Lobi land) reinforces the sacredness of the earth.[1] According to Sié Eric Dah, land must not be sold. As God's gift it can only be lent and should also be given freely to anyone in need.[2]

---

1 Ini Dorcas Dah, *Women Do More Work Than Men; Birifor Women as Change Agents in the Mission and Expansion of the Church in West Africa (Burkina Faso, Côte d'Ivoire and Ghana)* (Akropong-Akuapem, Ghana: Regnum Africa, 2017), 48.

2 Sié Eric Dah, "L'Eglise, Champ de Dieu: Intelligence du Mystère à partir de l'Image du Champ en Milieu Birifor" [The church, field of God: Intelligence of the mystery from the image of the field in Birifor environment] (Mémoire en Théologie, 6ème Année, Koumi, Juin 1998), 13-14. Note that giving the land for free was for it to be used for farming and not for excavation in search for gold as it is done today in the area.

Early French monographs from 1902 document of the presence of gold in "Lobi land" and indicate that only women engaged in occasional, small-scale gold mining.[3] The women exchanged the gold for useful commodities for the upkeep of their families.[4] It was rare to see people wearing gold in the area because they believed that gold had the power to swallow their souls.[5] For them, God placed gold inside the rocks on the hills. Thus no one broke rocks in search for gold.[6] Even when the Lobi found a rock containing a large gold nugget they would take it to the top of a hill and leave it there as a sacred stone.[7]

There were also myths about how gold used to walk around or crawl like a snake. Anyone who collected gold would die. To prevent death, a person had to urinate on it; however, as a consequence they would become impotent. This idea of urinating on gold and becoming impotent was cause for reflection in a society where wealth is neither measured by the size of one's bank account nor the abundance of material possessions, but by the size of one's family. As Dah points out, "there is always joy in families when a new baby is born because children are a sign of wealth."[8] If the size of one's family was seen as the symbol of wealth, then no traditional Lobi would have wanted to become impotent by urinating on or touching walking or crawling gold. However, the attitude to gold would change over time in the new generation of Lobi influenced by foreigners.

3 Monographie de Bondoukou, Colonie de la Côte d'Ivoire, Haute Côte d'Ivoire Orientale (deuxième Cahier, troisième cahier et quatrième cahier), Les Etats de Bouna (Suite) par le Lieutenant Chaudron du 1er Régiment de Tirailleurs Senegalais-Commandant la Circonscription de Bouna, 1902, Archives Nationales de Côte d'Ivoire, Abidjan [Monograph of Bondoukou, Colony of Côte d'Ivoire, Haute Côte d'Ivoire Orientale (second notebook, third notebook, and fourth notebook), The States of Bouna (continued) by Lieutenant Cauldron of the 1st Regiment of Senegalese Tirailleurs-Commander of the District of Bouna, 1902, National Archives of Côte d'Ivoire, Abidjan](ANCI-Abidjan).

4 Monographie de Bondoukou [Monograph of Bondoukou].

5 Cécile de Rouville, *Organisation Sociale des Lobi, Une Société bilinéaire du Burkina Faso et de Côte d'Ivoire* [Social organization of the Lobi: A bilinear society of Burkina Faso and Côte d'Ivoire] (Paris: L'Harmattan, 1987), 42.

6 Klaus Schneider, "Extraction et traitement rituel de l'or" [Extraction and ritual treatment of gold] in *Images d'Afrique et sciences sociales: Les pays Lobi, Birifor et Dagara (Burkina Faso, Côte d'Ivoire et Ghana), Actes du Colloques de Ouagadougou (10-15 décembre 1990)* [Images of Africa and the social sciences: The countries of Lobi, Birifor and Dagara (Burkina Faso, Côte d'Ivoire and Ghana), Proceedings of the Colloquium of Ouagadougou (December 10-15,1990)], sous la direction de Michèle Fiéloux, Jacques Lombard, avec Jeanne-Marie Kambou-Ferrand (Éditions Karthala et Orstom, 1993), 191.

7 Schneider, 191.

8 Dah, *Women Do More Work*, 41.

Change in Attitude Toward "Lobi Gold"

From the 1990s onward, things started changing drastically in Lobi land. The Lobi people could no longer control the occupation of their land by foreign artisanal miners from all over Burkina Faso, including people from the subregion.[9] According to Ebenezer Blasu, when people in their communities notice that the deities are no longer punishing those who violate taboos, they also stop respecting the traditional rules that were set up for the protection of their environment.[10]

Negative Consequences Associated with Gold Mining in the Southwest of Burkina Faso

Threat to Food Security

The younger generation has abandoned farming and become deeply involved in gold mining, to the point that it has almost replaced farming activities in the Southwest of Burkina Faso.[11] Four hundred forty-eight functional artisanal gold production sites were identified in Burkina Faso in 2017.[12] The Southwestern Region is one of the areas most affected by this artisanal gold mining, with more than sixty-one sites listed. In all four provinces of the region there is an exponential development of gold panning activity. This situation has grave repercussions on the agricultural sector, which drives economic development and occupies more than 80 percent of the population.

---

9   Ini Dorcas Dah, "Desacralisation of Gold in South West Burkina Faso: A Christian Response to Gold Mining and Its Consequences on Creation," in *Essays on the Land, Ecotheology and Traditions in Africa*, ed. Benjamin Abotchie Ntreh, Mark S. Aidoo, and Daniel Nii Aboagye Aryeh (Eugene, OR: Wipf and Stock, 2019), 193.

10 Ebenezer Yaw Blasu, "Christian Higher Education as Holistic Mission and Moral Transformation: An Assessment of Studying Environmental Science at the Presbyterian University College, Ghana and the Ecological Thought of the Sokpoe-Eʋe for the Development of an African Theocology Curriculum" (PhD diss., Akrofi-Christaller Institute, Akuapem-Akropong, 2017), 93; see also Ogbu U. Kalu, "The Sacred Egg: Worldview, Ecology, and Development in West Africa," in *Indigenous Traditions and Ecology*, ed. John A. Grim (Cambridge, MA: Harvard Univ. Press, 2001), 241.

11 Sié Mickael Da, "Région du sud-ouest: Le métal jaune une menace pour la sécurité alimentaire" [Southwest Region: The yellow metal a threat to food security] *Bafujii Infos*, Oct. 31, 2019, https://bafujiinfos.com/region-du-sud-ouest-le-metal-jaune-une-menace-pour-lagriculture/.

12 In the national survey on the gold panning sector organized by the National Institute of Statistics and Demography in collaboration with the Ministry in charge of mines and the Ministry of Territorial Administration and Decentralization.

Land Invasion by Gold Miners

It has become common to wake up one morning to find that your property has been confiscated by gold miners, without any notice. This is the testimony of Sanwnayir Kambiré, whose land was invaded and occupied by gold miners. He narrates that he woke up one morning to the presence of gold miners on his land. He had been growing millet, which was at the spike stage, but when the miners arrived they destroyed everything. Kambiré therefore demanded compensation, which some of the miners gave but others refused.[13] This indicates that the situation has reached a point where gold miners no longer care for or respect landownership in the area.

On the other hand some, people are selling their land for a quick profit. Sié Mickael Da reported the case of Sam Kambiré, who has rented his land to the miners for a large amount of money. When Da asked him how long that money would last for him to take care of his family, Kambiré said he would rely on divine providence when the money ran out.[14] The obsession with gold has narrowed some people's minds to the point that they undervalue the natural resources that they have been given for free and they still think that God will rain down provision from the sky after they deliberately destroy everything. It is obvious that Kambiré is not even thinking about his descendants after the miners have destroyed the family property.

Death as a Major Consequence

According to Sangaré, many people die in the pits every day in the search for gold.[15] I indicated above that the Lobi people believed that gold would swallow their souls if they wore it. Even though the younger generation does not seem to be facing punishment for the violation of the taboos, there have been numerous incidents resulting in injuries and death in many mining sites and the deaths of individuals connected with gold mining.[16] I will give one example of these tragedies.

---

13 Sié Mickael Da, "Région du sud-ouest" [Southwest Region].

14 Sié Mickael Da.

15 Hamed Nanema, "Sud-ouest du Burkina: Oumar Sangaré examine l'impact de l'orpaillage sur la vie sociale" [South-West Burkina Faso: Oumar Sangaré examines the impact of gold panning on social life], *LeFaso.net*, Nov. 10, 2022, https://lefaso.net/spip.php?article117233.

16 In November 2021, a young man from Tambili, a village located about four kilometers from Gaoua, had his leg amputated. Yerri Isabelle Kambou, who is from Gaoua but married in Tambili, narrated that this young man challenged his adopted father, who told him that gold was sacred for their family. Kambou indicated that the young man told his adopted father that he was not his biological father and so he should leave him alone and let him go and search for gold. He eventually found some gold and went to sell it in town. On his way back a three-wheel motorbike knocked him down. A second three-wheel motorbike, which was

Bonbagnè Palenfo recorded a case where over sixty people died and another sixty were injured due to an explosion. The tragedy occurred on February 21, 2022, in Gongombiro, a village in the Municipality of Gbomblora located about fifteen kilometers from Gaoua. The provisional death toll was sixty, according to information from Bafujii Infos.[17] All the miners had to move to the town of Gaoua that day. The culprits of this tragedy were eventually arrested and prosecuted. When the judge asked the families of the victims to claim compensation, all of them refused.[18] The culprits apologized to the family members and prayed for the souls of the victims and speedy recovery for the injured.

Connection between Terrorism and Gold Mining

The historical trajectory of Burkina Faso changed in 2015. This new trajectory has been most painful because human life has been secularized and undervalued in the country. Currently the entire country is painted as a dangerous zone in West Africa because of terrorist attacks.[19] According to Harouna Bambara, research shows that artisanal gold miners not only fund terrorists, but these sites are also used to recruit young people into terrorism, including children.[20] Even though child labor is strictly prohibited by the Mining Code, the Burkina Faso administration is unable to control

---

following the first one, ran over his leg and broke it into pieces. The money he got for the gold was not enough to take care of the hospital bills. The same adopted father, whom he literally insulted, had to step in to take care of the bills. This is a vivid case of the greedy pursuit after gold that is not really benefiting the population, as the younger generation thinks. This young man will end up homebound and be a burden for his family all his life if he is not brave enough to accept his handicap. He will also always feel guilty for insulting his father's brother, the man who raised him, because of gold.

17 This number reached sixty-three in the end as some of the injured people also lost their lives.

18 Sié Gildas Nazaire Palenfo, "Procès drame du site d'or de Gongonbiro: Les réquisitions du substitut du procureur Seydou Ouèdraogo du TGI de Gaoua" [Trial drama of the gold site of Gongonbiro: The requisitions of the deputy prosecutor Seydou Ouèdraogo of the TGI of Gaoua], *Bafujii Infos*, Apr. 6, 2022, https://bafujiinfos.com/proces-drame-du-site-dor-de-gongonbiro-les-requisitions-du-substitut-du-procureur-seydou-ouedraogo-du-tgi-de-gaoua/.

19 There have been many investigations into how these terrorists are funded. This chapter is not about the terrorist attacks in the country. However, I cannot avoid talking about it briefly here since terrorism arises as one of the consequences connected to gold mining in the country.

20 "L'orpaillage: sous emprise terroriste" [Gold panning: Under terrorist influence], *L'économiste du Faso*, Dec. 28, 2022, https://www.leconomistedufaso.com/2022/12/28/lorpaillage-sous-emprise-terroriste/. This recruitment of children threatens education and the fulfilment of UN Sustainable Development Goal 4, which is to ensure that everyone has quality and decent education by 2030.

the situation.[21] I met children on one of my visits to a mining site in Djikando, a village two kilometers from Gaoua town. I proceeded to visit the primary school in the village and the headmaster indicated the number of pupils in the school had dropped from seventy to forty due the proximity of the mining site to the school.[22]

Apart from funding, Bambara notes that "mining sites are used for other purposes by terrorists—as places to hide their weapons, supply chemicals, and manufacture improvised explosive devices."[23] This claim is warranted, given the death of over sixty people in one day (the calamity I mentioned above) was because some hidden explosive devices caught fire at that particular mining site.[24] This indicates that there are serious issues connected to artisanal mining in the country that call for serious attention from the authorities.

The Economic Impact on Local Communities

Mining contributed CFAF 182.2 billion to the national economy in 2008. According to Sangaré, Burkina Faso is also fourth in terms of gold production in Africa.[25] However, it is obvious that the money gained cannot repair the environmental damage caused by both industrial and traditional mining in the country.[26] The local populations experience all sorts of negative consequences directly linked with especially traditional mining, as mentioned above and in an earlier publication.[27]

Another difficulty is that some of the counties suffer before the miners contribute to the local coffers. For Sié Jean de la Croix Poda, mayor of Kampti, the mining in the area does not provide much benefit for the development of the community.[28] Sangaré also raised the issue of little

21 "L'orpaillage: sous emprise terroriste" [Gold panning: Under terrorist influence].

22 Massofa Kambou, interview by author, Djikando, Gaoua, Burkina Faso, Apr. 20, 2017. You can also find details in Dah, "Desacralisation of Gold," 200-201.

23 "L'orpaillage: sous emprise terroriste" [Gold panning: Under terrorist influence].

24 Note that I am not saying that the person who hid the explosives was a terrorist.

25 Hamed Nanema, "Sud-ouest du Burkina [South-West Burkina Faso].

26 Gountiéni Lankoandé et al., "Evaluation Economique de L'environnement et des Ressources Naturelles au Burkina Faso: Analyse Economico-Environnementale au Niveau National [Economic assessment of the environment and natural resources in Burkina Faso: Economic-Environmental analysis at the national level] (Conseil National pour l'Environnement et le Développement Durable: Ouagadougou, 2011), https://www.researchgate.net/publication/306429184, accessed 31-12-2022.

27 Dah, "Desacralisation of Gold," 194–201.

28 Bombagnè Palenfo, "Kampti: 'L'orpaillage n'apporte rien à la commune' dixit le maire Jean de la Croix Pooda" [Kampti: "Gold panning brings nothing to the municipality" says Mayor Jean de la Croix Pooda], *Bafujii Infos*, Nov. 29, 2021, https://bafujiinfos.com/kampti-lorpaillage-napporte-rien-a-la-commune-dixit-le-maire-jean-de-la-croix-pooda/.

benefit to the local population. Thus, he argues that the policies governing the sector should be enforced and state officials should be present at the sites and take appropriate measures to ensure communities benefit from gold panning at the local level.[29]

Connection between Humans and the Environment

Demystifying gold, therefore, has serious consequences for humanity because of the interdependence between human beings and other than-human creation. The different accounts about the current situation related to gold mining in the Southwest of Burkina Faso show that there is a connection between human beings and their environment. This undeniable fact is often expressed traditionally through taboos. Taboos are "moral rules that regulate human behavior, especially as it impacts negatively on the environment."[30] In other words, taboos are established to regulate society for its well-being in its own ecosystem. The exploration of the violation of the sacred rule about gold in Lobi land shows that there is a connection between the Lobi and their environment, which they depend on for living, and thus they have the responsibility to protect and care for it.

In addition to the different calamities mentioned above, climate change is affecting the area and thus contributing to global warming. There is no area in the country where the heat is controllable, including the Southwest, which once was one of the coolest areas. Many trees have been cut down and water bodies are polluted. Although it still rains in the area, sometimes its distribution causes more harm than good for farmers.

Christian Mission: The Great Commission and Structural Evil

One can define Christian mission as "the teaching of Christianity" or "the work of teaching people about Christianity, especially in a foreign country."[31] I see Christian mission as every Christian contributing to the spread of the holistic gospel. Thus, Christian mission in Lobi land concerns the indigenous Christian community as well as the foreign missionaries.

---

29 Hamed Nanema, "Sud-ouest du Burkina [South-West Burkina Faso].

30 M. Clemence and V. Chimininge, "Totem, Taboos and Sacred Places: An Analysis of Karanga People's Environmental Conservation and Management Practice," *International Journal of Humanities and Social Science Invention* 4 (2015): 9.

31 A. S. Hornby, *Oxford Advanced Learner's Dictionary*, 6th ed., ed. S. Wehmeier and M. Ashby (Oxford: Oxford Univ. Press, 2000), 816. (Although I do not reject the definition that mission is about people going to a foreign country to teach about Christianity, in this chapter I consider Christian mission as both being taught by foreign missionaries as well as local missionaries [Christians] reaching out to people).

Once we talk about Christian mission we are talking about the Great Commission, the command that Jesus gave to his disciples in the book of Matthew. Eddie Arthur states:

> The command in Matthew 28 is to make disciples of all nations. It is not to preach to all nations; it is not to establish churches in all nations or to translate the Scriptures into every language that needs it. Making disciples is a continuous job. No one is ever fully a disciple, and even when the Gospel is well established in a country it doesn't mean that the nation is full of disciples.[32]

This implies that the words of Jesus in Matthew 28 are not only about preaching and planting churches, but they are also about continual mentoring of people to reflect the image of God in various geographical locations. As Arthur further argues, "the Great Commission is not a one-off task that can one day be checked off the church's to-do list."[33] Jonathan Williams sees the Great Commission as something that started in the garden of Eden with Adam and all biblical leaders who came after him.[34] Although he focuses more on multiplying and filling the earth, God's injunction in Genesis 2:15 cannot be limited to this aspect only. In our current situation, the preservation of the earth is at stake and calls for special attention in Christian mission.[35]

One major issue is the lack of proper education and training of the miners, which leads to all sorts of negative activities that put the entire country in danger. Sangaré raises these concerns and thinks that gold mining could contribute to local community development if the activity was properly supervised. He blames the government for their inadequate supervision of artisanal mining sites and points out that the lack of training is responsible for all the other misconducts in the region, as he opines that the artisanal mining sites look like jungles because of lack of government intervention.[36] This is an indication that failure of leadership is responsible for the decay in the area, to the point of desecration of the land and human life in general. These abnormal practices can be classified as structural evils because nobody seems to be concerned about them anymore.

---

32 Eddie Arthur, *The Great Commission*, 4, accessed Dec. 26, 2022, https://www.academia.edu/1998918/The_Great_Commission.

33 Arthur, 4.

34 Jonathan Williams, *The Glory of the Great Commission* (San Antonio, TX: WGS Ministries, 2017), 7-11.

35 We cannot do an exegesis of Genesis 2:15 here due to word limit.

36 Hamed Nanema, "Sud-ouest du Burkina [South-West Burkina Faso].

According to Cynthia D. Moe-Lobeda, structural evil consists of "chains that bind us into systemic exploitation of others and of the earth,"[37] which are "intricate and cleverly hidden."[38] She further opines that these forces are intricate webs of interrelated power arrangements, ideologies, values, practices, policies, and ways of perceiving reality that span generations and have unintended snowballing consequences.[39] She further argues that "structural evil may be beyond the power of individuals to counter, it is composed of power arrangements and other factors that are humanly constructed."[40] In other words, it is the evil practices that are accepted as normal due to the lack of proper decisions from leadership. Far from dictating rules to the church in Burkina Faso, I think it is time to think about how one does mission in the country. It is important to develop strategies that can touch the people holistically (spiritually, socially, physically, and so on) to bring about a transformation that contributes to the well-being of people in their socioreligious environment for better care of creation in general.

Conclusion

Sangaré says, "It is a pity that gold, which has a mystical character for the Lobi, it is deplorable that the earth, which represents a status of divinity, are considered today as vulgar commodities."[41] Even though traditional mining in Burkina Faso contributes to the economic development of the country, the negative consequences of the activity are beyond measure. The life of both current and future generations is endangered because of the unsustainability of artisanal gold mining. Traditional norms and values are no longer respected by the younger generation, which is obsessed with economic gain. The entire governmental and societal structure seems to have accepted that it is powerless in this situation and so the leadership is not taking any decisive action to correct the situation for the well-being of both current and future generations. This is an alert to the church in the area that we need to rethink what is preached from the pulpit and what we teach in our Bible colleges because tradition seems to have better guidelines for the protection of human beings and the environment, even though this was achieved through taboos. The main Christian churches and denominations in the Southwest

---

37 Cynthia D. Moe-Lobeda, *Resisting Structural Evil; Love as Ecological-Economic Vocation* (Minneapolis: Fortress Press, 2013), 2.

38 Moe-Lobeda, 2.

39 Moe-Lobeda, 2.

40 Moe-Lobeda, 3.

41 Hamed Nanema, "Sud-ouest du Burkina [South-West Burkina Faso].

of Burkina Faso should follow the example of the Presbyterian Church of Ghana by educating both church members and students to be aware of care for creation.[42]

Discussion Questions

1. What do you think about the Lobi people's traditional belief about gold?

2. How can we bridge the gap between traditional Lobi beliefs and taboos designed to protect creation and Christian beliefs about creation care?

3. What lessons can we draw from Lobi land for other parts of the world?

42 Ebenezer Yaw Blasu, *African Theocology: Studies in African Religious Creation Care* (Eugene, OR: Wipf and Stock, 2020), 2.

Response

by Jonathan J. Bonk

Everything that happens has happened before;
nothing is new, nothing under the sun.
—Ecclesiastes 2:9, CEV

Dorcas Dah begins her case study by describing the sacralization of gold in traditional Lobi culture, and the attendant restraint with which it was mined. She then shows how this religious circumspection was swept aside by a swelling tide of gold rush opportunists, from foreign mining interests and prospectors to impoverished regional interlopers, including children, hoping for a better life.

Artisanal gold extraction sites in Burkina Faso known to exist in 2017—some 448 in all—have almost certainly increased in number and scale since that tabulation was made. Mining's baleful but entirely predictable results include food scarcity, degradation of fertile land, high rates of injury and death among laborers, often children, and a sharp rise in general lawlessness and terrorism. The destruction of flora and the poisoning of water resources above and below ground compounds the more visible social degeneration and environmental deterioration.

While Dr. Dah's case study focuses on a decimated region of Burkina Faso, what she describes is neither unique nor surprising. The overwhelming of local sensibilities, restraints, and controls by the scale and insatiability of outside entities is an all-too-familiar story across the "developing" world, as it has been throughout the past half-millennium of European migratory settlement and expropriation of the western hemisphere and the continent of Australia.[43] The "civilizing" missions of European colonizers and empire builders were always—though not exclusively—a front for exploitation.

---

43 By 1914, seven European countries "controlled" 90 percent of Africa. Only Liberia and Ethiopia remained independent nations See, for example: Mark Simner, *The Lion and the Dragon: Britain's Opium Wars with China, 1839-1860* (Stroud, Gloucestershire: Fonthill Media, 2019); Adam Hochschild, *King Leopold's Ghost: A Story of Greed, Terrorism, and Heroism in Colonial Africa* (Boston: Houghton Mifflin Harcourt, 1998); Thomas Pakenham, *The Scramble for Africa* (New York. HarperCollins, 1992); William Easterly, *The White Man's Burden: Why the West's Efforts to Aid the Rest Have Done So Much Ill and So Little Good* (New York: Penguin, 2006), and Easterly's more recent *The Tyranny of Experts: Economists, Dictators, and the Forgotten Rights of the Poor* (New York: Basic, 2014); and finally, Siddharth Kara, *Cobalt Red: How the Blood of the Congo Powers our Lives* (New York: St. Martin's Press, 2023). These books make challenging reading for those of us blessed with cell phones, computers, and hybrid or electric vehicles.

The economic extraction systems were designed to permanently benefit powerful business and political entities in distant lands, regardless of local human and environmental costs.[44]

But these insidiously complicated and ultimately ruinous systems become entangled inextricably with what is good and essential for human survival. It is true that a person needs more than food to live; but a person without food is soon dead. And that is what makes the achievement of justice and equity so complicated. As Dr. Dah observes, the evil is *structural* ... built into the very systems from which human beings eke out their existence.

When our Lord commissioned his followers to "go into all the world and make disciples" or "go into all the world and preach the gospel," he did not have in mind the exploitation of the weak, the genocide of civilizations, the expropriation of lands, the dispossession of peoples, or the pillaging of regional and local resources. Those who initially obeyed his "Great Commission" were themselves poor and without political or economic influence. The Good News at that time was not about "civilization" and enculturation to a Western understanding and domination of the world and its peoples. But then came Christendom. Constantine declared Christianity a legitimate religion of the Roman Empire and put clergy on the government payroll with his Edict of Milan in 313 CE. With the Edict of Thessalonica in 380 CE, Emperor Theodosius I made Christianity the empire's only legally permitted religion. Not surprisingly, by 632 CE, state Christianity had spread throughout the Mediterranean basin and much of Europe, including the British Isles, and parts of Asia and Africa.

But it was the violence of Europe's "civilizing" missions from the sixteenth through the twentieth centuries, rationalized by the "doctrine of discovery," that "Christianized" the western hemisphere.[45] Along the way, an estimated sixty to one hundred twenty million indigenous incumbents were exterminated[46] and millions of blacks from Africa were enslaved. It was this bloody process that resulted in Christianity's dominance as a world religion today. The missionary movement from the West—of which

---

44 See Courtney Faal, "The Partition of Africa," Blackpast, Feb. 21, 2009, https://www.blackpast.org/global-african-history/partition-africa/.

45 A series of five hundred-year-old papal decrees used to justify colonization and embedded in United States and international law. These doctrines were religiously grounded in papal bulls authorizing various European powers—especially Portugal and Spain—to subjugate, occupy, and exploit lands inhabited by non-Christians. This included the enslavement of inhabitants and the exploitation of the territory's natural resources.

46 American historian David Stannard (University of Hawaii) estimates that the extermination of Indigenous peoples took the lives of at least one hundred million people. See his *American Holocaust: The Conquest of the New World* (New York: Oxford Univ. Press, 1992).

my parents were a part—would not have been possible without the violent military subjugation of a majority of the planet's inhabitants and their lands. Throughout this genocidal land grab Europeans employed the rationale and the vocabulary of "civilization," more lately evolved into "development."

Although England and France did not cite papal bulls as their justification for exploiting non-Christian territories, they deemed that discovery alone was sufficient to justify the subjugation of pagan peoples. Protestant missions, while frequently addressing the injustices of enslavement and economic exploitation, nevertheless followed on the coat tails of this exploitation and took full advantage of their privileged status as citizens of the colonizing countries. Making disciples came to mean not only converting pagans to the Christian religion, but enculturating survivors into the global economic juggernaut that we now know as market consumerism.[47]

Dorcas Dah presents one example of this structural evil. The difficulty is that *evil* is never *pure* evil. It is inevitably intertwined with good. Gold mining in Burkina Faso provides livelihoods and benefits, however meager, at the grass roots level of children and migrant workers. It is their livelihood—their stake in survival and dreams of a better future. It also becomes entrenched in the larger economic and social infrastructure of the region and the country, not only corrupting officials and various lawbreakers, but providing benefits on an ever-increasing scale to the ascending ladder of operators, managers, and company owners on up to the shareholders in Toronto or New York or London or Seoul, who are too many layers removed to notice anything amiss.

The great conundrum facing all advocates of social, economic, and climate shalom is the brief life cycle of a human being's mortality, with its relentless need to feed, protect, and rest the body at every stage along its life journey, from infancy through terminal old age. No human life can be put on pause until laws change and justice prevails, infrastructure develops, schools emerge, and children no longer have to work to sustain their own lives. In the meanwhile, food must be eaten, clothing must be worn, and shelter must be found ... even if the means to these basic ends require that a child tend cattle or sheep, work in an artisanal mine, or toil in a sweatshop sewing designer jeans for teenagers in New York or Seoul.

---

47 By 1925, the British Empire controlled 25 percent of the world's population and land area, and dominated the seas. Christian missionaries from the West accepted this as providential, even though they had serious scruples about the brutality and unfairness of genocidal wars and evil treaties and enforced trade. The two aptly named "Opium Wars"—the first in 1839-42 and the second in 1856-60 involving France as well as Britain—forced China to purchase opium from British merchants in the name of free trade, and permitted Christian missionaries to evangelize in China's interior without being fully subject to Chinese laws.

Artisanal mining in Burkina Faso is just one tiny, ulcerous pustule, a symptom of the massive tumor inextricably embedded within the lungs of our socioeconomic world. This deadly parasite cannot be removed without killing the patient. None of us, however sincere our Christian faith, is unaffected. We share these quandaries: How is one to live morally within economic and social structures that are suffused with evil? What does it mean to be followers of Jesus who are among the prime beneficiaries of that evil? These are difficult questions, and our responses and proffers of know-how must always be mindful of our own fated complicity.

What can we do as missionaries and church leaders from the wealthiest countries in the world? Given the intractability of structural evil, where does the gospel of hope fit in, and what are our roles in its proclamation? Despite our good intentions as church and mission leaders from Korea, England, Canada, Australia, New Zealand, and the United States, it is difficult to imagine any credible resolution coming from men and women like us, citizens of cultures that lead the world in the production, marketing, and consumption of sophisticated goods that require vast quantities of these minerals.

The traditional Lobi were right, and so is our gospel: gold has the power to swallow souls (Mark 8:36).

Section D

Responses to Climate Change and Its Effects, Historical and Current

CHAPTER 14

Partnering with God to Restore Creation
A Story of Hope

by Tony Rinaudo

Testimony of God's Call and Answered Prayers

Formative Years

Growing up in the Ovens Valley in South East Australia, I was surrounded by the beauty of God's creation. My playgrounds were the mountain streams, fertile farms, and rolling hills covered with eucalyptus trees. With this backdrop, three things shaped the person I am today.

The first was disregard for and destruction of creation was the norm. There was widespread clearing of the forests I loved. Pesticides sprayed on crops poisoned the streams that I—and many others—drank from, swam in, and fished from. The destruction was bad enough, but the fact that this behavior in the eyes of most adults was "normal" and unquestioned disturbed me deeply.

The second influence was my strong interest in other countries and world events. As a child I soon learned that other children who happened to be born elsewhere were going to bed hungry, while our farmers used good land to grow tobacco. To me, this was unjust. Society's priorities—putting money and progress above the needs of people and the environment—seemed misplaced.

The third thing that impacted me was my mother's strong faith and teachings from God's word. I learned that there are more important things to life than money (Matt. 6:25–34), that we have a duty of care for those less fortunate than ourselves (Matt. 25:31–46), and that we are to be good stewards of creation (Gen.1:26–28; 2:15; Rev. 11:18).

Angry at the way things were and frustrated at my powerlessness to change anything, I did the one thing I could do—I prayed a child's prayer simply asking God to use me somehow, somewhere to make a difference.

I went on to study agriculture at university but was often plagued by doubts. Who did I think I was? What difference did this country boy think he would make in the world? But God's word gave me a great sense of peace and assurance: "For we are God's handiwork, created in Christ Jesus to do good works, which God prepared in advance for us to do" (Eph. 2:10). Hadn't God already prepared good works for me to do? I did not know all the hows, whats, whens, and wheres of the future, but God did, and that was sufficient.

At university I met my wife to be, Liz Fearon, who had her own sense of call to be a missionary in Africa. At that time, we learned about the evangelical missionary organization, Serving in Mission (SIM). SIM has a holistic approach to ministry, serving God and people through ministering to both spiritual and physical needs.

Environmental Degradation and Poverty

After studying Bible and Missions, we were accepted by SIM for service in Niger Republic, an extremely poor country suffering from desertification due to large-scale deforestation and climate change. Arriving in Niger in 1981, I was confronted by a landscape at the brink of ecological collapse, one which was barely able to support life. The land had undergone massive deforestation. Soil fertility was depleted, and people were struggling to survive due to increased frequency and severity of drought in an already harsh environment. The people were poor and regularly experienced hunger. It was common for men to leave home for at least part of the year to supplement their incomes. The scale of environmental destruction was so vast, the conditions so harsh, and the reluctance of the people to change so great, that I wondered whether it would be possible to have any significant impact at all.

Futile Efforts at Restoration

Even so, I reasoned that if deforestation was one of the root causes of these problems, then reforestation should go a long way towards solving them. I threw all my energy into the task—reading reforestation documents, consulting experts, and experimenting with different methods and species. Nothing worked in an economically viable or sustainable way. Eighty percent of the trees planted died, and for the most part, the people I was trying to help weren't interested. Many called me the crazy white farmer!

After two and a half years of striving, I felt like a failure and that my efforts were a waste of time and money. I was so discouraged that it would have been very easy to give up and go home. However, I believed that God doesn't make mistakes. I remembered my childhood prayer and all the confirmations I'd received along my spiritual journey and reasoned that there must be a solution.

A God Who Renews the Earth

Niger appeared to reflect the exact opposite of the biblical picture of God's provision and bounty (Ps. 65:9–13). I wondered if God had forgotten Niger. "His divine power has granted to us all things that pertain to life and godliness, through the knowledge of him who called us to his own glory and excellence" (2 Pet. 1:3, RSV). Where was the provision of everything we needed for life (our physical needs) and godliness?

The land seemed to be cursed and our efforts were regularly destroyed by a variable assortment of woes—drought, windstorms, insect attacks, and the people themselves. At times I wondered if I needed to simply accept the status quo until Jesus returned. It seemed that due to the Fall, we were condemned to perpetual suffering, to a life of toil and misery, rising temperatures, increased drought, and severe storms.

The consequences of sin are real. Life is hard and fraught with illness, toil, and death. But I believe God is still a God of love and compassion, and even though the earth is under a curse, he still reaches out to us and wishes to bless us. Despite our sin, God is merciful. "He does not treat us as our sins deserve or repay us according to our iniquities" (Ps. 103:10). With the psalmist, I believe "I will see the goodness of the LORD in the land of the living." (Ps. 27:13). That is, I would not have to wait until Jesus returns to see God's blessing in the here and now.

In my devotions I read, "When you send your Spirit, they are created, and you renew the face of the ground" (Ps. 104:30). While the idea of God's Spirit renewing the earth caught my attention, the significance didn't dawn on me till later that day. Driving through a barren landscape, my heart was crying out that God would give me the wisdom and ability to restore even this moonscape. I stopped the vehicle on a barren, compacted area that could have served as car park. I wondered if this land could ever be restored. Then, looking down at my feet I saw a tiny germinating plant pushing through a crack in the dry, hard ground and immediately recalled the morning's reading. I realized that God is not only in the business of saving lost souls and healing broken humanity. God is also in the business of renewing and healing his broken creation. With this revelation, I felt a great burden lift— the task of restoring the earth was not my burden alone. This was God's work and I could go to him for guidance, help, and strength.

Not long after this, I was driving a pickup truck and trailer loaded with tree seedlings for the villagers. Knowing full well most trees would die and that the people didn't care, I was feeling particularly down. I stopped and reduced the air pressure in the tires to prevent getting bogged down in the deep sand. Looking out over the barren landscape it seemed hopeless—I wondered how many years, how many million dollars, how many hundreds of staff it would take to make any meaningful impact. Not having an answer, I turned to God in prayer, asking him to forgive us for destroying the gift of his creation, as a consequence of which people were now hungry, poor, and fearful for the future. I reminded God that he still loved us and asked him to open my eyes, show me what to do, help me.

Looking across the landscape again, a seemingly useless bush caught my attention, and I walked over to take a closer look. As soon as I saw the shape of the leaves, I realized that it wasn't a bush at all. It was a tree that had been cut down and was resprouting from the living stump. I knew that there were millions of such "bushes" in the landscape and now realized they constituted a vast underground forest just waiting to regrow. In that instant everything changed. I was no longer fighting the Sahara Desert; I didn't need a miracle species of tree that could withstand the goats and cutting and drought—everything I needed was literally at my feet—an "underground forest." My approach shifted from being primarily technical (reverse deforestation with tree planting) to tackling spiritual, social, and cultural norms. I reasoned that if peoples' false beliefs about the value of trees on their land led to negative attitudes and destructive practices that brought the landscape to the point where it could barely support life, then the real battle was primarily against false beliefs. I knew that if I could convince people that it was in their best interest to work with creation instead of destroying it and that they could build a better future for themselves and their children, restoration would be relatively easy. After all, everything needed for reforestation was literally at their feet!

The technique of growing trees from living stumps and self-sown seed is today called Farmer Managed Natural Regeneration (FMNR).[1] From 1984, FMNR spread largely from farmer to farmer at an estimated rate of 250 thousand hectares per year for the next twenty years. On-farm tree density increased from four trees per hectare to forty, resulting in some 200 million trees restored across five million hectares of degraded land without planting a single tree.[2] Windspeeds, temperatures, and evaporation rates decreased.

1 Tony Rinaudo, "FMNR Frequently Asked Questions with Tony Rinaudo," The Climate Action and Resilience Team, World Vision Australia, accessed Jan. 9, 2023, https://fmnrhub.com.au/frequently-asked-questions/#.Y7tdS3YzZRY.

2 Tony Rinaudo et al., "Farmer Managed Natural Regeneration: Community Driven, Low Cost and Scalable Reforestation Approach for Climate Change Mitigation and Adaptation," abstract, in *Handbook of Climate Change Management*, ed. W. L. Filho, J. Luetz, and D. Ayal (Cham, Switzerland: Springer, 2021), https://link.springer.com/referenceworkentry/10.1007%2F978-3-030-22759-3_281-1.

Soil fertility increased. As the trees grew, habitats for beneficial predators, such as insect eating birds, lizards, and spiders were created, bringing back greater balance in nature and reducing crop damage from insect pests. Because of improved soil fertility and moisture levels, and a more favorable microclimate, crop yields increased, and in time farmers were able to grow and raise more and different types of crops and livestock. With greater diversity came greater resilience to climatic shocks. More children were able to attend school. The burden on women was reduced as firewood could now be found closer to home.

It is estimated that gross incomes in the immediate project area increased by $1,000 per household each year.[3] Extrapolating this added income from FMNR to the entire five million hectares implies aggregate income benefits of $900 million per year,[4] benefiting approximately nine hundred thousand households or four and a half million people. Observations backed by subsequent research showed that increase in millet yields ranged from 49 to 153 percent. Through FMNR Nigerien farmers were producing five hundred thousand more tons of cereal per year than in the 1970s and 1980s. As a result, two and a half million people are now more food secure.[5]

Indeed, God had not forgotten Niger. He has provided all that is needed for the physical life of its inhabitants. What was missing was a culture of caring for God's creation.

Reflection: Why Care?

What was going through God's and the angels' minds at the time of creation? The "I" in Proverbs 8:30 is wisdom talking in first person, where wisdom is a type or prefigurement of Christ. In effect, Jesus was delighting in mankind and rejoicing in his creation (Prov. 8:30–31). God tells Job that as the earth's foundations were being laid, "the morning stars sang together and all the

---

3 C. Pye-Smith, *The Quiet Revolution: How Niger's Farmers are Re-greening the Parklands of the Sahel*, ICRAF Trees for Change, no. 12 (Nairobi: World Agroforestry Centre, 2013), 20.

4 J. Sendzimir, C. P. Reij, and P. Magnuszewski, "Rebuilding Resilience in the Sahel: Regreening in the Maradi and Zinder Regions of Niger," *Ecology and Society* 16, no. 3 (2011): 1, http://www.ecologyandsociety.org/vol16/iss3/art1/.

5 C. Reij, G. Tappan, and M. Smale, "Agroenvironmental Transformation in the Sahel: Another Kind of 'Green Revolution,'" IFPRI Discussion Paper 00914 (Washington, DC: International Food Policy Research Institute, 2009), 18; C. Reij, G. Tappan, and M. Smale, "Re-Greening the Sahel: Farmer-Led Innovation in Burkina Faso and Niger," in *Millions Fed: Proven Successes in Agricultural Development*, ed. David J. Spielman and Rajul Pandya-Lorch (Washington, DC: International Food Policy Research Institute, 2009), 56; and Babou Ndour, Alioune Sarr, and Abdou Mbaye, "Projets BEYSATOL/SFLEI, Rapport d'Activités," Institut Sénégalais de Recherches Agricoles Centre National de Recherches Agronomiques (ISRA) (unpublished report, 2010).

angels shouted for joy" (Job 38:7). When you consider that there are "ten thousand times ten thousand" angels (Rev. 5:11), that is, a numberless host, the sound must have been deafening. Clearly, the response in heaven to God's act of creation was not to hold a sedate garden tea party. The picture painted here is more in alignment with the unbridled joy of the end of football season, a back slapping and foot stomping all-out victory celebration.

How do God and the angels feel when they look at the state of creation today and see how humanity is trashing it? What is going through their minds? I certainly don't think I would hear any angels shouting for joy! And, where are the people of God in all this? Not only are we all too often silent about the deliberate and both random and systematic destruction of God's wonderful creation, for most of us our lifestyle, our profligate waste and toxic pollution, and our investments often support its destruction. Why is it so rare to hear words of righteous anger at the destruction of God's creation coming from our pulpits?

Why should Christians care for God's creation? "Is the health of birds, plants, soil, watersheds, forests, air and the earth's atmosphere too worldly or mundane to merit the attention of faithful disciples? For John Stott, active care for the Earth and all its inhabitants is not a special domain for some believers with an interest in nature, it is integral to the normal life of Christian discipleship. Creation care matters because 'God intends ... our care of the creation to reflect our love for the Creator.'"[6]

Firstly, Christians should care for creation because creation belongs to God and is important to him. The 2010 Lausanne Congress on World Evangelization report, The Cape Town Commitment, contains this statement: "'The earth is the Lord's and everything in it.' The earth is the property of the God we claim to love and obey. We care for the earth, most simply, because it belongs to the one whom we call Lord."[7]

That creation is important to God is symbolically suggested in Genesis 1 and 2. The term "God said" occurs nine times. "And God said, 'Let there be light'" (Gen. 1:3); "and God said, "'Let there be a vault between the waters to separate water from water'" (Gen. 1:6), and so on. Curiously, Genesis 2:8 says, "And the LORD God planted a garden in Eden" (RSV). Why would the God who has the power to speak things into being bother to plant a garden? What is the significance? When you plant a garden it involves all

---

6 John Stott, *The Radical Disciple: Some Neglected Aspects of Our Calling* (Downers Grove, IL: IVP, 2010), 59, quoted in R. J. Berry with L. S. Meitzner Yoder, *John Stott on Creation Care* (London: IVP, 2021), 1.

7 "The Cape Town Commitment," Lausanne Movement, accessed Jan. 20, 2023, https://lausanne.org/content/ctc/ctcommitment.

of yourself. You develop a very special relationship with the soil, plants, and animals in your garden. You give and you receive in return. You do not plant a garden and look after it if you don't care about gardens. Those who don't care garden begrudgingly, pay someone else to do it, or simply buy their vegetables at the store. This passage suggests to me that if God himself, creator of heaven and earth, thought it important enough to plant a garden, we as his followers at the very least should value and care for his creation—a creation that, post-Fall, is in grave danger of being destroyed unless humans intervene. John Stott writes, "Christian people should surely have been in the vanguard of the movement for environmental responsibility, because of our doctrines of creation and stewardship. Did God make the world? Does he sustain it? Has he committed its resources to our care? His personal concern for his own creation should be sufficient to inspire us to be equally concerned."[8] Further, in a forward to *The Care of Creation*, Stott writes that "our care of creation will reflect our love of the creator."[9]

Secondly, knowing that environmental destruction leads to human suffering, we care for creation as an act of love towards our neighbor, and incidentally, towards ourselves since we are not immune to the impacts of environmental destruction. With the knowledge that through environmental restoration we can reduce hunger, lift people out of poverty, and reduce the risks of environmental disasters, surely it is imperative that Christians be at the forefront of environmental protection and restorative action. Such actions, depending on the context, increase availability and quality of food and water, reduce the likelihood and impact of severe storms, landslides, flood, and drought, and both mitigate against and help people adapt to climate change. People living in proximity to healthy, functioning ecosystems tend to have more livelihood options and are more resilient to climatic shocks and natural disasters. In this light, loving our neighbor as ourselves is inseparable from caring for creation.

Thirdly, in that God deemed all that he made was very good (Gen. 1:31), we care for creation because it is intrinsically good. Creation has value in its own right, apart from economic or functional value. The sheer beauty, intricacy, variety, interconnectedness, and wonder of creation is reason enough to care for it.

Fourthly, and this may be contentious, the earth, albeit a renewed earth, will be our home for eternity. "A balanced biblical understanding recognizes

---

8 P. Harris, *Under the Bright Wings* (London: Hodder and Stoughton, 1993), 181–82.

9 R. J. Berry, ed., *The Care of Creation. Focusing Concern and Action* (Leicester: IVP, 2000), 8–9.

that God's judgment of all that is fallen, evil and sinful will mean a radical cleansing of the whole creation, but that God's saving love towards all he has made will eventually lead to the remaking, reshaping and renewal of creation."[10] Bookless continues, "the 'new heavens and new earth' referred to by Peter (2 Pet. 3:13) or the book of Revelation (Rev. 21:1) do not necessarily imply that the current universe is thrown on the scrap heap. Rather, they speak of the renewal of creation. Just as God is into recycling broken, spoiled, messed-up people, and making them into new creations in Christ, so this whole damaged and groaning creation will be made new again."[11] Just as we care for and maintain our own homes, surely we should take the same level of care for the only planet we know of where life is possible?

Epilogue

My first FMNR-related visit to Talensi, Upper East Region of Ghana, was in 2009. As in Niger decades earlier, deforestation and climate change were taking their toll. Women were walking up to four hours to collect firewood. The lack of fodder resulted in farmers walking their cattle to distant hills where they were susceptible to theft. Crops were often destroyed, alternately by flood or drought. Winds became strong enough to remove hut roofs. Children weren't in school, and hunger stalked the land. Communities were contemplating abandoning their land for good. After an introductory workshop, communities agreed to trial FMNR on communal land.

I returned two years later to witness the celebrations over what had been achieved. Through adoption of FMNR, women now had fuelwood close at hand, livestock were thriving with plenty of fodder within a short walking distance, the trees were already ameliorating the impacts of both too much and too little rain, wind speeds had dropped, children were back in school, and food production had increased. During the ceremony, the old chief stood and declared that "this gift of FMNR is from the almighty God and therefore, wherever you bring it you bring life and joy." Over the years I've had the privilege of visiting many communities that have transformed their land and their lives. While the regreened landscapes are impressive, the biggest change I see is the restoration of hope in the people themselves. Invariably there is a spontaneous outburst of joy expressed in song, dancing, and clapping. Interestingly, this is very similar to the responses in heaven to the act of creation! Could it be that by partaking in creation stewardship and restoration, we experience a foretaste of heaven on earth?

---

10 D. Bookless, *Planet Wise: Dare to Care for God's World* (Nottingham: IVP, 2008), 146.

11 Bookless, 80.

Discussion Questions

1. What is the individual Christian's responsibility regarding creation care?

2. Does the church give enough attention to creation care in its teaching?

3. Is caring for creation a valid expression of showing our love for God and for our neighbor?

Response

by Gihong Park

> And though a tenth remain in it, it will be burned again,
> like a terebinth or an oak, whose stump remains when it is felled.
> The holy seed is its stump.
> —Isaiah 6:13, ESV

Burned Again

"It was hopeless, and I [Tony] was on the verge of going home."[12] After two and a half years of mounting frustrations, the young missionary of twenty-three years was ready to give up. Upon arrival in Niger Republic in 1981, which was suffering from a series of droughts, Tony inherited a small reforestation project serving God and the Niger people. But most of the trees he planted died due to drought, sandstorms, animals, and termites. The "common knowledge" of farmers about reforestation, however, was a bigger cause of the failures because they believed that trees and crops are incompatible—trees shading crops resulted in lower yields. Furthermore, out of desperation people would cut down even the last trees to sell the firewood to buy food. Despite throwing all his energy into the project, such as reading reforestation documents, consulting experts, and experimenting with different methods and species, his efforts made no significant difference. To many Niger farmers, Tony was the "mad white farmer" and his ideas were just silly. At a particularly low point when the hopelessness of the situation weighed heavily on Tony, he stopped driving and looked over the barren landscapes and asked God "to forgive us for destroying the gift of his beautiful creation" and "to open my eyes and to show me what to do."[13]

The Stump Remains

Looking across the seemingly "useless bushes" on the barren landscape again, Tony realized that they were not bushes at all but resprouting trees from the remaining stumps. There was hope—one which had never registered its significance before—"a vast underground forest" existed beneath the surface of the seemingly hopeless land and had been waiting to regrow. It was the moment of discovering that reforestation was no longer

---

12 Johannes Dieterich, ed., *Tony Rinaudo: The Forest-Maker* (Zurich: Rüffer & Rub, 2018), 59.

13 Tony Rinaudo, *The Forest Underground: Hope for a Planet in Crisis* (Forest Hill, Victoria: ISCAST, 2021), 105.

the reverse of deforestation, that is, reforestation would not occur by tree planting with enough funds, staff, and time, but by convincing people to battle with their false beliefs and to work with God's creation for themselves and their children.

In fact, God leaves a stump in times of tribulation. The remaining stumps could refer to the Bible's idiomatic use of "remnant" (e.g., Isa. 10:20–23; 11:11). The Hebrew root *sh'r* (√ שָׁאַר) literally means "remnant," "remained," or "left." Noah was the first to be called a remnant throughout the flood (Gen. 7:23); God sent Joseph to preserve a remnant "to save your lives by a great deliverance" (Gen. 45:7); Paul also indicated that a remnant is God's gracious choice (Rom. 11:5); and Elijah misunderstood that he alone was left (1 Kgs. 19:14), when God had reserved seven thousand, representative of a faithful remnant (1 Kgs. 19:18). Thus, the remaining stump is God's hidden plan and purpose for restoration, which becomes a hope and blessing to the earth.

The Holy Seed

The holy seed is its stump for reforestation. Like the seemingly useless stone that the builders, even the specialists, rejected, the stump has become the cornerstone, and this is God's doing. So Tony, when he understood the idea of God's Spirit renewing the earth (Ps. 104:30), realized all that he needed for reforestation was literally at his feet and that actually he was surrounded by an underground forest. In fact, resprouting trees have the capacity for rapid regrowth because the stump contains a large store of starch, with access to soil nutrients and water by a mature root that has already adapted to local conditions. Using the holy seed, a method of revegetation developed by Roland Bunch[14] was applied by selecting and pruning the strongest stems and culling surplus stems while they are growing, with a near 100 percent survival rate. This technique, called Farmer Managed Natural Regeneration (FMNR), was cheaper, easier, and more successful than transplanting seedlings, which had only a 20 percent survival rate. FMNR resulted in a tenfold increase in tree density for two decades, compared to the average of four trees per hectare in the early 1980s in Niger Republic.[15] The expression "holy seed" (zera‘ qōdhesh/זֶרַע קֹדֶשׁ) is close to the meaning of "blessed seed," which characterizes hope for the survival of God's people in the holy

---

14 Center for Regenerative Agriculture and Resilient Systems, "Roland Bunch," California State University, Chico, https://www.csuchico.edu/regenerativeagriculture/international-research/roland-bunch.shtml.

15 Rinaudo, *The Forest Underground*, 9.

remnant.[16] By God's gracious choice, the seed was separated from other seeds. Likewise, FMNR selects and prunes chosen stems for a hopeful future. As expressed in Tony's subtitle, "A Story of Hope," there is hope in partnership with God to restore creation, and there is restoration of hope in the people.

+1.5 Degrees Celsius

The IPCC emphasizes that limiting the global temperature rise to 1.5 degrees Celsius is the Maginot Line to avoid the tipping point of 2 degrees Celsius, to protect the natural and human systems.[17] Some climate scientists, however, warn that at the current rate of global warming there is already a 50 percent chance that the global temperature will rise by 1.5 degrees Celsius within the next five years.[18] In this context, the term "global heating" has been used more in recent years because the expression "global warming" does not present a strong-enough warning of the impending calamity of climate change. Ironically the world's overconsuming rich are causing the most negative impacts, yet the world's poorest along with many of its creatures are paying the highest price.

Moreover, informed ecosystem management under future climate conditions will require understanding of both terrestrial and marine ecosystems. My recent studies have considered how phytoplankton populations have the potential to adapt rapidly in response to climate change due to their short generation times and large population sizes. Like phytoplankton, we found zooplankton populations also show rapid but limited adaptation to ocean warming and acidification conditions.[19] The fact that even these small plankton are affected means that all ecosystems are exposed to the threat of climate-related challenges, waiting with eager longing for the revealing of the sons of God, the remnant, who responsibly live out their faith in Christ (Rom. 8:19).

---

16 Grzegorz Szamocki, "'Holy Seed' in Isaiah 6:13: Echo of an Exclusive Concept of Israel's Identity," *Verbum Vitae* 40, no. 4 (2022): 1055, https://doi.org/10.31743/vv.14605.

17 Ove Hoegh-Guldberg, Daniela Jacob, Michael Taylor et al., "Impacts of 1.5°C of Global Warming on Natural and Human Systems," in *Global Warming of 1.5°C: IPCC Special Report on Impacts of Global Warming of 1.5°C above Pre-industrial Levels in Context of Strengthening Response to Climate Change, Sustainable Development, and Efforts to Eradicate Poverty*, ed. Valérie Masson-Delmotte et al. (Cambridge: Cambridge Univ. Press, 2022), 177-231, https://doi.org/10.1017/9781009157940.005.

18 M. T. Dvorak et al., "Estimating the Timing of Geophysical Commitment to 1.5 and 2.0°C of Global Warming," *Nature Climate Change* 12, no. 6 (2022): 547, https://doi.org/10.1038/s41558-022-01372-y.

19 Hans G. Dam, Gihong Park et al., "Rapid, but Limited, Zooplankton Adaptation to Simultaneous Warming and Acidification," *Nature Climate Change* 11 (2021): 780-86, https://doi.org/10.1038/s41558-021-01131-5.

Why Care?

Through environmental and human calamities, such as COVID-19, many people have felt that the tipping point has already come, and they will not be able to live normal lives as before. Similarly, a series of devastating droughts and famine in the 1980s must have felt like a tipping point. Yet when the Niger people were introduced to the concept of FMNR, many farmers were surprised that their crops grew better among the trees, which was the opposite of what they expected based on their common knowledge. In consequence, FMNR went viral from farmer to farmer at an estimated rate of 250 thousand hectares per year. Never waste a good crisis!

Although two and a half million people are now more food secure, Tony realized the most fundamental thing is understanding the culture of caring for God's creation, that is, why should Christians care for God's creation? Tony answered: (1) creation belongs to God and that creation is important to God; (2) loving our neighbor as ourselves is inseparable from caring for creation; (3) creation is intrinsically good and it has value in its own right; and (4) God makes broken, spoiled, and messed up people into new creations in Christ. Our God is an expert in recycling, because with God nothing ever gets wasted.[20] When things are in their Maker's hands, there is hope of redemption. If we hope for what we do not see, we should wait for it with patience in Christ, and act in God's everlasting love. This is the story of reforestation and land restoration visionary Tony Rinaudo. No one calls him "mad white farmer" anymore, but "forest maker" and "famine fighter," as a holy seed.

---

20 Dave Bookless, *God Doesn't Do Waste: Redeeming the Whole of Life* (London: IVP, 2012), 62–63.

Discussion Questions

Based on Tony's questions for discussion, I would suggest three more to help build a better future for the next generations:

1. What is your educational responsibility regarding creation care for your children?

2. Does your Sunday school give enough attention to creation care?

3. If loving your neighbor is inseparable from caring for creation, how do you strike a balance between saving souls and caring for creation on the mission field?

CHAPTER 15

Onnuri Church's Environmental Mission and Strategy

by Woon-Oh Jung, Regina Ryu, and Woo-Yong Kim

In early 2014, Onnuri Church established its Social Justice Ministry with the intent to expand its social missions. Church leaders wished to settle the debate over whether evangelism has priority over social missions, as both are needed to advance the kingdom of God. Senior Pastor Jae Hoon Lee referred to evangelism and social missions as "two wings" that must work together for the church to "soar" with God for his kingdom.[1] The establishment of the Social Justice Ministry marked a crucial milestone for Onnuri Church toward a holistic mission in alignment with the spirit of the Cape Town Commitment: "The salvation we proclaim should be transforming us in the totality of our personal and social responsibilities. Faith without works is dead."[2] Onnuri's Social Justice Ministry was thus founded, based on Micah 6:8: "He has shown you, O mortal, what is good. And what does the LORD require of you? To act justly and to love mercy and to walk humbly with your God." Various church ministry teams were organized under the umbrella of the Social Justice Ministry, the "Life and Environment" team being one among them.

The two main missions of the team are: first, in response to the prevailing disregard for human life, apparent in the surge of suicide, abortion, homosexuality, and child abuse cases (all of which are deemed ills caused by the influences of atheism, evolution theory, and a perverted sense of humanism), we hope to increase the awareness of and recover the dignity of human life created in God's likeness; second, we hope to make concrete efforts to restore order in the created world that has long been exploited and destroyed by the greed of human beings steeped in materialism and consumerism. We will particularly endeavor to promote our congregation's awareness of the ongoing life-threatening climate crisis and suggest action plans to slow down its progress.

---

1 Senior Pastor Jae Hoon Lee, "Humble Church" (sermon, delivered at the Revival Vision Conference for the Thirtieth Anniversary of Onnuri Church, October 7, 2015).

2 "The Cape Town Commitment," Lausanne Movement, 2011 (pt. 1, sec. 10, par. B [citing the "Lausanne Covenant," par. 5]), https://lausanne.org/content/ctc/ctcommitment.

The primary aim of this chapter is to introduce the vision, mission, and strategy of the Life and Environment Team, and to present a summary of the most notable ministries conducted from its inception up until the present. Consistent with the theme of this year's forum, this chapter will focus on the team's environmental ministries.

Life and Environment Team's Vision, Mission, and Strategy

The vision of the Life and Environment Team is to preserve the beauty of the ecosystem in created nature. A healthy ecosystem is necessary to fulfill God's command in Genesis 1:28: "Be fruitful and increase in number; fill the earth and subdue it." The team's mission is to raise awareness among the congregation of the urgency of combating environmental pollution and climate change, which has rapidly worsened in the twenty-first century, and to lead the congregation to participate in such work to prevent the ongoing destruction of the ecosystem. The team's strategy is aligned with that of the church's Social Justice Ministry, which is well reflected in its "Loving U" slogan, where the letter "U" carries a threefold meaning of "Unfamiliar," "Uncomfortable," and "Unsafe."

"Unfamiliar" calls the congregation to approach and befriend unfamiliar people, to meet their material, psychological, and spiritual needs while sharing the gospel. Unfamiliar people are those who are typically overlooked in society, such as the "aliens" living in our midst. Just as the kingdom of God broke through human history by way of Christ's incarnation, the true church must penetrate with Christ into the present world, humbly reaching unfamiliar souls. "Uncomfortable" proposes leaving behind the lifestyle and habits of comfort and convenience. This means willingly embracing discomfort and inconvenience in order to live out the gospel of the kingdom of God. It runs counter to the modern lifestyle of overspending and excessive use of disposable goods (e.g., plastics), which is a key threat to the ecosystem. "Unsafe" calls for leaving one's comfort zone and taking risks to build the kingdom of God in places ridden with systemic injustice, poverty, and oppression. "Loving U" is a fitting strategy for Onnuri's Social Justice Ministry, because what is most unsafe on earth is believing in Jesus, and the church is the most unsafe community in the world.[3]

For the team's environmental ministry, the most relevant strategy is "uncomfortable," the one which embraces discomfort and inconvenience. People will have to grow accustomed to many discomforts to help protect

---

3 Senior Pastor Jae Hoon Lee, "Unsafe Church" (sermon, delivered at the Revival Vision Conference for the Thirtieth Anniversary of Onnuri Church, October 6, 2015).

the environment. For example, people will have to take public transportation when coming to church and carry personal water bottles instead of using disposable cups. Willingly sorting trash for effective recycling will become possible only when people learn to "love" being uncomfortable.

At the inception of Onnuri Church's social justice ministry, we encountered some negative response and misunderstanding. For many, our claim that environmental issues did in fact belong in the realm of faith was difficult to accept. In particular, those who understood salvation as a purely personal and private matter found it difficult to connect the gospel with the responsibility to practice social justice. Even leaders in the church had difficulty comprehending how environmental protection and responding to the climate crisis could relate to the gospel.

To resolve this problem, we referred to not only Scripture but also to the "Cape Town Commitment: A Confession of Faith and a Call to Action" from the Third Lausanne Congress. Its seventh confession of faith, "We love God's world," states that loving the world that God created means "caring for what belongs to him" and that all who love God must do this.[4] Since the world and everything in it belongs to God whom we say we love, if we abuse and destroy the world, we cannot say that we love God. Therefore, we must take care of the created world and use its resources responsibly. We must take care of the world, not because of humanistic reasons but because of our love for God. Therefore, the task of taking care of the created world becomes a matter of practicing the gospel in relation to God's sovereignty. This confession is a manifestation of our holistic mission: The created world, along with individuals and human society, are broken by and suffer from sin, and all these three entities are targets of *missio Dei*. This spirit of holistic mission is a basic principle that supports the Life and Environment Team and becomes the basis of calling its ministry an "environmental mission."

Early Ministry: Public Transportation Campaign

In the early days, the team focused more on understanding social justice ministry and establishing our identity, so the environmental ministry was not immediately active. The "Public Transportation Campaign" was the only active ministry at the time. Onnuri Church designated one Sunday each quarter as the day for the entire congregation[5] to take public transportation to church, and vehicles would not be permitted to enter the church premises. This campaign also brought about the added benefit of alleviating the

---

4 "The Cape Town Commitment" (pt. 1, sec. 7, par. A).

5 Exceptions were made for certain members with special needs.

typical Sunday traffic congestion in the neighborhood caused by the tens of thousands of worshipers coming to church in cars, which was a tremendous inconvenience for nearby residents. The team used this day as an opportunity to raise awareness regarding the climate crisis and other environmental issues, encouraging the use of public transportation as a means of reducing carbon emissions.

Later Ministry

The Life and Environment Team's ministry finally began making some visible progress starting in 2018, after more firmly establishing its identity and building up its inner capacity. In January, we held two workshops to reaffirm our conviction that a proper response to the climate crisis is a matter of acting upon the gospel. These workshops culminated in the following plans for the team's ministry.

Green Station

The installation of the Green Station was the team's first significant ministry. In February 2018, upon examining the church's garbage disposal and recycling procedure, we found it to be lacking. Effective recycling requires a thorough separation of trash, for which at least eight or nine different categories of recycling bins are needed. We found, however, that very few recycling bins were being used. Furthermore, in the process of transporting the trash to the outdoor garbage pick-up location, all trash was dumped together and got mixed up, requiring it to be sorted and separated again for recycling. To overcome this inefficient and ineffective recycling, we installed multiple bins at a central garbage collection location and named it the "Green Station." We also made efforts to reduce the number of indoor trash bins.

In June 2019, we finished the installation of the Green Station. With four trash bins, the Green Station had a length of 4.5m, a width of 2.5m, and a height of 2.8m, covered on all sides except for the front. Although we were unable to install the originally intended number of bins due to limited space, the Green Station was the first step toward more effective recycling. Unfortunately, the outbreak of COVID-19 in late 2019 changed the fate of the Green Station. As church buildings were closed and the congregation could not worship in them, the usage of the Green Station dropped rapidly. Even worse, due to construction of a park on one side of the church, the Green Station has temporarily been relocated and is currently being used as a storage area for miscellaneous objects.

Loving U Campaign and Tumbler Use Incentives

This campaign was launched in 2018 and focused on encouraging the use of personal water bottles and tumblers to reduce the use of disposable goods in the church cafes. The team arranged to have the church cafes replace paper and plastic cups with mugs and offer discounts to tumbler users. This, however, required washing mugs after each use, which was not feasible due to the limited number of workers and lack of adequate dishwashing equipment. Realizing that it would not be possible to execute this plan within a short time period, a different incentive for tumbler users was arranged instead.

The team also sold about four hundred tumblers with the Onnuri Church logo inscribed, in hopes that church members would cherish and use them more often. A brochure entitled "Why Use a Tumbler?" was also created and distributed, detailing the reasons for and the benefit of using tumblers, and explaining how best to maintain them. Purchasers were also given coffee coupons as an additional incentive to purchase the tumblers.

Environmental Awareness and Zero Waste Campaign

Since its inception in 2014, the team endeavored to raise awareness in the church regarding environmental issues. It was only starting in 2018, however, that the team was able to promote its environmental ministry more proactively on a church-wide scale. In designating specific Sundays for the Public Transportation Campaign, we purposefully included Children's Sunday[6] and Church Foundation Sunday and set up activity booths for children in the vacant church parking lot. This enabled us to provide young visitors with opportunities such as observing and drawing resource circulation maps,[7] making candles using empty discarded cans, and constructing cactus pots using recycled plastic cups. To increase participation, we also rewarded participants with official records of volunteer service time.

In 2019, we employed the slogans "Zero Waste," "Zero Plastic," and "Zero Leftovers" to advocate environmental awareness more effectively. These slogans were aimed at eliminating (or at least reducing) garbage, plastic usage, and leftover food. We produced a three-minute promotional video and played it during Onnuri Church's Sunday service to kick off the Zero Waste Campaign. On that day, volunteers lined the church lobby holding campaign posters, directing church members to campaign information and

---

6 Korean churches traditionally observe the first Sunday in May as Children's Sunday, in celebration of Children's Day, which is a national holiday that falls on May 5.

7 A resource circulation map would detail the process from the origination of garbage to its final destination, showing where and how much garbage emerges and how it is processed.

activities. In collaboration with the church's Children's Ministry, the team also hosted a drawing competition for elementary school kids, entitled "Reducing Disposable Goods and Using Tumblers." Final selections were framed and displayed next to the twenty-four water dispensers in the church, directing the congregation to consider the environment as they use paper cups.

Green Outreach and Plogging[8]

Green Outreach is an outreach project focused on environmental missions, which the team conducts two to three times a year, starting in 2019. The places visited include areas where environmental accidents have occurred, regions with ongoing environmental issues, or churches and organizations that successfully practice environmental missions. On the outreach trips, we engaged in environment-friendly activities such as plogging and avoided the use of disposable goods and practiced leaving no leftover food. One placed the team visited was the Korea Maritime Transportation Safety Authority, located on Taean Peninsula.[9] We learned about the gravity of ocean pollution and about possible recovery efforts. Social distancing and lockdowns caused by the COVID-19 pandemic, however, halted all Green Outreach in 2020 and 2021. It resumed only in the fall of 2022 after social distancing regulations were lifted.

"Restoring the Creation Order" Campaign

This campaign was planned in 2021 after the team decided to join the "carbon fast" movement designed to reduce carbon dioxide emissions, a root cause of climate change. Carbon fasts had already spread among many churches with a keen awareness of the climate crisis. Since the campaign called for fasting, it was deemed appropriate for Lent and scheduled for Lent in 2022. In an effort to properly reflect the scriptural mandate behind this campaign, as well as to address the general unfamiliarity on the part of the congregation with the concept of carbon fasting, the campaign was named "Restoring the Creation Order," with the subtitle, "And it was good."

We first brainstormed ideas for possible carbon-reducing activities. Then, focusing on the concept of restoring and preserving the God's created world as originally intended, we selected seven creation themes from Genesis, one for each week during Lent. These themes were roughly assigned the chronological order of creation: light, air, water, earth, seasons, flora &

---

8 "Plogging" is a term used to express the act of picking up litter while jogging. It is a portmanteau of the Swedish term "plocka upp," which means "to pick up," and the English word "jogging."

9 In December 2007, 12,547 kl of oil was spilled in the ocean near Taean Peninsula.

fauna, and humans. We then grouped together related activities according to these seven themes and allocated one to each day of the week. The following table summarizes the initial plan.

Table 15.1: "Restoring the Creation Order" campaign (2022 original)

Week	Monday	Tuesday	Wednesday	Thursday	Friday	Saturday
1 Light			Unplugging home appliances when not in use	Using stairs instead of elevators	Reducing cell phone (media) usage	Turning off lights in unoccupied rooms
2 Air	Using public transporta-tion	Reducing garbage output	Purchasing local fruits and vegetables	Opening windows for air circulation	Eating vegetables	Walking or biking
3 Water	Reducing the length of time spent in the shower	Shutting off the water during soaping/ shampooing	Filling the washing machine full before running a cycle	Using kitchen products without microplastic	Using naturally fermented cleaners	Using a bin during dishwashing; separating waste cooking oil
4 Earth	Washing recyclable garbage thoroughly before discarding	Not using disposable wet tissues and sweeper wipes	Using handker-chiefs; using the back side of used papers	Not using plastic wraps, straws, disposable	Drinking boiled or purified water instead of bottled water	Reducing online shopping
5 Seasons	Dressing properly for the season; reducing the use of heaters	Taking a walk and basking in the sun	Turning off lights at 9 p.m. and going to bed	Eating seasonal fruits and vegetables	Maintaining indoor temperature at 20°C	Enjoying spring flowers and thanking God
6 Flora & fauna	Learning about biodiversity	Raising indoor plants and flowers	Caring for pets	Learning about roadkills	Supporting organizations that take care of abandoned pets	Planting flowers and/ or trees
7 Humans	Buying only absolute necessities	Cleaning the home and workplace	Sorting out unnecessary possessions	Sharing and donating unnecessary items	Good Friday: fasting (one meal)	Praying for the restoration of the creation order

The initial campaign plan as presented in table 15.1 was subsequently revised, however, following review by the church's Ministry Planning Board and Senior Pastor Lee. The plan was revised as follows: first, the focus on carbon fast and the climate crisis was expanded to incorporate a pro-life agenda, emphasizing respect for human life created in God's image and especially the rights of fetuses who cannot defend themselves; second, the original plan was modified due to certain implementation problems, which would have rendered the campaign impractical.

The revised campaign plan is presented in table 15.2. Under this new scheme, campaign participants may freely select one or more activities under any category and practice them any time during Lent. Furthermore, the theme "Flora and Fauna" was changed to "Life." As for "Humans," the original focus on carbon fast by way of minimalism was replace by an emphasis on "respect for life."

Table 15.2: "Restoring the Creation Order" campaign (2022 final)

Themes	Activities
Light	Turning off lights when not in use Unplugging appliances when not in use Taking stairs instead of using elevators
Air	Riding public transportation instead of personal automobiles Consuming locally grown produce Walking and biking
Water	Turning off the water during shampooing and soaping (in the shower) Using a cup while brushing teeth (instead of running the tap) Washing clothes only after the washing machine is full of laundry Conserving water during dishwashing by using dishwashing bins
Earth	Using the back side of used paper Reducing the usage of toilet paper and wet tissues Reducing the usage of disposable goods
Seasons	Eating seasonal fruits and vegetables Maintaining indoor temperatures at 20°C Enjoying spring flowers and thanking God for them
Life	Participating in the "40 Days for Life" prayer campaign to end abortion Learning about adoption and foster care Learning about biodiversity
Humans	Loving oneself—declaring "I am precious" once a day Loving others—acting and speaking respectfully toward others Sending an encouraging note to someone facing a crisis

With this revised plan, we launched Onnuri Church's first "Restoring the Creation Order" Lent campaign on Ash Wednesday in 2022. For the month leading up to Ash Wednesday, we published articles in the church newspaper each week, explaining how restoration of God's creation was a biblically mandated matter of faith. Finally, on the Lord's Day before Ash Wednesday, we kicked off the new, church-wide campaign with a three-minute promotional video during the main worship service. Campaign participants were encouraged to provide feedback in the form of participation photos and short text messages, which would be rewarded with nominal mobile gifts. The progress of the campaign was reported not only in the church newspaper but also by way of Onnuri Church's various social media channels.

Epilogue

In reviewing the Life and Environment Team's ministry, we acknowledge weaknesses in many respects. We will, however, persevere in our mission. We will work harder to raise awareness that restoring and taking care of the created world is a matter of faith. "Restoring the Creation Order" campaign will continue each year. The Green Station that stopped functioning during the park construction will soon be reinstated. We will also consider declaring our church a "green church," in order to participate in the carbon fast movement more proactively. Additionally, we will need to reach out more to Generation Z and beyond, since they will suffer the most from the climate crisis.

A crucial aspect of the climate crisis is that the real source of the problem comes from human greed exacerbated by materialism. For this reason, the Cape Town Commitment calls for repentance of the destruction and pollution of the earth's resources and condoning the worship of consumerism.[10] Materialism is a reductionistic worldview that asserts consuming and possessing material things can satisfy physical, mental, and even spiritual needs. It sneaks into people's minds, instigating overconsumption, which can only be supported by overproduction, which in turn causes carbon emissions and the climate crisis. Overconsumption upstream is a primary cause of the climate crisis, resulting in undue suffering downstream. To address this upstream problem, we hope to promote a minimalistic lifestyle, to encourage minimizing spending and possessions. This would urge the congregation to be more circumspect about consumption and also proactively recycle and share their possessions.

---

10 "The Cape Town Commitment" (pt. 1, sec. 7, par. A).

Discussion Questions

1. In much of the evangelical Korean church today, as is likely the case in many evangelical circles across the world, environmental issues have traditionally been neglected in discussions concerning the church's mission. Although in recent years creation care has increasingly emerged as a missional priority, the existing anthropocentric interpretation and understanding of Scripture presents much challenge. What would be some effective ways to convince the church that environmental concerns do indeed belong in the realm of faith, that creation care is in fact a gospel mandate?

2. One of the explanations given for the evangelical Korean church's negative reaction to environmental matters (e.g., carbon fast), is the nation's political history. Interestingly, much of the evangelical Korean church has historically been aligned with the political right, whereas the environmental agenda has largely belonged to the political left. While the church clearly does not believe that politics ought to guide its mission, this invisible barrier is very real and has proven difficult to overcome. Are there any experiences from other parts of the world from which we may draw some insight as to how we may resolve this dilemma?

3. Onnuri Church's Life and Environment Team believes that human greed, exacerbated by the pervasiveness of materialism and consumerism in much of the world today, lies at the root of our abuse and destruction of God's creation and the resulting climate crisis we face today. How could this connection be made more obvious to and relevant for Christians today, encouraging them to focus more on upstream efforts (e.g., minimalism, carbon fast) in addition to the more traditional downstream efforts (e.g., recycling, upcycling) as part of the mission to restore the creation order? How could we also capitalize on our COVID shutdown experience and its positive impact—albeit short-term— upon the environment to help make our point?

Response

by Laura S. Meitzner Yoder

I am grateful for this opportunity to learn about the first decade of Onnuri Church's environmental mission and strategy in the chapter by Woon-Oh Jung, Regina Ryu, and Woo-Yong Kim. Started in 2014, the Social Justice Ministry's Life and Environment Team (LET) seeks to increase holistic mission, with the support of and guidance by senior pastoral leadership. Two chief purposes are (1) to uphold the dignity of human life and to restore creation in concrete ways, and (2) to acknowledge human materialism and consumerism as root causes of ecological degradation, while promoting actions to ameliorate climate change.

The LET aims to incorporate concrete, individual, and congregational actions for environmental care, protection, and repair within the liturgical rhythms and ordinary aspects of church life. The team's initiatives are very thoughtfully timed and executed, in tandem with raising awareness in the congregation for the first few years. There are a variety of elements and some commitments that I find laudably challenging! These include launching LET's program with a bold initiative I think few churches in my own home context could achieve: a public transportation promotion campaign one Sunday per quarter in which private vehicles are not allowed to enter the church premises. Strategically, this is scheduled for prominent Sundays, including national Children's Day, and it significantly reduces traffic for the church building's neighbors. Other activities have included designing a "Green Station" to separate waste for recycling, reducing disposables in church cafes, children's environmental education, visiting sites of environmental disasters, such as an oil spill, and litter cleanups. A Lenten carbon fast integrates environmental action with the church calendar. Pastoral leadership asked that this initiative link to the church's pro-life focus, as the defenseless unborn are the primary victims of climate change. Our current overconsumption, rooted in the socially accepted sin of greed, increases suffering for future generations.

Of theological importance, the work of this team is part of the Onnuri Church's wider effort to reconcile and to heal the un-Christlike separation of evangelism and social mission that has crept into many churches worldwide, limiting our sharing of the good news as both are central to gospel witness. The authors mention that this message can be hard for congregants and church leaders alike to absorb and to enact, as overcoming a long-internalized distinction takes time and deliberate work. It can be difficult for people to understand the reason for undoing divisions of categories that many have come to see as natural—and this is as true in my own context as the Onnuri authors note for theirs. Following Jesus who took on flesh and made his home with us is a fully embodied experience.

Additional early challenges were encountered at the intersection of theology and politics. Early uptake was slow because many did not see environmental issues as relevant to their faith lives, or how climate action connected to the gospel. The authors describe the politicized association of environmental concerns as an "invisible barrier [that] is very real and has proven difficult to overcome." This chapter gives us glimpses into the processes by which the program took shape within the LET, in relation to church leadership and for the congregation.

It is notable that the organizing impetus for the social justice ministries is encapsulated as "Loving [Three] U's"—"Unfamiliar," "Uncomfortable," and "Unsafe." The first reminds congregants to befriend unfamiliar (and overlooked) people. Being uncomfortable entails "leaving behind the lifestyle and habits of comfort and convenience. This means willingly embracing discomfort and inconvenience in order to live out the gospel of the kingdom of God." This goal is remarkable, going against the near taboo (even in churches) of speaking against consumerism and materialism, a critique of our culturally valued corporate sin. Being unsafe, just as countercultural in a risk-averse society, is "leaving one's comfort zone and taking risks to build the kingdom of God in places … [of] systemic injustice, poverty, and oppression"—and recognizing that sometimes we fail to see where these are present even within or adjacent to our churches.

Building on the foundation already begun, I encourage the LET and Onnuri Church leadership to further integrate the three U's to expand the impact of this ministry. On getting close to the unfamiliar, this can be extended to knowledge we often prefer to keep distant or willfully ignore. It was a bold and critical move for the LET to lead and to accompany the congregation in, first of all, coming *to see and to know* the ways, places, and people both far and near affected by our lifestyles. With the positive neighborhood effects of the public transportation promotion campaign, could that initiative be combined with inviting near neighbors to the church?

Another expansion would be to *add communal/collective, systemic, and advocacy aspects* to the LET's mandate. It seems that many of the early initiatives have focused on personal practices carried out independently. This is important because our lives and lifestyles do need to change in many ways as we follow God's prompting to reorient our highly consumptive lifestyles; specific commitments can help us develop new habits. But a primary focus on what individuals can do privately may distract from the critically important arena of public advocacy, and of grappling with and carrying out environmental justice actions together with, alongside of, and on behalf of the poor and marginalized—the unfamiliar people and unsafe spaces that (we) church people often avoid. Do the activities of the Lenten carbon fast lead congregants to embrace discomfort and inconvenience in ways visible to the watching world, including the church?

In future years, the LET can add actions that challenge congregants to work together or to collaborate with others to address systemic poverty and oppression. The recommendations could focus on systems that directly help or harm neighbors, as demonstrated already by the positive effects of the public transportation campaign on the church's immediate neighbors. Might a third (or even fourth) column be added to the Lenten campaign, suggesting collective actions that benefit others, highlighting systemic elements, or promoting public advocacy points on each of the Lenten themes? For example, the individual activity may be walking/biking, but the collective activity could be participating in path maintenance or advocating for increasing the number of paths accessible to people with disabilities or with limited means for transport. Another individual activity might be eating seasonal produce, but the collective/systemic/advocacy activity could be volunteering at a garden or food distribution center, or joining an advocacy campaign to expand produce accessibility for low-income families.

To engage the pastoral request to link the Lenten activities to a life-honoring emphasis, congregants could focus on the effects of pollution and environmental contamination on the unborn, who will be living with our disposables, plastics, and effects of our released carbon long after we have passed. A future year's Lenten fast could ask congregants to consider for each of the weekly themes of air, water, earth, seasons, and so forth, *How can we extend God's love to future generations?* Connecting creation care and climate concern within the church to family and duty and responsibility of care for (future) relatives may be broadly resonant and help congregants draw more concrete connections between climate concern and the well-being of others who are as yet unknown and distant from us, in space and in time.

I will close this response with a personal anecdote. I myself was drawn to the church not so much by the smoothly run programs and beautiful services of my home congregation while growing up, but by seeing the life testimonies of the teachers in my Christian schools, characterized by joyful and creative embrace *in community* of the inconveniences of carpooling and public transit, of spending time growing food, of adopting children in need, of serving their neighbors in crises and in ordinary times, of sharing their resources, of eating simply, of washing dishes together to avoid using disposables, and of orienting their whole lives, including time and finances, to caring for family, neighbors, strangers, and God's earth in integrated ways. Our lifestyles bear powerful witness to the importance of the gospel in our lives!

Discussion Questions

1. How have you observed or experienced the process of expanding congregational understanding of holistic mission, including environmental action as part of the gospel witness and neighbor-loving ministry of the church? What events, talks, activities, etc. have been most meaningful in this regard?

2. What are important elements of a theology of discomfort and inconvenience?

3. What other collective activities would you pair with individual Lenten actions, which may include working directly alongside people in situations of marginalization, injustice, and oppression?

4. What are the two or three most important advocacy points for church leadership and congregants to engage in the public square?

5. Can participants share their experiences promoting neighbor love within the church that extends to future generations, including but not limited to one's own family, and acting now to protect or to improve the environment they will inhabit?

CHAPTER 16

Economically Viable Green Energy from Waste Plastic

A Fourth River Energy Proposal to Support Missions and Bless the Environment

by Ben Torrey and Bong Ju Lee

This is a general proposal to build a hydrogen (H_2) production plant and fuel cell charging station with a capacity of producing one metric ton of H_2 per day. The plant will consume ten tonnes of waste plastic and vinyl per day. It will use a microwave plasma torch to gasify the fuel stock (waste plastic, etc.) to produce "green" H_2. Retail sales of H_2 will be through the charging station for hydrogen fuel cell vehicles located adjacent to the production facility. These vehicles, also known as fuel cell electric vehicles (FCEV), use hydrogen to generate electricity for propulsion. This will provide operating and expansion funding for the Three Seas Training Center—the home of The Fourth River Project, preparing for the opening of North Korea to the gospel.

The technology used will be a microwave-generated plasma torch for gasification of the feedstock (waste plastic and vinyl). This technology has been developed by Dr. Bong Ju Lee and will be provided through his company, Green Science, located in Taebaek, Gangwon-do.

Viability of H_2 Production and Comparisons

The use of H_2 as a source of energy has been recognized for quite some time. It is the lightest, smallest, and most abundant element, and is neither toxic nor corrosive. Hydrogen fuel cells are in use around the world as an economic and nonpolluting means to power large and small vehicles, heavy equipment, railroads, etc., and to provide electric power for buildings, data centers, etc. A hydrogen fuel cell uses hydrogen through a chemical reaction with oxygen to produce electricity, heat, and water. There are no other emissions.

Currently, hydrogen is produced using four main sources: natural gas (48 percent of world H_2 production), oil (30 percent), coal (18 percent), and by electrolysis of water (4 percent).[1] Production using fossil fuels results in what is termed "gray" hydrogen and greenhouse gases. When CO_2 is sequestered, the result is termed "blue" hydrogen. Electrolysis of water produces "green" hydrogen with no emissions.[2] Two of the main problems with electrolysis are the high levels of electricity required in the process and the source of that electricity. For these reasons, it is only being considered in combination with other renewable energy sources—with wind power, for instance.

In the 1980s, a process using plasma was developed in Norway for the production of H_2 and carbon black from liquid hydrocarbons. Later on, a variation of this process was developed using electric arcs to produce an extremely high temperature plasma that can gasify any hydrocarbon (such as municipal waste or plastics) in an oxygen-starved environment. The major problems with the electric arc method are the high costs of the electrodes required, their short duration, and the accompanying high maintenance costs. This method has been tried in various countries and is not, to our knowledge, economically viable anywhere at this time. We are aware of plans for new construction based on this technology but these appear to be heavily dependent on government subsidies.

The unique contribution of Dr. Lee's method is the use of microwaves (not electric arc) to produce a higher than 1,400°C plasma torch in order to gasify hydrocarbons. This process can run twenty-four hours a day for over 330 days a year with little maintenance. In commercial production, the plant need only operate sixteen hours per day, in three shifts. It also provides a very efficient way to eliminate waste, such as municipal solid waste, plastics, vinyl, agricultural by-products, etc.

Table 16.1: Comparison of microwave and conventional (arc) plasma torches

	Microwave plasma	Conventional (arc) plasma torch
Electricity costs for the case of 10 kW applied to gasify waste	10 kWh	250 kWh
Highest temperature of a torch	> 6,500°C	> 10,000°C
Maintenance costs	Low	High (require the change of electrodes every 300 h)
Operating hours	24 h/d, 330 d/y	270 d/y

1 Roman J. Press et al., *Introduction to Hydrogen Technology* (Hoboken, NJ: John Wiley, 2008), 249; also quoted in Wikipedia, s.v. "Hydrogen Production," last modified Jan. 30, 2023, https://en.wikipedia.org/wiki/Hydrogen_production.

2 Len Rosen, "Grey, Blue and Green Hydrogen: What's the Difference and What It Could Mean for Fighting Climate Change," 21st Century Tech Blog, Mar. 15, 2021, https://www.21stcentech.com/grey-blue-green-hydrogen-difference-fighting-climate-change/.

The cost benefit of microwave compared to electric arc technology is seen in three areas: electricity usage, reactor liner maintenance, and the nonuse of electrodes. A microwave plasma torch uses about 1/25 the amount of electricity to operate compared to an electric arc plasma torch.

An electric arc plasma torch operates at temperatures of 4,000–6,000 °C whereas a microwave plasma torch operates at a more efficient 1,400°C, which is adequate for the purpose of gasifying solid wastes. This results in less corrosion of the reaction chamber liner. The liner for an electric arc plasma torch reactor chamber needs to be replaced more frequently. In addition to chamber liner maintenance, an electric arc torch requires frequent replacement of the electrodes. Based on the type of gases used, electrode life can be measured anywhere from hours to weeks. A recent study on the economics of a plasma torch to treat plastic waste contained this statement: "Maintenance costs for a PG facility will be difficult to estimate because companies developing the technology are hesitant to release information. This is likely because the maintenance costs are heavily dependent on the lifetime of the plasma electrode."[3] Electrode costs are estimated to be in the neighborhood of $1,000 each. A microwave plasma torch does not use electrodes that need replacing. It is clear that the operating and maintenance costs of a microwave plasma torch are orders of magnitude less than the only other feasible method for gasifying plastics and other wastes or organic materials.

In addition to the operating and maintenance costs, there are considerable savings in capital expenditures. Electric arc plasma installations are generally conceived or have been built and operated on a much larger scale than a microwave torch facility in order to approach economic viability. A microwave torch system can be built on a much smaller scale with considerably less capital expenditure. Scaling would be accomplished, not by building one large expensive central facility but by building multiple smaller, less expensive facilities located where they are most needed. (For a complete financial analysis, see the Financial Analysis section below.)

Government and Industry Priorities

The Korean government and the Province of Gangwon placed a very high priority on converting to H_2 fueled vehicles where feasible. It is the intention of both the provincial and central government to work toward the transformation of trucks, buses, and heavy equipment to H_2 fuel cells. As of 2022, both the central government and Gangwon Province intend to provide 50 percent each of the capital costs to construct an H_2 retail charging station.

---

3 Zachary Homolka, "Treatment of Plastic Wastes Using Plasma Gasification Technology" (Honors Thesis, Univ. of Nebraska-Lincoln, 2019), 11, https://digitalcommons.unl.edu/cgi/viewcontent.cgi?article=1081&context=honorstheses.

Gangwon Province has an interest in a stable market for hydrogen and is expected to help facilitate such a market.

Korea Gas Corporation (kogas.or.kr) has established a hydrogen exchange to purchase H_2 from producers at approximately ₩8,000/kg for distribution to a nationwide network of H_2 charging stations.[4] The province will pay tipping fees of about $175 per metric ton to deliver plastic waste. The province and city have plans to develop a technology incubator in Taebaek to promote the development and application of this technology. They are working to establish a "green hydrogen cluster" in the city of Taebaek.

The following is excerpted from a special report from Gangwon Province released in January 2021 titled, "Creating a Green Plasma Cluster," which is a plan to create the cluster in the city of Taebaek.[5]

Table 16.2 shows a breakdown of the estimated consumption of hydrogen by 2025 in tonnes per day (hereafter t/d) for Gangwon Province.

Table 16.2: Consumption of hydrogen by 2025

Total t/d	Vehicles (automobiles, buses, trucks, etc.)	Major fuel cell users (ships, power generation, etc.)	Other (railroads, drones, etc.)
38.6	20.6	8.0	10.0

Gangwon Province is currently in the initial planning and implementation stages of hydrogen production (nothing is currently online), including (with city names in parentheses)

- planned production of 4.1 t/d, leaving a shortfall of 34.5 t/d;

- (Chuncheon) Ministry of Construction and Industry Hydrogen Extraction Facilities taking bids for an investment of ₩16.2 billion to produce 2.5 t/d;

- (Donghae) P2G Hydrogen Production Demonstration Complex seeking private investment of ₩48.6 billion to produce 350 kg/d;

- (Sokcho) Ministry of Environment soliciting public bids for ₩4.6 billion to produce 250 kg/d; and

- (Samcheok) Hydrogen Production Facility seeking national government and provincial funding of ₩7 billion to produce 1 t/d.

---

4 H_2Exchange Beta Version, accessed Dec. 20, 2022, https://www.h2exchange.kr/hd/hdb/HDB10320/insertBidPlanVw.do?pageFlag210=Y&bidNo=2022121601007&bidOdr=01&bidId=20221215007:jsessionid=1E872BA495770F6DB49552C280EF02ED.tomcat1. 플라즈마 그린수소 클러스터 조성 [Creating a green plasma cluster] (Gangwon Province, January 2021), 5; translation by Ben Torrey.

5 플라즈마 그린수소 클러스터 조성 [Creating a green plasma cluster] (Gangwon Province, January 2021), 5; translation by Ben Torrey.

Space Needed

The amount of space needed for the construction and operation of a 1 t/d H_2 production plant, including storage space for 50 tonnes of plastic feedstock (a five-day supply—one tonne of waste plastic is compressed into a one cubic meter cube for transportation), is 16,000 sq. ft. (167 sq. m). The space needed to operate a fuel cell charging station, including adequate parking for vehicles, is the same. The total space required for the Fourth River Energy production and sales facility is 32,000 sq. ft. (334 sq. m).

Ongoing Supply of Waste Plastic

According to a 2018 report from the Korean Environmental Department, Gangwon Province generates some 170 t/d of waste plastic. The special report from Gangwon Province released in January of 2021 puts the total at 177 t/d.[6] This waste plastic is accumulating in landfills, which is the only acceptable way to dispose of it. As noted above, the province will pay tipping fees to have the plastic taken off its hands. The amount of waste plastic has been growing for years, ever since the incineration of plastic was outlawed. Some 6,000 tonnes of waste plastic is generated every day throughout Korea.

Management and Staffing

Management and staffing may be contracted out to an engineering, procurement and construction, or operations and maintenance contractor. Green Science, the developer of the microwave plasma technology, will provide technical training for the operation and management of the facility. Oversight will be provided by Fourth River Energy Corporation under the control of The Fourth River Project, Inc. It is also possible that this facility could be used for the training of personnel in the development, management, and maintenance of this type of facility in other locations or overseas.

Investment

The Fourth River Project, Inc. is currently seeking investors in this project. Anyone interested may contact Ben Torrey at bentorrey@thefourthriver.org.

---

6 플라즈마 그린수소 클러스터 조성 [Creating a green plasma cluster], 13.

Financial Analysis

Table 16.3: Facility planning and total investment costs

Type and quantity	Description		Cost (₩1,000)
Plant construction cost	Basic (detail) design and simulation		1,500,000
Excavation and construction			*2,000,000
Technical construction			*2,000,000
Equipment:			4,000,000
Microwave heater pyrolyzer (4)		600,000	
Pyrolysis reactor and char gasifier		530,000	
Quencher		50,000	
Water replacement		100,000	
Demister		30,000	
Pressure swing adsorption		1,000,000	
60 kW microplasma torch (2)		800,000	
3 kW microwave generator (72)		400,000	
Mist generator		20,000	
Compressor (for PSA)		300,000	
Chiller (80RT)		70,000	
Misc.		100,000	
Estimated investments for plant			9,500,000
Reserve			500,000
Total Cost			10,000,000

*Excavation and construction costs are estimates. Numbers will depend on the actual site selected.

Estimated Revenue

Hydrogen sales. The price of hydrogen at a charging station ranges between ₩7,000-₩9,000/kg, depending on the region. Gangwon province indicates that they may purchase hydrogen at a price of ₩7,000/kg. KOGAS plans to purchase H_2 at about ₩8,000/kg for distribution to charging stations throughout the country. In our proposal, we are using a conservative estimate of ₩6,000/kg.

Tipping fee income. The Ministry of Environment states that the price of collection, transportation, and treatment of waste plastic/vinyl is about ₩270,000/t. Prices are set by the private sector depending on the type of waste. The treatment process costs around ₩180,000-₩270,000/t. The price prediction model for this income is excluded from the report and is set at ₩200,000/t as a conservative estimate.

Table 16.4: Estimation of efficiency rate and annual sales volume

Type	Unit		Remarks
Uptime	h	16	
Output	t/d	10	
Downtime	d	20	
Efficiency	%	94.52%	Stabilizing the maintenance period for fiscal year one (FY1)
Daily H_2 production	t/d	1	
At efficiency sales volume	t/y	345	

Table 16.5: Estimated sales volume and price

Type	Unit	H_2 Production	Remarks
After FY2	Tonne	345	Full capacity
H_2 price	₩/kg	₩6,000	

Table 16.6: Estimated annual revenue

Type	Multiplier unit (₩)	Sales	Remarks
Tipping fee	1,000	690,000	₩200,000/t, 10 t/d
H_2 sales	1,000	2,070,000	At efficiency
Total	1,000	2,760,000	At efficiency

Estimated Production Costs

Table 16.7: Processing and production cost per unit (kg) under normal operation

Type	Multiplier unit (₩)	Cost per year	Remarks
Labor	1,000	550,000	
O_2 usage	1,000	4,830	At efficiency
Overhead	1,000	35,000	At efficiency
Electricity	1,000	256,960	
H_2O usage	1,000	10,046	At efficiency
Treatment fee	1,000	6,900	At efficiency
Misc.	1,000	110,000	
Net cost	1,000	973,736	
Production	t/y	345	At efficiency
Unit price (changes)	1,000/kg	2,822	
Depreciation	1,000	500,000	
Total	1,000	1,473,736	
Total Cost	1,000/kg	4,272	W depreciation

Table 16.8: Annual water usage and cost

Type	Usages (t/d)	Usages (t/y)	Remarks
For mist	6.4	2,336	
For cooling	12.8	4,672	50% recycling rate
Others	1.6	584	
Total	20.8	7,592	16/d, Taebaek
Unit price (₩)		1,400	
Cost (₩)		10,629	100% operating

Table 16.9: Chemical treatment volume and cost

Type	Usage (t/d)	Usage (t/y; cost/y)	Remarks
Est. treatment volume	0.02	7	NaOH oil absorbent
Unit price (₩)		1,000,000	
Cost (₩1,000)	1,000	7,000	

Table 16.10: Oxygen usage and cost

Type	Unit (t/d)	Usage (t/y; cost/y)	Remarks
Est. O_2 usage	0.1	37	
Unit price (₩)		140,000	Unit price/t
Cost (₩1,000)		5,180	

Table 16.11: Electricity cost

Type	Usages (kW/h)	Usages (MW/y)	Remarks
Electricity usages	6,400	2,336	
Unit price (₩/MW)		110,000	Weighted avg. price
Cost (₩1,000)		256,960	100% operation

Table 16.12: Maintenance cost

Type	Expenses/y (₩1,000)	Remarks
Quartz heating plate, etc.	15,000	
3 kW magnetron	10,000	Weighted avg. price
Other maintenance	10,000	
Total	35,000	100% operation

Table 16.13: Labor details and cost

Labor cost	Type	Persons	Group	Shift	Persons	Remarks
	Drivers	2	3	3	6	
	Main control room operator	1	3	3	3	
	Maintenance and misc.	1	1	NA	1	
	Manager	1	1	NA	1	
				Total	11	
Avg. Salary (₩1,000)	1,000				50,000/y	
Total (₩1,000)	1,000				550,000/y	Fixed
Misc. exp. (₩1,000)	20% of avg. salary				110,000/y	

Table 16.14: Summary

Type	Remarks
Processing capacity	10 t/d (1 tonne of H_2 produced/d)
H_2 sales price and income	₩6,000/kg, tipping fee ₩200,000/t
H_2 unit cost	₩2,822/kg (W/O depreciation), ₩4,272/kg (W depreciation)
Est. yearly profit	₩2,760,000,000 (est. annual avg. net profit)
Est. NPV	₩158,000,000 (WACC 4.5%, 20 years operation)
Est. IRR	14.20%
Est. ROI	5 years
Assumptions made	Economic variables and inflation not considered. Corporate tax to be reduced by 50%

IRR = Internal Rate of Return; NPV = Net Present Value; ROI = Return on Investment; WACC = Weighted Cost of Capital

Fuel Cell Technology

Fuel cells were invented in 1838 and entered into commercial use in 1932 with the invention of the hydrogen fuel cell. Fuel cells generate electricity from the chemical reaction between the fuel and oxygen. In the case of a hydrogen fuel cell, the fuel is hydrogen. Oxygen is derived from air. The chemical reaction in the fuel cell generates electricity and water. The electricity is used to operate machinery. For vehicles using H_2 fuel cells, the internal combustion engine is replaced with an electric motor.

Plasma Gasification

Plasma is the fourth state of matter—solid, liquid, gas, plasma. Beginning with the solid state, each new state is achieved through a phase transition brought about by the application of heat. For example, H_2O is a solid at temperatures below 0°C, ice. With the application of heat raising the temperature above 0°C, the ice becomes liquid, water. When the water is heated to 100°C it becomes steam. Continued heating to a very high temperature will cause the constituent molecules of H_2O to break down to hydrogen and oxygen atoms. When the temperature gets high enough (roughly 100,000°C for water) the atoms are stripped of their electrons resulting in plasma, a loose collection of positive ions and negative electrons (e.g., the sun is a plasma). For our purposes using carbon-based feedstock, the required temperature to produce plasma is only 1,400°C.

Gasification is the process of converting various carbon-based materials into useful gases by using a plasma torch. The plasma torch is created using microwaves and operates within a gasification chamber into which the feedstock is fed. In the case of producing hydrogen from waste plastics, the waste material is fed into a microwave-powered rotary kiln where the solids are heated to a gaseous state. This mixture of gases is then fed into the gasification chamber where it is converted into a synthetic gas—a mixture of carbon monoxide (CO) and hydrogen (H_2). This is fed into a pressure swing adsorption system (PSA) where the constituent molecules are adsorbed separately. The H_2 is extracted for end use. The CO is converted to pure carbon (C) and oxygen (O_2). The pure carbon (often called carbon black) has a variety of industrial uses. The O_2 is vented into the atmosphere.

If the feedstock contains polyvinylchloride (PVC), any chlorine gas produced by the gasification process is dissolved in water to form a very weak solution of hydrochloric acid (HCl). The quantity is negligible and inexpensively and easily disposed of.

The Fourth River Project and the Three Seas Center

The Fourth River Project

The need. In anticipation of a greater opening of North Korea in the near future, it is imperative that those who go in be prepared with a deep understanding of the culture, society, psychology, history, and language of North Korea. Without such understanding, attempts to share the love of Jesus Christ in the North are quite likely to do more harm than good.

Mission. The mission of The Fourth River Project is to work toward the healing of the divisions of the Korean nation by preparing servant workers in all walks of life to bear witness to our Lord and work for the building of a new Korea on the foundation of Jesus Christ.

Vision. The vision of The Fourth River Project is that there be teams of men and women from all walks of life prepared to enter and live in North Korea and express the love of Christ, seek reconciliation, proclaim the whole gospel, build the church of Jesus Christ and, with a deep understanding of the value of biblical principles, assist in rebuilding Korean society.

The Ultimate Objectives. Our ultimate objectives are that there be

- a new Korean nation that is built on Christian principles;
- a new society with a culture based on and expressing a Christian world view; and
- a united Korean people carrying the gospel onward to the most dangerous parts of the world.

The Three Seas Training Center

Purpose. The purpose of the Three Seas Training Center is to provide a place, strategically located, to equip members of the body of Christ for service to God in South Korea, North Korea, and to the ends of the earth through study, training, labor, prayer, and a common life. Specifically, the center will be a place for

- raising up the "unification generation," Korea's young people whose heritage is this divided land, through various programs;

- providing workers with language, cultural, and other training to prepare them to go live and work inside North Korea as it opens up;

- providing a safe and welcoming environment for the healing of relationships between individuals from both North and South Korea; and

- enabling synergies by networking with other groups, organizations, and churches engaged in similar efforts and helping them work together to accomplish more than the sum of their separate works.

Location. The location of this center is both symbolic and strategic:

- at the apex of the three-way watershed, where the three major river systems of South Korea, flowing into the three seas surrounding Korea— east, west, and south—have their sources; it is the "source" as Christ is our source from which wells up the river of life.

- on the Paektu Trail running the length of the Korean peninsula, symbolizing both the river of life flowing north to North Korea and the call to God's people to go north with the gospel. This is the Fourth River.

- near Jesus Abbey geographically and functioning as an extension of the Abbey. Jesus Abbey is a community dedicated to

    ◊ intercessory prayer—vitally important for the success of all endeavors;

    ◊ communal life—sharing with one another and submitting to one another in the power of the Holy Spirit. Jesus Abbey has over fifty years of experience in communal living. This is important for engaging those with a Communist—ideologically communitarian—worldview. It is also of great benefit to those living and working in North Korea. And

    ◊ the value of labor—another theoretical ideal of Communism demonstrated as being a biblical and Christian value. This is important for engaging those with a Communist worldview as well as providing important spiritual encouragement to those who are engaged in this work.

The Three Seas is a residential community as well as a conference and training center. In addition to permanent residents, who provide staff for the center and The Fourth River Project, there are temporary residents participating in research and program development as well as training and equipping. It is also a place for larger numbers of people to gather and participate in conferences and shorter training sessions.

Discussion Questions

1. This project is proposed as a way to support missions; "Business *for* Missions" rather than the common concept of "Business *as* Mission." Is this a viable concept for this day and age?

2. Microwave plasma torch technology is very new. At this time there is only one commercial application on line, an electricity generating plant in Taebaek, Gangwon-do, Korea. Strong interest has been shown by a number of organizations around the world, both commercial and governmental; however, it is difficult to get investors to actually invest in this type of project. What might make this pioneering effort attractive to investors?

3. What are some particular blessings in relation to caring for God's creation that can be achieved through producing hydrogen (H_2) from waste plastic commercially using the microwave plasma torch?

Response

by Jeffrey T. M. Yoder

I wish to express my appreciation to Ben Torrey and Bong Ju Lee for their chapter, "Economically Viable Green Energy from Waste Plastic: A Fourth River Energy Proposal to Support Missions and Bless the Environment." It is my privilege to respond to their proposal, which presents an initiative that addresses priorities both inside and outside the church today, centered on creation care and supporting church/institutional mission. In their proposal, Torrey and Lee seek investors in a venture to capture hydrogen and sell it retail as an energy source for hydrogen-powered vehicles. Their method of hydrogen capture relies on an emerging technology, a microwave plasma torch, used to gasify hydrocarbons in waste plastic, and then ultimately to separate out the hydrogen for eventual retail sale. The revenue from sales would then help to fund the Three Seas Training Center—the home of The Fourth River Project. The project's mission is to "prepare for the opening of North Korea by equipping servant workers in all walks of life for the rebuilding of the nation and the proclamation of the gospel."[7]

In my response, I will broadly reflect on the hydrogen capture and sale process, then on pairing a newer or emerging mission (in this case, creation care) with a longer-term mission of the church (in this case, addressing mission in the currently closed region of North Korea).

From Waste to Resource

While modern technologies and industrial processes have contributed to our current ecological degradation, finding innovative ways to apply new technologies to redress such effects is critically important in our current age. Take, for example, an existing technological device, the incandescent lightbulb, whose primary purpose is to illuminate a room. While the incandescent lightbulb achieves this task, it does so at high levels of energy consumption. Creation care and addressing the global climate crisis demand that we look for less energy-consumptive technologies to achieve the task of illumination. That drives us to other technologies and, in this case, the development of fluorescent lights, and eventually the LED lightbulb, which consumes far less energy than the incandescent lightbulb while accomplishing the same task. This is the same kind of responsible

---

7 The Fourth River Project, *Jesus Abbey's Three Seas Center*, accessed May 19, 2023, http://www.thefourthriver.org/PDF%20Documents/Main%20Brochure%20English.pdf.

environmental stewardship that Torrey and Lee promote as they explore new methods for capturing hydrogen.

Hydrogen has been viewed as a clean energy source since the 1800s. When it reacts with oxygen, its only byproduct is water. That is, in a hydrogen-powered vehicle there is no carbon or substance other than water released while the car is in operation. However, the process of capturing hydrogen so that it may be used, for example, as energy to power a vehicle, is usually very energy intensive. As Torrey and Lee point out, most hydrogen capture processes involve using natural gas, oil, or coal, with a much smaller percentage captured by electrolysis of water. The goal is then to "green" the hydrogen capture process through a less energy-intensive process.

Torrey and Lee identify waste plastic as a stock source for the hydrogen they will capture. The plastic is heated to a plasma state, allowing its elements, including hydrogen, to separate and the hydrogen to be captured and stored for later use. In Torrey and Lee's proposal, this plasma state is achieved using an as yet experimental microwave plasma torch, at a much lower energy consumption rate and maintenance cost than current plasma torch technologies provide—an idea similar to moving from incandescent to LED lightbulbs.

Torrey and Lee identified plastic waste as a stock source because it is found in great and ongoing abundance in cities worldwide. In this particular case, the local government is willing to pay for its disposal, thus creating a viable long-term stock source. Using waste plastic may achieve the goal of reducing plastic waste through reuse.

Thus, for hydrogen capture, the proposal addresses several creation care/crisis reduction goals by

- building on a current technology to develop a more energy-efficient method for hydrogen capture;
- addressing the waste plastic disposal problems—offering a zero waste-to-landfill reuse solution to the ever-increasing volume of waste plastic; and
- supporting the move to "greener" hydrogen vehicle transportation, where the only emission is water.

This creates missional outcomes and blessings for the people who use hydrogen as an energy source for their vehicles, the city as it is able to find an environmentally friendly way to dispose of its plastic waste, and the world at large as further development of hydrogen energy becomes a mitigating force against the climate crisis.

However, plastics consist of elements such as carbon, hydrogen, oxygen, nitrogen, chlorine, and sulfur. It is also important to be mindful of environmental justice elements of all industrial processes, including for example other waste products from plastic conversion, and what people and places disproportionately bear any costs and benefits—extending to solid waste storage, air quality, and exposure to risks for laborers and nearby residents.

Supporting a Ministry and Creating Dual Blessings

While the creation care element of this project is evident, Torrey and Lee focus their rationale for hydrogen capture on the financial support that it offers to The Fourth River Project. Finding creative ways to support a project, such as hydrogen sales to support The Fourth River Project, is important, and there is synergy when both the fundraising and the funded projects are each missional in their own right. I would like to point to a similar dual missional benefit coming from my North American Mennonite context.

In the 1920s, Mennonite Central Committee (MCC) was formed to help provide famine relief to Mennonites in what is now Ukraine. When the famine ended, MCC began serving other peoples around the world in relief, development, and peacemaking in the name of Christ, as it does today. In the 1960s, many people donated used clothing to MCC, who in turn shipped the clothing to their partners in other countries of need. When MCC changed its missional model in 1972, citing the benefits of purchasing deliverables locally, a community in Altona, Manitoba, Canada decided to continue collecting clothing and used items from within the community, but instead of shipping them overseas they sold the items locally and donated the proceeds to MCC. This was the genesis of the MCC thrift shop: selling used goods to benefit MCC's mission. Today there are eighty-five MCC thrift shops in North America, which have donated more than $250 million to MCC over the past fifty years.[8]

Beyond the cash benefit that the thrift shops gave to MCC's (initial) mission, the thrift shops themselves became a mission and a blessing in their own communities. They

- allowed people to buy relatively good clothes and to reuse other items at a low cost;
- kept existing products in local circulation, reducing landfilled waste and energy needed to produce and transport new items;

---

8 Lori Giesbrecht, "MCC Thrift Shops Celebrate 50 Years," *Anabaptist World*, March 23, 2022, https://anabaptistworld.org/mcc-thrift-shops-celebrate-50-years/.

- provided outlets for people to "clear their shelves" of items and clothes that they were no longer using, knowing that those items would be a blessing to others who could use them;
- acted as a community center for volunteers who wanted to donate their time to a worthy cause; and
- provided an identity and ethos for the community as a people who serve others.

The MCC thrift shops, which began as a way to fund MCC's programs, became missions of their own with wide ancillary benefits throughout many communities. In the same way, a hydrogen fueling center, which may be developed in order to fund The Four Rivers Project, can become a mission of its own, blessing a world that needs to find ways to reduce its environmental impact as a part of creation care and addressing our current climate crisis.

Conclusion

In their proposal, Torrey and Lee grapple with two human-created crises: a climate/environmental crisis and a political division of the Korean peninsula. They address the climate/environmental crisis through an energy-efficient method of capturing hydrogen using waste plastic, then selling it as fuel for hydrogen-powered vehicles. They address the crisis of a divided Korea by using the revenue from hydrogen sales to fund The Fourth River Project.

Just as we recognize that people possess different spiritual gifts and that each gift is valuable (1 Cor. 12), the same can be said about gifts to address crises; the gifts are not all the same, but each one is important. For some, the gift is an ability to find energy-efficient ways to capture hydrogen while for others it is the gift of unifying and empowering people in the Korean peninsula. By bringing multiple missions together under one system, such initiatives can begin to address the multiple urgent crises of our time.

CHAPTER 17

Environment, Natural Disasters, and the Experience of the Dandelion Community

by Insoo Kim

As the inevitable evils of industrial development and unrestrained economic growth, environmental pollution and natural disasters are the most serious existential threats mankind has ever faced. And like the saying that the stones will cry out (Luke 19:40), there is a common outcry heard in the forests, lakes, seas, and skies, and even in the mouths of children.[1] Christian visionaries have constantly warned about the seriousness of these threats but they have largely been ignored, even more so than climate activists in the secular world. Since the mission community clings to the dualistic position that prioritizes the salvation of souls, the subject of the environment and nature is not even a part of the holistic gospel. Although the deep ecology argument that growth and development must cease is persuasive, we still place too much emphasis on the pursuit of sustainable growth and on mission as development. We are now facing the challenges of how to reflect on the past, how to transform reality, and how to prepare for the future.

We must find communal solutions and then experiment, share, and preserve them, while restoring admiration, reverence, and respect for this world, God, and man. Above all, we must not produce the evils of unbalanced "development" based on highly specialized knowledge, technology, and science, but cultivate rather a culture of broad generalization that seeks to protect the vulnerable environment itself. Such generalization can become a way of life for the people who preserve the ecological environment, social community, and spirituality through the application of human science or appropriate life skills. In the context of experimenting with missional life in Korea and rural Asia, I hope the Dandelion Community will be a modest community model of holism, restoration, and vitality, serving as an exemplary ark of safety within the deluge of environmental pollution and natural disasters.

---

1 Greta Thunberg's attendance at the UN Climate Action Summit led the global climate alliance movement in 2019. Since then, voices and appeals from children and adolescents have been popping up all around the world.

Transformation of Life and Faith

The very terms "environmental pollution" and "natural disasters" undermine the beauty, richness, and sustainability of God's creation. Because of man's disobedience and sin, the harmony and balance of the world and nature has become imperfect. However, today's environmental pollution, climate change, and frequent natural catastrophes result from the development of material civilization over the past two hundred years, which indulged humanity's sinful greed and its human-centered worldview and lifestyle. Of course, there was the age-old tradition of treating nature as a conquered colony, all within the reasonable thinking of the ancient Greeks and the practical skill of the Romans.[2] You could ask them about the origins of environmental destruction, but it is undeniable in our time that natural destruction and catastrophe on a global scale has resulted from our modern civilization and lifestyles.

Mankind is facing a dilemma—it cannot continue down the path of apparent destruction, nor can it turn back.[3] In this situation, it is significant that a transition movement has also begun in the UK, the epicenter of modern industry and environmental destruction.[4] Even in the face of the crisis of civilization caused by peak oil and climate change, it is possible to live in friendship with nature. A transition movement that seeks to build nonviolent social relationships and alternative lifestyles can lead to a renewal for humanity. In this era of transition, the Christian missionary movement must consider the following three reorientations. These are also ongoing life experiments in the Dandelion Community.

Transition to a Soil-Based Farming Life

Since ancient times in Korea, an idea called *Nong Ja Cheon Hali Dae Bon* (농자천하지대본 農者天下之大本) was well-known not only to peasants but to the general population. It means that farming is "the great foundation of

---

2 J. Donald Hughes, *Ecology in Ancient Civilizations* (Albuquerque: Univ. of New Mexico Press, 1975).

3 Masahiro Morioka, 무통문명 [Painless civilization] (모멘토, 2003), 10–47.

4 A course called "Life After Oil" was launched at Schumacher College, an alternative university, and a village-level transition movement began and spread in Totnes and Devon. It is worth looking at the development philosophy of the college after whom the school is named, E. F. Schumacher ("E. F. Schumacher's Founding Philosophy and How It Still Guides Us Today," Practical Action, June 30, 2021, https://practicalaction. org/news-media/2021/06/30/e-f-schumachers-founding-philosophy-and-how-it-still-guides-us-today/#:~:text=discussed%20and%20championed-,E.F.,rather%20than%20a%20select%20few). His pioneering thinking is profoundly practical and applicable and consistent with Christian orientation and values.

the lives of people under the heavens," implying an agrarian worldview. In contrast, the great foundation of our modern lifestyle is the vast infrastructure that supports financial transactions (e.g., banks and investments), so that making lots of money becomes the most important thing in life.

Mankind has built cities and civilizations through the development of technology and science, but these were not constructed in symbiosis with the soil. Rather, the process involved plundering the soil's value, reducing its vitality, and even killing it. Can you believe that every year a land area one hundred times the size of Seoul is turned into infertile, desert land on the earth?[5] Urbanization and civilization can never preserve the land's fertility.

By its very nature, the city has been possessed by the spirits of consumption, rape, despoiling, and killing.[6] As cities expand, nearby agricultural land and mountain and fishing villages are destroyed, renewable energy resources are depleted, the earth's environment deteriorates, and even humans are consumed and killed. The more you study, the more you go to an advanced school, the more you go to a prestigious university, and the more you earn money, gain fame, and hold power in your hands, the more you become detached from the earth, despise the soil, abandon your hometown, and lose your moorings.

"Humus," another name for soil, is from the word "human, humanity", and we must realize that even humility, the final process of our spirituality, is inseparable from the soil.[7] Historically, a soil-based farming life destined one to live in relative poverty. We must learn how to live in poverty and learn the grace to share our destiny with the poor. Agricultural life is fundamental to the restoration of true spirituality, which protects us from structures that consume life and extinguish the soil's vitality in the process of urbanization and civilization.

Transition to Discipleship Based on a Simpler Way to Live

The church's mission is to make disciples as followers of Jesus. However, in its mission it has not deviated from the industrial development, the temptation to abundant growth, and the urban lifestyle that are the backbones

---

5 John Madeley, *Food for All: The Need for a New Agriculture* (London: Zed Books, 2002), 134.

6 For his groundbreaking biblical theology of the city and modern technological society, see the reprints of Jacques Ellul's, *The Meaning of the City*, trans. Dennis Pardee (Eugene, OR: Wipf and Stock, 2011) and *The Technological System*, trans. Joachim Neugrosche (Eugene, OR: Wipf and Stock, 2018).

7 In fact, the Benedictine Rule states that one can reach God's love by setting and performing the twelve steps of humility.

of mainstream civilization. In addition, the more missionaries are trained and educated, the more they tend to separate nature from their destiny. Is it not time to seek the authenticity of discipleship in Galilee and not in Jerusalem? The numerous methodologies and practices of discipleship in history have certainly promoted global mission with quantifiable results. However, What kind of society has our gospel produced? is a difficult question with no easy answer. Love and unity, the inner essence of discipleship,[8] are difficult to observe in society and the gospel cannot free itself from the criticisms of being a pioneering mission of modern Christian civilization and promoting Christian capitalism as a servant of colonialism.

In fact, our Christian discipleship has promoted the pursuit of wealth and civilization, and unwittingly moved us away from harmony with nature. We should have followed the path of Jesus and his disciples, not wealth. Theirs was a simple life and we should have resolved to live the same way, in poverty with integrity. We must face the fact that many disasters happen because we hate a simple life. We should wonder if the purpose and direction of our discipleship is wrong since although Christianity has been around for 2,000 years, there have continually been the poor and the oppressed among us in the world.

If God is calling us to redeem his creation and to preach the gospel to the poor, not to a better civilization and a more convenient life, shouldn't we first listen to the earth's lessons, nature's voice, and the cries of the poor? This requires us to have a poetic imagination. The languages of earth, nature, and the poor are different from ours. They can only be approached by the language of the heart, expressed in empathy, in awe, in admiration, and in reverence, rather than by the language of understanding. It should not be a language of logic and persuasion, but a language that takes it all in. In that sense, the time has come for a new psalm to be sung.

Transition to Friendship in the Mission Field

We cherish the mission field that we worked so hard to build. Many theological, humanistic, political-economic, and technological talents were put into it, and our labor was filled with blood, sweat, and tears. But we must question again; we must ask whether the customary results and merits of our work are perhaps holding us back. We must reflect on the purpose, process, and methodology of our mission, even if we do not repent. What are we doing as ministers and missionaries? and, Why are we doing this?

---

8 "By this everyone will know that you are my disciples, if you love one another" (John 13:35); "Father, just as you are in me and I am in you. May they also be in us so that the world may believe that you have sent me" (John 17:21).

True faith movements formed communities of true friendship— friendship with God, fellow human beings, and nature. Today, however, missionaries are burdened with loneliness. Discord and division among missionary communities, psychological pain, and frustration are common themes in missionaries' lives. There is anxiety and nervousness in our hearts that can easily creep in without sponsorship and financial support. We should move toward a life of sincere friendship with others, not with friendship evangelism, so-called "making friendships for evangelism."

As missionaries, we must not speak and give; we must let the poor speak and give. Even though they are poor, we have to let them lead us and let them preach. As Hans Carlier put it, Are we willing to accept the illiterate and poor peasant of the Third World as our teacher?[9] When they begin to speak to us and lead us, a true friendship will sprout between them and us, and we will be able to humbly let go of our foolish idea to advance the gospel with money, talent, and strategies, and move one step at a time toward the truth. This is possible not only with the poor, but also with the land in which we find ourselves, with its grasses and flowing waters. Only then will we feel admiration for the land and nature, respect for the poor, and overwhelming wonder for the true God, as warm as the rising sun.

The Life and Experience of the Dandelion Community

Our community has been around for thirty-two years, and we have many things to be honored and proud of. But we have been frustrated at every step, have been at odds with our colleagues, and are still immature at integrating the past, present, and future. However, when we look back, we can see the lifestyle that we have worked so hard to preserve: we have never forgotten the Lord's command to preach the gospel to the poor, we have not rejected the poor and afflicted when they came, and we have never undermined the graces of nature but stayed rooted in the soil, farming, and living simply. Since we learned by "doing and then learning" rather than by "learning and then doing," there was a lot of trial and error, which finally became our teacher. We can say without shame that the Bible not only taught us, but also the mountains, fields, and waters taught us, and that the poor are our teachers. Here are some of the lifestyles and insights we've gained from living in the Dandelion Community.

Formation of Self-Reliant Communities

The Dandelion Community strives to implement five basic self-sufficiencies: food, energy, economics, education and culture, and faith and conscience.

---

9 Madeley, *Food for All*, 20.

We would like to share these efforts with our fellow churches on the mission field:

1. Food self-sufficiency is centered on the main grain crops and adheres to eco-friendly farming methods, without pesticides or chemical fertilizers.

2. Energy self-sufficiency is still a difficult task because we already live with a convenient power system. But in the future, we plan that all buildings will be converted to a distributed power system, and the appropriate modern and traditional (구들) technologies, such as old ecological architecture, will be utilized. Every fall, Dandelion School students are given the opportunity to create and utilize energy on their own through the "Energy Independence Training" course.

3. Economic self-reliance is based on non-competitive communal cooperation as much as possible, with income derived from agriculture and handcrafts, while also considering the creation of community enterprises. Education, ecology, alternative living, agriculture, experiential learning, different crafts, etc. seem to be other possible business areas where we could do well. Above all, we do not want to owe money, but rather campaign to pay debts of individual debtors and some organizations.

4. Self-sufficiency in education and culture is achieved through elementary, middle, and high school courses in the Dandelion School community. And through Dandelion University, rural mission leaders in Asia and Africa and young people in Korea grow together, teaching and learning simultaneously (교학상장: 教學相長, "learn from each other"), and are nurtured as rural leaders. Also, rather than passively submitting to the wider culture through purchase and consumption of goods and services, the community is actively involved in producing and nurturing its own culture as a craft community.

5. Self-sufficiency in faith and conscience fosters a spirit of resistance to the world and a symbiotic relationship with the earth as a movement of truth, evidenced by a community life without bias toward any denomination or theology.

A Lifestyle That Minimizes the Power of Money

Modern society and the church operate and depend on the power of money. The entrenched belief is that more money can expand ministry and do more good. In human history, however, the people who helped the poor were none other than the other poor around them. We want to cultivate the economics of friendship, not the inexorable economics in which only excellence and competitiveness survive, and to live a life in coincidence with labor, free from the risk that money easily becomes power. We want to make the whole process of production, processing, and sales a labor of ownership. A lifestyle that minimizes the power of money inevitably leads us to peaceful relationships with a land, a region, its resources, and its people, and makes faith rooted in life a reality. This approach also leads us to a more humble and contented life.

It is easy to fall prey to crisis and disaster in human society or community. They occur when we ignore the biblical grand principles, "Love God and love your neighbor," and the suffering of the last days comes when we love money instead of God and only ourselves instead of our neighbor. 2 Timothy 3:1–5 accurately points to this fact—"But mark this: There will be terrible times in the last days. People will be lovers of themselves, lovers of money … ." James 5:3 also warns that "You have hoarded wealth in the last days," pointing out the overriding danger we have to guard against in the last days. This exhortation is very different from modern advice on how to prepare for an impending crisis and a dangerous future. Most people don't want a community that is built on long-standing trust and love; money as a sure guarantee is more important. But money becomes useless in extreme catastrophes. We cannot eat gold or money. But as a loving community, brothers and sisters can ensure each other's destiny.

When we enjoy the happiness of sharing rather than possessions, we can expect that the way we look at nature will change, and not only will we enjoy the riches of nature, but the door for those who suffer will be opened wider. In many cases, the neuropsychiatric illnesses of our modern age can be referred to as the diseases of civilization. And often they don't need excellent medical technology, counseling, and medicines, but the warmness of absolute friendship. So, communities of light and friendship must be established everywhere.

The Valley Where We Live (Insoo Kim)

In the valley where we live, I like the light.
The sun rises early and sets late, the light is bright and plentiful,
full of warmth and heat.

The trees grow well, the grass grows well,
the people are at peace, and the difficult sickness is healed
occasionally.
A land where waterfowl come and mountain birds come,
where light gathers and warmth shines in the land,
Let light gather in our hearts.

With its warmth and heat, we become kind-hearted and love
one another.
Let us live together removing the shadows, melting the cold
in the heart,
and living in the valley of light where we live.

Reducing Life/Livelihood Mileage

The Food Miles movement, which is concerned with health, energy, and environmental issues, is already well-received around the world. Nearby gardens and locally produced crops become channels of friendship that promote health, knowing who produced them. We should reduce food and housing mileage through increased self-sufficiency, learning to consume environmentally sustainable amounts of food and using environmentally friendly construction materials. We should also drink purified local water and rainwater instead of water brought in from distant rivers or lakes and use eco-friendly sewage treatment methods as practical ways to save surrounding wetlands, to protect rice fields, and to save the creeks and streams. In the Dandelion Community, some of the treatment of domestic sewage is carried out using naturally-ventilated, vertical and horizontal-flow wetlands installed with eco-friendly water purification technology. Also, a diversity of environment-friendly energy sources (biomass, electric, photovoltaic, wind, geothermal, etc.) should be developed, passive houses should be constructed that use maximum natural energy, and energy-saving lifestyles (complemented by warm clothing) should be adopted.

It's also best to find places to dine as close as possible, while people who come from far away should absolutely be welcomed. In particular, the creation of a community that welcomes people suffering from economic hardship, political repression, oppressive environmental scourges, and mental stress and anxiety is more urgent than ever (1 Cor. 1:26–28; 1 Sam. 22:1–2). In order to be able to live a simple but self-sufficient life with hospitality, we have to find the way to live in harmony with nature and its resources and with neighboring communities rooted in the earth, and then expand on that path.

Maintaining the Fertility of the Land

It takes at least one to three hundred years for one centimeter of arable topsoil to form naturally. The topsoil layer of arable land is usually about thirty centimeters deep, which takes about three to ten thousand years to form. However, the amount of topsoil lost every year could cover an entire island.

The first command given to the first humans was to to cultivate and tend the garden of Eden (Gen. 2:15). It is surprising that the King James Version, more than four hundred years old, translates the Hebrew word for "to cultivate" as "to dress." I don't know if there was more meaning to "dress" at that time, but "dress" literally means "to put on clothes." Here it means "clothe the earth" and "protect the topsoil from sunlight and heavy rains to preserve its fertility." This illustrates the importance of mulch as a soil cover in natural agriculture. In modern translation, it preserves the fertility of the land.

Ignorance and greed sparked the beginning of mankind's tragic history. Industrial approaches to the soil have depleted its fertility, which has been the reason for the decline and fall of all civilizations. Edward Hyams in *Soil and Civilization* consistently argues that the decline of self-sufficient farming and the depletion of soil fertility were the direct causes of the decline and fall of major ancient civilizations, especially Greco-Roman civilization.[10]

The Dandelion Community adheres to sustainable agriculture based on natural farming methods, without using any chemical fertilizers or pesticides. Natural farming is a concept developed from the community's own organic farm. It enhances soil structure and fertility by activating native microorganisms in the soil, and has added benefits such as reducing labor and farming costs and improving water quality. Currently, rice, wheat, potatoes, beans, peppers, vegetables, herbs, etc. are grown, chickens are raised naturally (free-range), and educational livestock programs are run. By sourcing most of the seeds, compost, natural pesticides, and irrigation locally, natural farming is becoming sustainable.

---

10 Edward Hyams, *Soil and Civilization* (New York: Thames and Hudson, 1952).

Land fertility contributes to the health and nutrition of crops and livestock and brings health and happiness to the people who are the final consumers. One of the most important factors for the health and healing of the Dandelion Community is healthy eating. Good air, clean water, healthy food, proper work, and a cheerful, open community life can heal the people. Many have reported improvements in insomnia, depression, addiction, respiratory problems, obesity, cancer, mental distress, and interpersonal relationships.

Preparation of the Craft Community

We reduce energy consumption and machine operation as much as possible and develop the habit of using local resources to produce the basic necessities of life with simple tools. These are not items produced with an eye to technological impressiveness or complexity, but for practical functionality and a stress on the dignity of the person using the tool.

Deep understanding of the properties of soil and stone, iron and wood, water and fire, and promoting their utilization will lead us from being consumption-oriented to being production-oriented, and in the long term, our crafting will be a source of wisdom that prepares us for times of disaster. Identifying as a craft community allows us to discover and cherish the hidden values of the environment and resources around us and leads us to a sustainable life in harmony with nature. In our experience, the most dignified and harmonious architecture uses surrounding, environmentally-friendly materials for practical functionality. And we also realized that the discipline of building a sound and moderate character in education depends on how we craft useful and beautiful things using hands and body.

Two Poems about Civilization

Suicide Civilization (Insoo Kim)

All human civilization,
in a place with clean water and easy transportation,
where people gather to eat well and live well,
where knowledge, learning, and education
push the limits of human beings,
push down the limits of nature,
and make many seemingly impossible areas a reality,
rather, where the phenomenon of reality becomes unreal
occurs,
humanity is preoccupied with the pleasures of the place.
This is the subversion of reality, the rebellion of
knowledge and technology,
and the phenomenon of the reverse attack of nature is
witnessed in the place.

Here, our lives are easy, fast, and abundant,
watching videos, having fun across time and space,
and enjoying omnipotence every day.
Thus, we have no worries about winter storms or summer
heat anymore,
rather, we have three meals a day full of delicacies carried
from all over the world.
Now, man is almost a god,
who has been found to satisfy the pleasures of the body,
the mind, and even the soul.
However, the earth is sick and ruined,
the forest is sick and ruined,
lakes and seas are sick and ruined,
the sky is sick and ruined,
and man is sick and ruined.
Even though the path of self-destruction,
that path of suicide civilization,
is now beginning to manifest itself clearly,
What would we do?
What will be done about this?
What would we do?
How will we avoid this embarrassment?

Our Civilization (Insoo Kim)

Nature is more thorough than human hands,
and instinct outlasts education.
Since the beginning of time,
mountains, fields, seas, and deserts have nurtured life
and have suffered all kinds of weather,
but nature never makes garbage
and never forgets the wonder and beauty.

Our civilization, however, has been built on pollution,
garbage,
and death for a long time,
and even the memory of celebrating life is fading.
Our civilization has taught its knowledge,
but we are afraid of the civilization that we have built,
and we are concerned about how the sky and land will save
our children.
Above all, we sleep hard at night worrying that
the knowledge our civilization teaches to our children
may be false, weak, and despaired.

Education should not easily sing hope.
Because even with the best education,
our children are only part of nature
and can only live by its grace.

Discussion Questions

1. How do earth's lessons, nature's voice, and the cries of the poor express in "heart language" that mankind must transition to farming life?

2. How should farming communities apply the traditional values of friendship and hospitality as counterculture to modern technology, materialism, and individualism?

3. How could such friendship communities serve as arks of refuge in times of disaster?

Response

by Douglas Day Kaufman

What a delight to learn about the Dandelion Community with their communal practices and missional theology. They offer a compelling alternative to the postmodern, global capitalist world that engenders natural disasters, climate catastrophe, and socioeconomic inequality. Theirs is also an alternative to mission that embraces and promotes this global dysfunction rather than offering a contrast to it. Like monastic communities and communalist Anabaptists, such as the Hutterites and the Bruderhof, they offer Christianity as alternative economics.[11] The Dandelion Community is an alternative political economy to global capitalism.

Though *ecology* and *economy* find roots in the same Greek word for house or household, *oikos*, economics focuses exclusively on one part of human life, while ecology includes all creation. The bifurcation between these two has tragic consequences.

Wendell Berry addresses this problem with the term *great economy*. The term originated in conversation with Wes Jackson about how the money economy is ruining farmland. As they struggled to find an economy comprehensive enough to include land, Jackson finally suggested the *kingdom of God*. Inspired by Jesus's words in Matthew 6:25–33, Berry calls this the great economy, and it includes everything, even the birds of the air (v. 26) and the lilies of the field (v. 28). What we think of as the economy, what can be counted by bookkeepers and economists, is the small economy and is dependent on this broader ecology of God.[12]

Insoo Kim beautifully connects these two economies/ecologies in describing their relationship with nature. Kim's is a theological economy/ecology. He writes of an economy of friendship—friendship with God, with fellow humans, and with nature. That these relationships are broken is why communities such as the Dandelion Community must exist. This brokenness in relationships is what fuels the looming threat of climate change.

Offering an alternative political economy is one of the most critical tasks for the church confronting climate and other calamities. My own journey into recognizing the problem of climate change is probably typical. At first, I recognized global warming as a scientific problem. Too many greenhouse

---

11 Eberhard Arnold, *Why We Live in Community* (Farmington, PA: Plough Publishing, 1995).

12 Wendell Berry, "Two Economies," *Review & Expositor* 81, no. 2 (1984): 209–12, https://doi.org/10.1177/003463738408100204.

gas emissions were causing it, so we simply needed to reduce those emissions. However, in the over thirty years since the global community first convened to address the issue,[13] greenhouse gas emissions have increased dramatically. In the face of an existential threat, humanity accelerates towards extinction. This caused me to research the social psychology of climate change. Why are humans doing the opposite of the rational and good thing?

Sociologist Kari Norgaard identified several different forms of denial around climate change.[14] While many focus on the hard denial of some conservatives, she noticed that many more people engage in a soft denial that recognizes climate science but ignores the implications, trying to avoid thinking about climate. This denial protects us from a host of uncomfortable thoughts and emotions, such as guilt, fear, and helplessness.[15] Finnish pastoral theologian Panu Pihkala offers spiritual responses to this dilemma with ritual, art, education, conversations, and more. The hope is that as humans come to know the enormity of the problem, we will change.[16]

But anyone working against climate change eventually runs into a sobering reality. Powerful globally entrenched interests prevent responsible change. That is, the problem is one of political economy. To address this problem within the faith community, we need a political theology of climate change.[17]

The Dandelion Community's alternative political economy is found in several key ideas, especially self-reliance in food, energy, enterprise, education, and faith. Yet this is *self* not in an individualistic or independent way, but a radical communalism and interdependence with the soil, the community, and one another. Along with the emphasis on "non-competitive

---

13 The Rio Summit in June 1992 was when commitments were made. However, the first global conference on climate precedes that by twenty years, held in Stockholm in 1972.

14 Kari Marie Norgaard, *Living in Denial: Climate Change, Emotions, and Everyday Life* (Cambridge, MA: MIT Press, 2011), Kindle.

15 Another, more theological, response to Norgaard's thesis, including the dilemma of humans doing the wrong thing, is Willa Swenson-Lengyel, "Moral Paralysis and Practical Denial: Environmental Ethics in Light of Human Failure," *Journal of the Society of Christian Ethics* 37, no. 2 (Fall/Winter 2017): 171–87, https://doi.org/10.1353/sce.2017.0039.

16 Panu Pihkala, "Eco-anxiety, Tragedy, and Hope: Psychological and Spiritual Dimensions of Climate Change," *Zygon: Journal of Religion and Science* 53, no. 2 (June 2018): 545–69, https://onlinelibrary.wiley.com/doi/abs/10.1111/zygo.12407, and "The Pastoral Challenge of the Environmental Crisis: Environmental Anxiety and Lutheran Eco-Reformation," *Dialog: A Journal of Theology* 55, no. 2 (Summer 2016): 131–40, https://doi.org/10.1111/dial.12239.

17 For example, Michael Northcott, *A Political Theology of Climate Change* (Grand Rapids: Eerdmans, 2013), and Daniel Castillo, *An Ecological Theology of Liberation: Salvation and Political Ecology* (Maryknoll, NY: Orbis Books, 2019).

communal cooperation," there is "the power of money." Kim writes: "We want to cultivate the economics of friendship, not the inexorable economics in which only excellence and competitiveness survive, and to live a life in coincidence with labor, free from the risk that money easily becomes power."

This alternative political economy, an economy based on friendship and sharing, leads to a different relationship with nature, where there is mutual learning. Kim writes: "We can say without shame that the Bible not only taught us, but also the mountains, fields, and waters taught us." This economy leads to more positive relationships. "A lifestyle that minimizes the power of money inevitably leads us to peaceful relationships with a land, a region, its resources, and its people, and makes faith rooted in life a reality." Their relationship with the poor is changed as well, as they learn from and not just teach the poor. When you have an economics of relationship, you do not need to save a surplus for your retirement. When greed is seen as a vice rather than a virtue, you do not need to take more than you need. Practices of mutual caring and sharing do not encourage people to gain more income than they need.

In line with learning from the mountains and listening to the cries of the stones (Luke 19:40), Daniel Quinn in his novel *Ishmael* imagines a human learning from an ape named Ishmael. The ape calls modern people *Takers*, those who take more than they need. They take what they want from the world without considering the consequences. They squander nature.[18] The Dandelion Community is a place of both giving and receiving, taking and leaving. This is an alternative way of life that is sustainable.

Yet how can this alternative become the norm? At one point Kim talks about the Dandelion Community as an "ark of safety." The metaphor is apt, except that the ark set down on a restored earth after the flood. In a climate-changed world, the floods will continue and there will be no off-ramp. While alternatives like the Dandelion Community and Bruderhof can be inspiring, how can their lessons reach those beyond the community? How can we move toward a broader social movement where most of us practice something closer to the economy and ecology of Jesus?

This quandary has shaped changes at Practical Action, the organization founded by E. F. Schumacher. "With complex and interrelated issues such as environmental degradation and climate change, we need our work to scale up to go beyond isolated action at a community level and meet a wider

---

18 Daniel Quinn, *Ishmael* (New York: Bantam Books, 1992).

array of challenges, addressing the systems and not just the symptoms."[19] The recent CEO of Practical Action, Paul Smith Lomas, describes the shift: "The real difference between then and now is that now we focus much more on bringing about systems change. Once you've found something that works, how do you find ways to make something go beyond the individual projects or individual program that we worked on in those days."[20]

This approach works if markets are indeed free and open, where special interests do not receive subsidies or tax breaks, where government processes are transparent, and elections are accountable. All these, whether they ever existed, seem under threat today, and the changing climate seems to accentuate these inequities.

So how do these alternatives become the new standards globally? Forms of confrontational, direct, and nonviolent action seem necessary. Yet if indeed the universe bends towards justice, then someone needs to be living more fully into that justice, even if on a small scale.

Many Christian missiologies today simply add some God-talk to individualistic, capitalist approaches. God will help you become a better capitalist who exploits labor and land. Like the Bruderhof before them, the Dandelion Community offers a social and ecological missiology. We need a true conversion to a way of life that embraces and learns from one another, from God, and from all creatures. This is the kind of polity and economics that will help all creation to thrive in harmony with the Creator.

---

19 "E. F. Schumacher's "Founding Philosophy and How It Still Guides Us Today," *Practical Action*, June 30, 2021, https://practicalaction.org/news-media/2021/06/30/ e-f-schumachers-founding-philosophy-and-how-it-still-guides-us-today/#:~: text=discussed%20and%20championed-,E.F.,rather%20than%20a%20select%20few.

20 "E. F. Schumacher's Founding Philosophy."

CHAPTER 18

Evangelizing All Creatures
Pastoral Ecology as Mission

by Douglas Day Kaufman

Today I invite you to broaden your view of evangelism, that we not only evangelize our fellow human beings but all our fellow creatures, human or not. I call this pastoral ecology, mission that engages not only neighboring humans but the whole ecosystem of a congregation.

Scriptural Basis

Evangelizing all creatures comes from a little-noticed phrase repeated a couple of times in the New Testament. In Colossians 1:23 the writer invites the brothers and sisters in Colossae to remain steadfast to "the gospel that you heard, which has been proclaimed to every creature under heaven" (NRSV). How is the gospel proclaimed to every creature? Is this just hyperbole? Does this not really mean every human?

That it is more than just overstatement is suggested by the context, with its repeated phrase "all things" in describing Christ's relationship with creation. Christ is "the image of the invisible God, the firstborn of all creation; for in him *all things* in heaven and on earth were created … *all thing*s have been created through him and for him (vv. 15–16)." Furthermore, "through him God was pleased to reconcile to himself *all things*, whether on earth or in heaven" (v. 20, NRSV). Here creation is not some backdrop or scenery for salvation history. Creation is a participant in the divine drama of creation and reconciliation. Perhaps creation even participates in the divine being.

A similar phrase appears in the longer ending of the Gospel of Mark, in 16:15, in the Marcan Great Commission. Jesus begins with the words, "Go into all the world and proclaim the good news to the whole creation" (NRSV). For some reason, the NRSV translates the Greek words differently here than in Colossians 1. The King James Version translates it as "every creature." Here we have more reason to think this is exaggeration. For Jesus goes on to say, "The one who believes and is baptized will be saved" (v. 16, NRSV). It is hard to know how another creature could be baptized in any meaningful way. At the same time, included in his list of signs accompanying believers is picking up snakes, a powerful example of threatening creatures (v. 18).

My Congregation's Story of River Baptisms

Baptism is what first caused me to ponder the place of creation in God's mission. Through baptism I learned to know the creatures in my congregation's neighborhood. Among these creatures are Caddisfly larvae, who live in the river bottom and build small houses around themselves. I find them by dipping a net into the river bottom. I see these creatures as my neighbors. But more than that, I see them as participants in the gospel in our neighborhood.

Why am I looking for creatures in our river bottom?

It began about twenty years ago. My congregation, Benton Mennonite Church in Goshen, Indiana, practices believers baptism, baptizing those who have made a commitment to follow Christ. Though we are not particular about the method, our congregations started baptizing people in the Elkhart River. Jesus himself was baptized in a river, and our congregation is located across the street from the river.

The first time we were preparing a river baptism, a congregant told me, "Doug, the Elkhart County Environmental Health Department does not recommend full body contact with the Elkhart River." This puzzled me, since we live in a rural area. I told the baptizands about this problem and one of them told me, "God won't let me get sick when I'm baptized." Knowing that following Christ also means suffering, I wasn't so sure. But we arranged for them to have showers after their baptisms.

Learning River Ecology

This started a search for me. I learned to know soil and water conservation leaders in our area; I learned the reason for the health warning was because at times the water becomes contaminated with too much manure. This made more sense, that in our rural area mismanagement of sewage from humans and from farm animals could cause the water to become unhealthy.

I also learned about Hoosier Riverwatch, with Hoosier being what someone from Indiana is called. This state organization gave us training and equipment to start monitoring the quality of the water of the Elkhart River. We performed chemical tests of the water, looking at the levels of oxygen, phosphate, nitrate, and pH. We examined the habitat looking for how natural it is. A river in the midst of parking lots, concrete, and roofs is not going to be as healthy as one surrounded by trees and meadows.

And finally we took biological tests, using nets to discover the many creatures who make their home in the river bottom. While the other tests tell us the water quality at the moment in time we are testing, the biological test tells us the quality of the water over time. It asks the crucial question, What creatures are able to inhabit and thrive in this river? We are looking for a diversity of creatures and whether that diversity includes some creatures who are sensitive to pollution. If there is a sudden change, what is happening to the river?

In our setting the most important test was also the hardest, discovering how much E. coli was in the water. This signals how much manure is in the water. We are volunteer scientists, and bacteria were not easy to grow in our small, improvised incubator originally used for hatching eggs.

We learned a lot about our river and how humans interact with him.[1] Most of the time the river is clean. But especially after rain, manure and dirt go into the water. The presence of dirt indicates soil erosion, how tilling the soil for farming and breaking earth for construction are taking away precious topsoil, sending it to Lake Michigan and eventually the Atlantic Ocean.

The basic lesson I learned is that if it doesn't rain before a baptism, then we are okay. If it does, let the baptizands know. I offer to get in the river and pour some water over their heads rather than immerse them, but so far no one has asked to avoid a full immersion in the river. So far that first baptizand was right. God has not permitted anyone to get sick from being baptized, at least not to my knowledge.[2]

Spirituality and Rivers

Along with engaging the science and ecology of our river, I also started reading the Bible differently. I wondered about the role of rivers in God's eyes. I was surprised to see how rivers are present at critical moments in salvation history: the river of Eden at the very beginning of the Bible, the bloodied Nile as the first of ten ecological plagues against the Egyptian Empire, crossing the Jordan into God's promise, being baptized in the Jordan, worshipping along the river in Philippi, and the river of the water of life in the New Jerusalem at the end of the Bible. This *Heilsgeographie* (salvation geography) is integral to God's vision for the world alongside the *Heilsgeschichte* (salvation history).

---

1 As you read the paper you will come to see that I use personal pronouns such as "he" rather than following standard English in using the impersonal pronoun "it" for other creatures. This is based on the conviction that "we must say of the universe that it is a communion of subjects, not a collection of objects" (Thomas Berry, *The Great Work: Our Way into the Future* [New York: Crown, 1999], 82, Kindle). Also, because my second language is Spanish, I often use the gender from that language.

2 This story is also told in Doug Kaufman, "Water Evangelism," *Purpose* 47, no. 6 (June 2014): 20–21 and is part of a broader survey of the Elkhart River watershed in Jamie Pitts, "The Hovering Spirit, the Elkhart River Watershed, and Political Institutions," *The Mennonite Quarterly Review* 46, no. 1 (January 2022): 39–40.

After fifteen years of water testing three times a year, we stopped during the COVID pandemic. If we had found a way to have more community partners working for a clean river, where our data was an important part of that, or if we had become more engaged in public advocacy for the river, I think we would have continued longer. But I tell stories of my congregation not because we have reached an ideal for being a green congregation, but simply because we are on this journey along with many others. I want to encourage others to be on this journey as well, a journey of sharing the good news with all creation.

As I think about those fifteen years of testing, I am less interested in the data that I could graph for you. We didn't discover meaningful trend lines. But we did make discoveries: stay out of the river when it rains and enjoy it when it hasn't. Take care of the land, because the land and rivers are interconnected. Take care of your neighbor, because the land and water are connected with all creatures in a watershed; those creatures include we humans.

I once preached on this theme in Toronto on Lake Ontario, located downriver from us. I imagined with them the holy creatures who might be passing by us on this Great Lake, creatures who had witnessed one of our baptisms months before. Perhaps in that sense the creatures near the holy water of baptism are themselves baptized.

I am most interested in how the river testing affected my and my congregation's relationship with the earth and her creatures. I felt like every time we dipped our nets and tested for river creatures, we were checking on our neighbors. How are you doing? Are the people here treating you right? In fact, they struggled the most when the river had a lot of soil suspended in it. This measurement is called turbidity, and usually the turbidity in our river was low. But especially when you combine snow melt and rain in the spring, the river is so brown that you see nothing below. At those times the creatures struggled, and we would have trouble finding the variety and immensity of life that we do when the river is running clean and clear.

I was changed by those fifteen years of relating to these tiny creatures, creatures I had honestly not realized even existed, making their place in the river bottom. Many of them, like the Caddisfly larvae, are water creatures in their adolescence and then have the privilege of being air creatures in their adulthood. Imagine, living in water and then one day flying off into the sky! What a fascinating life of transition God has granted these creatures!

Hans Hut and the Gospel of All Creatures

This whole experience gave me a special affinity when I first read about the gospel of all creatures, written by the early Anabaptist Hans Hut in 1526. Anabaptists are the direct predecessors of my own Mennonite tradition, as well as the Amish and Hutterites.

Hut had followed Luther for some time, but his vision became more social and ecological.[3] Living as a bookseller in southern Germany, he was baptized by Hans Denck as the Anabaptist movement was spreading from its origins in 1525 in Zurich, Switzerland.

The phrase "gospel of all creatures" first appears in his tract "On the Mystery of Baptism,"[4] but it continues in other Anabaptist writings for a generation after. The phrase "gospel of all creatures" was taken from the German translation of Mark 16:15. Both German and Greek have case endings. Whereas in the original Greek text it is dative, gospel *to* all creatures, in German the ending is more ambiguous; it could either be dative like the Greek, or genitive, gospel *of* all creatures. Is this a misunderstanding of the text? In my view the gospel of all creatures is also a gospel to all creatures.

In this I agree with Canadian Mennonite theologian Max Kennel, who sees in the gospel of all creatures a corrective to certain metaphysical and political problems arising from the strong church-world dualism in much Mennonite theology.[5] Kennel takes the ambiguity that at first troubled me and makes a virtue of it, noting that in English the word "of" "may refer to the presence of the gospel *in* all creatures and/or the measure of the gospel proclaimed or declared *by* all creatures."[6] As noted before, the German version makes this ambiguity even broader. Kennel writes, "The distinction between the way in which the gospel is *for* all creatures (directed toward creation), and the way in which the gospel is *in* all creatures (coming from

---

3 Hut's biographer, Gottfried Seebaß, makes the comment about the social order; I added the ecological aspect, from his "Hans Hut: The Suffering Avenger," in *Profiles of Radical Reformers*, ed. Hans-Jürgen Goertz and Walter Klaassen (Scottdale, PA: Herald Press, 1982), 54.

4 Hans Hut, "On the Mystery of Baptism: Baptism as Symbol and as Essence, the Beginning of a True Christian Life. John 5," in *Early Anabaptist Spirituality: Selected Writings*, ed. and trans. Daniel Liechty (New York: Paulist Press, 1994), 67.

5 Maxwell Kennel, "The Gospel of All Creatures: An Anabaptist Natural Theology for Mennonite Political Theology," *Journal of Mennonite Studies* 37 (2019): 354. This is the most comprehensive elucidation of the contemporary meaning of the gospel of all creatures and was published at about the same time as my essay that included a lengthy section more fully developing the ecological implications; see Douglas Kaufman, "Caring about Climate Change: An Anabaptist Cruciform Response," *Mennonite Quarterly Review*, 94, no. 1 (January 2020): 89–95.

6 Kennel, "The Gospel of All Creatures," 355.

within creation), gives way to an ambiguity that refuses modern categories."[7]

But exactly what is this gospel of all creatures? Quoting Hut, "the gospel of all creatures is about nothing other than simply Christ the crucified one. But not only Christ the Head was crucified, but rather Christ in all his members. This Christ is what is preached and taught by all creatures. The whole Christ suffers in all members."[8]

The good news is we do not suffer alone. The suffering of Jesus was not just a onetime event on the cross, but an ongoing participation in the suffering of all creation, including we humans. For baptist theologian James William McClendon, Hut's import is his refusal to simply link suffering to guilt. McClendon notes, "Hut related suffering, instead, to ongoing creation: to exist is to suffer."[9] Yet Mennonite pastor Isaac Villegas makes this suffering more specific, writing that "the woundedness of life remembers the crucified love of God."[10]

Hut specifically mentions predation as an aspect of this suffering. He was not a vegetarian. Not that Hut would have been against vegetarianism; he probably didn't imagine it. Humans slaughtering and eating animals is part of the created order, and in offering themselves in this way, the animals participate in the suffering of Christ.

When it comes to human suffering and the sufferings of Christ, he saw Christians needing to follow Christ in affliction. He contrasts his view to Luther, who saw Christ fulfilling all things. Hut sees ongoing suffering in creation. But the suffering Hut has in mind is a process of justification and purification, becoming who God desires us to be. This is the evangelistic part.

He writes, "If God has use of us or will have benefit of us, we must first be justified and made pure by Him, both inwardly and outwardly; inwardly from greed and lust, outwardly from injustice in our way of living and our misuse of the creatures."[11] This is a process that is not just introspective, but one that moves us towards justice in how we relate to others, including other creatures. In this way we become and live the good news. Villegas reminds us that Hut's treatise is about baptism: "The submersion of baptism, according to the gospel of all creatures, is union with the Christ who empowers

---

7   Kennel, 356.

8   Hut, "On the Mystery of Baptism," 67.

9   James Wm. McClendon Jr., *Systematic Theology*, vol. 2: *Doctrine* (Nashville: Abingdon Press, 1994), 163. In defining his own Anabaptist vision, McClendon preferred small "b" baptist.

10 Isaac Villegas, "Wounded Life," *The Conrad Grebel Review* 39, no. 1 (Winter 2021), 45. This reflection on the gospel of all creatures beautifully connects baptism, ecclesiology, ecology, and cruciformity.

11 Hut, "On the Mystery of Baptism," 70.

a movement for liberation, a struggle against oppressive dominions whose power over life derives from the threat of death."[12]

Because you can see the good news in the creatures, Hut writes that "all that can be shown in the scriptures is already shown in the creatures."[13] He is again criticizing the scholarly mainline reformers. Even the common illiterate person—most of the population of Europe at the time—can understand the gospel by viewing the good news found in the suffering of the creatures.

A number of other reformers and medieval predecessors said similar things to Hut about our connection with all creatures. His biographers have suggested various precedents in both German and Spanish mysticism. I see affinities with Franciscan spirituality. Martin Luther too wrote in a similar vein, "God is substantially present everywhere, in and through all creatures, in all their parts and places, so that the world is full of God and he fills all, but without being encompassed and surrounded by it. He is at the same time outside and above all creatures."[14]

Yet Hut's approach to God's presence within the creatures emphasizes suffering. Given our contemporary creation calamities, this is appropriate. But we can also see creation linked with Christ in resurrection as well. We see both suffering and resurrection, depression and joy, grief and hope in ourselves and in creation. From death and suffering comes new life and new creation.[15]

This is a regular process in soil ecology. Soil scientist Rattan Lal, whose background is Hindu, once spoke about the rhizosphere, the network of roots and microorganisms associated with them in the soil. He called the rhizosphere the place in the universe where death is regularly resurrected into life.[16] The creation herself enacts redemption and new creation. Christ's sacrifice has meaning and is found throughout the creation, certainly among humans but also among all creatures.

Evangelizing All Creatures Today

Hut's vision of Christ's ecological union in suffering is especially important in the midst of the ecological crises of our day. If our gospel is not good news for all creatures, then it falls short of God's vision for the created order.

---

12 Villegas, "Wounded Life," 43.

13 Hut, "On the Mystery of Baptism," 72.

14 Heinrich Bornkamm, *Luther's World of Thought* (Saint Louis, MO: Concordia, 1958), 189.

15 Villegas connects grief and hope with baptism ("Wounded Life," 42).

16 Rattan Lal, "The Soil Will Save Our Soul" (paper presented at the conference On Food and Faith: Ministry in a Time of Climate Change, Methodist Theological School of Ohio, Delaware, OH, May 31, 2019).

The need to clarify this grows out of the calamity we face as our ability to devastate God's creation has outpaced our desire to nurture creation as creation has nurtured us. Congregations must cooperate with human and other than-human neighbors to restore, reclaim, and revive our ecosystems for the good of all.

Contemporary society is killing creatures at an unprecedented rate. While the deaths of individual creatures are unavoidable, the myriad deaths of entire species are avoidable. The contemporary extinction crisis is the largest since an asteroid caused the extinction of the dinosaurs. This is not good news to all creation.

Good news is more like the symbol I saw at the front of the Jepara Javanese Mennonite Church (GITJ). A cross stands in the center of a *Wayan*, a Javanese symbol of the cosmos, along with several wild and domesticated animals. The cross reconciles all creation (Col. 1). A friend wondered if this symbol was syncretistic, but we use that word selectively. A more dangerous syncretism today is that of a global Christianity compromised with an international political economy destroying the planet.

Pastoral ecology is simply a way of ministering missionally that includes the whole ecosystem, not just the human creatures in a congregation's community. Pastoral ecology affects our worship, in that our liturgical life—sermons and prayers and hymns—will include the whole creation. It is integrated with our mission. Our community mission projects include river cleanups, tree plantings, invasive species removal, installing solar panels, flood resilience, and many other projects. It includes ministry to the most vulnerable people, living in the floodplains and other areas most affected by ecological calamities. Pastoral ecology includes political advocacy, speaking in support of solar installations, of dam removal, and of policies that help the most vulnerable be resilient to climate calamities. And it includes psychology and helping people through ritual and discussion to move from despairing inactivity to hopeful action.

All this is gospel. From the very beginning, I sensed that this river work was evangelistic, even if not in the way I usually thought. I once attended a river watershed event where I was the only person interested in river quality so I could baptize people. One of the people joked that we could have baptisms after the event. Yet my interest and care for our local watershed was an expression of God's interest and care for the river and his creatures.

Some have asked whether I am saying that churches must do yet something more. Pastoring is already too hard. We study psychology and communications, now must we also add ecology and political science? Yes, I think so.

But as anyone knows who engages in holistic ministry, following God's call means good news for yourself and others. We do not save the planet; God does. But we love the world (*kosmos* in the Greek of John 3:16). God loves as we plant trees in our neighborhoods, along with other members of our communities. A river cleanup brings us together with kayakers and fishers. We are loving the cosmos when we engage in pastoral ecology, caring for creation as creation cares for us.

Discussion Questions

1. How would the gospel of all creatures help address the ecological crises? How could it be misunderstood?

2. What actions have you taken or could you take—individually or congregationally—that could be good news for all creatures in your region or nation?

3. Can you think of other Scriptures and theological themes that connect with the gospel of all creatures?

Response

by Hansung Kim

I must admit that I knew little of the Mennonite tradition, and therefore, reading Douglas Day Kaufman's article was a big learning curve for me. As many probably know, the Presbyterian and the Methodist Church are the two majority denominations in South Korea and the Mennonite Church is very small here. Most Korean Christians learned about the Anabaptist tradition, the Mennonite Church, the Amish, and the Hutterites only in a few pages of some church history books and Hollywood movies, like *Witness*. However, it was really interesting to learn about Hans Hut's use of "the gospel of all creatures" and Kaufman's new take on it. Coming from a cultural background where honoring one's teacher means learning what the teacher said and staying within the shadow of the teacher, it was also an intercultural experience to see how Kaufman dealt with Hut's concept of the gospel of all creatures.

I will first sum up Kaufman's article. Secondly, I will discuss what Hut might have meant by "the gospel of all creatures," on which Kaufman developed his argument. Lastly, I will add my own thoughts, which admittedly will reflect the eastern way of thinking.

Kaufman suggested that we expand the scope of evangelism beyond mankind to all creatures. In that regard, he creatively interwove his involvement in environmental monitoring of a local river and Hans Hut's tract, *On the Mystery of Baptism*. He built his argument on two footings: baptism and "the gospel of all creatures." He connected his own experience of baptisms with Hut's teaching on baptism and searched for the meaning of "the gospel of all creatures." At the end, Kaufman proposed a new meaning for the gospel of all creatures—caring for creation.

It was very inspiring to read Kaufman's account of how a pastor of a local church became involved in pastoral ecology. As he performed a religious ritual in a way that might have more symbolic meanings for the congregation, he became aware of an environmental problem. He, along with some members from the same church, began regularly monitoring the condition of the river for the safety of the congregation. Instead of limiting his interest in this issue to the practical level, he sought a theological understanding of the phenomenon. I thought this was a good example of the harmony of practice and theory. Those at schools and those at church must seek the meaning beyond a phenomenon.

My reading of Hut's *On the Mystery of Baptism* is the following: Hut used the expression "the gospel of all creatures" in his teaching of baptism. Some historical background knowledge will help us understand why he did so. The Bible in the vernacular was not readily available for ordinary Christians at that time.[17] Besides, most of them were illiterate.[18] The established church also claimed the authority of the Bible.[19] In this context, Hut used animals and plants, easily within reach and readily understood, as an alternative and effective means of communication to explain his own views on baptism.

Hut suggested that all creatures direct people to Jesus: "The gospel of all creatures is nothing other than the power of God to bless all those who believe."[20] He believed that the suffering of Christ was the core of the gospel message and all creatures mirror Christ the crucified one: "The gospel of all creatures is about nothing other than simply Christ the crucified one." When people see suffering creatures they may see Christ the crucified one. "These [Jesus's] parables note well that the creatures are made to suffer in human work…. So the whole scripture and all the creatures illustrate the suffering of Christ in all his members."[21] All creatures suffer when men clean, change, kill, and use them for their own benefit. Hut made a connection between the suffering of Christ and the suffering of all creatures to remind Christians of the gospel. He thought all creatures communicated the gospel to people.

Hut did not suggest that the church should seek the well-being of all creatures. For him, suffering was inevitable and could not be avoided. He was aware that mankind was the cause for the suffering of all creatures. As the suffering of all creatures in Hut's time was mostly out of necessity, this was understandable. The global population was much smaller than today's and therefore consumption was comparatively much lower. There were no cash crops, confined animal feeding operations (COFOS), or mass production that hurt many creatures. There were no cars, airplanes, and ships to pollute the air and water. There were no chemicals, petroleum, plastics, and nuclear waste that threatened the lives and well-being of all creatures.

---

17 Martin Luther translated the New Testament into German and published it in 1522. His Bible with Old Testament, New Testament, and Apocrypha was published in 1534.

18 The literacy rate in Britain and Germany in 1450 was only 7 percent and rose to around 16 percent by 1550 (Natalie Calder, "Literacy and Print in Early Modern Germany and England," Medieval Forum, Queen's University, Belfast, uploaded Aug. 19, 2015, accessed May 27, 2023, https://blogs.qub.ac.uk/medievalforum/2015/08/19/literacy-and-print-in-early-modern-germany-and-england/). So in 1526, when *On the Mystery of Baptism* was published, the literacy rate would have been lower than 16 percent.

19 Hans Hut was critical of the state and the church and their use of the Bible in *On the Mystery of Baptism*.

20 Hut, "On the Mystery of Baptism," 69.

21 Hut, 69.

Things are different today. Today, all creatures are suffering for the comfort and pleasure of the exploding population. People have more convenient lives, travel to more distant places more often, and possess and consume more goods and services. Many people today have access to more goods, services, and opportunities than the kings and queens in Hut's time. For example, my small car has more horsepower than any powerful king or queen's carriage had in the sixteenth century. And this is bad news for all creatures: what is good for mankind is bad for other living beings.

Kaufman's concern should become the concern of the church today. God's creation has suffered since the sin of Adam and Eve: "You [the serpent] are cursed more than all animals, domestic and wild" (Gen 3:14); and "The ground is cursed because of you" (Gen 3:17). In pursuit of a better life, which is driven by human selfishness, modern men and women have made the suffering of all creatures even worse.

As a Korean who sees things holistically and has a pietistic revivalist spirituality, I understand "the gospel of all creatures" a little differently. I think that the sustainability of the church and the sustainability of all creatures are equally important. The presence of Christians is a must for the well-being of nature, and the church is a vital instrument in God's mission. The church today must make a concrete effort in the regeneration of the souls in near and far places to reproduce God's people. The church is growing in places where the gospel of Jesus is preached to Christians and non-Christians. The church is not growing in places where the gospel is taken for granted. The ministry of caring for all creatures hinges on the sustainability of the church—the more Christians, the more voices for all creatures in more places on earth.

The church today needs to be intentional about creation care because it is the right thing to do. Mankind is a part of the ecosystem and we, all creatures, need each other for our survival. Caring for creation is also a way of building trust and credibility with the young generation. The sustainability of creation may be a good contact point for evangelism with young people.

We may learn from the early church. With the expectation of the return of Jesus, they preached the crucified Christ because the cross was not shame but glory and they participated in suffering so that more people might know Jesus who was crucified for them. They lived out Christ's love in disasters when others ran for their lives. They were committed to telling others about Jesus and bringing hope to their neighbors. Our commitment to making Jesus known is the same as always, and yet, the scope of our neighbors may need to expand to all creatures.

CHAPTER 19

Can the Desert Be Green?
An Environmental Mission to Plant Hope in the Wilderness

by Lawrence Ko

Introduction: A Journey of a Thousand Miles in Asia

China and India's economic growth and development have benefited the entire continent, so much so that the twenty-first century has been called the Asian Century. With the rise in financial strength, political self-determination will also intensify. The result could be a rise in ethnic nationalism and identity politics, strengthening the call for greater indigenization in some countries. As Christianity is still viewed as foreign and indeed a Western religion, Christian missions and activities in these countries will become more restricted if they are viewed as threats to local cultural development, including possible interference in domestic politics.

Over the past two decades, a greater awareness is growing in Asia that the gospel of Christ is holistic and missions need to be holistic too. The love of God for his creation and the peoples of all cultures requires a concrete demonstration of love and compassion to address the felt needs of the masses living lives of quiet desperation. It is time for an Asian narrative of the gospel of Christ that grows out of the social and cultural milieu of Asia. Engaging local communities through environmental projects can prove to be an effective witness to the gospel of Christ as it incarnates the holistic Messianic mission and the kingdom vision and values of God, our Creator and Redeemer.

The First Step in Environmental Missions

In 2002, Asian Journeys Ltd. embarked on environmental projects in Asian cities, beginning with the Yangtze River Conservation Project in Shanghai, where thirty-three youths studied the problem of pollution in the Suzhou River. The successful completion of the project led to an exploration of the reforestation project in Inner Mongolia. Three months later, the Green Desert Project was born.

Asian Journeys, a social enterprise in Singapore, was established to help young people discover and recover Asian resources for faith and peace. Its objective is to help the youths in Singapore step out into the region to serve and learn, with an aim to understand and appreciate the wealth of Asian civilizational resources for both personal and collective development in a rapidly modernizing Asian milieu.

Tapping into government funding, Asian Journeys began to organize urban community projects as well as environmental projects. Through these three-week long service projects where youth volunteers were immersed in local host communities, they could interact freely with the locals and explore their cultures as well as the complex social issues in context.

Planting an Acre of Desert Land and Restoring a Piece of Blue Sky in the City

Since 2002, over one thousand youth volunteers have journeyed with us on these experiential learning trips, with the majority involved in our signature project, the Green Desert Project. Since it began, the Green Desert Project has mobilized over seven hundred youth participants, from ages thirteen to thirty, in planting thirty thousand trees in the desertified grassland of Inner Mongolia. Participants come from universities and institutes of higher education as well as from churches and agencies.

In 2002, at the invitation of the mayor of Duolun County, I visited the Mongolian grassland to see the effects of desertification on the previously green grassland. Over forty sandstorms each spring engulfed the county rendering agriculture impossible in the farmsteads, while the rapid loss of pasturelands made herding sheep a great challenge to the nomadic Mongolian herders.

A year before in 2001, a reforestation project was initiated by then Chinese premier, Mr. Zhu Rongji, who had visited Duolun in the spring of 2000. Looking at the degraded grassland, he directed that combating desertification must begin immediately. Thus, efforts began to "plant an acre of desert land in Duolun and restore the blue sky in Beijing," a slogan used by the state media CCTV to raise national awareness and funding for the project.

This was timely, as it was announced earlier that year that the 2008 Olympic Games has been awarded to Beijing. Hence, keeping Beijing clean and green had become a priority on the nation's agenda. I later had the privilege to dine with the chairman of the China Green Foundation, which spearheaded the efforts to mobilize the local residents in Inner Mongolia to plant trees in the desert. Volunteers from Beijing and Tianjin also participated in these efforts, since these two cities bore the brunt of the sandstorms each year.

The Green Desert Project

This was the context in which Asian Journeys was invited to participate in the reforestation project, working closely with the local government and NGO. We named the project the Green Desert Project, which opened doors for us to work also in Chinese cities, including Shanghai, Nanjing, Wuhan, and Beijing. But in the eyes of donors and grant makers, apparently it was an exercise in futility. Can anything grow in the desert? I was asked this pointed question when I approached foundations to help fund the project. Hence, I entitled my book on this environmental project, *Can the Desert Be Green?*[1]

The term "green desert" is an oxymoron and an eye-catching paradox. Deserts are necessarily not green. But green desert connotes hope and a vision of possibility, transforming dry arid desert lands into green oases and green pasturelands. It challenges young people to dare to dream, to dare to act, and to dare to make a difference by turning deserts into grasslands again. It evokes the hope of transformation, which is the heart of mission.

Planting Hope in the Wilderness

The Green Desert Project was founded on a vision of rivers in the desert. In the fall of 2002, I was invited by the mayor of Duolun County to visit the 3,500 sq. km of desertified grassland. There we would be assigned a three hundred-acre plot of land to be known as Asian Journeys Tree-Planting Base, with a monument erected in 2010. I had also seen rivers in the desert dammed up into a huge reservoir called Duolun Lake. I also saw the fountainhead of the Luan River, which would grow into a huge river flowing out of Inner Mongolia into Tianjin city. Water was a critical resource for the success of reforestation projects.

But it was in Dalateqi County, where I was visiting with the local mayor and traversing the desert lands, that I chanced upon another river. When I was told this was the Huanghe (Yellow River), I requested to stop the vehicle immediately and quickly got out to take a photo and spend a moment by the riverside. Some of the Chinese poems and proverbs of the Yellow River came to mind as I stood there, amazed at how the river could make a sudden 90 degree turn to flow northwards into Inner Mongolia. It must have been the finger of God directing it to water the grassland, now become desert. It was a moment of worship for me and thanksgiving for his creativity.

The visions of rivers in the desert reminded me of God's gracious providence from Isaiah 43:18–20, where he is doing a new thing, to make

---

1 Lawrence Ko, *Can the Desert Be Green? Planting Hope in the Wilderness* (Singapore: Singapore Centre for Global Missions, and Asian Journeys, 2014)

a way in the wilderness and streams in the desert. These environmental missions are not merely redeeming and restoring physical environments but also addressing social injustices. Isaiah 42:1–4 encourages believers in serving to bring justice. Similarly, Isaiah 35 points us prophetically to the hope of deserts blooming and streams flowing, turning wildernesses into wetlands. Thus would be revealed the Messianic mission of healing, restoration, and salvation on earth, affirmed in Luke 4:18–19, in which believers are invited to participate.

Through the Green Desert Project, we worked directly with local governments and host communities in a shared vision of combating not only desertification and the climate crisis, but also speaking against social injustice as we shared a sense of solidarity with the poor of the land, such as the Mongolian herders and Hui Muslim farmers—indeed, the unrich people groups. Even the government officials resonate with us when we say we care for the earth because "this is our Father's world." During our work on the grassland, we would take time to worship and pray. Prayer is an act of hope in God, and they were glad when we told them we pray for God's blessings on the land.

Planting Hope and Shaping Young Lives

In July 2019, the local government of Duolun County organized an environmental forum to commemorate the tenth anniversary of our partnership with the local government, which was covered in the local news media. We presented the local government with a Chinese calligraphy scroll to celebrate the occasion. The scroll, which says "A Decade to Plant a Tree and a Century to Shape a Life," declared our ultimate aim of planting hope in the environment and shaping young lives in the community.

In the past twenty years, the Green Desert Project has reached out to schools and churches in Singapore and has spawned Green Desert clubs for youths to organize the annual Youth Environmental Stewards (YES) Forum, established in 2011. In 2017, the Green Urban Youth Forum was instituted, as we created platforms for youth volunteers to engage in serving the poor in urban slums and addressing the issues of urban poverty. Green Desert kids clubs were also established in 2009 for children to learn to appreciate trees and live sustainable lifestyles, beginning from their homes in the cities.

From the Desert to the Cities

Over the years, I have been invited to share in schools, church mission conferences, leadership forums, corporate events, and university workshops.

Once I was also interviewed on a local radio station show. It was a great way to raise awareness that Christians are contributing to climate action in creative ways.

In 2019, I accepted an invitation by Ethos Institute, a Christian think tank in Singapore, to write a book on creation care for the Christian community. In that book, *From the Desert to the City: Christians in Creation Care*,[2] I discussed the importance of planting hope in the wilderness as well as living green lifestyles in the cities. Unless we change our consumeristic urban lifestyles, cities will continue to consume energy relentlessly and contribute wastes, which will worsen the current climate crisis. As stewards of the environment, we must be responsive to this climate challenge, and as priests of God's creation, we must be creative in our responsibility to lift creation up in worship of our creator God.

In the book, I emphasized the importance of Christian participation in climate action, which requires the church to first get its theology correct, especially a sound eschatology of the renewed creation and conjoined heaven and earth. This theological basis will help us recover our creation mandate and hence our mission mandate. This is crucial for our spirituality and discipleship so that the church can truly be an eschatological community that sees the mission of the crucified Christ as bona fide hope of a helpless and harassed world waiting to be saved and transformed. It calls for repentance from our anthropocentric view of life and our recovery of a theocentric vision that cares for creation because the earth is the Lord's and everything in it.

Conclusion

The Green Desert Project is an example of a Christian faith-based environmental mission that can help the church respond in a time of environmental and ecological crisis. As we mobilize participants from both within the church and without, participating in a posture of service and learning, we will be readily welcomed into nations and cities to work with the most needy and vulnerable communities alongside local government and community leaders. The gospel needs to be incarnated at street level, and through these environmental projects Christians can reach out to the poor and experience firsthand the plight of living amid a degraded environment, and learn to share in the fellowship of suffering and pour out God's love.

Environmental missions can begin through prayer and lead to lamentation, repentance, and a new resolve to live simply and responsibly

---

2 Lawrence Ko, *From the Desert to the City: Christians in Creation Care* (Singapore: Ethos Institute for Public Christianity, Sower Publishing Centre, 2020).

as disciples of Christ. As we combat climate change, we are participating in shaping history, the arena where God acts. Environmental mission reveals the full gospel narrative of Christ, as we witness to the Creator's love in Genesis 1 and the eschatological hope in Christ in Revelation 22. As we go about caring for God's creation with justice and mercy, we are pointing to the glorious Shalom vision of the kingdom, which is here on earth but not yet fully.

Response

by Myung-Soo Lee

Asian Journeys's Vision and Impact

The foundation of Asian Journeys was built upon Ko's vision, aimed at nurturing urban youth in Singapore. This vision included encouraging exploration of vast landscapes, deep Chinese cultural heritage, and fostering a sense of care for nature and indigenous communities. The overarching aim was to cultivate a love for nature, oneself, others, and God. Through the Green Desert Project, Singaporean youth have become witnesses to the magnificence of God's creation and his redemptive work within nature. This experience also shapes their holistic Messianic mission in life, which encompasses both sociopolitical engagement and evangelism as essential components of Christian duty. This innovative approach has facilitated access to countries initially unfriendly to Christian missions. It has also instilled hope among urban youth, who engage in environmental stewardship and seek purpose in their lives.

The Green Desert Project, led by Asian Journeys, stands as an exemplary illustration of a comprehensive Christian mission, aligned with a problem-solving perspective. In this paper, I will analyze the pivotal components of this project through a problem-solving lens. Additionally, I will address the unique challenges posed by specific issues within the Korean context.

Consideration of the Green Desert Project in the Korean Context

1. Fundamental Components for Overall Project Success

The Green Desert Project offers valuable components for an effective problem-solving approach, which should be considered when designing and implementing projects in the Korean context.

(a) Focus on collective problem solving. Addressing complex environmental issues requires collaboration among multiple stakeholders. Identifying these stakeholders and finding common interests is essential for successful cooperation. In the Green Desert Project, the reforestation of Inner Mongolia's desertified land became a shared objective for the Chinese central government, local government, and NGOs. Examining governmental policies related to the environment, climate change, youth welfare, multiculturalism, etc., can uncover common interests, enabling churches and Christian organizations to contribute to solutions for significant societal challenges.

(b) Equality among stakeholders. A harmonious and interdependent partnership among all stakeholders is crucial. When working with foreign governments and NGOs, respecting each other's interests and embracing differences fosters project success. Avoiding an attitude of superiority and unilateral solutions ensures a more optimized outcome. Openness to diverse perspectives prevents entrenchment and fosters a cooperative mindset.

(c) Effective communication. Communication between project participants and local populations is paramount. Overcoming initial positional differences requires understanding that these disparities are the starting point for collaborative efforts. Shared language, such as the use of Chinese in the Green Desert Project, serves as a vital medium for communication between participants and local residents in Inner Mongolia. This shared linguistic and cultural background enhances a sense of commonality among participants and aids in understanding indigenous perspectives.

2. Key Challenges in the Korean Context

(a) The power of the gospel and God's words: vision change for a servant. Ko, the initiator of the project, believed from its inception that God is doing a new thing to make a way in the wilderness and streams in the desert (Isa. 43:19). Confronting numerous challenges, Ko chose to proclaim God's words and the gospel of Christ as a primary guiding force. When individuals align their hearts with God and experience his benevolent love, their perspectives transcend mere visual observation. Even amid societal skepticism they can perceive and embrace the promise of life, reflecting the beauty of God's holiness reminiscent of his original creation. Bearing witness to God's redemptive work in both the environment and human lives transformed individuals to become faithful stewards and collaborators in this divine workmanship. A parallel can be drawn from Korea's history, particularly in the 1950s through to the 1990s, when numerous servants of God personally experienced the profound impact of Christ's death and resurrection. They fervently invoked the touch of the Holy Spirit to infuse hope into the hearts of Korean people to rise from the ravages of war and poverty.

However, as Korea experienced miraculous economic development and its churches transformed into megasized institutions, the approach of following a singular servant's vision rooted in God's words has become less common. This shift can be attributed to the rational and collective decision-making processes within churches, influenced by intellectually sophisticated congregants. Nonetheless, adhering to the convictions of a single servant can still be viable, particularly within small churches or

Christian NGOs. This raises an essential question: How can we support such a devoted servant in maintaining their conviction until they witness the fruits of their labor? Moreover, what mechanisms can ensure that the collective efforts of numerous dedicated individuals, each working in their unique directions to tackle significant shared problems, are effectively harnessed and coordinated?

(b) Working with urban youth: shifting perspectives. When Singaporean youth planted trees in desertified lands, they also sowed hope within themselves. Engaging in volunteer work in remote, desolate foreign environments motivated these urban youth to address broader societal challenges, transcending their personal struggles in their home country. The foreign setting allowed for a change in perspective, empowering them to overcome feelings of hopelessness. This enabled them to focus on raising environmental awareness and contributing to healing the land and life back home.

Bringing Korean urban youth into nature outside of Korea, however, presents significant challenges: (i) spiritual leaders within churches or Christian NGOs must convince Korean parents to entrust their children to God's care, despite the time constraints imposed by university entrance exams and job markets; (ii) engaging in physically demanding volunteering for environmental projects may prove difficult; and (iii) if these young individuals come from impoverished regions, their existing sense of hopelessness, coupled with the daunting prospect of confronting seemingly insurmountable tasks, adds to the challenge.

Urbanization, materialism, Western-influenced extreme individualism, and the intense drive for self-improvement within Korea have led to broken homes, where many Christian parents lose influence over their children. However, the transformation of the hearts of parents and youth starts with God's servants, those whose eyes are open to see a path in the wilderness and rivers in the desert through God's redemptive work in their own lives.

In the multicultural community in Korea, a novel approach has emerged through the M Center of Onnuri Church, where foreign mothers teach their own children their mother tongues. Instead of grappling with identity issues as Koreans or experiencing shame due to their parents' difficulty adapting to Korea, these children have grown to appreciate the value of learning their mothers' languages and embracing their cultural roots.

I earnestly hope for numerous opportunities to emerge for Korean urban youth to travel overseas or explore nature within the country, demonstrating concern for others rather than endlessly pursuing self-improvement.

I envision South Korean youth restoring North Korea's mountainous land with prayers, worship, and communication with North Koreans. Additionally, I desire to see South Korean youths whose parents hail from various Asian countries working collaboratively to bless their parents' lands. Similar to Singaporean youth, through experiencing Korea's natural landscapes or foreign lands combined with God's teachings, Korean urban youth can become good stewards for their communities.

3. Collaboration among Christians and Christian Organizations: A Vision for the Church—Holistic Messianic Mission

I aspire for the proclamation of the pure gospel by Korean pastors and missionaries to inspire Christians and Christian NGOs to transform their visions and come into the unity of the Spirit. Just as Ko cooperated with foreign governments and NGOs for the enduring success of the Green Desert Project and received support from his own government for youth funding, Korean Christian NGOs and churches must work interdependently, unified as one body of Christ. They should also engage with governments and non-Christian organizations in a spirit of mutual respect and collaboration. Not all results from mission activities may be immediately visible or quantifiable, but the exaltation of God and the dissemination of his words through his Spirit should remain the primary focus. While securing funding for missions often requires demonstrating effectiveness and efficiency, God's divine work transcends our financial calculations.

Conclusion

Environmental change is intricately tied to individual transformation. People are both the central aspect of the problem and the key to its solution. Altering the environment necessitates a change in people's mindset. I firmly believe that the collective body of Christ holds the pivotal solution to transform people and the environment. Christians and diverse Christian organizations must remember that they are integral parts of the broader church of Christ. By keeping their focus on God's ultimate purpose, they can inspire, support, and collaborate effectively.

Section E

Testimonies

CHAPTER 20

The Founding of Shine Church and Its Environmental Missionary Work

by Hyoungmin Kim

After five years of missionary work in the Middle East, I founded Shine Church. We started meeting in a small, modified shipping container, and currently hold services in the Konkuk University auditorium. As of 2023, Shine Church has successfully set up eighteen other churches and four schools by the grace of God.

I started believing in Jesus Christ after graduating high school. I have had faith in him for forty-three years. In the meantime, like Joseph, I have received generous blessings. Now that I think about it, these were things that God did not have to grant me. These were a part of the grace of God.

I have experienced many miracles throughout my deep relationship with God. These were things that could not have happened with human efforts. Yet God accomplished them all with the passing of time.

When I was a student, I did not have any life dreams and I was not a happy person. Back then, if someone had come to me and informed me about what would become of me now, I would have carefully prepared for my future. I hope everyone listening to my testimony today will be able to see their own future. Also, if you have seen it, I hope you do not doubt yourself and prepare for your future with confidence.

The Establishment of the Church and the Missionary Work

Praising God Is a Fundamental Principle for Human Beings (Isa. 43:21)

According to 2 Corinthians 4:15, being grateful is the way of glorifying God. If we desire to give glory to God, we should thank him. When you express thankfulness through songs, it is much better. This is called praise. The prophet Isaiah said that the reason God created us was that he wanted us to praise him (Isa. 43:21). Thanking or praising God should not be done silently. These can be expressed in various ways, such as music, dance, and paintings. It is also possible to praise God through poetry as King David did. Therefore, the conclusion I reached after having faith in Jesus Christ was this: Christianity was gratitude. As I thanked and praised God, all sorts of miracles occurred. I would like to tell you about three of them.

The first miracle was that I, who could not speak English and did not have much money, was able to receive a scholarship from a good university and go abroad for studies. I, who was poor, began unconditionally thanking and praising God from the day I set foot in the United States. One day, an older person who was jogging asked permission to come into my house to shelter from the rain. This person was deeply moved after seeing me pray and praise God in tears. He asked me what I was praying for, and I said I wanted to study in the United States and attend Southwest Baptist University. He said he wanted to see me again and when he returned he gave me a special four-year scholarship to attend the university. This person turned out to be the university's president, Dr. Charles Chaney. This miracle happened while I was praising God with gratitude at home.

The second miracle occurred while I was attending church in the Middle East. We operated under the guise of a kindergarten and organized services for Koreans as well as other foreigners. Moreover, it was our mission to preach to the people in country S, in secret. However, as our missionary work was about to bear fruit, we suddenly experienced great difficulty as a fellow worker was sent to prison and the church was split. Nonetheless, we had strong faith as we were armed with early morning and regular prayers. Amid such hardships, we praised God even more strongly than before. Then, slowly the darkness began to disappear. The believers of Christ prospered and the children were blessed. As a result of these events, the Korean ambassador, who previously found the church objectionable, later accepted Jesus Christ thanks to my evangelism.

My coworker also experienced a miracle. He was released from prison in a very peculiar way, as follows. An aide of a United States senator, whom I met through a high school student who was attending the church, helped us to contact two senators he used to serve. After a few months, our situation began to improve when the assistant secretary of the U.S. Department of State came to country S on official duty. The assistant secretary met the minister of religious affairs of country S, and in this country where it is illegal for people to gather for worship, our church received permission to conduct service with the private, official, and tacit approval of the Ministry of Religious Affairs. Our coworker was also released from prison and came back home. This happy news was delivered by the US ambassador to the Korean ambassador, and then to us. When you express gratitude, your anger changes into a blessing.

Our worship service had been held in secret in a dilapidated building, but then we could hold a beautiful worship service in a compound that included a pool, soccer field, and even a kindergarten building. Previously, church members had been risking their lives introducing the Bible and videos on Christianity to Muslim households or trying to broadcast Christian content through satellites. Although our church was eventually shut down by the religious police, there was an amazing gift from God hidden in our hardships. When you face hardships, declare it with an opposite spirit! "Therefore, it will be much better! Hallelujah!"

The third miracle began with an opportunity to start a Christian alternative school twelve years ago. An elementary school student moved to Seoul with her grandmother because of family problems. As a result of this urgent decision, it was unclear to which school she would transfer. Therefore, the child and I, just the two of us, put up a signboard with the name of a new school and held the admission ceremony. We then invited the pastors of the church and they helped her continue her studies, arranging cooked meals at the church and commutes with our church van. However, as time passed the school was attended by not only one student but dozens of students. The church storage room became the first classroom. Later, we began to spend more and more time worshipping and less time studying. The miracle occurred while the children were singing praises. An unbelievable event happened when mothers touched the door handle to enter the room where their children were singing praises and were suddenly thrown over a meter into the air and collapsed.

There were also other miracles: a child's autism was cured, and the eyes of another child who was suffering from an incurable disease were also cured. Our school now has grown into the largest Christian alternative school thanks to God's blessing. It also received the education brand grand prize from Kukmin Ilbo as the school with the strongest colors (Christian spirit) of Christianity.

Praising God Is the Duty of All Creations (Ps. 100:1; Ps. 148:3–7)

The angels in heaven and mankind on earth are not the only created things that praise God. When we look at Psalm 148, everything in the universe was created with the purpose of praising God. The sun, the moon, and planet earth are included in this (Ps. 148:3, 7). As science advances, we are even able to record the sound of a black hole. Its sound is like the sound of a drum, violin, or cello. Everything in the universe sings. Even meteorites that fly through space generate sound. These sound waves are what the Bible refers to when it says, "Praise him, all you shining stars. Praise him, you highest heavens" (Ps. 148:3–4).

Other inanimate objects praise God. The Pharisees hated Jesus and interrupted people who honored and praised the Lord. Jesus spoke to the Pharisees as follows: "If they keep quiet, these stones will start shouting!" (Luke 19:40, CEV). This means if people stop praising Jesus, then the stones will instead praise him.

The things in the sea also praise God. Everything created by God is unique and special. The forms of their existence are praise to God in themselves. I personally like humpback whales. These whales compose and sing songs. Their songs go round and round as they sing them. When they finish their songs, they make new ones and sing them.

Land creatures also praise God. If we were to increase the speed of the sound of crickets, we would hear a beautiful sound like that of an orchestra. Indeed, all living creatures sing in various ways. They may not have an awareness of God; nevertheless, they are beautiful in the eyes of God. For this reason it is terrible to kill elephants for ivory. Elephants know how to thank people whom they feel indebted to, and they can draw paintings if trained. Therefore, in God's eyes they must be capable of praising him in their own unique way.

God who has granted us happiness should really be happy. We hope for the happiness of God who has sacrificed his Son, Jesus Christ. Our parents and our creator both have a right to happiness. Our God, who has designed the earth with intellect and love, is good and charitable. He has gifted us this beautiful earth and entrusted us with autonomy.

However, mankind mocks God and acts like a master, even though "everything belongs to the Lord your God, not only the earth and everything on it, but also the sky and the highest heavens" (Deut. 10:14, CEV). Humanity's grade as earth's manager is an "F."

It is necessary for human beings to humbly return to their original place. Romans 8:19 says "creation waits with eager longing for the revealing of the children of God" (NRSVUE). If we believe in Jesus, we should return to the ecological mandate in Genesis 1:26–28 This is the mission of a servant. Be it small or large, a church should not leave this task with environmental organizations around the world but should actively engage in environmental missions and support the protection of the ecosystem.

Environmental Missionary Work of Shine Church

Shine Church, the first church in Korea to start an environmental mission, established its Christian Environmental Graduate School to train environmental missionaries. In addition, we established an environmental research center ten years ago and created Shine Gardens in public schools in Cambodia and Honduras, made of recycled environmental waste products.

We developed a curriculum for educating children on the environment and installed eco-friendly waste incinerators in developing countries. We also helped a school by installing a solar power electricity facility in a village in Manila, Philippines. We have built eco-friendly bathrooms in many public schools in developing countries. We also provide education on hygiene to children in countries with inadequate public health standards, and together with environmental organizations, we volunteer to clean up the garbage on beaches. We visit poor communities and organize activities where we create mural paintings with environmental themes. We are also establishing schools through a small project aimed at villages where children do not have educational opportunities.

Conclusion

The current global environment is at a critical juncture for protecting us and our descendants. All creatures living on earth are suffering due to air pollution, heat waves, fires, deadly climate, food and water shortages, and viruses such as the coronavirus. If the earth's temperature increases by another 0.3 degrees Celsius, it will enter the last stage before the disaster. Earth's ecosystems have already begun to be destroyed. Most scholars worldwide estimate that these ecosystems will be totally destroyed by 2100 unless people realize this and take action. The created beings do not have original sin. For the sake of all creatures who perish without sin, and for us, we need to return to our position of humbly praising God.

CHAPTER 21

My Journey of Growth and Hope

From God's Word, to Works and Wonders, to World Care

by Laurence Gatawa

> But grow in the grace and knowledge
> of our Lord and Savior Jesus Christ.
> —2 Peter 3:18

I was born within a tribal community with deep respect for nature. Our poverty, though marked by a lack of material wealth, was overshadowed by our profound connection to the environment. We regarded nature as sacred, with the essence of the natural world believed to house spiritual beings. From an early age, I was oriented to approach the natural realm with caution, aware of the undesirable consequences that recklessness could bring. This outlook permeated every aspect of our lives, positively contributing to the preservation of the environment. However, fear compelled us to appease the spirits believed to dwell in our surroundings by performing ancient pagan rituals passed down through generations.

There were also moments of fear as we heard of encounters between government forces and rebels seeking sanctuary within the expanses of the mountains. While a few voices were championing their cause, a majority were very cautious. Amid the uncertainty, I remember an occasion when my family was obliged to open our doors to them. With meager provisions, we shared our meals, forging connections around our table. We listened to their tales of strife and their pleas for social justice and equality. Those occasions sparked and kindled conviction in our youthful hearts, and later one of my elder playmates joined the battle, standing shoulder-to-shoulder with those same rebels.

The dearth of material wealth drove my family, like numerous others, to seek employment in the mines. Through my father's stories of toiling beneath the earth's surface, I gained insight into the allure of financial security at the expense of nature. Nonetheless, while growing up I bore witness to the expansion of mining endeavors, including open-pit operations, which laid bare the full extent of the devastation. The once flourishing land was transformed into a desolate terrain, showing the consequences driven by poverty and greed. As I recount my odyssey, I intend to share my growth in learning God's word, engaging in social work, testifying about God's wonders, and campaigning for the cause of world care.

Word

> All Scripture is breathed out by God and profitable for teaching,
> for reproof, for correction, and for training in righteousness.
> (2 Timothy 3:16, ESV)

Amid the embrace of my cultural heritage, I found myself face-to-face with the transformative message of the gospel, heralded by a missionary who had journeyed far in obedience to the call of Christ. At the age of fourteen, swayed by the proposal of my elder brother, I responded to the missionary's invitation, surrendering my heart to Jesus Christ as my Lord and Savior. This conversion experience offered me a renewed sense of purpose, igniting within me an ardent desire to delve deeper into the sacred teachings of the Bible.

As I delved into the depths of my newfound faith, I encountered a Bible preacher who testified that before his conversion, he held high reverence for the environment. He had been hesitant to cut down trees, particularly those believed to be inhabited by spirits, apprehensive of the potential repercussions. However, upon embracing Christianity he discovered a newfound liberation from fear. Armed with a chainsaw, he boldly brought down huge trees, only to find that there were no adverse consequences. Although seemingly detached from the realm of creation care, this narrative sowed the seeds of curiosity within me, hinting at the broader implications of my faith in relation to the environment.

As my faith matured and as I got involved in church ministry, I felt the need to pursue theological studies at an evangelical Bible college. While there was an emphasis on theology, biblical studies, and evangelism, there was a failure to present a comprehensive understanding of our fundamental role as stewards of God's creation. It became increasingly apparent to me that the lack of emphasis on creation care was, in part, rooted in the questionable application of the doctrine of the last things (eschatology). Such heralding the imminent destruction of the present earth and the promise of a new heaven and new earth had caused certain individuals to question the relevance of nurturing the environment. After all, if the current creation is destined for annihilation, why invest our precious time and energy in its preservation?

Works

> For we are his workmanship, created in Christ Jesus for good
> works, which God prepared beforehand, that we should walk
> in them. —Ephesians 2:10, ESV

In my Christian journey, the church and theological education played a central role in deepening my conviction about the importance of holistic ministry. I am ever mindful of James 2:14–17, that faith without works is dead. This highlights the imperative of addressing the practical needs of others, inspired by the love and compassion embodied by Jesus, who ministered to the entirety of the human experience. Thus, within the church where I serve, we established the ministry of compassion as the social significance of our faith, recognizing that true transformation occurs when we tend to every facet of an individual's well-being.

In connection with emphasizing the public significance of the gospel, I had the privilege of participating in a book writing project that delved into the implications of the Lord's Prayer. My task was to expound upon the plea, "Lead us not into temptation but deliver us from evil," within the context of the Philippine public sphere. I sought to illuminate the pressing need for redemption in a society plagued by systemic evils, while also acknowledging the presence of Satan and his malevolent influence. In my discussion, prayer becomes the cornerstone of my efforts to address societal injustices and advocate for the benefit of the poor and oppressed. Furthermore, I myself need to live a transformed lifestyle that reflects the ethics of the heavenly kingdom, consciously shunning all forms of evil.

However, amid my involvement in the church and the pursuit of holistic ministry, I couldn't help but notice a certain oversight regarding creation care. While evangelism and social ministry took precedence, the significance of caring for God's creation remained obscured. Even within the vibrant ministries of my colleagues, there seemed to be a dearth of biblical teachings on the sacred responsibility of stewarding the environment. Though many pastors occasionally expressed sorrow over the destruction of the environment, rarely was it approached from a scriptural standpoint. This realization underscored the need for a more comprehensive understanding of our role as stewards of God's creation, intertwining our social ministry with a commitment to creation care.

Wonders

> Call to me and I will answer you, and will tell you
> great and hidden things that you have not known.
> (Jeremiah 33:3, ESV)

During my formative years in the faith, I had the privilege of observing my pastor casting out demons when we ministered to far-flung villages. There were times during prayer when individuals would shake as they were set free from the bondage of darkness. I encountered a similar incident while pursuing further studies and doing pastoral ministry. A lady who had arrived from a remote province in the Philippines attended one of our prayer meetings. During prayer time, her countenance turned wild, her face darkened with her tongue stretched out, and she emitted sounds without words. Fear gripped my heart, but I mustered the courage to intercede for her deliverance in Jesus's name. After about an hour of prayer she calmed down, testifying that the two spirits that had held her captive were now gone. She explained that these spirits had taken hold of her during a time of isolation and loneliness in the depths of the forest, where she had carelessly invoked their names.

I also encountered a distressing situation that tested my faith while pursuing a research degree in the UK. With each passing day, I experienced an increasing discomfort in my throat, caused by a growing polyp. When I turned to the internet for answers, I read disturbing opinions about the possibility of cancer. The thought of departing this world and leaving behind my beloved wife and young children heightened my anxiety and uncertainty. So, I cried and prostrated myself before the Lord, shedding tears until eventually succumbing to deep sleep. As I awoke the next morning, the first thing I did was examine my mouth, only to discover that the polyp had disappeared. The inexplicable nature of what had occurred left me in awe. Whether the polyp had dissolved and been swallowed during the night or if it had miraculously compressed, I could not ascertain. However, one thing remained certain—the Lord had heard my prayer, igniting within me the courage to believe that he still held a plan and purpose for my life.

I have been a witness to the wonders of the Lord, manifesting in various forms. His divine hand has consistently shown itself to me, whether through the workings of nature, medical interventions, or supernatural occurrences. I carry with me countless testimonies of God's miraculous works and provisions for myself, my family, and my ministry. Even in my role as the leader of the seminary, I have experienced firsthand God's special provision. When the seminary was burdened with debts, a woman unexpectedly sought me out, presenting a check for $14,000. Though doubtful initially, I had our business manager verify the check, only to discover that it was indeed valid. More recently, when our financial needs grew urgent, I turned to the Lord in earnest prayer, feeling both helpless and hopeful. The following day, our business manager informed me that a government scholarship had deposited $14,000 into our account. Shortly thereafter, he shared news of an additional $7,000 deposit, the source of which remained unknown to him. But I hold the firm conviction that these provisions came from the Lord, a tangible testament to his unwavering faithfulness and care, bolstering my faith and fueling my resolve to continue walking the path he has laid out before me.

World Care

> The LORD God took the man and put him in the garden of
> Eden to work it and keep it.   (Genesis 2:15, ESV)

As I engaged in conversations with like-minded individuals and pursued research, a new understanding began to take root. I realized that the gospel of hope, which forms the bedrock of our faith, should inspire us to be agents of transformation not only in the spiritual and social realms but also in the physical world we inhabit. This realization started at a Reformed seminary, where professors diligently stressed the absence of a division between the sacred and secular realms. In addition, they emphasized the significance of both the evangelistic mandate and the cultural mandate. Moreover, Francis Schaeffer articulated through his writings the connection of faith, culture, and the environment. In his works, he highlighted the astonishing reality that adherents of other religious traditions, such as Buddhists, often exhibited a greater level of care for the natural world than many Christians. This discovery struck me deeply, serving as a wake-up call to reevaluate my own beliefs and actions.

One of my professors lectured on the concept of transforming the world into a garden, which resonated deeply with me, reminding me of the garden of Eden and our divine calling to care for the earth. Additionally, a presentation on Jesus as the gardener further illuminated the biblical narrative of creation care. It pointed back to the Old Testament's account of God planting a garden and placing Adam and Eve as caretakers, while also offering a glimpse into the future paradise of the new heaven and new earth. This understanding challenged me to view creation through the lens of its ultimate restoration and to treat it responsibly in the present.

In response to this growing understanding, I took action. As the president of PTS College and Advanced Studies, I initiated the creation of a prayer garden—a physical manifestation of our commitment to spirituality and creation care. This landmark not only aligns with the nature theme of our institution but also serves as a reminder of what we ought to be and do; that is, I envisioned a community where the pursuit of spirituality and the embrace of creation care coexisted harmoniously, nurturing future generations of Christians who would be equipped to actively contribute to the substantial healing of the environment, given the current ecological crisis in the Philippines brought about by climate change and human irresponsibility.

In Retrospect

> Remember the former things, those of long ago; I am God,
> and there is no other; I am God, and there is none like me.
> (Isaiah 46:9)

I recall a turning point in my life when I faced a crossroads. Overwhelmed with difficulty, I contemplated abandoning my theological studies and religious vocation. When I decided to pursue another profession, I suddenly burst into tears and cried for about thirty minutes. Then I heard my colleague calling my name, but I ran to hide myself and continued to cry for another thirty minutes. At that moment, I realized that the Lord captured my heart and would not let me go, reaffirming my calling to serve him in Christian ministry. Since that moment, I have remained steadfast in following the Lord, progressing from an emphasis on the Word of God to engaging in works of ministry and witnessing the wonders of God's miracles, and am now involved in world care.

Looking back on my journey of growth, I am filled with gratitude for the transformative power of the gospel. It has not only reconciled me with God but also opened my eyes to the profound interconnectedness between my faith, the environment, and the well-being of humanity. As I continue to walk this path, I am inspired by the gospel—a hope that compels us to engage in missional responses to environmental and human calamities, bringing healing and restoration to our world until we hear the Lord say, "Well done, good and faithful servant! ... Come and share your master's happiness!" (Matt. 25:23). *Soli Deo gloria!*

CHAPTER 22

KGMLF Missional Koinonia

by Sun Man Kim

Hi, my name is Sun Man Kim and I really thank God for giving me this opportunity to share my testimony here at KGMLF. I want to share the impact the gospel of hope has had on my life. And as one of many who personally witnessed the beginning and progress of the KGMLF, I'd like to give a short testimony about it as well.

I immigrated to the United States in 1983. I was very surprised when I visited my home country about twenty years later because Korea was no exception in terms of environmental pollution. I believe that only when humans have a right relationship with God can we fulfill our stewardship responsibilities over the environment: "For God was pleased to have all his fullness dwell in him, and through him to reconcile to himself all things, whether things on earth or things in heaven, by making peace through his blood, shed on the cross" (Col. 1:19–20). If peace is the state of human beings restored to a right relationship with God, I have experienced it being reconciled through Christ.

When I was in my third year of high school, I was pessimistic about the world and drank poison. After three days in a coma, God miraculously saved me. It was the first time in my life that I realized that Jesus died for me and my sins. For the first time I admitted I was a sinner and confessed it. From that moment, I shed a lot of tears of repentance. I wanted to die like that, but now, on the contrary, I so desired to live. "Therefore, if anyone is in Christ, he is a new creation; the old has gone, the new has come!" (2 Cor. 5:17, NIV 1984).

However, after immigrating to the United States, I was totally preoccupied with the issues of living. Then, God called me on a crowded street of Manhattan, New York, in the winter of the first year of immigration. An unknown evangelist was proclaiming the gospel, "Believe in Jesus!" One evening, he saw me and asked, "You're Korean, aren't you?" "Yes, I am," I answered. "Please take my spot," he asked, and gave me his microphone and ran off somewhere. I had to stand on the spot, and soon after I found myself repeating the same words of the evangelist. I came home that night and organized my immigration bag. Among the things in the bag, there was a small gift box my high school friend gave me. It was a cassette tape of him praying on his knees for me. One phrase of request hit me hard in my heart: "Please help my friend Sun Man to be a person who proclaims the gospel without being hidden by the forest of skyscrapers in New York … . !" I was brokenhearted and rededicated my life to Jesus that night.

I was called by God in my mid-twenties, and I've become a pastor of an immigrant church. Now I am at an age to think about retirement. And I still thank God and I am happy. Looking back, I have no regrets because it is God who called me, "for God's gifts and his call are irrevocable" (Rom. 11:29).

When I was ministering in Hartford, Connecticut, the Overseas Ministries Study Center (OMSC) was nearby. I used to visit the missionary families staying there and frequently invited them to church. At that time, the OMSC director was Dr. Jonathan J. Bonk, later succeeded Dr. J. Nelson Jennings. They used to hold mission seminars and forums by inviting local church pastors, and also published the International Bulletin of Missionary Research (IBMR) on a regular basis.

During those years, I met Jinbong Kim in 2006, a missionary in residence from Guinea in Africa. One day while eating *jajangmyeon* with Jinbong, he raised a missionary issue: Western or non-Korean missionaries were very interested in Korean missions. However, it's very difficult for them to overcome language barriers. So, we talked about whether it would be good for Korean mission leaders and Western or non-Korean mission leaders to hold a forum together and publish the results in an English book. Eventually, the first forum was held in February 2011, and as a result, Korean and English editions of *Accountability in Missions* were published.[1] Besides, this forum gave birth to the mission organization Global Mission Leaders Forum (GMLF) and the biennial KGMLF. Every time the forum is held, an edition of a Korean and English book or e-book is published, accessible anywhere in the world. I believe this was entirely the product of a so-called missional koinonia.

However, right after the second forum in 2013, OMSC faced a trial. One of the board members sparked infighting over OMSC's policies and finances. After several board meetings, no solution was found. At the last meeting, all of the board members failed to come to one mind over the issues. In the end, the board members who could not agree with them had to

---

1 Jonathan J. Bonk, Sang-Chul Moon et al., eds., 선교 책무 : 21세기 한국과 북미 선교 연구 [Mission Responsibilities: Twenty-First century Korean and North American mission studies], trans. Sang-Chul Moon, Nam-Yong Sung, and Yong-Kyu Park (Seoul: 생명의말씀사 [Word of Life], 2011). The English edition is Jonathan J. Bonk et al., eds., *Accountability in Missions: Korean and Western Case Studies* (Eugene, OR: Wipf & Stock, 2011).

resign, and the leaders also had to set out to find a new path. It was a great pain and wound. However, we have experienced that nothing can stop the mission of saving people with the gospel: "We always carry around in our body the death of Jesus, so that the life of Jesus may also be revealed in our body" (2 Cor. 4:10).

In this respect, the value of the KGMLF forums, which have continued after this painful event, has been very great indeed. As one of the past board members of OMSC, I now realize the precious accountability of the mission given to KGMLF. We give all glory and thanks to God who has led us this far under his sovereign providence. At the same time, I would like to deeply thank Dr. Jonathan Bonk, Dr. Nelson Jennings, and Dr. Jinbong Kim, who served Jesus with one mind but also with strong friendship. Thank you very much for your selfless support and prayers.

Section F

Summary and Conclusion

CHAPTER 23

The Gospel of Hope in a Hopeless World

by Jonathan J. Bonk

> I consider that the sufferings of this present time are not worth comparing with the glory about to be revealed to us. For the creation waits with eager longing for the revealing of the children of God, for the creation was subjected to futility, not of its own will, but by the will of the one who subjected it, in hope that the creation itself will be set free from its enslavement to decay and will obtain the freedom of the glory of the children of God. We know that the whole creation has been groaning together as it suffers together the pains of labor.
> —Romans 8:18–22 (NRSVUE)

We live in the Anthropocene epoch,[1] an era marked by escalating global calamities rooted in human behavior. Our sins have found us out (Num. 32:14, 23)!

In the Opinion section of the July 15, 2023, online version of *The Guardian,* George Monbiot offered this gloomy prediction: "With our food systems on the verge of collapse, it's the plutocrats v life on Earth." A scientific paper published the week before had shown that "the chances of simultaneous crop losses in the world's major growing regions, caused by climate breakdown, appear to have been dangerously underestimated.... We face an epochal, unthinkable prospect: of perhaps the two greatest existential threats—environmental breakdown and food system failure—converging, as one triggers the other."[2] Another highly respected author writing in *The New York Times Magazine* for July 30, 2023, was similarly gloomy: "One grim climate lesson from the Canadian wildfires," he noted, is that "for all our plans to control emissions, humans are no longer fully

---

1 "The Anthropocene is a proposed geological epoch dating from the commencement of significant human impact on Earth's geology and ecosystems, including, but not limited to, anthropogenic climate change" (Wikipedia, s.v. "Anthropocene," last edited on Aug. 4, 2023, https://en.wikipedia.org/wiki/Anthropocene).

2 George Monbiot, "With Our Food Systems on the Verge of Collapse, It's the Plutocrats v Life on Earth," *The Guardian,* July 15, 2023, https://www.theguardian.com/commentisfree/2023/jul/15/food-systems-collapse-plutocrats-life-on-earth-climate-breakdown.

in charge."[3] Such realities underline the poignancy of the question raised by Zhou Li in his paper, "Who Will Feed the World in the Twenty-First Century?"

Prophets of doom have rarely been warmly received by their fellow countrymen, especially those who are convinced that their understanding of revealed truth trumps inconvenient evidence. Isaiah's audience, like many in our time, preferred the reassuringly soothing message of a Hananiah (Jer. 28) or a Robert Schuller to the truth of God:

> [The people] have turned against the LORD and can't be trusted. They have refused his teaching and have said to his messengers and prophets: "Don't tell us what God has shown you and don't preach the truth. Just say what we want to hear, even if it's false. Stop telling us what God has said! We don't want to hear any more about the holy One of Israel." (Isa. 30:9–11, CEV)

My assignment is to write a concluding summation of the forum, highlighting and summarizing its salient emphases. Given the broad reach of the presentations and the programmatic density of the forum itself, my remarks are organized around four broad motifs that have overlapped and merged at numerous points across the spectrum of presentations, responses, and discussions: biblical and theological truth;[4] historical and cultural perspectives;[5] material and social dimensions;[6] and hopeful signs.[7]

---

3 David Wallace-Wells, "One Grim Lesson from the Canadian Wildfires: For All Our Plans to Control Emissions, Humans Are No Longer Fully in Charge," *The New York Times Magazine*, July 30, 2023, 16–17. Wallace-Wells is a staff writer at the magazine and author of *The Uninhabitable Earth: Life after Warming* (New York: Tim Duggan Books, 2019).

4 (*a*) Bible studies on Jeremiah 1, Jeremiah 7, and Isaiah 24–25 by Christopher J. H. Wright: "God's Word to a Nation in Denial and Rebellion"; "God's Word in a Culture of Delusion and False Security"; and "God's Word of Global Judgment and Salvation"; (*b*) "Toward a Biblical Theology of Calamity" by Michel G. Distefano"; and (*c*) "Biblical Foundations for Creation Care" by Dave Bookless.

5 (a) "Learning from the Past and Finding Hope for the Future" by Allison Howell; (*b*) "Indigenous Epistemologies: Connecting with Christ and Creation" by Jay Mātenga; (*c*) "Creation Care: The Gospel's Third Dimension" by Ed Brown; and (*d*) "Environmental and Human Calamities in Korea and Implications for Mission" by Bright Myeong-Seok Lee.

6 (*a*) "Climate Crisis and Stewardship: A Christian Economist's Perspective" by Jong Ho Hong; (*b*) "The Transformation of Korean Missionaries' Epistemological Beliefs on Environmental and Human Calamities: A Critical Analysis" by Jooyun Eum; (*c*) "Who Will Feed the World in the Twenty-First Century? Lessons and Questions from a Brief Comparison of China's, India's, and Africa's Food Systems and Food Sovereignty" by Zhou Li; and (*d*) "Gold Mining in the Southwest of Burkina Faso and Christian Mission: The Great Commission and Structural Evil" by Ini Dorcas Dah.

7 (*a*) "Partnering with God to Restore Creation: A Story of Hope" by Tony Rinaudo; (*b*) "Onnuri Church's Environmental Mission and Strategy" by Woon-Oh Jung, Regina

Biblical and Theological Truth

> The LORD God came down in a cloud and stood beside
> Moses there on the mountain. God spoke his holy name,
> "the LORD." Then he passed in front of Moses and called out,
> "I am the LORD God. I am merciful and very patient with my
> people. I show great love, and I can be trusted. I keep my
> promises to my people forever, but I also punish anyone who
> sins. When people sin, I punish them and their children, and
> also their grandchildren and great-grandchildren."
> (Exodus 34:5–7, CEV)

All of the presentations, in particular those with explicitly biblical and
theological focus, reminded us that creation itself is suffused with morality.
What human beings *do* or *fail to do* matters. This vulnerable world, created
and sustained by God, is inhabited by a morally responsible caretaker,
humankind. Within this metaframework, we human beings are obliged to
suffer the consequences of disasters of our ancestors' and our own making.
God takes responsibility for designing this world in which human behavior
can precipitate calamity. To quote Chris Wright, "it is the word of God …
that governs human history."

Michel Distefano's study is sobering, since the writers of Scripture
were under no illusions about the ultimate *Source* of all calamities.
As Distefano noted, "divine sovereignty and human moral responsibility
are so intertwined" as to be inseparable in human deciphering of calamity.
Morality infuses every dimension of God's creation—known and unknown,
and every action and interaction of God's human creatures contributes to
immediate or eventual consequences, for good or for ill.

We live with the sobering reality that since humankind's original and
continuing alienation from God, the purpose for which we were created—
to care for that part of God's creation within which we ourselves reside—
has been profoundly subverted, turning humanity into our living world's
most destructively invasive species. Nothing on earth has escaped our
devastating touch: flora, fauna, minerals, water, and atmosphere. Our God-

---

Ryu, and Woo-Yong Kim; (*c*) "Economically Viable Green Energy from Waste Plastic:
A Fourth River Energy Proposal to Support Missions and Bless the Environment" by Ben
Torrey and Bong Ju Lee; (*d*) "Environment, Natural Disasters, and the Experience of the
Dandelion Community" by Insoo Kim; (*e*) "Evangelizing all Creatures: Pastoral Ecology
as Mission" by Douglas D. Kaufman; (*f*) "Can the Desert Be Green? An Environmental
Mission to Plant Hope in the Wilderness" by Lawrence Ko; (*g*) "The Founding of Shine
Church and Its Environmental Missionary Work" by Hyoungmin Kim; (*h*) "My Journey of
Growth and Hope: From God's Word, to Works and Wonders, to World Care" by Laurence
Gatawa; and (*i*) "KGMLF Missional Koinonia" by Sun Man Kim.

gifted ingenuity; our capacity to learn, transmit, accumulate, and amplify that learning—good or evil—across time through the utterly unique gift of language; and our fallen predisposition to employ lies, greed, and violence to achieve or maintain imagined personal or group advantage—such human capacities and behavior have contributed to the sad state in which we now find ourselves. Putting on the brakes of the juggernaut that we have designed and driven and shifting it into reverse will take centuries, and probably millennia.

This is congruent with the Bible's explanation of calamity in nature and in human affairs. We are sinners, who find ways of deliberately or unconsciously defying God. It is no surprise that in the days of Jesus, the official religion into which Jesus was born had so reified that religious leaders discovered grounds for crucifying the One they ostensibly worshipped. The custodians of *God as they imagined him to be* executed *God when he showed them what he was really like.* Today, likewise, it is often the most stridently religious who do their utmost to make sure that their nations do not follow the challenging but life-giving paths of righteousness.

Historical and Cultural Perspectives

> Time present and time past
> Are both perhaps present in time future,
> And time future contained in time past.
> —T. S. Eliot, *The Four Quartets*

Allison Howell introduces those of us with meagre historical memory to climate change-induced calamities from the not-so-distant past. Years long volcanic shading of the sun generated crop failures and famines, rat and flee generated plagues, massive loss of life, the collapse of social order, and genocidal wars that extinguished entire populations. In her helpful response, Jung-Sook Lee makes the connection between the cataclysmic Icelandic volcanic eruptions between 536 and 547 CE and the seeming lull in Christian missionary activity during that period. She also makes a direct connection between the more recent El Niño-Southern Oscillation (ENSO) between 1876 and 1879 and unprecedented drought conditions in Korea that issued in eighteen officially decreed special prayer rituals!

Climate-related calamities have been a frequently recurring feature of life on this planet. If present day calamities are unique, it is because the lifestyles and entitlements of the most affluent human societies play a direct role in generating and accelerating seemingly irreversible climate calamity on a planetary rather than regional scale.

The neat dispensational eschatologies that we have so artfully constructed—inadvertently or intentionally exempting believers from kingdom priorities in the here and now—are shown by Dave Bookless to be hermeneutically flawed, with predictable consequences. The loudly self-professed "most Christian" nations in the world turn out to be at the root of much of this planet's present agonies. Far from caring for creation with a view to restoration, these nations (and their cultural satellites)—by means of their aggressively promoted, ideologically compelling economic *gospel of never enough*—have led the way in fostering the will and devising the means of delivering a series of massive blows to our now-stricken world.

The "Enlightenment," Jay Mātenga reminded us, not only opened our eyes to hitherto-unknown realities, but engendered a dense mental fog of theological incomprehension. The West's *Meaning Map* (the Bible) was degraded to an artifact of a bygone era as it was displaced by science. Scientists became the priests and highly effective proselytizers of a dynamic cult ideally suited to socioeconomic systems requiring ever-increasing creation and consumption of material goods. Those who still required religion could hang on to their quaint anthropomorphic projections, of course, provided these didn't interfere with consumer world necessities. A form of godliness was fine, if neutered of any *real* power to generate economic, political, and ethical curbs or conditions.

Alas! Perhaps too late we have come to the realization that human history is not the story of the steady, inexorable improvement of the human *being*. The idea of "progress" is a secular version of the Christian doctrine of providence, but human nature itself shows no signs of progressing in sync with material or social changes. We have not become better through time or with more money. Political systems of betterment turn out to be always contingent, subject to the rot and decay of moral decline evinced by greed, selfishness, pride, violence, and racism. As Professor John Gray, himself an atheist, astutely observed:

> Human life as a whole is not a cumulative activity; what is gained in one generation may be lost in the next... . Science increases human power—and magnifies the flaws in human nature. It enables us to live longer and have higher living standards than in the past. At the same time it allows us to wreak destruction—on each other and the Earth—on a larger scale than ever before.
>
> The idea of progress rests on the belief that the growth of knowledge and the advance of the species go together—if not now, then in the long run. The biblical myth of the Fall of Man contains the forbidden truth. Knowledge does not make

us free. It leaves us as we have always been, prey to every kind of folly.[8]

Western human beings have presumed to imagine that they can recreate themselves or the world in which they fleetingly reside. They have forgotten that the aim of life is not to change the material world, but to see it rightly and live in it together harmoniously as a humble part of a much larger, more mysterious reality. This fundamental truth is reflected in the meaning maps of many indigenous peoples. We modern secularists—including Christians—have much to learn from so-called indigenous theologies of the womb in which we exist, the earth itself.

That, in part, is why it is so encouraging to read Edward Brown's account of the Cape Town Commitment's inclusion of creation care as an integral part of God's gospel. It shows that our myopic and sadly reified theologies *can* be born again! We evangelicals *can* embrace the liberating truth that our theological mandate does not include the need to prove that we have been right all along! The Micah Declaration is evidence that *even evangelicals can repent and be converted*. We *can* jettison wrong theologies, adjust misguided perspectives, and flesh out theological skeletons. This is encouraging, and it reflects Paul's advice to early believers in Romans 12:2: "Don't be like the people of this world, but let God change the way you think. Then you will know how to do everything that is good and pleasing to him" (CEV).

Myeong-Seok Lee's sober yet ultimately hopeful recounting of the disastrous consequences of decades of corrupt and inept governance by Korea's premodern elite who willfully disregarded weather and tsunami warnings has its analogues throughout human history across cultures and political constructs. The same stubborn refusal to heed prophetic warnings was and is a hallmark of Judeo-Christian societies everywhere, often because of the short-term interests of societies' political and wealthy elite, and the complicity of ordinary folks like you and me.

The persecution and elimination of those advocating beliefs and actions most likely to save society from its kamikaze rush to doom was as predictable then as it is today. The salutary benefits of good (ethical and just) governance at all levels of society cannot be overstated. Contrarily, no society can thrive when self-serving corruption and inequity are the rule. It is not surprising that the selfless service of Christian missionaries in many parts of the world should have served as a seed from which sprouted a flourishing better way.

---

8 John Gray, *Straw Dogs: Thoughts on Humans and Other Animals* (New York: Farrar, Straus and Giroux, 2002), xiii-xv.

Material and Social Dimensions

> These are the two great commandments of American society:
> "Create more desire; Thou shalt consume."
> —Jules Henry, *Culture Against Man*[9]

> Among the many models of the good society, no one has urged
> the squirrel wheel.
> —John Kenneth Galbraith, *The Affluent Society*[10]

Economist Jong Ho Hong's case study from Korea and Ini Dorcas Dah's from Burkina Faso touch on the unintended harms and global-scale disasters that issue from the short-term, parochial economic interests of individuals, corporations, countries, trade blocks, or entire civilizations.[11] In Christian theology, *greed*—socially embedded entitlement to more than enough in contexts where neighbors (whom we are to love as ourselves) have less than enough—is one of the "head" or "deadly" sins from which many other sins naturally issue.[12] Concomitant damages—some of them catastrophic to entire populations or to future generations of plant or animal life—are at times unintended and often underestimated. But at other times damages are deliberate, an inevitability of national or religious interests most starkly but not exclusively evident in wars.

The economic rewards of officially sanctioned and rewarded greed are fleeting and inevitably Pyrrhic, since their attendant desolations render prolonged thriving of life impossible. Creation care becomes a remote

---

9   Jules Henry, *Culture Against Man* (New York: Random House, 1963): 19–20

10 John Kenneth Galbraith, *The Affluent Society*, 3rd ed., rev. (New York: New American Library, 1976), 124.

11 Such incidents are common in Canada, and wherever in the world mineral extraction and forestry take place. For example, in Leyland Cecco's "Mercury Exposure Linked to High Youth Suicides in Canada First Nation: Grassy Narrows' Exposure to Toxic Metal Helped Cause a Suicide Rate Three Times Higher than Other Communities, Research Finds," *The Guardian*, July 20, 2023, https://www.theguardian.com/world/2023/jul/20/canada-mercury-poisoning-first-nations-indigenous-youth-suicides, he explains that "Grassy Narrows was the site of mercury dumping for nearly a decade after 1963, when a paper company released more than 20,000lb of mercury into the Wabigoon and English river systems. Fish, including walleye, were soon too poisonous to consume. The dumping is believed to have contaminated more than 150 miles of watershed. A single gram of mercury is sufficient to make all fish in a 20–hectare radius unsafe for consumption—but the Grassy Narrows dumping was 9m times higher."

12 "These are the fundamental bad habits of mind recognized and defined by the Church as the well-heads from which all sinful behaviour ultimately springs. They may also be called: the Seven Roots of Sinfulness"; see Dorothy L. Sayers's introductory remarks in Dante, *Divine Comedy*, vol. II, *Purgatory*, trans. Dorothy L. Sayers," in *Delphi Complete Works of Dorothy L. Sayers* (Delphi Classics, 2021), 7185, Kindle.

and irrelevant abstraction and creation destruction becomes a paramount focus of entire economies. The siren call of idolatrous nationalism sweeps all other interests, including creation care, aside.[13] Less dramatic than war but every bit as lethal is the chemical poisoning of the natural environment with disastrous long-term effects on human, animal, and organic life. Dave Bookless's constructive response to Hong complements and deepens the paper's intellectual, theological, and social fidelity. These chapters deserve to be reread, studied, and discussed.

It is no surprise that those of us with conservative theologies should be somewhat laggard in appropriating the insights of secular or theologically suspect experts, as Jooyun Eum's analysis of Korean missionaries' thinking about environmental issues demonstrates. On the other hand, it is foolish to deny that in our Scriptures, Yahweh never hesitates to own the calamities precipitated by humanity's disobedience and penchant for deeply unjust and exploitative social and economic systems that fly in the face of biblical shalom.

To the question posed in the missiological implications section of Eum's survey of missionaries—"Should the preservation of creation be included in mission?"—the answer, implicit and explicit, provided by the presenters in this forum is an unequivocal "Yes!" But perhaps "preserving" is too weak a term to describe our Creator's mandate. A gardener does far more than "preserve"; a gardener works hard to keep a garden healthy and productive— plants and soil and produce. It is no surprise that missionaries working in drought-ravaged rural communities are more aware of climate change as a key consideration in their mission theory and practice. Like Jesus, they do not tell people what they need; they "ask" people (or discern) how they can be of help in their life predicaments.

"Onnuri Church's Environmental Mission and Strategy"—tracing its roots to the Cape Town Commitment—is a model for each of us individually and for the churches, agencies, and educational institutions that we represent. Grounded in a popular evangelical theology that became more deeply biblical as the congregation's understanding of God's world grew, its "Loving U" slogan—loving the unfamiliar, the uncomfortable, and the unsafe—turned out to be applicable in any conceivable context in which churches, any Christian organization, or followers of Jesus might be called to minister. It is one of the many ways in which this church models faithfulness consistent with its growing understanding of God's love for the world.

---

13 See for example, Donovan Webster, *Aftermath: The Remnants of War: From Landmines to Chemical Warfare—The Devastating Effects of Modern Combat* (New York: Vintage Books, 1998), and Dan Kaszeta, *Toxic: A History of Nerve Agents, from Nazi Germany to Putin's Russia* (New York: Oxford Univ. Press, 2021).

Not far from Onnuri on the theological spectrum, albeit with a mandate more narrowly focused, is The Fourth River Project.[14] The prospect of a thoroughly evangelical mission organization pioneering in the design and construction of "a hydrogen (H_2) production plant and fuel cell charging station with a capacity of producing one metric ton of H_2 per day [by consuming] ten tonnes of waste plastic and vinyl per day" seems at first glance to be a long way from William Carey and more recent interpretations of the "Great Commission" to "preach the gospel." But his magnum opus was prescient, given its title.[15] It is our theologically truncated understanding of the gospel that lies at the root of our surprise.

This imaginative proposal is well within the bounds of our God-given mandate to care for creation; should it come to fruition it would certainly fall into the category of "good news for the poor"; and it reminds us that when Jesus walked this earth, he not only proclaimed the Good News as a kind of a priori entity; he asked the men and women who crowded around him to tell him what they understood the good news to be, and he acted in response to their understanding: "He wants to see" said the friends of a blind man; "We want to be made clean" said the lepers; "I want my bleeding to stop" breathed the frightened woman; "We need food" said the multitude; "We want this man to hear and speak" said some anonymous friends of the deaf mute brought to Jesus's attention; "I beg you to drive the demon out of my little daughter" begged a distraught and exhausted mother; and so on. This was the pattern characterizing our Lord's three brief years of parochial ministry in Judea. The gospel was defined by the people he encountered; and before he left this earth, he made it clear that his sheep, as distinct from mere goats, will always proclaim the gospel this way (Matt. 25:31–46).

---

14 "The mission of The Fourth River Project is to prepare for the opening of North Korea to the Gospel by equipping servant workers in all walks of life for the rebuilding of North Korea on the foundation of Jesus Christ. To this end, we encourage research into North Korea and seek to share the results of research and experience through knowledge exchange, education and training" ("Profile: The Fourth River Project," *Jesus Abbey's Three Seas Center*, accessed Aug. 5, 2023, http://www.thefourthriver.org/PDF%20 Documents/Profile.pdf).

15 William Carey, *An Enquiry into the Obligations of Christians to Use Means for the Conversion of the Heathens* (1792; repr., London: Carey Kingsgate Press, 1961).

Hopeful Signs

> The kind of hope that I often think about ... I understand above all as a state of mind, not a state of the world. Either we have hope within us, or we don't. It is a dimension of the soul. It's not essentially dependent upon some particular observation of the world or estimate of the situation. Hope is not the conviction that something will turn out well, but the certainty that something makes sense, regardless of how it turns out.
> —Václav Havel, Disturbing the Peace[16]

> "I know the plans I have in mind for you," declares the LORD; "they are plans for peace, not disaster, to give you a future filled with hope."
> (Jeremiah 29:11, CEB)

Tony Rinaudo's remarkable account of reforestation in Niger, by any measure among the most starkly improbable settings on earth for any semblance of a green revolution, did not begin with success, but with villager indifference and an enervating sense of hopelessness. How remarkable that a significant catalyst in his own conversion to environmental activism should have been Psalm 104:30: "When you send your Spirit, they [all things, including vegetation] are created, and you renew the face of the ground." As the source of all life, God is constantly creating and recreating. The scale of this re-creation in Niger is mind-boggling! A quarter million hectares per year for twenty years totals five million hectares. Five million hectares is fifty thousand square kilometers, which is almost half of the surface area of South Korea (100,032 sq. km)! With renewal of creation came an abundance of benefits for the entire population, all triggered by a young man from the Australian outback stumbling upon a biblical text written several millennia ago! God's Spirit renewed the face of the earth! Creation is important to its Creator, and it should be of utmost importance to those who worship its Creator, as John Stott taught as evangelical truth many years ago. Tony's paper made me sing the Doxology! What good news!

Perhaps it is Insoo Kim who most prophetically captures the roots and prospects of our present crises, and who presents us with a constructive alternative. Our present climate and environment related disasters could

---

16 Václav Havel [Czech playwright, president], "Vaclav Havel Quotes," AZ QUOTES, accessed Aug. 5, 2023, https://www.azquotes.com/author/6389–Vaclav_Havel. Havel. The quote is from Václav Havel and Karel Hvížďala, *Disturbing the Peace: A Conversation with Karel Hvížďala*, trans. Paul Wilson (New York: Knopf, 1990), 181.

not be explained without referencing what we call "western civilization" itself, in all its consumer manifestations. The fact is that we do not create our culture and its values. We are created by it, and by our behavior we perpetuate and promote it both consciously—as teachers, exemplars, and scholars—and unconsciously—as social beings formed and acculturated to surging forces of material consumer cultures. We cannot escape, even though we know something is seriously wrong. The empty ways of our forefathers permeates our thinking, our language, our mission strategies, our personal lifestyles, and our ambitions for our children. Our dreams for our children are, after all, a response to the siren call of a competitive consumer society— top grades, prestigious schools, distinguished positions, great respect, lavish consumption—dreams shaped by our consumer societies' terms, not God's. There seems to be no escape.

It appears that like Jeremiah, we are heading into exile as our consumer culture creeps inexorably forward on the path of self-immolation. We can see no way of escape; and can offer only laughably inconsequential alternatives. We are like bits of flotsam on the crest of a civilizational tsunami, having no control over its power, velocity, or destructive force. Any hope that we have must be lived out in this reality.

Douglas Kaufman's response to Kim and Kaufman's own paper chronicling his ongoing journey toward a fuller understanding of the depth and breadth of our Creator's love for all of his creation help us to glimpse the extent of the gospel that we, his new creation in Christ Jesus, are to live and proclaim wherever we are. "God loved the people of this world so much that he gave his only Son, so that everyone who has faith in him will have eternal life and never really die" (CEV). As Hansung Kim reminded us in his response to Kaufman's presentation, the good news begins with humankind, because it is humankind that has besmirched, degraded, and brought suffering and destruction to creation. Unless God's human creation repents and is renewed, there can be no hope for the rest of creation. But with God's new way of seeing and being and prioritizing, the crown of his creation will once again assume its God-given mandate with its attendant responsibilities of stewardship of and care for all of creation. From being a deformed and deforming invasive species on earth, humankind will return to its salvific, stewarding role of taking care of God's garden and all of the creatures in it.

Admittedly it is hard to imagine this happening. We are so laden down by the weight of inherited cultural and social baggage and so entangled in its sinful values and orientations that we can hardly move beyond the starting line as we run the race that is set before us. But run we must, with perseverance, witnessed by our contemporaries and by those who ran before, and against the formidable opposition of cynical believers and unbelievers alike, proclaiming what Hans Hut recognized as the "gospel of all creatures."

Is there any basis for realistic, well-founded hope? We must believe so. Despite our focus on the mess that we humans have made, creation waits in eager expectation of its ultimate liberation. Evil cannot triumph (Rom. 7:7–25; 8:18–24). The image of God can be marred but never be eradicated in humankind. We are precious to God. We are loved. And we are redeemable. As Dave Bookless so powerfully argues in his "Biblical Foundations for Creation Care," "God's final plan is not to destroy and replace the creation … but to renew, refine, and restore it… . Humanity's first task in bearing God's image relates to the conservation and protection of the natural world and its creatures." In our age of calamity, this is our hope.

APPENDIX
Resources for Mission and Congregation

Books

Christian

Bell, Colin and Robert S. White, eds. *Creation Care and the Gospel: Reconsidering the Mission of the Church*. Lausanne Library. Peabody, MA: Hendrickson, 2016.

Berry, R. J. (Sam) with Laura S. Meitzner Yoder. *John Stott on Creation Care*. London: IVP, 2021.

Hayhoe, Katharine. *Saving Us: A Climate Scientist's Case for Hope and Healing in a Divided World*. New York: One Signal Publishers, an imprint of Simon & Schuster, 2021.

Ingleby, Jonathan. *Christians and Catastrophe*. Gloucester: Wide Margin, 2010.

Jenkins, Philip. *Climate, Catastrophe, and Faith: How Changes in Climate Drive Religious Upheaval*. New York: Oxford Univ. Press, 2021.

Moo, Douglas J. and Jonathan A. Moo. *Creation Care: A Biblical Theology of the Natural World*. Grand Rapids: Zondervan, 2018.

Yoder, Laura S. Meitzner, ed. *Living Radical Discipleship: Inspired by John Stott*. Carlisle, Cumbria, UK: Langham Global Library, an imprint of Langham Publishing, 2021.

Secular

Carson, Rachel. *Silent Spring*. New York: Houghton Mifflin, 1962.

Eisenstein, Charles. *Climate: A New Story*. Berkeley, CA: North Atlantic Books, 2018.

Goodell, Jeff. *The Heat Will Kill You First: Life and Death on a Scorched Planet*. New York: Little, Brown and Company, 2023.

Horrell, David. *Ecological Hermeneutics: Biblical, Historical and Theological Perspectives*. London: T. & T. Clark, 2010.

Jackson, Wes and Robert Jensen. *An Inconvenient Apocalypse: Environmental Collapse, Climate Crisis, and the Fate of Humanity*. Notre Dame, IN: Univ. of Notre Dame Press, 2022.

Kara, Siddharth. *Cobalt Red: How the Blood of the Congo Powers Our Lives*. New York: St. Martins Press, 2023.

Klein, Seth. *A Good War: Mobilizing Canada for the Climate Emergency*. Toronto: ECW Press, 2020.

Magnason, Andri Snaer. *On Time and Water*. Translated by Lytton Smith. Rochester, NY: Open Letter, 2021.

McGuire, Bill. *Hothouse Earth: An Inhabitant's Guide*. London: Icon, 2022.

Thunberg, Greta. *The Climate Book: The Facts and the Solutions*. New York: Penguin, 2023.

Vince, Gaia. *Nomad Century: How Climate Migration Will Reshape Our World*. New York: Flatiron, 2022.

Von Brackel, Benjamin. *Nowhere Left to Go: How Climate Change is Driving Species to the Ends of the Earth*. Translated by Ayça Türkoğlu. New York: The Experiment, LLC, 2022.

Walia, Harsha. *Border and Rule: Global Migration, Capitalism, and the Rise of Racist Nationalism*. Chicago: Haymarket, 2021.

Wallace-Wells, David. *The Uninhabitable Earth: Life after Warming*. New York: Tim Duggan Books, 2019.

Watson, Brian T. *Headed into the Abyss: The Story of Our Time, and the Future We'll Face*. Swampscott, MA: Anvilside, 2019.

Fiction

Doerr, Anthony. *Cloud Cuckoo Land: A Novel*. New York: Scribner, 2021.

Robinson, Kim Stanley. The High Sierra: A Love Story. New York: Little, Brown and Company, 2022.

Williams, Joy. *Harrow*. New York: Alfred A. Knopf, 2021.

Article

Rosen, Julia. "The Science of Climate Change Explained: Facts, Evidence and Proof: Definitive Answers to the Big Questions." *The New York Times*, April 19, 2021, updated Nov. 6, 2021.

Websites and Online International Scientific and Government Reports

Padilla-DeBorst, Ruth. "Fleeing the Hot Spots: Climate Change, Migration and Mission."

Alexander Duff Lecture for COP26, November 16, 2021. YouTube video, https://media.ed.ac.uk/media/Ruth+Padilla+DeBorstA+Fleeing+the+hot +spotsA+Climate+change%2C+migration+and+mission/1_9uswa9v9/42247861.

Francis (pope). "Laudato Si': On Care for Our Common Home." Encyclical letter, Vatican Press, May 24, 2015, https://www. vatican.va/content/francesco/en/encyclicals/documents/papa-francesco_20150524_enciclica-laudato-si.html.

Pope Francis. "The Pope, the Environmental Crisis, and Frontline Leaders | The Letter: Laudato Si Film." YouTube video, Oct. 4, 2022, https:// www.youtube.com/watch?v=Rps9bs85BII. Trailer: "Official Trailer | The Letter: Laudato Si Film." YouTube video, Sept. 27, 2022, https:// www.youtube.com/watch?v=l3EBHebH17Y.

UK Church Mission Society. "Sustainability and Mission." Anvil 38, no. 2 (November 2022), https://churchmissionsociety.org/anvil-journal-theology-and-mission/sustainability-and-mission-anvil-journal-of-theology-and-mission-vol-38-issue-2/.

UK Tearfund. "Policy positions—Closing the Loop: The Benefits of the Circular Economy for Developing Countries and Emerging Economies." 2016, https://learn.tearfund.org/en/resources/policy-reports/closing-the-loop.

UN. Intergovernmental Panel on Climate Change (IPCC). https://www.ipcc.ch/.

Yale-Edinburgh Group. "Creation, Climate Change, and World Christianity." Yale-Edinburgh Conference, New College, Edinburgh, June 21–23, 2023, http://www.cswc.div.ed.ac.uk/events/yale-edinburgh-2023/.

Documentary Film

Baichwal, Jennifer, Nicholas de Pencier, and Edward Burtynsky. "Anthropocene: The Human Epoch." Canadian documentary film, 2018. Trailer: "Anthropocene—Official U.S. Trailer." YouTube video, May 16, 2019, https://www.youtube.com/watch?v=ikMlCxzO-94.

Participants

Dr. Bonk, Jonathan J.
Outgoing President, Global Mission
Leaders Forum
Research Professor of Mission,
Boston University School of
Theology
Winnipeg, Manitoba, Canada
bonkgmlf@gmail.com

Rev. Dr. Bookless, Dave
Director of Theology,
A Rocha International
Catalyst for Creation Care,
Lausanne Movement
Southall, London, UK
dave.bookless@arocha.org

Rev. Brown, Edward (Ed) R.
Executive Director, Care of Creation
Inc., Madison, Wisconsin, USA
ed@careofcreation.org

Prof. Chung, Seung-hyun (Nathan)
Professor of Missiology, Juan
International University
Incheon, South Korea
kahdohshi@gmail.com

Dr. Dah, Ini Dorcas
Experienced Researcher, Alexander
von Humboldt Foundation
Münster, Germany
dorcasdah@gmail.com

Dr. Distefano, Michel G.
Independent Scholar,
formerly at McGill
KGMLF Editor
Near Homewood, Manitoba, Canada
michel.distefano@gmail.com

Dr. Eum, Jooyun
Professor, Global Missionary
Training Center (GMTC)
Director, Mission and Policy (MaP)
lovegmtc@gmail.com

Dr. Gatawa, Laurence
President at PTS College and
Advanced Studies
(formerly Presbyterian Theological
Seminary)
Chairman of the Board of Trustees,
Asia Graduate School of Theology,
Philippines
Dasmarinas, Cavite, Philippines
lgatawa@gmail.com

Prof. Hong, Jong Ho
Graduate School of Environmental
Studies
Seoul National University
Seoul, Korea
hongjongho@snu.ac.kr

Dr. Howell, Allison M.
Nov. 10, 1951–Nov. 14, 2023
Former Associate Professor, Adjunct
Staff, Akrofi-Christaller Institute
of Theology, Mission and Culture,
Akropong-Akuapem, Ghana

Rev. Dr. Jennings, J. Nelson
Vice President, Global Mission
Leaders Forum, Inc.
Editor, *Global Missiology—English*
Hamden, Connecticut, USA
jnelsonjennings@gmail.com

Prof. Emer. Jung, Woon-Oh
College of Business Administration
Seoul National University, Gwanak
Campus
Seoul, Republic of Korea
wjung@snu.ac.kr

Rev. Kaufman, Douglas Day
Executive Director, Anabaptist
Climate Collaborative
Goshen, Indiana, USA
director@anabaptistclimate.org

Prof. Kim, Hansung
Professor of Missiology, ACTS/
Ashin University
Yangpyung, Kyungkido, South
Korea
easy05@acts.ac.kr

Rev. Kim, Hyoungmin
Senior Pastor, Shine Church
Seoul, South Korea
ejh8140@gmail.com

Dr. Kim, Insoo
Director, Dandelion Community
Principal, Dandelion School
Sancheong, Gyeongnam, Korea
ewlkis@daum.net

Rev. Dr. Kim, Jinbong
Managing Director, GMLF
Coordinator, KGMLF
Shelton, Connecticut, USA
kim@globalmlf.org

Rev. Kim, Sun Man
Senior Pastor, Dallas Korean Church
of Love
Carrollton, Texas, USA
sunmankim59@gmail.com

Mr. Kim, Woo-Yong
Researcher, Korea Baptist Theology
Institute
Student (ThM in Missiology),
Korea Baptist Theology University/
Seminary
Seoul, Korea
peterspress@naver.com

Mr. Ko, Lawrence J. C.
Founder/Director, Asian Journeys
Ltd.
lawrence@asianjourneys.org

Prof. Lee, Bong Ju
Handong Global University
Green Science Corporation
Pohang, Kyungsangbuk-Do, Korea
bongju.Lee@gmail.com

Dr. Lee, Bright Myeong-Seok
General Secretary, International
Association for Mission Studies
Co-President, Korea IAMS
Fellowship
Chaplain/Assistant Professor, ACTS
University International Graduate
School
Yangpyeong, Gyeonggido, Korea
brightlee@acts.ac.kr

Prof. Lee, Han Young
Executive Vice President &
Old Testament Professor, ACTS
University
Dean of ACTS International
Graduate School
Yangpyeong, Korea
hyl@acts.ac.kr

Prof. Lee, Jung-Sook
Professor of Church History
Torch Trinity Graduate University
Seoul, South Korea
js.lee@ttgu.ac.kr

Dr. Lee, Myung-Soo
Senior Fellow, US-Asia Law
Institute,
New York University School of Law
Seoul, Republic of Korea
myungsoo.lee@gmail.com

Dr. Mātenga, Jay
Director, Mātenga Global Witness
Dept.
Executive Director, Mission
Commission, World Evangelical
Alliance
Director, Missions Interlink
New Zealand
Auckland, New Zealand
jay@worldea.org

Ms. Mudahy, Anna lisa
Research Assistant, University of
Connecticut
Groton, Connecticut, USA
amudahy@gmail.com

Dr. Park, Gihong
Research Scientist, Department of
Marine Sciences,
University of Connecticut
Waterford, Connecticut, USA
gihong.park@uconn.edu

Mr. Rinaudo, Tony
Principal Climate Action Advisor,
World Vision Australia
Melbourne, Australia
tony.rinaudo@worldvision.com.au

Rev. Ryu, Regina
Pastor, Onnuri Church (Social
Justice Ministry)
Seoul, South Korea
lttlshp@gmail.com

Dr. Shin, Youngmi
Research Scientist, Department of
Marine Sciences,
University of Connecticut
Researcher, US EPA,
Stamford, Connecticut
Waterford, Connecticut, USA
youngmi.shin@uconn.edu

The Reverend Torrey, Ben
Executive Director, The Fourth
River Project, Inc.
Director, The Three Seas Center
Taebaek, Gangwon, Korea
bentorrey@thefourthriver.org

Rev. Dr. Wright, Christopher J. H.
Global Ambassador, Langham
Partnership International
London, United Kingdom
chris.wright@langham.org

Mr. Yoder, Jeffrey T. M.
Engineering Program Director,
Wheaton College
Wheaton, IL, USA
jeff.yoder@wheaton.edu

Dr. Yoder, Laura S. Meitzner
John Stott Chair and HNGR Director
Professor of Environmental Studies,
Wheaton College
Wheaton, IL, USA
laura.yoder@wheaton.edu

Prof. Zhou, Li
School of Agricultural and Rural
Development
Renmin University of China
Haidian, Beijing, China
zhouli@ruc.edu.cn

Contributors

JONATHAN J. BONK is research professor of mission at Boston University, where he is director emeritus of the *Dictionary of African Christian Biography* (www.dacb.org). He is executive director emeritus of the Overseas Ministries Study Center (www.omsc.org) where he served from 1997 until his retirement in July 2013. He was editor of the *International Bulletin of Missionary Research* (www.internationalbulletin.org) from July 1997 until June 2013. He has authored five books, edited eleven collaborative volumes, and published nearly two hundred scholarly articles, book chapters, reviews, and editorials. His best-known book is *Missions and Money: Affluence as a Western Missionary Problem* (Orbis 1991 and 2006). Past president of the APM, ASM, EMS, and IAMS, he has served on the executive of the Global Mission Leaders Forum since 2011. Each of the previous six forums has resulted in books published in English and in Korean. He retired as GMLF President following this seventh forum. He is a lay minister of the Fort Garry Mennonite Fellowship in Winnipeg, Manitoba, Canada. He was raised in Ethiopia by missionary parents.

DAVE BOOKLESS (PhD, University of Cambridge) is director of theology for A Rocha International, and catalyst for creation care with the Lausanne Movement. He was born and raised in India, where his parents both taught theology, and has lived in multiracial Southall, London since 1991. His books include *Planetwise: Dare to Care for God's World* (IVP, 2008), translated into Chinese, Dutch, French, German, Korean, and Spanish. He has contributed to over thirty books, lectured in over forty countries across six continents, serves on several global boards and committees, and teaches ecotheology in several seminaries. His academic interests include ecological missiology, intercultural and outdoor expressions of church, and the theology of wildlife conservation. Dave, when he's not travelling, helps his wife Anne lead an Anglican church in Southall. To relax, he enjoys walking, running, birdwatching, and Indian food and films.

EDWARD (ED) R. BROWN (MDiv, Gordon Conwell, Hon. DD, ACTS Institution of Higher Education, Bangalore) is the founding executive director of Care of Creation, a US-based NGO whose mission is to mobilize the church around the world to care for God's creation. From 2012 to 2022, he was an honorary fellow at the Nelson Institute of Environmental Studies at the University of Wisconsin, Madison. Ed was a Lausanne catalyst for creation care and in that role led a global campaign for creation care and the gospel, which gave birth to the worldwide Lausanne/WEA Creation Care

Network. He is the author of two books, *Our Father's World: Mobilizing the Church to Care for God's Creation* and *When Heaven and Nature Sing: Exploring God's Goals for His People and His World*. He has contributed chapters and articles to several books and journals, including the Spring 2023 issue of Evangelical Missions Quarterly. Ed and his wife Susanna live in Madison, WI, USA, and have four adult children and three grandchildren.

SEUNG-HYUN CHUNG has been serving as a professor of missiology at Juan International University, Incheon, South Korea since 2011. He received his PhD from Fuller Theological Seminary in 2007. Then he ministered at Jakarta Theological Seminary (Sekolah Tinggi Filsafat Theologi Jakarta), Indonesia, as a professor of missiology from 2008 to 2010. Currently, he is an editorial staff member of *Mission and Theology*, *Korea Presbyterian Journal of Theology*, and *Muslim-Christian Encounter*. His research and teaching interests include mission theology, missional church, Islam, and creation theology.

INI DORCAS DAH (PhD, Akrofi-Christaller Institute of Theology, Mission and Culture [ACI], Akropong-Akuapem, Ghana) is a lay preacher. She is the founder and president of L'Association Evangélique Sowtaa: AES (Association Evangélique pour la Joie et le Développement de la Femme, Burkina Faso: AEJDF). She is an experienced researcher of the Alexander von Humboldt Foundation at Arbeitselle für Theologische Genderforschung (Katholisch-Theologische Fakultät), Münster University, Germany. She is the course facilitator for Executive Certificate in Theology, Deeper Life International Bible Training College, Kumasi, Ghana. She is also the institutional research coordinator (Francophone Africa) for the Alliance of Mission Researchers and Institutions Project, Oxford Centre for Mission Studies (UK)/ACI (Ghana), a professeur associée (visiteur) of L'Institut Pastoral Hébron (IPH), Bouaflé, Côte d'Ivoire, and an adjunct research fellow at ACI. She has published books on Christian mission and articles on women in Christian mission, theology, human need and environment, and spirituality and hope in Africa. Her research interests are Christian history, gospel and culture, and holistic mission and development. Dah is from Burkina Faso and currently lives in Münster, Germany.

MICHEL G. DISTEFANO (PhD, McGill) thought he was on a fast track for a career in Hebrew Bible, but after Bible college (Providence) and seminary (TEDS) in the 1980s that plan was interrupted for over a decade. So he quickly studied nursing and worked in neonatal intensive care. In the 2000s, he got his PhD and was an instructor in Hebrew Bible and ANE religions at McGill. In the 2010s, his plans were interrupted again and he became a homesteader, and lately also an independent scholar. He has been involved with KGMLF since 2019. He has known Prof. Jonathan Bonk ("Dad") for more than forty years, and it has been a great privilege to work with him and the rest of the executive again. Michel and his wife, whom he also met at Bible college, are Canadians and have three children, a son-in-law, a daughter-in-law, and the cutest grandchildren.

JOOYUN EUM (PhD, Oxford Centre for Mission Studies) is professor of the Global Missionary Training Center (GMTC), Seoul, South Korea. He also serves as the director of Mission and Policy (MaP), a specialized research and consulting institution that analyzes and advises Korean churches and mission organizations on their mission policies. He was as a missionary to urban Muslims in the Philippines. He has translated and published several books on missiology, theology of religion, and mission strategy, and has published missiological research articles in many national and international missions journals. He currently lectures on various topics related to missions for the Korean church and many missional communities around the world. His wife, Kyung-Hwa Son, serves as the director of Women's Leadership Focus (WLF), an organization that researches and supports women's leadership in the Korean church and missions community.

LAURENCE GATAWA (PhD, University of Middlesex London via Oxford Centre for Mission Studies) is president at PTS College and Advanced Studies (formerly Presbyterian Theological Seminary) and chairman of the board of trustees for Asia Graduate School of Theology, Philippines. As an ordained minister of the Presbyterian Church of the Philippines, he is assigned as moderator at Emmanuel Christian Church, Cavite. He studied for his PhD through the support of Langham Partnership and published articles with Langham Publishing and other publishers. He is a Filipino married to Arcelyn C. Gatawa, and they are blessed with two kids, Renz and Lynette. His family lives in Dasmarinas, Cavite, Philippines.

JONG HO HONG is a professor of economics and former dean of the Graduate School of Environmental Studies at Seoul National University (SNU). His teaching and research are focused on environmental/energy economics and sustainable economy and policy. His involvement within the school extends to serving as the former director of the Environmental Planning Institute and the Institute for Sustainable Development. After receiving his PhD in economics from Cornell University, he held research and academic positions at Korea Development Institute (KDI) and Hanyang University in Korea. He also has broad experience working as a consultant for international organizations, such as the World Bank and Asian Development Bank. He has previously served as the president of the Asian Association of Environmental and Resource Economics (AAERE), Korea Environmental Economics Association, and Korean Association of Public Finance. He is also devoted to activities related to environmental groups, serving as a co-president of the Korean Federation for Environmental Movement. Currently, he serves as chairman of the Energy Transition Forum Korea.

ALLISON M. HOWELL (Nov. 10, 1951 - Nov. 14, 2023) prerecorded her presentation but was unable otherwise to take part in the forum. Allison (PhD, Edinburgh University) served in Ghana for thirty-eight years, first as a missionary with SIM and then as an associate professor at the Akrofi-Christaller Institute of Theology, Culture and Mission. As an adjunct faculty member, she continued to supervise PhD candidates and participated in online activities. Allison wrote a number of books and articles; "Allison Howell's Papers" up to 2019 are listed at https://aci.edu.gh/images/Archives-FAs/ALLISON_M_HOWELL_PAPERS_9.pdf. The fourth edition of her *A Daily Guide for Culture and Language Learning* was published through CAPRO International in Nigeria at the beginning of 2023. In her later years Allison resided in her native country of Australia and served on the board of Australians in Mission Together (AMT). She passed away four days after the conclusion of the forum at the age of seventy-two.

J. NELSON JENNINGS (PhD, Edinburgh University) is vice president of the Korean Global Mission Leaders Forum. He is editor of *Global Missiology—English* (globalmissiology.org) and is involved in several other online mission research projects, including the Dictionary of Christian Biography in Asia (dcbasia.org) and the Alliance of Mission Researchers and Institutions (amriconnect.net). He and his family served in Japan for thirteen years (1986–1999), first in church planting, then in teaching at Tokyo Christian University. Jennings taught world mission for twelve years at Covenant Theological Seminary (and again since 2018 in an adjunct capacity), served at the Overseas Ministries Study Center (2011–2015), and was a mission consultant for Onnuri Church (2015–2021). He has published numerous books and articles and has also served as editor of *Missiology: An International Review* and *International Bulletin of Missionary [now Mission] Research*. Jennings and his wife, Kathy, are both US-Americans and live in Hamden, Connecticut, USA.

WOON-OH JUNG is an elder at Onnuri Church in Seoul, South Korea, where he currently serves as leader of the Life and Environment Team under the church's Social Justice Ministry. He is a professor emeritus of the College of Business Administration at Seoul National University (SNU). While he was on the SNU faculty, he held Samil PricewaterhouseCoopers' Distinguished Professorship in Accounting. His teaching and research range from financial accounting and tax planning to business ethics. Prior to SNU, he was a tenured associate professor in the College of Commerce at the University of Illinois in Urbana-Champaign. He served for three years on the Korea Accounting Standards Board, the promulgator of Korean accounting standards. He also served as president of the Korean Academic Society of Taxation. In addition, he has years of industry experience, serving on the boards of directors of LG Household and Health Care, LX International (formerly LG International), and Kumho Petrochemical. He completed his BA in Economics at SNU, earned his MBA degree from Cornell University, and his PhD in Management at UCLA.

DOUGLAS DAY KAUFMAN recently became executive director of the Anabaptist Climate Collaborative, an organization inspiring climate action. For twenty-three years he served as co-pastor of Benton Mennonite Church, Goshen, Indiana, USA. Earning a ThM in ecology from the University of Toronto, he has trained hundreds of pastors on climate. He became active in creation care when he discovered that the river where he baptized new believers was often compromised with too much manure. He is father to three young adult sons.

HANSUNG KIM (DMiss, Biola University) is professor of missiology at the Asian Center for Theological Studies and Mission, South Korea. He was a missionary to South Asia with OM. He is the author of a number of books and articles on missions. His recent publications are *The Korean Church's Mission Work in Nepal* (2017, in Korean), *Church Planting in the Mission Field: Building or People?* (2020, in Korean), *Korean Pioneers of Nepal Missions* (2022, in Korean), and *From Nepal Mission to Mission Nepal* (2022, in English). His interests include the missions of the majority world church, the history of the cross-cultural missions of the Korean church,

Business as Mission, and cross-cultural missionary cooperation. Hansung (South Korean), Virginia (Canadian), and their three children live in Sejong City, South Korea.

INSOO KIM (PhD, Seoul National University) is the founder and director of Dandelion Community since 1991. His early ministry had been focused on rural evangelism and church planting. Enhancing the wellness of rural church members and spreading life-giving agriculture (eco-friendly farming) have been his major concerns unto now. The Dandelion Team extended its mission to Cambodia (ISAC, Institute of Sustainable Agriculture and Community Development) and the Himalayas (Mission Partnership with CRBC, Council of Rengma Baptist Churches), and supports countries with rural resource development and related issues. Now he is leading the Dandelion Community Development Course (hopefully Dandelion College Program) for African and Asian Mission and Rural Leaders. Insoo and his wife, Kwon, Keunsook, live in Sancheong, Kyeongnam, Korea.

JINBONG KIM, the coordinator of KGMLF, proposed its creation in 2008 and is now the managing director of the umbrella organization, Global Mission Leaders Forum. Beginning in 1990, he served for a number of years as a missionary in West Africa. He and his wife, Soon Young Jung, joined GMS in 1994 and in 1998 joined WEC International as well. They spent two terms working among Fulani Muslims in Guinea, Afterward, Kim served for six years as the director of International Church Relations at Overseas Ministries Study Center. Kim pursued mission studies in England (ANCC) and he also interned at a church in France. In 2006, he earned the degree of doctor of intercultural studies in the US. He and his wife are blessed with two young adult sons.

SUN MAN KIM is the senior pastor of Sarang Church in Dallas, Texas (formerly McKinney Shalom Church). He also delivers the Word on the hour "Today's Meditation," a Korean-American radio station in Dallas (2017-present). He served as a board member of the Overseas Mission Study Center (OMSC) in New Haven, Connecticut (2012 to 2015), president of the Connecticut Korean Church Council and Pastors' Council (2014), moderator of the New England Presbytery (KAPC), and senior pastor of the First Presbyterian Church of Hartford, Connecticut (2006–2016). He also served as a professor and board member of the Eastern Reformed Presbyterian Theological Seminary in Flushing, New York (2010–2015). He is the author of *Sermon on the Book of Revelation* (CLC, 2014). He and his wife have four grown children and two grandchildren. As of 2023, he is serving as the president of the Tarran County Korean Church Council.

WOO-YONG KIM is working toward a ThM in missiology at Korea Baptist Theological University/Seminary, and serves as a researcher at its Korea Baptist Theology Institute. He is studying 10,000 Ministry (a lay ministry) and the Anabaptist tradition, focusing on the missional church. He served as CEO of DML Corp., a construction heavy equipment company, and is a member of Onnuri Church. He serves as the general secretary of the Life and Environment Team of the Social Justice Mission Ministry, the team leader of the 10,000 Ministry of the 2000 Mission HQ, and the representative of the S-Bridge community. He is a lay leader of Acts29, a vision of missional Onnuri Church.

LAWRENCE J. C. KO is founder/director of Asian Journeys Ltd., a social enterprise in Singapore engaged in environmental and urban projects. He has organized service learning and environmental education for youth leaders from tertiary institutions for the past twenty-five years, and is the author of two books, *Can the Desert Be Green? Planting Hope in the Wilderness* (2014) and *From the Desert to the City: Christians in Creation Care* (2020). He was the former national director of the Singapore Centre for Global Missions (2012–2022) and has been teaching in seminaries on Christian mission. He also served on the boards of the Asia Lausanne Committee, the International Council for Higher Education, and the Asia Evangelical Alliance Mission Commission. Lawrence has been an associate trainer with the Civil Service College in Singapore since 2007, and is the international adviser for Mastercoach Institute.

BONG JU LEE (PhD, University of Wisconsin-Madison) is a plasma scientist. He is a professor at Handong Global University, and CEO of Green Science Co. and Inc. and Innopowder Co. After he returned to S. Korea in 1997 from the US, he devoted himself to establishing 100,000 mission centers based on his plasma power plants utilizing all kinds of burnable waste in the world. His plasma power plant converts hydrocarbon fuel, including waste, into clean energy without exhausting toxic gases, such as dioxin and furan, etc.

BRIGHT MYEONG-SEOK LEE (PhD, Akrofi-Christaller Institute) is the general secretary of the International Association for Mission Studies. He is co-president of the Korea IAMS Fellowship and is involved in online mission research projects with the Alliance of Mission Researchers and Institutions. He is teaching at ACTS University as a chaplain and assistant professor. He and his family served in Ghana for nineteen years (2002–2021) as an ecumenical coworker in collaboration with the Palatinate Church in Germany. Lee served migrant workers in Korea for eight years

(1994–2002), established C3TV (a Christian broadcasting system, now GoodTV) as a founding member and general manager (1997–2002), and taught at Presbyterian University and Theological Seminary and Torch Trinity Graduate University in Korea in an adjunct capacity. Lee and his wife, Grace, are both Koreans and live in Yangpyeong, Korea.

HAN YOUNG LEE (PhD, North West University, South Africa) is vice president of ACTS University. He is also professor of Old Testament at the same institute, research pastor at Seobu Church, and on the board of trustees of Global Fraternity Mission, Seoul, Korea. He grew up in Brazil as an MK, studied in the US, and worked as a medical doctor prior to his theological pursuit and teaching ministry. He has published numerous books, biblical commentaries, and articles, including a devotional book, *Sister Myong-Ja*, which has become a Christian bestseller in Korea. Han Young and his wife, Sook, are both US citizens. Han Young was a former US Army chaplain while Sook has been serving as a US Army physician for the last twenty-three years.

JUNG-SOOK LEE (PhD, Princeton Theological Seminary) is professor of church history at Torch Trinity Graduate University (TTGU), Seoul, Korea, where she served as the fifth president. She serves as vice president for Asia Theological Association (ATA), board member for the Oxford Centre for Mission Studies, and international advisor to the International Museum of the Reformation, Geneva. Until recently she served as praesidium member for the International Congress on Calvin Research, representing Asia. Besides TTGU president, she served as the first woman president of the Church History Society in Korea, Korea Association of Accredited Theological Schools, and Korea Society of Evangelical Theological Colleges and Seminaries. She lectures several series of church history and Bible study on Christian TVs in Korea, and has translated books and written book chapters and articles in both English and Korean about the Protestant Reformation and its legacy, Christian art, and women in ministry. She is ordained and married with two grown-up children.

MYUNG-SOO LEE was born in Seoul, Korea, and studied law at Korea University (BA & ML) and public international law and conflict resolution/negotiation at Harvard Law School (LLM & SJD). She was assistant director/director of research of East Asian Legal Studies of Harvard Law School, and a research fellow at New York University (NYU) School of Law. She served on the board of the Geneva School of Manhattan, a private Christian school, and as a core member of World Aid New York, a humanitarian aid organization. She also served as the co-leader of Women's Ministry at Times

Square Church. She is currently a senior fellow at the US-Asia Law Institute of NYU School of Law and serves on the board of the Council on Diplomacy for Korean Unification (CDKU).

JAY MĀTENGA (DIS, Fuller School of Intercultural Studies) is a Māori theologian of missions practice based in Auckland, who serves as the director of Missions Interlink, the alliance of missions-passionate organizations in Aotearoa, New Zealand. He is seconded from Missions Interlink for half of his time to the World Evangelical Alliance, which he serves as director of the Global Witness department and executive director of the WEA's Mission Commission. Prior to serving alliances, Jay led Pioneers, a missionary-deploying agency in Aotearoa, New Zealand (2000–2015). Jay is coauthor of *Mission in Motion: Speaking Frankly of Mobilization* (2016) and numerous articles, most of which are archived on Jay's website, jaymatenga.com. The website also hosts Jay's monthly reflections about missions through an indigenous lens.

ANNA LISA MUDAHY is a graduate of the University of Connecticut where she studied marine sciences and oceanography. Her primary field of focus is water quality monitoring and environmental modeling. She has a strong passion for social and environmental justice and fulfilling the gospel mission in whatever way the Lord provides.

GIHONG PARK (PhD, University of Connecticut), a Korean-English translator/editor of KGMLF 2023, is also a marine plankton ecologist. He has been studying plankton adaptation to climate change, reciprocal predator-toxic prey adaptation, and harmful algal blooms at the University of Connecticut since 2011. He has been involved in the water quality monitoring of Long Island Sound, particularly micro/mesozooplankton as water quality indicators (granted by Connecticut Department of Energy and Environmental Protection). He is still searching for a way that ecology can explain our Father's will. He also is serving as an InterVarsity volunteer staff member along with his wife, Youngmi Shin, in the New England region. Gihong, his wife, Youngmi, and three boys, Gordon, Eden, and Lyndon, are living in Waterford, Connecticut, USA.

TONY RINAUDO served as an agriculturalist and missionary with Serving in Mission in Niger Republic from 1981 to 1999. There, he oversaw long-term rural development and periodic, large-scale relief programs. Through these he contributed to a transformation in how Nigeriens farm, and the reforesting of over six million hectares of land, which still inspires regreening movements globally. For his eighteen years of service to humanity and the environment, the government of Niger awarded him its highest honor for an expatriate, The Order of Agriculture with Merit (Merite Agricole du Niger). Since joining World Vision Australia in 1999, Tony initiated and/or oversaw important land regeneration projects worldwide. Serving now as principal climate action advisor, he promotes forestry and agroforestry initiatives globally within the World Vision partnership and beyond. Among major awards Tony and FMNR have recently received are the 2018 Right Livelihood Award "for demonstrating on a large scale how drylands can be greened at minimal cost, improving the livelihoods of millions of people," and the World Future Council Agroecology Award. In 2019, Tony was appointed as a Member (AM) of the Order of Australia (General Division). Tony currently has a book, *The Forest Underground*, available for purchase and on any audiobook platform, and a documentary called "The Forest Maker," available online.

REGINA RYU is an ordained pastor at Onnuri Church in Seoul, Korea, where she has served as a founding member of the church's Social Justice Ministry (since 2014), comprising twenty-six different ministry teams, including the Life and Environment Team. Prior to entering ministry and joining Onnuri, she practiced corporate law, first at Paul, Weiss, Rifkind, Wharton & Garrison in New York City and then at Kim & Chang in Seoul, Korea. Regina holds an AB in history from Princeton University and a JD from New York University School of Law. After twelve years of private law practice, she began her theological studies at the Presbyterian University and Theological Seminary in Seoul, Korea, earning her MDiv and ThM in public theology. Regina is a firm believer that a holistic understanding of the gospel of the kingdom of God proclaimed by Jesus must constitute the theological and biblical basis of, and the very raison d'être of the church's social mission, an integral part of *missio Dei* in which all churches must engage.

YOUNGMI SHIN (PhD, Oceanography) is working as an environmental scientist in the Department of Marine Science (DMS) at UConn (University of Connecticut) and in the US EPA. She has been serving as an InterVarsity volunteer staff member in the GFM (Graduate and Faculty Ministries, https://gfm.intervarsity.org/) in the New England region. She is also a Korean-English translator/editor of KGMLF 2023. As a scientist, her research focuses on investigating the physical processes that drive ocean water and monitoring the water quality of coastal oceans with biogeochemical dynamics in response to climate change and extreme water events. As an InterVarsity staff member, she has been leading/coordinating Bible study and Christian fellowship for graduated/faculty ministry in the UConn Avery Campus. Youngmi, her husband, Gihong, and three boys, Gordon, Eden, and Lyndon, are living in Waterford, Connecticut, USA.

BEN TORREY is director of the Three Seas Center, a ministry of Jesus Abbey in Taebaek, Gangwon, Korea. He is also the executive director of The Fourth River Project, Inc., a US nonprofit corporation dedicated to preparing for the opening of North Korea. Ben grew up in Korea where his parents, Archer and Jane Torrey, were missionaries. After reestablishing the Anglican Seminary in Seoul following the Korean War, the Torreys moved to Taebaek, where they founded Jesus Abbey as an intentional intercessory prayer community in 1965. Ben was a teenager at the time. He returned to the US in 1969 for college and career. Following pastoral ministry in the United States and establishing a Christian middle and high school, the Lord called him and his wife, Liz, in 2002 to return to Korea to prepare for the opening of North Korea. At that time, he began planning and construction of the Three Seas Center as a place to carry out the work of The Fourth River Project. Ben and Liz spend most of their time in Taebaek but return to the US from time to time.

CHRISTOPHER J. H. WRIGHT is a missiologist, an Anglican clergyman, and an Old Testament scholar. As global ambassador of Langham Partnership International, he represents and promotes the vision and work of Langham around the world through his international travel and speaking and his writing ministry as a Christian scholar and author, and shares in the spiritual and strategic leadership of the organization. An ordained pastor in the Church of England, Chris spent five years teaching the Old Testament in India (1983–88) and thirteen years as academic dean and then principal of All Nations Christian College in England (1988–2001) before taking over the leadership of Langham Partnership at the request of its founder, John Stott. With his wife, Liz, Chris is an honorary member of staff at All Souls Church, Langham Place in London, UK. A prolific author, he has published scores of books and articles and is a well-known voice in the world of evangelical and mission scholarship. His most recent contribution in this field is *The Great Story and the Great Commission: Participating in the Biblical Drama of Mission* (Baker, 2023).

JEFFREY YODER is a civil engineer, an educator, and director of the engineering program at Wheaton College, Illinois, USA. He is committed to improving water supply and sanitation in rural communities without reliable infrastructure. He served with Mennonite Central Committee, IRC, Oxfam, local churches, national universities, and bilateral agencies for relief and development in Zambia, Timor-Leste, Thailand, and West Papua, Indonesia. He also directed disaster recovery programs in post-tsunami Aceh, Indonesia, working in partnership with local organizations. He addressed US flood response with the Federal Emergency Management Agency. His family is active in a local Mennonite Church.

LAURA S. MEITZNER YODER is a political ecologist, John Stott Chair of Human Needs & Global Resources, and professor of environmental studies at Wheaton College, Illinois, USA. Her students intern with local Christian organizations in South/Southeast Asia, Africa, and Latin America. She researches human-environment interactions, focusing on the experiences of smallholder farmers and forest dwellers in situations of conflict, disaster, or political marginalization. She served with Mennonite Central Committee in West Papua and in post-tsunami Aceh, Indonesia, and does long-term research on land/forest control in the enclave district of Oecusse, Timor-Leste. Her family is active in a local Mennonite Church.

LI ZHOU (PhD in economics, Fudan University; postdoctoral fellow in management, Tsinghua University) is professor of the School of Agricultural and Rural Development, Renmin University of China, and chief expert of the Major Project of the National Social Science Foundation of China. He is an expert committee member on the construction of the national public cultural service system and a researcher at the China Bankers Association. He is a visiting scholar of the French Social Science Foundation (MSH), the University of California, Los Angeles (UCLA), the Institute for Agricultural and Trade Policy (IATP) in the US, Griffith University in Australia, and Lincoln University in New Zealand. He has field research experience to more than thirty countries, including India, Thailand, Brazil, South and North Korea, and Kenya. His wife, Lyu Yongqing, is an assistant pastor in Beijing, China.

Indices

Subject Index

Names Index

N

Nanema, Hamed 198n15, 200n25, 201n29, 202n36, 203n41

Ndour, Babou 215n5

Nebuchadnezzar 4, 15

Neta, Ram 162n8

Neugrosche, Joachim 259n6

Noah 23–24, 30, 35, 55, 58, 69, 73, 83, 221

Norgaard, Kari Marie 271, 271nn14–15

Northcott, Michael 271n17

Ntreh, Benjamin Abotchie 197n9

O

Oelschlager, Max 117

Osendarp, S. 186n17

Ouèdraogo, Seydou 199n18

P

Paalo, Sebastian Angzoorokuu 134n36

Pachauri, R. K. 146n1

Padilla, René 118–19, 119nn12–13

Padilla DeBorst, Ruth ii, 331

Pakenham, Thomas 205n43

Palais, James B. 131n20, 132n28, 132n30

Palenfo, Bonbagnè 199, 200n28

Palenfo, Sié Gildas Nazaire 199n18

Palmer, Clare 159, 159n19

Pandya-Lorch, Rajul 215n5

Pardee, Dennis 259n6

Park, Gihong xx, 220–24, 222n19, 335, 345, 347

Park, Seona 136n42

Park, Yong-Kyu 312n1

Paul 9, 12, 16, 140

Pedlar, James 123n17

Perry, John S. 128n8

Pharaoh 39, 51, 189

Philip 16

Pihkala, Panu 271, 271n16

Pintrich, Paul R. 163n9

Pitts, Jamie 277n2

Poda, Sié Jean de la Croix 200

Prance, Ghillean T. 162n6

Press, Roman J. 240n1

Procopius 81, 81n2, 82n7

Pseudo-Dionysius 81n1, 82nn7–9, 83nn10–11, 83nn13–14, 84 n19, 84n15

Pye-Smith, C. 215n3

Pyŏn, Won-lim 131n18, 132, 132n22

Q

Quinn, Daniel 272, 272n18

R

Raworth, Kate 159, 159n17

Reij, C. P. 215nn4–5

Richard, Timothy 85, 85nn27–28, 86n30, 87–88, 88nn40–41, 89, 89n45, 90, 90n49, 90n51, 91–92, 94

Rinaudo, Tony 211–19, 214nn1–2, 220–24, 220nn12–13, 222n15, 318n7, 326, 335, 345–46

Robinson, Kim Stanley 330

Rockström, Johan 158n13

Rongji, Zhu 288

Rosen, Julia 330

Rosen, Len 240n2

Rosen, William 82nn5–6, 84n23

Royal, Te Ahukaramu Charles 105n13

Ryu, Regina 75–78, 225–34, 235, 318n7, 335, 346

S

Samuel 29

Sánchez, M. V. 188n24

Sangaré, Oumar 198, 198n15, 200, 202–3

Sarr, Alioune 215n5

Satan 37–38, 55, 123–24, 307

Sayers, Dorothy L. 323n12

Schaeffer, Francis 309

Schneider, Klaus 196nn6–7

Schroeder, Roger 101

Schuller, Robert 318

Schultz, T. W. 187, 187n22

Schumacher, E. F. 258n4, 272, 273nn19–20

Seebaß, Gottfried 279n3

Selby, Rachael 106, 106n15

Sendzimir, J. 215n4

Sennacherib 25

Seo, Ji-hyun 135n37

Shead, Andrew 13, 13n2

Shem 69

Shin, Ho-cheol 131n19

Shin, Susan 131n17

Shin, Youngmi xx, 122–25, 125n19, 335, 345, 346–47

Si, Z. 188n23

Simner, Mark 205n43

Sittler, Joseph 162n4

Smale, M., 215n5

Solomon 25, 27, 110

Song, Byung-Nak 149n4

Spaulding, Nicole E. 81n3

Spielman, David J. 215n5

Stanley, Jason 162n8

Stannard, David 206n46

Stark, Rodney 133, 133n33, 136, 136n43

Steffen, Will 157n10, 158n14

Steup, Matthias 162n8

Stott, John 216, 216n6, 217, 326, 329, 335, 347, 348

Stradivarius 96n60

Suh, Jung-hoon 111

Sung, Nam-Yong 312n1

Swenson-Lengyel, Willa 271n15

Swindoll, Charles R. 63, 63n15

Symeon, Saint 84

Szamocki, Grzegorz 222n16

T

Tappan, G. 215n5

Taylor, Charles 104, 104nn11–12

Taylor, Michael 222n17

Testerman, Dennis E. 162n6

Theodosius I 206

Thorpe, Lewis 82n7

Thunberg, Greta 257n1, 330

Timothy 9

Ting, Governor 90n49

Titus 16

Torrey, Ben 239–52, 242n5, 243, 253–56, 319n7, 335, 347

Torrey, Liz 347

Townend, Stuart 44n2

Tzu, Y. S. 129n13

U

Underwood, Lillias H. 133nn31–32

V

Van Dijk, M. 186n18

Venn, Henry 177

Villegas, Isaac 280, 280n10, 281n12, 281n15

Vince, Gaia 330

Von Brackel, Benjamin 330

von Rad, Gerhard 69n3

W

Wagner, C. Peter 141n50

Walia, Harsha 330

Wallace-Wells, David 318n3, 330

Walton, John H. 122–23, 123n16

Wang, S. 186n14

Scripture Index

Old Testament

New Testament